THE CASE FOR
PROGRESSIVE
DISPENSATIONALISM

THE CASE FOR
PROGRESSIVE
DISPENSATIONALISM

■

The Interface Between
Dispensational & Non-Dispensational Theology

ROBERT L. SAUCY

ZondervanPublishingHouse

Academic andProfessionalBooks

Grand Rapids, Michigan

A Division of HarperCollinsPublishers

Requests for information should be addressed to:
Zondervan Publishing House
Academic and Professional Books
Grand Rapids, Michigan 49530

Library of Congress Cataloging-in-Publication Data
Saucy, Robert L.
    The case for progressive dispensationalism : the interface between dispensa-
tional and non-dispensational theology / Robert L. Saucy.
        p.   cm.
    Includes bibliographical references and index.
    ISBN 0-310-30441-5
    1. Dispensationalism. 2. Evangelicalism. 3. History (Theology) I. Title.
BT157.S28   1993   92-44315
230'.046—dc20   CIP

Cover design by Kurt Dietsch & Associates

Printed in the United States of America

93 94 95 96 97 98 / CH / 10 9 8 7 6 5 4 3 2 1

*To the memory of our daughter Becky,
who now sees Him face to face.
(1963–1991)*

Contents

Preface

Over the past several decades the system of theological interpretation commonly known as dispensationalism has undergone considerable development and refinement. The impetus for change has come largely from among dispensationalists themselves as, through mutual discussion, they have felt the need to revise classic dispensationalism at several points. The process has been aided considerably by an increasing dialogue between dispensationalists and those from non-dispensational traditions. One senses a new openness to listen and learn from one another on the part of many in these traditions.

Because, as we will argue in this work, the nature of the fulfillment of the prophecies concerning Israel remains the crucial issue dividing many dispensationalists from non-dispensationalists, the existence of the state of Israel has, no doubt, also contributed to this dialogue. The Jewish experience leading to the establishment of the state of Israel and the continuing world focus on the problems of the Near East have brought renewed interest in the theological question of the place of Israel in God's plan for the world.

Our purpose in this work is to bring additional clarification to a contemporary form of dispensationalism that, although differing in some details among its adherents, is in general shared by many today. It is hoped that this will both give traditional dispensationalists a greater understanding of what some of their colleagues are saying, and aid the ongoing dialogue with non-dispensationalists. For many of us, references to dispensational interpretations by those not holding this position no longer speak to the real issues over which we differ. It is hoped that this work will help clarify the changes that have taken place within dispensationalism so that we can focus on the issues that still need resolution. In this regard, the question of the time of the rapture has not been included in the work. While most dispensationalists probably hold to a pretribula-

8

tion rapture of the church as being in certain respects more harmonious with dispensationalism in general, many would not desire to make this a determining touchstone of dispensationalism today. For these the broad dispensational interpretation of biblical history does not ultimately stand or fall on the time of the rapture.

As will be evident throughout our work, the changes in dispensationalism have been largely in the direction of a greater continuity within God's program of historical salvation. Instead of a strict parenthesis that has no relation with the messianic kingdom prophecies of the Old Testament, many dispensationalists now acknowledge the present age of the church as the first-stage partial fulfillment of these prophecies. Israel and the church are no longer viewed as representing two different purposes and plans of God, as some earlier dispensationalists taught; they are now seen as sharing in the same messianic kingdom of salvation history. These changes have obviously brought more congruence between dispensationalism and non-dispensationalism at many points.

The question may be raised as to whether such a revised dispensationalism is still legitimately "dispensationalism." We have chosen to keep this terminology because of its association with dispensationalism's traditional interpretation of the prophecies concerning the nation of Israel. Anyone who asserts not only the restoration of Israel as a national entity but also a future role for that nation in God's kingdom program has been generally identified as dispensationalist. The new dispensationalism retains such a future for Israel. In fact, because it has minimized many other previous distinctions held by dispensationalism, the revised form of dispensationalism may be said to be even more essentially defined by this understanding of the prophecies of Israel. Thus we still use the term "dispensational" to describe the position set forth in its contrast to non-dispensationalism. The addition of "progressive" in the title of the work is meant here only to distinguish the newer interpretations from the older version of dispensationalism, which we refer to in this book as "classical" or "traditional" dispensationalism.

We are not concerned in this work with labels. Labels, if understood, are useful for communication. Therefore, we use the terms "dispensational" and "non-dispensational" here as helpful designations of differing interpretations. But we trust that they will not obscure the real intent, which is to engage the reader in the discussion of biblical interpretation.

We wish to express our appreciation to the many who have helped in various ways to bring this work to completion. I want to express my heartfelt thanks to my colleagues on the faculty and the administration and staff of Talbot School of Theology for helpful discussions of some of the issues related to the work, and especially for the many expressions of support and encouragement along the way. A debt of gratitude is also due to the students at Talbot who over the years were compelled to listen to much of the content of this book in classes. The final product is better because of your questions and discussion.

The people at Zondervan Publishing House have also been a delight to work with. Thanks in particular to Dr. Stan Gundry for originally initiating this project with me longer ago than I wish to remember and to Mr. James Ruark, whose editorial skills made many of my theological contortions more readable fare.

Appreciation is also due Richard Zuelich and Tori Swingrover for making the book more useful by providing a subject index and a Scripture index respectively.

Finally, I want to express my deepest gratitude to my wife Nancy whose consistent faithful support, encouragement, and occasional prodding have been a rich channel of God's blessing to me, not only in this work, but in all of life.

PART I

INTRODUCTION

Chapter 1

The Crucial Issue
Between Dispensational
and Non-Dispensational Systems

I. INTRODUCTION

THROUGHOUT THE HISTORY of discussion between dispensationalists and non-dispensationalists numerous points of contention have been raised. These differences stemmed largely from the particular emphasis of each system in its understanding of biblical history. As its name indicates, the dispensational view tended to emphasize the differences in the various periods of human history brought about through the progressive revelation of God's salvation program. Non-dispensationalists, on the other hand, inclined toward an emphasis on the unity of God's work in biblical history.

Continued study of the Scriptures has seen development and modification of both perspectives. Most dispensationalists would acknowledge that some of the early statements of distinctions were overstated. This is often the case when a position is first espoused against another position as was the situation of early dispensationalism against traditional covenant amillenial theology. At the same time the rise of the discipline of biblical theology with its emphasis on interpreting the Scriptures in their historical environment has contributed to a greater appreciation of the development within the historical redemptive plan and the resultant differences entailed on the part of many non-dispensationalists.

These developments within the two schools of interpretation have worked to bring closer, if not total, agreement on many points of prior disagreement. There yet remain, however, some broad areas of difference which focus on the understanding of the fulfillment of God's historical plan of redemption. Before looking at this crucial area, it will be beneficial to note first those areas which for many interpreters are no longer major areas of dispute.

A. Resolved Issues

Law and Grace. A primary point of difference in earlier years was the relationship of law and grace. The belief that Israel and the church play different roles in biblical history led dispensationalists to make many rather sharp distinctions regarding God's methods of dealing with the two entities. They viewed Israel as operating under the economy of the Mosaic law; the church, under the dispensation of grace.

Although dispensationalists apparently never intended to teach a dichotomy between law and grace as principles of God's salvation, some statements of early advocates were easily construed that way. C. I. Scofield wrote in his notes to the Bible, "The point of testing is no longer legal obedience as the condition of salvation, but acceptance or rejection of Christ with good works as a fruit of salvation. . . ."[1] His comment on the petition for forgiveness in the so-called Lord's Prayer likewise promoted this dichotomy: "This is law. Forgiveness is conditioned upon a legal ground. . . . Under law forgiveness is conditioned upon a like spirit in us; under grace we are forgiven for Christ's sake, and exhorted to forgive because we have been forgiven."[2] Since forgiveness of sins lies at the heart of salvation, it was easy for non-dispensationalists to construe this view as teaching a law-based means of salvation in Old Testament times.

Charles C. Ryrie acknowledges that such "unguarded statements" were the "primary reason for the persistence of the charge" that dispensationalists were teaching more than one way of salvation. Ryrie responds that these early dispensationalists did not mean to teach what might be implied from these statements and, had they known the issue would arouse such acrimony, would have been more careful in what they said.[3]

While it cannot be denied that there is some unresolved tension in these earlier statements, dispensationalists have more recently been careful to explain that the progression in the dispensations involves no change in the fundamental principle of salvation by grace. Rather, they have affirmed more clearly that a single divine method of salvation by

---

[1]C. I. Scofield, ed., *The Scofield Reference Bible* (New York: Oxford Univ. Press, 1917), 115, n. 1.

[2]Scofield, *The Scofield Reference Bible*, 1002, n. 1.

[3]Charles C. Ryrie, *Dispensationalism Today* (Chicago: Moody Press, 1965), 112.

grace through faith has been in effect for all time; they have recognized an element of grace in the Mosaic economy; and they have asserted that the distinctions in the dispensations of law and grace refer to the rule of life rather than the means of justification before God. The two Scofield notes we cited have been radically altered in the New Scofield Reference Bible (1967). One note states that "prior to the cross man's salvation was through faith (Gen. 15:6; Rom. 4:3), being grounded on Christ's atoning sacrifice."[4]

Contention over the issue of law and grace has, therefore, been rendered passé. This is acknowledged by Ryrie, who views the law as a revelation of God relating both to spiritual salvation and to life under the temporal theocracy of the nation of Israel. He concludes that "under the law God provided ways whereby man could be temporally acceptable before Him. . . . Therefore it is entirely harmonious to say that the means of eternal salvation was by grace and the means of temporal life was by law."[5]

The new spirit in discussion is also affirmed by Daniel Fuller, a non-dispensationalist who sees modern dispensationalism and covenant theology coalescing on the problem of law and grace. Citing statements made in the New Scofield Reference Bible and in Ryrie's book *Dispensationalism Today*, Fuller comments, "In comparing these contemporary statements of dispensationalism with covenant theology, we conclude that there is no longer any substantive difference between the two on the subject of the law and the gospel."[6]

Curtis Crenshaw and Grover Gunn reach the same conclusion. They assert that "the neo-dispensationalists" have eliminated the problem of seemingly teaching "divergent ways of salvation in different ages" by "clearly teaching an Old Testament by-faith salvation."[7]

Finally, several recent works on dispensationalism by non-dispensationalists make no mention of different ways of salvation, suggesting by their silence that this is no longer a divisive issue.[8]

---

[4]C. I. Scofield, ed., *The New Scofield Reference Bible* (New York: Oxford Univ. Press, 1967), 1124, n. 1.

[5]Ryrie, *Dispensationalism Today*, 126.

[6]Daniel Fuller, *Gospel and Law: Contrast or Continuum?* (Grand Rapids: Eerdmans, 1980), 45. Fuller also says, "Although today's dispensationalism explains the relationship between law and grace in wording that is different from that of covenant theology, there is no substantial difference in meaning" (51).

[7]Curtis I. Creshaw and Grover E. Gunn III, *Dispensationalism Today, Yesterday, and Tomorrow* (Memphis: Footstool Publications, 1985), 365–66.

[8]See Vern S. Poythress, *Understanding Dispensationalists* (Grand Rapids: Zondervan, 1987); Greg L. Bahnsen and Kenneth L. Gentry, Jr., *House Divided: The Break-up of Dispensational Theology* (Tyler, Tex.: Institute for Christian Economics, 1989). The recent work by John Gerstner, *Wrongly Dividing the Word of Truth* (Brentwood, Tenn.: Wolgemuth & Hyatt, 1991), which makes soteriology the fundamental error of dispensationalism seem difficult to understand in the light of recent discussions. In our opinion Gerstner makes some

It would be going too far, however, to say that all differences on the relationship of law and grace have been erased. Dispensationalism's affirmation of the distinction between the church and Israel and its greater emphasis on the progressive working of God throughout salvation history cause it to place greater emphasis on the distinctions between the pre-Christian era and that of the new covenant following Christ's redemptive work. But none of these differences involves the fundamental way of salvation.[9]

One such distinction that is often noted is the change in the specific object of faith which took place as the revelation of God's salvation unfolded. According to dispensationalists, the Old Testament saints could not have expressly placed their faith in Christ and the saving work of his death and resurrection in the same way believers could after those events took place.

Some differences also remain regarding the rule of the believer's life. Non-dispensationalists tend to emphasize the similarities in the role of the law in the Old Testament economy and the requirements for righteousness placed on believers in the New; they say little or nothing about differences. A full discussion of this issue lies beyond the purpose of this book, but we note that some scriptural statements suggest differences (e.g., Jn 1:17; Gal 3:17ff.), especially a contrast between the old and new covenants.

---

valid observations about the error of "non-lordship salvation." Yet, two things should be noted in this regard: First, the radical non-lordship position of some contemporary dispensationalists, denying the need in salvation of a "faith that works" based on James 2:14–26, has never been a part of traditional or classic dispensationalism. Second, since many dispensationalists today accept some form of lordship salvation, this issue cannot be said to mark dispensationalism as a system of theology (see, for example, John F. MacArthur, *The Gospel According to Jesus* [Grand Rapids, Zondervan, 1988]; James Montgomery Boice, *Christ's Call to Discipleship* [Chicago: Moody, 1986]).

In general, it is difficult to reconcile Gerstner's strong castigation of dispensationalism's soteriology, especially its alleged "spurious Calvinism," with (1) the absence of this issue in the writings of the other non-dispensationalists cited above, and (2) the conclusion of another non-dispensationalist (after an entire section discussing "Dispensationalism and Calvinism") that "the basic theological affinities of dispensationalism are Calvinistic" (C. Norman Kraus, *Dispensationalism in America* [Richmond: John Knox, 1958], 59).

[9]For a discussion of these issues, see John S. Feinberg, "Salvation in the Old Testament," in *Tradition and Testament: Essays in Honor of Charles Lee Feinberg* (Chicago: Moody Press, 1981), 39–77; Allen P. Ross, "The Biblical Method of Salvation: A Case for Discontinuity," in *Continuity and Discontinuity* (Westchester, Ill.: Crossway, 1988), 161–78. Recently differences have arisen between dispensationalists and the non-dispensationalist position commonly known as "dominion theology" or "theonomy" over the application of the Mosaic law to the present age. Again, the issue is the law as the rule of life and not distinctions over the way of salvation. Because many non-dispensationalists also oppose the application of the Mosaic law as taught by dominion theology, the dispensational stance cannot be made a distinctive feature of dispensationalism.

Some see a similarity in the place of the law under the old covenant and the works of faith under the new (e.g., Jas 2), and we concur.[10] But is this all that needs to be said? Surely some added measure of enabling grace is included in the new covenant that was absent under the old economy. The Mosaic covenant includes no promise from God such as that recorded by the prophet Ezekiel: "And I will put My Spirit within you and cause you to walk in My statutes" (Eze 36:27 NASB; cf. Jer 31:33–34). It was this very lack in the old covenant that made a new one necessary to bring people to final perfection (Heb 8:7ff.). Because this difference can only be considered in relation to God's grace, this factor must be included to some extent in discussing the two economies of life.[11]

The Sermon on the Mount. A significant issue closely related to the law-grace question is the interpretation of the Sermon on the Mount. Traditional dispensationalists see Jesus' teaching as applying primarily to the kingdom that he was announcing as being "at hand" (KJV and NASB; "near," NIV). Chafer advocated this position: "In this manifesto the King declares the essential character of the kingdom, the conduct which will be required in the kingdom, and the directions of entrance into the kingdom." He noted further that the teachings are "purely legal" and present "a new degree and standard of law which is adapted to the conditions which shall obtain in the kingdom." Chafer then said that "when His kingdom was rejected and its realization delayed until the return of the King, the application of all Scripture which conditions life in the kingdom was delayed as well."[12] This does not deny that "a secondary application" of "lessons and principles may be drawn from it" for the church today, but it means that its primary application belongs to the dispensation of the kingdom.[13]

Ryrie has expressed essentially the same view. He argues that everyone who seeks to find a direct application of injunctions such as "turning the other cheek" to life today has to abandon a strict literal interpretation of Scripture and make some adjustments. Thus, he writes, "the full, nonfudging, unadjusted fulfillment of the Sermon relates to the

---

[10]Fuller, *Gospel and Law*, 65–120; John Murray, *Principles of Conduct* (Grand Rapids: Eerdmans, 1957), 181–201.

[11]This difference in enabling grace is overlooked by Fuller in his attempt to totally equate the relation of the believer to the commands of the law with the New Testament believer's relation to the imperatives of Christ and the apostles. Under the old economy the believer was commanded to a life of absolute holiness, even as the New Testament believer is. But the old covenant did not include the ultimate fulfillment through enabling grace that is supplied under the new covenant. If the concept of a law-demand without complete enablement for fulfillment constitutes a form of the covenant of works, then it is difficult to deny some aspect of this covenant form under the Mosaic economy.

[12]Lewis Sperry Chafer, *Systematic Theology*, 8 vols. (Dallas: Dallas Seminary Press, 1948), 4:177–78.

[13]Chafer, *Systematic Theology*, 5:97.

kingdom of Messiah . . . ," although it all has relevance for today.[14] However, the question may legitimately be raised whether Jesus intended his teaching to be interpreted in strict literalness. Most scholars suggest that Jesus used some extreme examples designed to teach fundamental principles rather than offering strict, actual cases that are to be interpreted absolutely without qualification.[15] If this is, in fact, the better understanding, then the argument for the impossibility of a primary application for the present age loses its force.

Other dispensationalists, by contrast, hold that the strong presence of manifest evil alluded to in the teaching of the Sermon on the Mount precludes a primary application to the kingdom. They view Jesus' teaching as directed only toward those living during that period when the kingdom was proclaimed as being at hand. Taking this position, Dwight Pentecost states that ". . . in its primary interpretation the Sermon on the Mount is directly applicable to those of our Lord's own day who . . . were anticipating the coming of the King and the kingdom." According to this view, because the kingdom was rejected by Israel and therefore was not established, the message of the Sermon will only be applicable again just prior to the second advent, when the establishment of the kingdom is again "near."[16]

Finally, other dispensationalists, acknowledging that the teachings of Jesus in the Sermon were intended directly for his disciples at the time, see the application as continuing throughout this age. With the previous position, this view understands the directives of the Lord as expressions of kingdom righteousness to be lived in the world before the actual establishment of that kingdom. As believers in the church live in anticipation of that kingdom and are presently called "sons of the kingdom" (Mt 13:18), the pattern of life set forth by Jesus in the Sermon applies directly to them during this age.[17] This latter position on the Sermon would appear to be becoming more popular within dispensationalism, thus excluding this issue as a point of distinction vis-a-vis non-dispensationalists.

---

[14]Ryrie, *Dispensationalism Today*, 106–8.

[15]John A. Broadus, *Commentary on the Gospel of Matthew* (Philadelphia: America Baptist Publication Society, 1886), 110; D. A. Carson, *The Sermon on the Mount* (Grand Rapids: Baker, 1978), 40, 47; Robert H. Stein, *Difficult Sayings in the Gospels* (Grand Rapids: Baker, 1985), 71; D. Martyn Lloyd-Jones, *Studies in the Sermon on the Mount* (Grand Rapids: Eerdmans, 1959), 1:28–30; John Nolland, *Luke 1:1–9:20*, Word Biblical Commentary, vol. 35A (Dallas: Word Books, 1989), 303; John F. Walvoord, *Matthew: Thy Kingdom Come* (Chicago: Moody Press, 1974), 49.

[16]J. Dwight Pentecost, "The Purpose of the Sermon on the Mount," *Bibliotheca Sacra* 115 (October–December 1958): 317; cf. Stanley D. Toussaint, *Behold the King* (Portland, Oreg.: Multnomah Press, 1980), 91–94.

[17]Harry A. Sturz, "The Sermon on the Mount and Its Application to the Present Age," *Grace Journal* 4 (Fall 1963): 3–15.

The Kingdom of Heaven and the Kingdom of God. A rather minor issue that is still occasionally regarded as a feature of dispensationalism,[18] but really should not be, is the distinction between "the kingdom of heaven" and "the kingdom of God." Traditional dispensationalists sometimes contended that the term *kingdom of God* referred to the sphere of reality and *kingdom of heaven* only to the sphere of profession, which encompassed both genuine believers and merely professing believers. In this view, also, the kingdom of God was cosmic and universal in its dimensions, having authority over all creation, while the kingdom of heaven was limited to the earth.[19]

Most recent advocates of a distinction acknowledge that the two expressions are "often used synonymously," yet are to be distinguished in certain contexts.[20] Others who would generally be identified with dispensationalism agree with most non-dispensationalists that no distinction between these expressions is intended by the biblical writers.[21] Matthew's use of "the kingdom of heaven" is to be explained as a Semitic idiom probably resulting from the Jewish reverence for the name of God and the tendency to use "heaven" or "heavens" as a substitute.[22] So, although some dispensationalists still distinguish the two terms in some passages, we agree with Ryrie that this issue is not a determinative feature of dispensationalism.[23]

B. The Focal Issue

Amid this greater harmony, one basic and fairly broad issue remains a point of contention between dispensationalists and non-dispensationalists—namely, God's purpose and plan in biblical history. Other fundamental distinctions have been made, particularly in relation to covenant theology,[24] but in our opinion these other issues should not be viewed as underlying differences.

Non-dispensationalists are often accused of using a spiritualizing or even an allegorizing method of biblical interpretation, especially in the areas of prophecy that relate to the issue of the church and Israel.

---

[18]Millard Erickson, *Contemporary Options in Eschatology* (Grand Rapids: Baker, 1977), 212; see previously George E. Ladd, *Crucial Questions About the Kingdom of God* (Grand Rapids: Eerdmans, 1952), 106.

[19]Chafer, *Systematic Theology*, 7:223–24; 5:316; John F. Walvoord, *The Millennial Kingdom* (Findlay, Ohio: Dunham, 1959), 171; Scofield, *The Scofield Reference Bible*, 1003.

[20]Scofield, *The New Scofield Reference Bible*, 994, 1002.

[21]Eric Sauer, *The Triumph of the Crucified* (Grand Rapids: Eerdmans, 1951), 23; Toussaint, *Behold the King*, 65–68.

[22]Gustaf Dalman, *The Words of Jesus* (Edinburgh: T & T Clark, 1909), 91–93.

[23]Ryrie, *Dispensationalism Today*, 170–71.

[24]Ryrie, *Dispensationalism Today*, 44–47.

Moreover, these critics say, a hermeneutical presupposition is involved, and therefore the differences between theologies entail fundamental approaches to biblical hermeneutics. An analysis of non-dispensational systems, however, reveals that their less-than-literal approach to Israel in the Old Testament prophecies does not really arise from an a priori spiritualistic or metaphorical hermeneutic. Rather, it is the result of their interpretation of the New Testament using the same grammatico-historical hermeneutic as that of dispensationalists. Coming to the conclusion that the New Testament teaches the equation of the church and Israel leads them to an interpretation of the Old Testament prophecies in harmony with their understanding of this New Testament teaching.

Again, it is beyond the scope of this book to explore why scholars using the same hermeneutical procedures come to different conclusions about a given passage of Scripture. Without question, all the factors that contribute to an interpreter's personality—the intellectual, emotional, and spiritual background as well as the *Zeitgeist* in which one works—affect the thought processes and the results.[25] It is here, not in a priori hermeneutical beliefs, that we should look to explain the differences in interpretation and application among dispensationalists and non-dispensationalists.

Another alleged distinction is sometimes seen in the ultimate purpose of God for history. Some dispensationalists have charged their opponents with defining God's purpose as "soteriological" while they themselves regard it as "doxological."[26] That is, non-dispensational (especially covenant) theologians are seen as viewing the salvation of the people of God as the unifying theme of Scripture whereas dispensationalists attribute this unity to the ascription of glory to God. While non-dispensationalists do tend to put more emphasis on the unity in God's program, they clearly view the ultimate goal as the glorification of God, even as dispensationalists do.

So the fundamental issue between dispensationalists and non-dispensationalists is neither a basic hermeneutical principle nor the ultimate purpose of human history. The basic issue is the way we understand the historical plan and the goal of that plan through which God will bring eternal glory to himself. More specifically, it is the question of the purpose and plan of God *within* human history, i.e., from this creation until the inauguration of the eternal state. This inquiry involves not only the basic goal of history, but the meaning and integration of the various aspects of God's work during this period. We must understand not only

---

[25]Stanley N. Gundry, "Hermeneutics or ZEITGEIST as the Determining Factor in the History of Eschatologies?" *Journal of the Evangelical Theological Society* 20 (March 1977): 45–55. See pages 29–35 for further comments on the hermeneutical question.

[26]Ryrie, *Dispensationalism Today*, 46, 98–104.

what God intends to do, but how he accomplishes it. The call of Abraham, the election and formation of the nation of Israel, God's dealing with the church and the nations, and the various covenant arrangements—all these are facets of the historical plan that must be integrated and understood.

There are differences among non-dispensationalists as to the historical goal and the meaning of the various facets, depending on whether they are premillennialists or amillennialists. However, the sharper distinctions occur between dispensationalists and non-dispensationalists.

II. THE NON-DISPENSATIONAL SYSTEM

A. *The Purpose of History*

Many biblical scholars past and present point to the concept of the kingdom of God as the theme of history.[27] Much recent non-dispensational thinking is illustrated by Anthony Hoekema, who writes that "the kingdom of God is the central theme of Jesus' preaching and, by implication, of the preaching and teaching of the apostles. . . . It is in the kingdom of God that we must see the real meaning of history."[28]

The nature of the kingdom of God within history, however, has different conceptions among non-dispensationalists, depending on whether or not they believe that the Scripture teaches a literal, earthly millennial reign of Christ. Because the amillennialist relates the reign of Christ to this present age before the second coming, he tends to view the kingdom purpose of God in history as fundamentally a spiritual reign over the people of God. Roderick Campbell, an earlier non-dispensationalist than Hoekema, declared, "Everything in history and life is subservient to spiritual redemption."[29]

But *spiritual redemption* is an ambiguous term. On the one hand, it can encompass all of God's redeeming activity (including human societal structures and ultimately the creation itself); on the other hand, it can be limited to the redemption summarized in the forgiveness of sins and the new life of the Spirit promised in the new covenant. Amillennialists subscribe to this latter, more limited meaning. Louis Berkhof, for example, argued that the temporal and earthly blessings promised to Abraham "did

[27]John Bright, *The Kingdom of God* (Nashville: Abingdon, 1953), 7; George N. H. Peters, *The Theocratic Kingdom* (Grand Rapids; Kregel, 1952), 1:31; Eric Sauer, *From Eternity to Eternity* (Grand Rapids; Eerdmans, 1972), 75; Walther Eichrodt, *Theology of the Old Testament* (Philadelphia: Westminster, 1961), 1:502ff.; Alva J. McClain, *The Greatness of the Kingdom* (Grand Rapids: Zondervan, 1959), 4–5.

[28]Anthony Hoekema, *The Bible and the Future* (Grand Rapids: Eerdmans, 1974), 41, 37.

[29]Roderick Campbell, *Israel and the New Covenant* (Philadelphia: Presbyterian Board of Christian Education, 1936), 14.

not constitute an end in themselves, but served to symbolize and typify spiritual and heavenly things."[30] In other words, the words that spoke of earthly physical blessing are to be applied presently to the church or to heaven.

Hoekema calls that exegesis unfortunate and seeks to affirm the earthly nature of these blessings by applying them to the new earth.[31] While in doing so, Hoekema does greater justice to the language of prophecy,* we must note that placing the fulfillment of these promises in the time of the new earth puts them beyond the pale of the history of this present earth and the messianic age of Christ's reign.

Hoekema contends that the Old Testament promises are fulfilled in two stages, which he calls "the present Messianic age and the age of the future."[32] According to amillennialists, Christ will deliver up the (messianic) kingdom at his second coming (1Co 15:24), and therefore the promises of a redeemed society of human nations and a world of nature redeemed from the curse will not be fulfilled within the realm of what is ordinarily associated with history and this creation. Instead these promises will be fulfilled in the new creation of the eternal state. Such an interpretation therefore still leaves the purpose of God within this history with the more limited concept of spiritual redemption.

By contrast, premillennial non-dispensationalists are able to view the historical redemption of the kingdom purpose as encompassing the societal and natural elements mentioned above. The messianic reign of Christ includes the establishment of God's will in the structures of human society and government before the mediatorial work of Christ is complete and the kingdom is delivered up to the Father for eternity.

B. The Emphasis on Unity

Non-dispensationalists, as we have stated, emphasize the unity of the historical working of God more than dispensationalists do. Although there may be some variations in how God administers the affairs of earth, these are basically stages in the development of a single program. They may be likened to the development of a person from an infant to adulthood. For traditional covenant theologians, the various economies of God are outworkings of the one covenant of grace.[33] For others, emphasizing the kingdom theme, these economies are stages in the development of

---

[30]Louis Berkhof, *Systematic Theology* (Grand Rapids: Eerdmans, 1953), 296.
[31]Hoekema, *The Bible and the Future*, 205–6, cf. also 274ff.
*In some instances it is difficult for millennialists to make a clear distinction between the millennium and the new earth.
[32]Hoekema, *The Bible and the Future*, 18.
[33]Berkhof, *Systematic Theology*, 290–300.

God's purpose to redeem his creation from the power of sin and and its effects.

Basic to all non-dispensationalist thought is a unity of the people of God that does not allow for a future place and purpose for the nation of Israel in the historical plan of God's redemption. Usually the term *Israel* is applied to the total people of God, Jews and Gentiles alike. However, two great events in this century—the Holocaust and the reestablishment of the state of Israel—have called attention to the continued historical existence of the Jews as a distinct people. This has evoked renewed theological discussion about the meaning and place of Israel in God's purposes, eliciting a wide array of opinions among non-dispensationalists.

Perhaps the view most commonly held among evangelical non-dispensationalists is that Israel's future is simply an incorporation of that people into the church. Hoekema speaks for many when he writes, ". . . the future of believing Israelites is not to be separated from the future of believing Gentiles." He states that Israel has no particular place in God's future salvation economy: "Israel's hope for the future is exactly the same as that of believing Gentiles: salvation and ultimate glorification through faith in Christ."[34]

Herman Ridderbos sets out the theological rationale for this position: "The church takes the place of Israel as the historical people of God" and has been "endowed with all the privileges and blessings of Israel."[35] This is essentially the stance adopted by the Roman Catholic Church at the Second Vatican Council. The council spoke of the future incorporation of Israel within the church, but made no reference to any role or purpose for Israel in God's plan.[36]

Some non-dispensationalists go a step further and say that Israel's incorporation is a means of great blessing to the world. Of Romans 11:15, John Murray states, "This restoration of Israel will have a marked beneficial effect, described as 'life from the dead.'" This is explained as "an unprecedented quickening for the world in the expansion and success of the gospel."[37] Ernst Käsemann likewise appears to see some significance for the rest of the world in the future conversion of Israel. "Israel," he writes, "is the bearer of the blessing both in the present and in the future." And "Israel is an integral part of the end of history. . . . Both the beginning and the end of the drama of salvation are determined by the destiny of Israel."[38] None of these expressions, however, seem to allow

---

[34]Hoekema, *The Bible and the Future*, 201.
[35]Herman Ridderbos, *Paul: An Outline of His Theology* (Grand Rapids: Eerdmans, 1975), 333–34, 360.
[36]Walter M. Abbott, ed., *The Documents of Vatican II* (New York: American Press, 1966), 664–65.
[37]John Murray, *The Epistle to the Romans* (Grand Rapids: Eerdmans, 1965), 2:81, 84.
[38]Ernst Käsemann, *Commentary on Romans* (Grand Rapids: Eerdmans, 1980), 305–7.

any place for the fulfillment of the biblical prophecies that ascribe to Israel a particular place among the nations.

Some scholars who would probably be classified as non-dispensationalists do appear to see some significance for the nation of Israel in the future. George Ladd envisions that through the salvation of Israel "a new wave of life will come to the whole world."[39] He suggested that this may be connected to a national existence: ". . . it may be that in the millennium, for the first time in human history, we will witness a truly Christian nation." However, Ladd seemed to deny giving any basis to this purpose in the Old Testament prophecies in adding that "eschatology simply affirms the future salvation of Israel and remains open to God's future as to the details."[40]

A similar openness to a significant national existence is suggested by Willem VanGemeren in his valuable study on the place of Israel in Reformed Theology. He shows that the Reformed tradition has not always limited the Old Testament prophecies about Israel to a spiritual fulfillment in the church. He calls for a hope that includes a greater fulfillment of the kingdom promises, including physical blessings. Like Ladd, however, VanGemeren seeks to leave completely open the nature of the fulfillment of these prophecies.[41]

The common thread running through these non-dispensational views is the emphasis on the unity of the people of God. True, the reestablishment of the nation of Israel has renewed their interest in the situation of the Jews and brought a greater appreciation for the biblical teaching of a future for Israel; but that future does not entail any distinction between the nation Israel and the other nations of the world. The concept of a special future role among the nations is somehow canceled out by the non-dispensationalists' regard for overriding unity.

III. THE TRADITIONAL DISPENSATIONAL SYSTEM

A. *The Purpose of History*

Traditional dispensationalism proposed a twofold purpose for God's program in history—one purpose related to the earth and worked out through Israel, the other related to heaven and worked out through the church. Chafer called this distinction the defining feature of dispensation-

---

[39]George E. Ladd, *A Theology of the New Testament* (Grand Rapids: Eerdmans, 1974), 562.

[40]George E. Ladd, "Historic Premillennialism," in *The Meaning of the Millennium: Four Views,* ed. Robert G. Clouse (Downers Grove, Ill.: InterVarsity Press, 1977), 28.

[41]Willem A. VanGemeren, "Israel as the Hermeneutical Crux in the Interpretation of Prophecy," *Westminster Theological Journal* (Spring 1983/Fall 1984): 45:132–44; 46:254–97.

alism: "The dispensationalist believes that throughout the ages God is pursuing two distinct purposes: one related to the earth with earthly people and earthly objectives involved which is Judaism; while the other is related to heaven with heavenly people and heavenly objectives involved, which is Christianity."[42]

This divided purpose has subsequently been modified by most dispensationalists in favor of some form of a unified historical plan. Ryrie explains that "any apparent dichotomy between heavenly and earthly purposes is not actual." Both Israel and the church ultimately have a heavenly hope together in the heavenly Jerusalem. The earthly purpose for Israel is to be fulfilled by natural Israel during the course of history, specifically in the millennium.[43]

The basis of this historical unity, according to some dispensationalists, lies in the concept of a theocratic kingdom. Pentecost advocates this view:

> From the outset of God's program to manifest His sovereignty by His rule in this earthly sphere until the consummation of that program, when universal sovereignty is acknowledged (1 Cor. 15:24), there has been one continuous, connected, progressive development of that program. While there might be various phases of the program and different media through which that sovereignty was exercised, it has been the development of one program. This whole program may be called the theocratic kingdom.[44]

Alva McClain likewise sees the kingdom concept as the unifying theme of biblical history, although he explains the term *meditorial kingdom* somewhat differently.[45]

Others, like Ryrie, prefer to see the unifying theme in the more comprehensive but less specific idea of the display of the glory of God. "The unifying principle of dispensationalism," Ryrie states, "is doxological, or the glory of God, and the dispensations reveal the glory of God as He manifests His character in the differing stewardships given to man."[46] While not denying that their opponents also see the glory of God as the chief end of all things, dispensationalists have insisted that limiting the means of that glorification to spiritual redemption—a common non-dispensational theme—is an unwarranted reduction of the many facets of God's historical work. John F. Walvoord states,

---

[42]Lewis Sperry Chafer, *Dispensationalism* (Dallas: Dallas Seminary Press, 1947), 107; cf. also Chafer, *Systematic Theology,* 4:47.

[43]Ryrie, *Dispensationalism Today,* 146–47; cf. J. Dwight Pentecost, *Things to Come* (Findlay, Ohio: Dunham, 1958), 542–46.

[44]Pentecost, *Things to Come,* 433.

[45]McClain, *The Greatness of the Kingdom.*

[46]Ryrie, *Dispensationalism Today,* 102–3.

> All the events of the created world are designed to manifest the glory of God. The error of covenant theologians is that they combine all the many facets of divine purpose in the one objective of fulfillment of the covenant of grace. . . . The various purposes of God for Israel, for the church which is His body, for the Gentile nations, for the unsaved, for Satan and the wicked angels, for the earth and for the heavens have each their contribution. How impossible it is to compress all of these factors into the mold of the covenant of grace![47]

So we see that while they have sometimes been accused of undermining the unity of the Bible,[48] traditional dispensationalists have sought to affirm a unity. But for them, the unity has generally been limited to overarching principles to which the various facets of history (e.g., God's work with Israel, the church, and Gentiles) can be vertically related, rather than any direct, horizontal relations within history itself.

B. The Discontinuity Within the Historical Program

Perhaps the key distinction of traditional dispensationalism, therefore, is its emphasis on the distinctions or discontinuities in the historical program of God. While affirming "an essential unity to divine dealing in human history," Walvoord explains that dispensationalism "distinguishes major stewardships or purposes of God, particularly as revealed in three important dispensations of law, grace, and kingdom."[49]

The most crucial distinction in traditional dispensationalism is between Israel and the church. Ryrie explicitly says so: "The essence of dispensationalism, then, is the distinction between Israel and the Church."[50] This separation is so sharp that the church is precluded from any present relationship to the messianic kingdom promises.

It is common for dispensationalists to refer to the "church age," the period between Pentecost and the rapture, as a parenthesis of time interrupting the messianic kingdom program.[51] Chafer preferred the term *intercalation* because, he said, "a parenthetical portion sustains some direct or indirect relation to that which goes before or that which follows; but the present age-purpose is not thus related. . . ."[52] Assigning this place to the church leads to the conclusion that it is not related to the messianic kingdom promises and the covenants on which this kingdom program rests. Although usually specifying the Davidic kingdom promises in

---

[47]Walvoord, *The Millennial Kingdom*, 92.
[48]See Ryrie, *Dispensationalism Today*, 98ff.
[49]Walvoord, *The Millennial Kingdom*, 223.
[50]Ryrie, *Dispensationalism Today*, 47.
[51]Walvoord, *The Millennial Kingdom*, 227–30.
[52]Chafer, *Systematic Theology*, 4:41.

particular, the fundamental teaching of traditional dispensationalism is that no part of the Old Testament kingdom predictions are being fulfilled in any way during this age.[53]

IV. A MEDIATING POSITION

In our opinion there is a mediating position between non-dispensationalism and traditional dispensationalism that provides a better understanding of Scripture. This view seeks to retain a natural understanding of the prophetic Scriptures that appear to assign a significant role to the nation Israel in the future, in accordance with a dispensational system. But it also sees the program of God as unified *within* history, in agreement with non-dispensationalists, and it denies a radical discontinuity between the present church age and the messianic kingdom promises.

At this point we will not explore all the Scripture and debatable issues related to this broad topic, but we will sketch the general outline.

A. The Unified Purpose of History

Various themes such as "covenant" or "promise" have been put forth as the unifying principle of biblical history. While the particular term one chooses is not crucial, we prefer, with many others, the concept of "the kingdom" as that which best encompasses the full meaning of God's work in the history of Scripture. George N. H. Peters offers this concept in his classic, three-volume work on premillennialism, *The Theocratic Kingdom:* "The kingdom deserves the first place in Biblical and the first rank in Systematic theology. . . . In view of its extent, the doctrine exceeds all others in magnitude, enfolding in itself nearly all doctrine."[54]

John Bright concurs. He writes, ". . . the concept of the Kingdom of God involves, in a real sense, the total message of the Bible. Not only does it loom large in the teachings of Jesus; it is to be found, in one form or another, through the length and breadth of the Bible."[55]

As the theme of biblical history, the kingdom is that program through which God effects his lordship on the earth in a comprehensive

---

[53]Walvoord, *The Millennial Kingdom*, 227; Ryrie, *Dispensationalism Today*, 172–73; Pentecost, *Things to Come*, 142–43.

[54]Peters, *The Theocractic Kingdom*, 1:31, 33.

[55]Bright, *The Kingdom of God*, 7; cf. Eric Sauer: "The 'kingdom' is the real basic theme of the Bible. . . . All ages and periods of the Divinely revealed ways; all groups and persons addressed, whether Israel, the nations, or the church; all temples, sanctuaries, and redeeming acts; all heavenly and demonic activites, whether in the foreground or background, stand in some way, either positively or negatively, in connexion with the history of the kingdom of God. The kingdom itself is the royal saving work of God to the carrying through of His counsels in creation and redemption" (*Eternity to Eternity*, 89).

salvation within history. According to the Scriptures, God has always been the sovereign King over all his creation. The truth stated by the psalmist is found repeatedly in Scripture: "The Lord has established His throne in the heavens; And His sovereignty [or kingdom] rules over all" (Ps 103:19 NASB; cf. Pss 29:10; 74:12; 145:13; 1Ch 29:11–12). This rule of God, however, has been opposed by both evil spirits and humans since the entrance of sin into the good creation of God through the fall of Satan and his angels.

According to biblical revelation, the focal point of the conflict between the powers of evil and the kingdom of God is the earth. Here the drama of redemption is played out and affects the far reaches of the universe. The earth appears in Scripture as a rebelling province in the universal kingdom of God. It is God's purpose to bring an end to this rebellion and its sinful effects, not only in human history, but in all creation. Thus God's kingdom, which today may be said to be *over* the earth, will one day be established *on* the earth. This fundamental purpose is expressed in the petition that Christ taught his disciples to pray: "Your kingdom come, your will be done on earth as it is in heaven" (Mt 6:10).

God's kingly rule is brought to the earth through the mediation of the kingdom of the Messiah. According to biblical prophecy, the coming of the kingdom involves the redemption of creation from all the effects of sin through the personal salvation of individuals, the socio-political salvation of the nations, and finally the salvation of the earth and heavens through re-creation. This pervasive mediatorial kingdom program, ultimately fulfilled through the reign of Christ, is the theme of Scripture and the unifying principle of all aspects of God's work in history.

The historical plan of God, therefore, is one unified plan. Contrary to traditional dispensationalism, it does not entail separate programs for the church and Israel that are somehow ultimately unified only in the display of God's glory or in eternity. The present age is not a historical parenthesis unrelated to the history that precedes and follows it; rather, it is an integrated phase in the development of the mediatorial kingdom. It is the beginning of the fulfillment of the eschatological promises. Thus the church today has its place and function in the same mediatorial messianic kingdom program that Israel was called to serve.

B. A Historical Unity with Distinctions

The unity of the historical kingdom program, however, must be interpreted in such a way as to allow for the natural understanding of all the biblical prophecies. These promises portray a restoration of the nation of Israel to the promised land and a central position for that nation in the final period of the mediatorial kingdom (Isa 2:1–4; chs. 60–62; Jer 33:14–15; Zec 14:16–21). Contrary to non-dispensationalism, the term *Israel* is not finally applied to all God's people irrespective of nationality. Rather, it retains its meaning for a particular national people in accordance with the early covenants and promises of Scripture. This particularity still has significance in the outworking of the mediatorial kingdom.

In our understanding of biblical history, then, Scripture teaches a "unity with distinctives," fusing together what might be termed the primary emphases of both dispensational and non-dispensational theology. Although traditional dispensationalism, as we see it, has tended to draw distinctives too sharply, it must be credited with calling attention to the particularities of biblical history that were ignored and virtually eliminated in other theological systems. By contrast, non-dispensational scholars have encouraged us to focus on the truth of the unity of God's historical work.

C. The Decisive Questions

Having sketched a course for biblical history that falls between traditional dispensational and non-dispensational systems, we still must deal with significant biblical issues that separate the two camps. These naturally focus on the relation of the church and the present age to the history that precedes and follows—which, according to Scripture, have in some sense a special place for Israel.

Is this present age in any sense the beginning of the fulfillment of the messianic kingdom promises? How is the eschatological time in which we are living, beginning with the first advent of Christ, related to the kingdom? What is the meaning of the "mystery" concerning the union of Jews and Gentiles in the church, and is it dispensational or soteriological? How are we to define the church and Israel and their relationship—are they two peoples of God or one? Finally—and most significant for dispensationalists—what is the distinctive role of Israel for the future, and what is the purpose in that role?

These questions relate to the basic differences between dispensationalism and non-dispensationalism. It is hoped that the increasing attention given to these issues by both groups today will lead to better understanding of Scripture and greater unity of thought.

V. SOME HERMENEUTICAL CONSIDERATIONS

In forging a mediating position that sees a historical unity of God's kingdom program of salvation, yet allows distinctions especially as regards Israel, we have suggested that this conclusion results from taking the Scriptures in their "natural understanding." We do not retract our earlier assertion that the basic hermeneutical procedure, especially in its beginning principles, is essentially the same for both dispensational and non-dispensational scholars. Both affirm a historical-grammatical hermeneutic. Differing judgments as to whether a particular statement should be interpreted literally are based on the prior application of the historical-grammatical hermeneutic to other passages.

There are, however, other considerations, which might be termed hermeneutical, that bear on one's interpretation. We will not explore these at length, but will deal with them briefly as they apply directly to the relationship of the Old and New Testaments and the overall interpretation of biblical history.

A. *The Old Testament Prophecies Include the Eschatological Realities*

For interpreting biblical prophecy it is necessary to understand the relationship of the two testaments. We must remember that the Old Testament is not just the record of the history that precedes the New Testament. The designations "Old" and "New" can give the false impression that the Old Testament is superseded historically by the New. The prophecies in the Old Testament, like those in the New, look to the future, which includes the eternal state of the new heavens and earth (e.g., Isa 65:17; 66:22). In other words, while the history of God's people related in the Old Testament reveals life under the old covenant, the Old Testament nevertheless depicts the ending of this old arrangement in favor of the blessings of a new covenant.

Recognizing that the Old Testament prophecies speak of the eschatological times and events, including the inauguration of the new covenant, precludes our seeing all of the Old Testament as merely shadows and types that become outmoded with the coming of Christ. The fulfilled reality of the coming of Christ transcended many elements contained in the old Mosaic covenant; but this cannot be said of the promises of the new covenant and other eschatological realities. These eschatological elements of the Old Testament promises, therefore, may be said to stand as antitypical in relation to the typical shadows of the old covenant. If such is the case, then, it would seem logical that these eschatological elements should be understood in their Old Testament meaning unless later revelation indicates a reinterpretation.

Another aspect of the eschatological elements in Old Testament prophecy is that these promises combined both "spiritual" and what might be called "material" elements. Some scholars conclude that with the coming of the spiritual realities in Christ and the Spirit, the physical, or material, loses its meaning. Thus Christ becomes the real meaning of the land or the temple or even Israel. According to this reasoning, the coming of the spiritual realities somehow requires eliminating the physical or material dimension of things. But the idea that a move away from the material to the spiritual is a genuine advancement in salvation history sounds suspiciously Platonic.

By contrast, the Old Testament prophets saw no problem with the physical and material existing together with the spiritual in eschatological times—analogous to the original creation, which included the material. For those prophets, the outpouring of the Spirit and even his indwelling in the human heart could exist alongside the material realities of Israel's restoration to the land, the city of Jerusalem, and the temple. Although the new spiritual realities brought changes—especially in the direct relationship of God, through the Spirit, with all people everywhere—these changes apparently did not rule out the reality and significance of the physical in God's eschatological plan. The present age of the church, with its lack of significance for physical realities (e.g., particular places or physical descent), ought not to rule out these material realities in the future. All agree that the present age is only the inauguration and partial fulfillment of the prophecies.

B. The Biblical Meaning and Use of Typology

Discussion of the church and Israel often turns to the matter of the biblical meaning and use of typology.[56] Without getting technical, we can say that Scripture clearly teaches that there is a correspondence between events, persons, and institutions related to Old Testament Israel and aspects of God's work in the New Testament church. But several things must be kept in mind in drawing conclusions from this relationship.

Typology, it is generally agreed, does not eliminate the historicity of the type. This is universally accepted with regard to historical Israel's living under the old covenant. But what about the Israel of the eschatological time portrayed in the prophets, the Israel related to the reign of the future Davidic king? The church is often viewed as typologically replacing Israel in these prophecies. What, then, happens to the historicity of the type if the type is not the historical Israel living under the old covenant, but the future Israel enjoying messianic salvation under the new covenant?

These questions lead us back to a prior question, namely, whether the New Testament teaches that Israel is a type of the church. The answer seems to depend on one's concept of the relationship between a type and its antitype. If a type is understood as shadow pointing forward to the

---

[56]For example, Leonhard Goppelt, *Typos: The Typological Interpretation of the Old Testament in the New* (Grand Rapids: Eerdmans, 1982), 136–51; Paul Feinberg, "Hermeneutics of Discontinuity," in *Continuity and Discontinuity*, 120–23; Mark W. Karlberg, "The Significance of Israel in Biblical Typology," *Journal of the Evangelical Theological Society* 31, no. 3 (1988): 257–69; Poythress, *Understanding Dispensationalists*, 97–117.

reality of an antitype, then it is questionable whether Israel is a type. It would mean, as with many matters under the old covenant, that the coming of the reality in Christ brought the existence of the type to an end—that is, the shadow was absorbed into the reality. By contrast, if a type is defined as a general historical and theological correspondence,[57] then the many analogies between Old Testament Israel and the New Testament people of God may well be explained by seeing Israel as a type of the church. But the correspondences with God's actions among Old Testament Israel would not in this understanding of typology deny the continued existence of that nation in the future.

C. The Finality of Christ

The revelation of God and in a very real sense the saving action of God reach their finality in Christ. All is finally summed up in him—all promises as well as all ministry for salvation. With the coming of Christ we have also reached the "last days" of history. Not only that, but we have reached the realm of the heavenlies having come to the heavenly Jerusalem (cf. Heb 12:22).

As profound as the truths of Christ's finality and our present relation to heavenly realities are, they cannot render totally insignificant the continuing historical fulfillment of the promises on earth. The truth that all the promises are fulfilled in Christ does not, as some say, dissolve their meaning into the person of Christ. Nor does it mean that all human ministry is outmoded. The fact that the Old Testament priesthood finds its fulfillment in Christ, as taught in the book of Hebrews, does not preclude a future priestly ministry for the nation of Israel in accord with the picture of the Old Testament prophets and the original call of that people. That such is the case is demonstrated in the present ministry of the church. Even though Christ came as the final High Priest, it is clear that the church is still commissioned as a priestly people in the service of God's salvation.

The fact that earthly human ministry still has significance after the finality of Christ's coming leads to a second truth with hermeneutical implications. The application of Christ's fulfillment of the eschatological promises is progressive. Christ's coming into the world and our coming to God's final eschatological salvation in him did not bring either the end of history or our perfection. Just as the new covenant, promising ultimate perfection, is worked out gradually in our lives, so also the application of

---

[57]This is essentially the definition of David L. Baker when he describes a type as "a biblical event, person or institution which serves as an example or pattern for other events, persons or institutions . . ." and then defines typology as "the study of types and the historical and theological correspondences between them" ("Typology and the Christian Use of the Old Testament," *Scottish Journal of Theology* 29 [1976]: 153).

God's salvation to human history involves the progressive fulfillment of promises on earth. Thus God's purpose in electing Israel may be said to be fulfilled in Christ, but this does not deny a place or time for Israel's participation in that fulfillment even as Christ presently fulfills his ministry through the church.

D. The Theology of the New Testament Writers

The interpretation of biblical prophecies that are central to our discussion revolves ultimately around the question of their progressive fulfillment. More specifically, the issue is how the prophecies in the Old Testament that relate to *the coming* of the Messiah are divided in the New Testament so as to be fulfilled in *two comings*. Everyone involved in the discussion would agree that the biblical writers are the final source of reference in this matter. Dispensationalists have sometimes been accused of putting a priority on Old Testament teaching while non-dispensationalists emphasize the teaching of the New Testament. In truth, both sides must use all the Bible with the recognition that the principle of progressive revelation obviously gives the New Testament writers the last word.

Thus the teaching of the apostles is crucial to the proper understanding of the fulfillment of the Old Testament prophecies. The apostles are the ones who must sort out the unified messianic prophecies of the Old Testament so that we can interpret them correctly. To understand the apostles' teaching, therefore, it is essential that the interpreter determine exactly what is taught as being fulfilled during this age and what remains for the future. Because the Old Testament prophecies were not divided, we must make careful judgments in our exegesis to determine what is present and what is future.

Peter's citation of Joel 2 in Acts 2:17ff. illustrates the problem, although this example is comparatively easy to solve. The immediate context and a knowledge of the New Testament teaching about the future lead to the unmistakable conclusion that Peter did not mean that all of Joel's prophecy was fulfilled at Pentecost.

It is common to give hermeneutical significance, either tacitly or explicitly, to the relative silence of the New Testament with regard to the prophetic picture portrayed so fully in the Old Testament. In particular, much is made of the lack of explicit teaching by the apostle Paul about the so-called nationalistic promises to Israel. For example, it is frequently assumed, if not stated outright, that the absence of a specific mention of the restoration of Israel as a nation and her return to the land in connection with her future salvation (Ro 11:26) signifies that these aspects of Old Testament prophecy are no longer valid. Another example is Paul's failure to give an explicit teaching about a millennial reign comparable to that given by John in Revelation 20.

We suggest that to assess this phenomenon of the comparative lack of repetition of the Old Testament prophetic picture in the New Testament, we should consider the historical situation of the New Testament writers. As Jews or other people closely related to Israel, the writers were people of the Old Testament Scriptures. For them, the apostolic tradition of the New Testament was something added onto their already existing Bible. As people well-versed in the Jewish Scriptures, the prophecies of the coming eschatological Davidic king and his reign were not only well-known to them but were also their hope. This is evident in the question the disciples asked about the restoration of the kingdom of Israel (Ac 1:6).

The Old Testament Scriptures were familiar not only to the writers of the New Testament, but also to the other people in the early church. The apostles continually referred to these Scriptures to support their teaching about Christ. Moreover, those who heard their teaching were commended for searching "the Scriptures"—that is, what we call the Old Testament—to see whether what the New Testament teachers were saying was true (Ac 17:11).

It should be noted that this relation of the early New Testament church to the Old Testament stands in contrast to most believers in the church who begin with the New Testament and only after considerable study in this portion of the Scriptures then venture into the Old Testament. Even then the prophetic portions of the Old Testament are often the last to receive much study. Along with this practice and perhaps to some extent resulting from it, the idea is fostered that the New Testament is the Christian Scriptures, whereas the Old Testament deals only with the history of ancient Israel. Little recognition is given to the fact that the Old Testament also deals with the Messiah, the Christ, in its prophecies. As indicated earlier, even the language, "Old" and "New" Testaments is somewhat misleading, somehow indicating that the old deals with that which has been outmoded even as the old covenant. For the people of the New Testament era, what we know as the Old Testament was considered their Christian Scriptures (e.g., 2Ti 3:16).

When we encounter the hermeneutical argument of silence, therefore, we must remember that the Old Testament prophecies were in the Scriptures and the minds of the New Testament writers and their audience. If that is the case, why should we think it necessary that the prophecies be reiterated in the New Testament? If they desired to teach their continued validity, it would seem sufficient for the apostles to simply affirm this fact without repeating all the prophecies.

At least two hermeneutical principles seem relevant to the historical and theological stance of the New Testament writers. First, the fact that these writers were familiar with the Old Testament prophecies suggests that we should be also to have an adequate foundation for interpreting the New Testament. Second, the lack of detail about the Old Testament prophecies in the New Testament does not necessarily mean they are invalid or superseded. To the contrary, the situation of the early church suggests that we should consider the prophecies valid unless there is explicit teaching to the contrary. The infrequent affirmations that do appear in the New Testament—such as Paul's statements of validation in Romans 9:3–5 and 11:26, 29—imply that these promises retain their Old Testament meaning unless otherwise stated.

The historical and theological setting of the New Testament writers compels us to put ourselves in their position even as we listen to them as our teachers. We must reckon with *their* Scriptures and not just the New Testament.

PART II

THE PRESENT AGE AND
OLD TESTAMENT PROPHECY

Chapter 2

The Abrahamic Covenant

A KEY ISSUE in discussion between dispensationalists and non-dispensationalists is the place of the present age in the Old Testament prophecies. Christian scholars agree that Jesus is the fulfillment of the Old Testament predictions of the Messiah who was to come. They likewise agree that the work of salvation that he accomplished on earth fulfilled the Old Testament Scriptures. The disagreement among interpreters centers primarily in the predictions about the messianic kingdom.

Dispensationalists traditionally have recognized Christ as the promised Messiah and his saving work as the fulfillment of the Old Testament predictions of spiritual salvation associated with the Messiah. However, they deny that any of the messianic kingdom promises are being fulfilled during the present age of the church. Since the church is not Israel, these promises, which feature a restored Israel, await their fulfillment in the future time of the millennium kingdom.

Non-dispensationalists, by contrast, affirm that these kingdom promises are fulfilled in part in the present age. The extent of that fulfillment relates to one's view of the millennium. Millennialists, believing that a millennial kingdom period will precede the eternal state, see the fulfillment of the prophecies as spanning the present church age, the millennium, and the eternal state.

Amillennialists hold to a fulfillment in two ages—the present church age and the eternal state (which is ushered in by the second coming of Christ). The amillennial emphasis on the fulfillment of Christ's messianic kingdom during the present age can be attributed to the apostle Paul's teaching that the mediatorial work of Christ's kingdom is in some sense complete at the second coming, when he hands over the kingdom to God the Father (1Co 15:24). Any predictions of the Messiah's reign over an imperfect world must be fulfilled during the present age, because the next age is the new heaven and new earth, where there is no unrighteousness.

The non-dispensational millennialist, on the other hand, has more room for the fulfillment of the promises. All of the prophecies of Christ's reign on earth before he hands the kingdom to the Father do not take place during the present time; there is yet a millennial phase of the kingdom when many of the predictions dealing with a literal reign are to be fulfilled.

The problem of relating the present age to the Old Testament messianic prophecies can be solved only by examining what the New Testament says. These prophecies, which outline God's purpose and plan for humankind and their world, are expressions of God's covenant promises—in particular, the Abrahamic, Davidic, and new covenants.[1] So we do well to consider first the fulfillment of the foundational covenants. Which aspects of these covenant promises, according to the Scriptures, are fulfilled in the present, and which ones remain to be fulfilled?

I. THE ABRAHAMIC COVENANT IN THE OLD TESTAMENT

Immediately after the Fall, God promised, in the protevangelium of Genesis 3:15, the future victory of humanity over evil. The "seed of the woman," Christ, would triumph over evil represented by "the seed of the serpent." As the conflict between good and evil is played out, the early chapters of Genesis tell of God's intervention in history to rescue mankind from total corruption in the Flood and at the tower of Babel. These actions, however, were essentially preservative rather than positive steps in a program of salvation. It would seem that God was letting mankind demonstrate its inability to fulfill the creation mandate of ruling the earth as his representative (cf. Ge 1:26, 28) before introducing his plan of salvation in the establishment of his kingdom.

Only with the call of Abraham does God step into human history to intitiate his own kingdom program of salvation. The gracious promises given to Abraham in covenant appear throughout Scripture as the foundation and essential ingredients in germinal form of all subsequent

---

[1]The Mosaic, or Sinaitic, covenant that dominated Israel's life in the Old Testament is superseded by the new covenant and therefore has no ongoing ramification for the fulfillment of God's purposes (cf. Jer 31:31–32; Heb 8:6–13, esp. v. 13).

salvation history.[2] In addition to the content, the paradigmatic divine-human relationship evident in the covenant with Abraham constitutes the root of all salvation. What H. J. Kraus aptly says in relation to Abraham and the Old Testament message can be extended equally to the remainder of biblical history:

> In this word of God to Abraham is to be found a master clue to the understanding of the whole of Old Testament history. The starting point of the history of man's salvation is God's call to man and nothing else. . . . This call, with its trenchant demand for separation, is at the same time promise. Out of Abraham a great people will grow, and this people will be the bearer of blessing to all peoples. *By way of Abraham and Israel God enters into the world of the nations.* The Old Testament message is based on the first call and on the first promise of which Abraham was the recipient.[3]

God's purpose through Abraham began with the gracious promises attached to a call for separation (Ge 12:1–3). It was subsequently ratified in formal covenant agreement (Ge 15:4–21) and later reiterated with more detail on three occasions during Abraham's lifetime (Ge 13:14–17; 17:1–21; 22:15–18). It was finally confirmed to Isaac (Ge 26:3–5, 24) and Jacob (Ge 28:13–15; 35:9–12; cf. 46:1–4), making it possible for Israel subsequently to speak of God's "covenant with Abraham, Isaac and Jacob" (2Ki 13:23).

This covenant promise is grounded in God's sovereign purpose. John Bright writes that

> this covenant is depicted simply as a binding promise—or, better, a promissory oath—on the part of God. No particular conditions are attached to it. True, it is assumed that Abraham would continue to trust God and walk before him in righteousness and obedience, and the point is now and then made that Abraham did so (e.g., 22:16; 16:50). But the giving of the promise itself is not made subject to conditions. There is no list of commandments that Abraham must obey, or obligations that he must fulfill, if it is to be made good. . . . The patriarchal covenant thus rests in God's unconditional promises for the future, and it asks of the recipient only that he trust.[4]

---

[2]William J. Dumbrell notes the comprehensiveness of the Abrahamic promise, declaring, "The Kingdom of God established in global terms is the goal of the Abrahamic covenant" (*Covenant and Creation* [Nashville: Nelson, 1984], 78).

[3]H. J. Kraus, *The People of God in the Old Testament* (New York: Association Press, 1958), 26–27.

[4]John Bright, *Covenant and Promise* (Philadelphia: Westmister, 1976), 25–26.

In the Abrahamic promise, therefore, God not only stipulated the basic format of his plan to establish his kingdom, but also assured its final fulfillment. The promises were eternal (Ge 13:15; 17:7–8, 19; 48:4).

A. The Promises of the Abrahamic Covenant

God began with promises and blessings for Abraham personally. The patriarch would become the primogenitor of a great nation; he would be blessed and his name made great; he would be a blessing to others; and all the families of the earth would be blessed in him (Ge 12:2–3).

It is only fitting that the one through whom God initiated his salvation program and who in his faith-response became the pattern of all true saving faith (cf. Ro 4:11–12, 16) should be blessed with great significance. But the personal blessing of Abraham and even the great nation of which he was primogenitor were not the final goal of God's promise. The construction of the Hebrew text of Genesis 12:2–3 reveals that the ultimate purpose was to bless all the peoples of the earth.[5] This ultimate purpose and the means to attain it are expressed in the later covenant statements with Abraham and its reiterations with Isaac and Jacob. These covenant promises reveal three essential elements: a seed, a land, and a blessing for all peoples.

1. The Seed. In the patriarchal narratives of Genesis 12–50, the most frequently mentioned aspect of the promise is a "seed." The initial promise refers to a "great nation" that will come from Abraham (Ge 12:2), but the term *seed* takes precedence in subsequent statements to the patriarchs. Beginning with the promise of a land for Abraham's "seed" in Genesis 12:7, the promise of a numerous posterity is stated again and again.[6]

The seed would be as innumerable as "the dust of the earth" (Ge 13:16) and "as numerous as the stars in the sky and as the sand on the

---

[5]Dumbrell's explanation of the Hebrew construction of Genesis 12:1–3 makes this evident. "There is a major summons in v. 1 in the form of a Heb. imperative ['Leave' or 'Go forth' (NASB)], followed in v. 2 by three Heb. subordinate clauses whose verbs are in the Heb. imperfect tense. Attached to them is the Heb. imperative with which v. 2 concludes ['You will be a blessing' or, perhaps more literally, 'Be thou a blessing']. Then there follow two more subordinate clauses, again with Heb. imperfect verbs, and finally a main statement, whose verb is in the Heb. perfect tense, concludes v. 3 ['all the peoples of the earth will be blessed . . .']. It is agreed that the principal statement of these three verses is contained in the final clause of v. 3. The Heb. syntax indicates this, and the clause is most probably to be taken as a result clause indicating what will be the consummation of the promises that the preceding verses have announced. That is to say, the personal promises given to Abram have final world blessing as their aim" (*Covenant and Creation,* 65).

[6]References to a posterity (most of which include the term *seed*) include Genesis 12:7; 13:15–16; 15:5; 17:2, 5–10, 13, 16, 19–20; 18:18; 21:12; 22:17–18; 26:3–4, 24; 28:13–14; 32:12; 35:11–12; 46:3; 48:4, 16.

seashore" (Ge 22:17; cf. 15:5). The New Testament discloses that this great "seed" ultimately includes all those who follow Abraham's pattern of faith that justifies, whether Jew or Gentile (cf. Ro 4:10–12).

Including Gentiles among Abraham's descendants through Christ, however, does not preclude the literal, physical dimension clearly evident in the promise. Abraham's seed was not identified merely by "faith"; it began with a clearly physical meaning. Abraham's "children" (literally "seed") would come from his "own body" (Ge 15:3–4). Beginning with Isaac, the "son of promise," the descendants of Abraham are traced by physical descent through Jacob and his sons until the Seed, Jesus the Christ, appears and the Gentiles are included in him.

It is significant that Abraham's posterity at first mention are termed "a great nation [יוֹג, goy]" (Ge 12:2; cf. also 18:18). The concept of "nation" in the Old Testament involved race, government, and territory.[7] Thus the term points to the physical nature of the seed that would come from Abraham. But it also signifies the political form that the seed was to take. Noting that the usual term for Israel as the seed is "people," a kinship term expressing the closeness of their relationship to God, William Dumbrell sees the use of "nation" in this initial promise to Abraham as signifying "Israel's later political constitution."[8] The use of "nation" for this aspect of Abraham's "seed" therefore separates it from other peoples, both racially and politically. The ultimate significance of applying this term to Israel, according to Dumbrell, is related to God's final purpose of establishing his kingdom on earth.

> . . . the choice of *goy* [nation] in these verses [Ge 12:1-3] may have been a studied one. "People of God," the usual designation later for Israel, operates as a separative term, without reference in itself to the set of wider purposes with which the call of Israel was bound up. But the biblical plan of redemption does not finally focus upon a saved people so much as it does upon a governed world. . . . In short the use of *am* [people] in this context may not have been an adequate one. It may not in itself have been thought to emphasize sufficiently the goal of redemption to which Gen. 12:1–3 directs itself. For though Israel is certainly the nation which the Abrahamic promises have immediately in view, Israel as a nation, as a symbol of divine rule manifested within a political framework, was intended itself to be an image of the shape of final world government, a symbol pointing beyond itself to the reality yet to be.[9]

[7]R. E. Clement, "יוֹג," *Theological Dictionary of the Old Testament* (Grand Rapids: Eerdmans, 1975), 2:428.
[8]Dumbrell, *Covenant and Creation*, 66.
[9]Dumbrell, *Covenant and Creation*, 66–67.

Both the promise of descendants from his own body and the term *nation* confirm that the promised seed involved people physically related to Abraham. In addition, the references to an innumerable seed anticipated including others in the promise beyond the physical relationship.

We should note also that the term *seed* carried with it a certain "doctrinal intention" that linked it with the original promise of a victorious "seed" for all mankind (Ge 3:15). The promise of a seed to Abraham was a continuation of this original promise.[10] As a collective singular noun, *seed* can refer both to one person and to numerous, related family descendants, implying a corporate solidarity between the one and the many. This double sense is evident in the term "seed of the woman," which moves from the collective many to the singular "he" (Ge 3:15). Thus it is with the seed of Abraham. The expression refers to the one, Christ (Gal 3:16), and the many in union with him (Gal 3:29).

Interestingly, the promised seed is presented both as a benefit (for Abraham and the entire world) and as the beneficiary of divine blessing (temporal and spiritual). The same may be said of the "seed of the woman."

2. *The Land.* The second component of the promise to Abraham was a land for the seed.[11] This is implied in the connection between the command to "go to the land I will show you" and the promise to make Abraham into "a great nation."[12] The promise is made explicit after Abraham reaches Canaan (Ge 12:7). The land promise is prominently repeated thereafter, running "through the patriarchal narratives like a red thread."[13]

Because the concept of "nation" carries a territorial aspect, the land must be viewed as the necessary corollary to the promised seed that would constitute the "great nation." Elmer Martens states, "The promise for descendants and the promise of land are complementary. Numerous descendants need living space; a land needs occupants. From the first, the

---

[10]For a fuller explanation of the connection between the "seed" of Genesis 3:15 and the Abrahamic "seed" promise, see Walter C. Kaiser, Jr., *Toward an Old Testament Theology* (Grand Rapids: Zondervan, 1978), 88–89.

[11]The exact territorial extent of the land is difficult to determine. For a thorough discussion of the boundaries of the promised land, see George Wesley Buchanan, *The Consequences of the Covenant* (Leiden: E. J. Brill, 1970), 91–109. Elmer Martens concludes that "the land was never defined with geographical precision" (*God's Design* [Grand Rapids: Baker, 1981], 100).

[12]For the connection evident in the grammatical structure of these verses, see Dumbrell, *Covenant and Creation,* 64–65.

[13]Magnus Ottosson, "אֶרֶץ," *Theological Dictionary of the Old Testament,* vol. 1 (Grand Rapids: Eerdmans, 1974), 403. The references to the land promise in the patriarchal narrative are in Genesis 12:7; 13:15, 17; 15:7–8, 18; 17:8; 24:7; 26:3–4 (pl. "lands"); 28:4, 13; 35:12; 48:4; 50:24.

people and land belong together; both belong to Yahweh."[14] This connection becomes prominent in Deuteronomy in relation to Israel's possession of the land. According to Magnus Ottosson,

> Deuteronomy understands the patriarchal narrative exclusively in the sense of land promise. "Possession of the land is a prerequisite for the existence of, and a condition for the continuation of, the people. Loss of the land means the end of the national existence."[15]

The land was promised as "an everlasting possession" for Abraham and his descendants (Ge 17:8; cf. 13:15). It is also mentioned in the context of the solemnizing of the covenant in Genesis 15 (cf. vv. 15–21). These statements demonstrate that the land promise cannot be singled out from the other aspects of the Abrahamic promise as only temporary or a type of something "spiritual" or "heavenly."[16] According to the Old Testament, the land promise was absolutely essential to the theology of Israel.

> The land in Old Testament faith is not something indifferent that could just as well be as not be. It is something that belongs to the

---

[14]Martens, *God's Design*, 99.

[15]Ottosson, "אֶרֶץ," *TDOT*, 1:404, citing J. G. Ploger, *Literarkritische, formgeschichtliche und stilkritische Untersuchungen zum Deuteronomium, Bonner Biblische Beitrage* 26 (1967): 91f. With the same focus on Deuteronomy, Gerhard von Rad states, ". . . it is evident that this notion of the land which Israel is to inhabit, and which matches Israel's nationhood, is a theological conception of the highest order. No one who has read *Deuteronomy* need have any doubt of this. In this work the land is undeniably the most important factor in the state of redemption to which Israel has been brought" ("There Remains Still a Rest for the People of God: An Investigation of a Biblical Conception," in *The Problem of the Hexateuch and Other Essays* [New York: McGraw-Hill, 1966], 95).

[16]Illustrative of this common interpretation is Louis Berkhof's statement: "The covenant with Abraham already included a symbolical element. On the one hand it had reference to temporal blessings, such as the land of Canaan, a numerous offspring, protection against and victory over the enemies; and on the other, it referred to spiritual blessings. It should be borne in mind, however, that the former were not co-ordinate with, but subordinate to, the latter. These temporal blessings did not constitute an end in themselves, but served to symbolize and typify spiritual and heavenly things" (*Systematic Theology* [Grand Rapids; Eerdmans, 1941], 296).

Kaiser's comment is well-founded: "Such material or temporal blessing was not to be torn apart from the spiritual aspects of God's great promise. Nor was it to be spiritualized or transmitted into some type of heavenly Canaan of which the earthly Canaan was only a model. The text was emphatic, especially chapter 17, that this covenant was to be eternal" (*Toward an Old Testament Theology*, 90).

Although Martens seems to equivocate somewhat on the literal meaning of the promise for the future, emphasizing the symbolic meaning of the land in the New Testament (see pp. 242, 247, 260–61), he nevertheless strongly affirms the natural meaning of "land" in the Old Testament promise: "But if land is more than acreage or territory and symbolic of promise, gift, blessing and life-style, it is nevertheless still soil and territory. It has theological aspects, but is it not thereby an ethereal thing, nor should it be spiritualized. Land is real. Earth is spatially definable. Life with Yahweh takes place here and now" (*God's Design*, 115).

complete relation of God to Israel. . . . The land is a gift of Yahweh, the Lord of the land, which has led Israel out of Egypt in order to bring her to the place of rest, as Deuteronomy 12.9 describes it. It acquires thereby something of a sacramental quality. It is the sign of the confirmation of God's love for Israel and of Israel's belonging to God.[17]

3. The Universal Blessing. The climax of the divine promise to Abraham came with the third provision, namely, that "all peoples on earth will be blessed through you" (Ge 12:3).[18] Repeated twice to Abraham (Ge 18:18; 22:18) and confirmed later to Isaac (Ge 26:4) and Jacob (Ge 28:14), this provision, coming as it does at the end, is the goal on which all the other aspects of the promise focus. On the basis of the Hebrew structure, Dumbrell calls this final promise "the principle statement" of Genesis 12:1–3. It is "most probably to be taken as a result clause indicating what will be the consummation of the promises that the preceding verses have announced. That is to say, the personal promises given to Abram have final world blessing as their aim."[19] This promise included the seed and the "great nation," Israel. The people of Israel were called to be a channel of God's grace to all peoples.

B. The Continuity of the Abrahamic Covenant in the Old Testament

Throughout the Old Testament, the history of God's people finds continuity in the Abrahamic promise. Passed on by Joseph to his brothers (Ge 50:24), the promise became the framework for all subsequent dealings between God and his people. Ronald E. Clements writes that "the covenant with Abraham is the ever abiding covenant by which Israel lives."[20] The establishment of the nation of Israel later under the Sinai covenant, with its goal of service for all nations (cf. Ex 19:5–6), was the beginning of the fulfillment of the promise to Abraham; the Davidic and new covenants gave further substance to the promise.

---

[17]Walther Zimmerli, *The Old Testament and the World* (Atlanta: John Knox, 1976), 77; also W. D. Davies: "Of all the promises made to the patriarchs it was that of the land that was most prominent and decisive. It is the linking together of the promise to the patriarchs with the fulfillment of it in the settlement that gives to the Hexateuch its distinctive theological character. For the Hexateuch the land is a promised land, and that inviolably" (*The Gospel and the Land* [Berkeley, Calif.: Univ. of California Press, 1974], 24).

[18]For a defense of the passive interpretation of the niphal form, נִבְרְכוּ, to bless, see Oswald T. Allis, "The Blessing of Abraham," *Princeton Theological Review* 25 (1927): 263–98; Kaiser, *Toward an Old Testament Theology*, 13. This interpretation is supported by the rendering of this verse in the LXX and the New Testament (Ac 3:25; Gal 3:8). The hithpael form is found in the statements in 22:18 and 26:4.

[19]Dumbrell, *Covenant and Creation*, 65.

[20]Ronald E. Clements, "אַבְרָהָם," *Theological Dictionary of the Old Testament*, vol. 1 (Grand Rapids: Eerdmans, 1974), 58; cf. also, Dumbrell, *Covenant and Creation*, 78.

As time passed, God's relationship with Israel was expressed predominantly in terms of the Sinai covenant and, under the monarchy, the Davidic covenant. However, the foundation of Israel's relation to God in the Abrahamic covenant was always present. God's favor rested on Israel, the "descendants of Abraham," because of his promise to his "servant," Abraham (Ps 105:6–11), who was also his "friend" (2Ch 20:7; cf. Isa 41:8).

Israel's very existence was sustained by the Abrahamic promise. When the people sinned by making the golden calf, Moses interceded in their behalf with an appeal to God's promise to Abraham (Ex 32:13; cf. Dt 9:27–28). God's warning of punishment for the people was always mitigated by a word of grace. Israel's judgment would never be absolute because God would remember his covenant with Abraham, Isaac, and Jacob (Lev 26:42–44; cf. Dt 29:13; 2Ki 13:22–23; 1Ch 16:16). Even the universal aspect of the promise was present as the psalmist celebrated the reign of Yahweh and anticipated the "nobles of the nations" assembling as "the people of the God of Abraham" (Ps 47:9).

In the time of the decline of the Davidic monarchy and subsequent exile, we find an increased reference to the Abrahamic covenant in the Scriptures of that period. According to Clements, this is owing both to the waning of the monarchy and to the concern for Israel's future, which was threatened by its transgression.

> That interest in Abraham was reawakened in the exilic and postexilic periods indicates the critical condition caused by the loss of the land and the downfall of the Davidic monarchy. It was natural for one to appeal to the covenant tradition guaranteeing Israel possession of the land by a divine oath. . . . While the covenant at Sinai-Horeb raised a question about Israel's future deliverance, since Israel had indeed transgressed the commandments (cf. Jer. 31:31–34; Ezk. 36:26–28), the Abraham covenant took on new significance as a unilateral divine oath, promising the growth of a national consciousness and possession of the land.[21]

Thus the prophets' message of a future for Israel, despite the present divine judgment, was anchored by references to Abraham (Isa 29:22–24; 41:8–10; Jer 33:1–26, esp. v. 26; Mic 7:20). Zion could take comfort in the fact that she was hewn from "the rock . . . Abraham" (Isa 51:2–3).

The land aspect of the Abrahamic promise had particular importance for the prophets of the declining and post-monarchy era. Because of apostasy, Israel was losing the land and consequently her nationhood, but

---

[21]Clements, *TDOT*, 1:57–58. This explanation is valid even if one puts the date for the references to Abraham found in Isaiah and Micah in the era of the declining monarchy rather than in the exile or postexilic eras, as Clements does.

that was not the last word. Through the prophecies of Jeremiah and Ezekiel in particular, God sustained the hope of the faithful with promises of a return to the land. Marten writes, "Israel heard again what it heard already at the exodus, that God's design, including his intention to give them the land, was still in force. Interest in the land component did not wane in the exilic time, but instead came to be of foremost importance for Israel."[22]

The emphasis given to the return to the land is but one specific illustration of the general promise of God to "restore the fortunes" of Israel, which meant the restoration of the nation (e.g., Jer 30:3 NASB).[23] The exiles who returned to the land under Ezra and Nehemiah rested their faith in the God of Abraham. Even while they were still under the domination of others (Ne 9:36–37), they based their hope of restoration on God's covenant with Abraham, as we see in their prayer of national confession and their determination to obey God's law (cf. Ne 9–10; see esp. 9:7–9).

So Old Testament history closed with the promise to Abraham very much alive in the message of the prophets and the faith of Israel. The original elements of the promise—namely, a seed, or descendants who constitute a special people distinct from the other nations, and a land—remained firmly in place. Although the final element—universal blessing through this seed and nation—was not yet fulfilled, it remained a vital part of the prophets' message of the future.

II. THE ABRAHAMIC COVENANT IN THE NEW TESTAMENT

With the coming of Christ and the beginning of New Testament history, we find the announcement of the fulfillment of the Abrahamic covenant. There had already been initial, partial fulfillments of the promises, especially the promises of descendants and the land. The prophetic announcements surrounding the birth of Jesus bespeak the final fulfillment. In her song, the "Magnificat," Mary rejoiced in the great things that the "Mighty One" was doing for her and her people "Israel." All this resulted from God's "remembering to be merciful to Abraham and his descendants forever, even as he said to our fathers" (Lk 1:54–55). Zechariah, the father of John the Baptist—the one who would prepare the

---

[22]Martens, *God's Design*, 237. The prominence of the announcements of the return to the land in Jeremiah and Ezekiel is evident in the following list of passages compiled by Martens: Jer 3:11–20; 12:14–17; 16:10–18; 23:1–8; 24; 28:1–4; 29:1–14; 30:1–3, 10–11; 31:2–14; 32:1–44; 42:1–22; 50:17–20; Eze 20:39–44; 34:1–16; 35:1–36:15; 36:16–36; 37:1–14, 15–28; 39:21–29 (n. 1, p. 238).

[23]On the preference of the alternative marginal translation of the NIV "restore the fortunes" over "bring . . . back from captivity" found in the text, see Martens, 238; J. A. Thompson, *The Book of Jeremiah*, NICOT (Grand Rapids: Eerdmans, 1980), 553–54.

way for the Messiah—likewise saw the coming of God to redeem and save Israel in God's remembering "his holy covenant, the oath he swore to our father Abraham" (Lk 1:72–73).

In the New Testament as in the Old, the Abrahamic promise is the foundation for all the other promises. The raising up of a "horn of salvation ... in the house of his servant David"—a reference to the Davidic covenant—is based on the covenant with Abraham (Lk 1:69–73). Peter refers to the promise to Abraham when he speaks of the fulfillment of the message of the prophets from Samuel forward, a message that includes the promised Davidic monarchy (Ac 3:25). God in all his work is seen as "the God of Abraham, the God of Isaac, and the God of Jacob" (Mk 12:26).

The foundational and comprehensive nature of the Abrahamic promise is grounded in the fact that Christ is the fulfillment of the promise. The prophetic activity that announced the fufillment of the Abrahamic promise was part of the supernatural event of the coming of Jesus. The apostolic preaching later on affirmed that God had "raised up his servant" to bring the blessing of all peoples that was promised to Abraham (Ac 3:13, 25–26). "He redeemed us in order that the blessing given to Abraham might come to the Gentiles through Christ Jesus" (Gal 3:14). According to the writer of Hebrews, the "Christ is the mediator of a new covenant, that those who are called may receive the promised eternal [Abrahamic] inheritance" (Heb 9:15; cf. 6:13–14; 11:11). Observing both a present and a future fulfillment of the promise in the message of Hebrews, Paul Minear states that "the promise is as near and as distant as its mediator."[24]

A. The Seed

In terms of the specific contents of the covenant, the "seed" promise continues in relation to the ethnic people of Israel, but is expanded to all those in Christ. The Jew according to the flesh is still recognized as the descendant of Abraham despite his spiritual status (Lk 13:16; 16:24; 19:9; Jn 8:37; Ac 13:26; Ro 11:1). However, the emphasis is now on the seed that actually inherits the promise, namely those who follow after the pattern of Abraham's faith.

The fulfillment of the promise is seen in the coming of "the seed," Christ (Gal 3:16). Abraham and his seed were to be both the heirs and mediators of the promise (cf. Ge 18:18; 22:18). The climax of this goal is reached in Christ, the one who inherits the blessing and mediates it to those who belong to him. Thus those of the faith of Abraham who are "in Christ," whether Jew or Gentile, are also constituted "Abraham's seed" (Gal 3:26–29).

---

[24]Paul S. Minear, "Promise," in *The Interpreter's Dictionary of the Bible* (Nashville: Abingdon, 1962), 3:895.

The fact that the true seed of Abraham includes both Jews and Gentiles does not rule out a continuing distinction for Israel in the New Testament. Nor should the calling of the Gentiles as the seed of Abraham be construed as the formation of a "new spiritual Israel" that supersedes the Old Testament nation of Israel. If Abraham were merely the father of Israel, we would have to conclude that the Gentiles who are now a part of his seed are therefore a part of Israel. But according to the New Testament, Abraham is more than that; he is portrayed as the father of both the people of Israel and of the Gentiles. On the grounds that Abraham was a believer before he was circumcised—that is, before he was recognized as a Hebrew—the apostle Paul declared him to be "the father of all who believe but have not been circumcised . . . and . . . also the father of the circumcised" (Ro 4:9–12; cf. v. 16).

Further evidence of this truth is found in the fact that the New Testament teaching of the inclusion of the Gentiles in the seed of Abraham is never related to the fulfillment of the promise of a "great nation" (Ge 12:2). Rather, it is always tied to the promise of universal blessing to all the nations (Gal 3:7–9). Thus the promises concerning the physical seed constituting the nation of Israel remain alongside this universal promise even as they did in the original statement in the Old Testament.[25]

B. The Land

The Abrahamic promise about the land receives little explicit mention in the New Testament. There are probably two reasons for this: (1) the land was vitally related to the nation of Israel, and that nation "has experienced a hardening in part" during much of the period of time covered by the New Testament writings (cf. Ro 11:7–25), and (2) the universal blessing for all nations becomes the focus of the apostolic teaching during the present age of the church. Yet the New Testament does contain some indirect witness to the continuing validity of the promise of the land.

Because the land is connected with the nation of Israel, any reference to God's continuing concern for that nation would have a territorial aspect. Therefore, when the Gospels link the coming of the Messiah and God's promises for Israel, we cannot ignore the inference that land is involved. The one born in Bethlehem was to be "the shepherd of my people Israel" (Mt 2:6, citing Mic 5:2).

Simeon prophesied that Christ would be "a light for revelation to the Gentiles and for glory to your people Israel" (Lk 2:32). I. Howard Marshall sees a geographical connotation in that statement: "For Israel the coming of the Messiah spells glory (cf. Is. 46:13; 45:25). The Gentiles will

---

[25]For the continuation of Israel's promises as a nation, see chaps. 10 and 11.

come to Israel as the *place* where God reveals his salvation, and Israel will share in the glory of the Messiah (Ps. Sol. 17:34f.)."[26] The promise of "salvation from our enemies" and "rescue" from their hands is likewise a clear reference to the freeing of land from the domination of alien gentile power (Lk 1:71–74).

Along with the statements regarding the nation Israel, the proclamation of the kingdom and its relation to the Davidic promise strongly suggest association with real land. Mary could not have mistaken the meaning of the angel Gabriel's message that God would give to her son Jesus "the throne of his father David, and he will reign over the house of Jacob forever, his kingdom will never end" (Lk 1:32–33). The connection with the Davidic promise in 2 Samuel 7:16 is evident in the mention of David's "house," "kingdom," and "throne."[27] The Old Testament's Davidic kingdom promise involving *land* is thus plainly related to the Messiah's work in the New Testament.

The biblical evidence does not support the idea that the kingdom, which is the central message of Jesus, has a more generalized, spiritual meaning rather than the implication of real land.[28] To be sure, the kingdom was first and foremost spiritual in that it involved the dynamic activity of God and his righteous power. But in its biblical setting it also contained a mundane, earthly dimension. According to Walter Brueggemann,

> The theme of "kingdom" is crucial for our consideration. It clearly includes among its nuances the idea of historical, political, physical realm, that is, land. It may and surely does mean more than that, but it is never so spiritualized that those elemental nuances are denied or overcome.[29]

The promise of land is also related to the apostle Paul's teaching that Abraham and his descendants "received the promise that he would be heir of the world" (Ro 4:13). This universal range is not found in the Old Testament promise, which did not extend beyond the land for the nation Israel (cf. Ge 12:2; 13:14f., 17; 15:7, 18–21; 17:8). However, the Old Testament teaching of the universality of blessing contained in the promise to Abraham, along with the predicted worldwide extent of the reign of the Messiah, lead easily to this conclusion.

The universal extent of Abraham's inheritance was already preva-

---

[26]I. Howard Marshall, *The Gospel of Luke*, New International Greek Testament Commentary (Grand Rapids: Eerdmans, 1978), 121 (italics added).

[27]Raymond E. Brown states: "Gabriel's words in 1:32–33 constitute a free interpretation of II Sam. 7:8–16, the promise of the prophet Nathan to David which came to serve as the foundation of messianic expectation" (*The Birth of the Messiah* [Garden City, N.Y.: Doubleday, 1977], 310).

[28]For a fuller explanation of the kingdom, see 82–90.

[29]Walter Brueggemann, *The Land* (Philadephia: Fortress, 1977), 171.

lent in Jewish tradition.[30] Ecclesiaticus 44:20–21 declares: "And when he was tested, he was found faithful. Therefore the Lord assured him on oath, that the nations would be blessed through his posterity, that he would multiply him like the dust of the earth and exalt his posterity like the stars, and cause them to inherit from sea to sea, and from the river unto the ends of the earth" (RSV). Mekilta Exodus says, "And so also you find that our father Abraham inherited both this world and the world beyond only as a reward for the faith with which he believed. . . ."[31] Similarly Jubilees 32:19 states, "I will give thy seed the whole earth which is under heaven . . . and they shall then inherit the whole earth and possess it forever."[32] The same universal extent is probably the meaning of Jesus' beatitude that the meek shall inherit the earth (Mt 5:5).[33]

While these universal statements transcend the extent of the specific land promise for Israel, they should not be reinterpreted as negating the nationalistic aspect of Israel's promise in favor of some kind of universal a-territorial fulfillment "in Christ."[34] Jewish tradition, indicated above, not only spoke of the inheritance of the whole earth, but retained the strong hope of the Old Testament prophets for Israel's restoration to their national land. According to Davies, "The understanding of the land found in the Old Testament reappears in the Apocrypha and Pseudepigrapha, . . . for the most part, there is continuity between these sources and the Old Testament in this area."[35] The same may be said of the Qumran and Rabbinic writings.[36]

Instead of cancelling the specific land promise for Israel, the apostle's teaching of Abraham as "heir of the world" goes beyond the limited inheritance of the nation of Israel to the fulfillment of the universal blessing for all people in Abraham. This fulfillment was nothing less than the restoration of mankind's lordship of all the earth promised in the creation account (cf. Ge 1:27f.).[37] Such a universal blessing was concomi-

---

[30]The considerable evidence that "already before Paul the concept [of the promised land] had been broadened out from Canaan to embrace the whole earth" is adduced by James Dunn: "Sir 44:21; *Jub.* 17.3; 22.14; 32.19; *1 Enoch* 5.7; Philo, *Som.* 1.175; *Mos.* 1.155; cf. *4 Ezra* 6.59; *Ap. Const.* 8.12.23; rabbinic references in Str-B, 3:203 the world to come—*2 Apoc. Bar.* 14.13; 51.3" (*Romans 1–8*, Word Biblical Commentary, vol. 38 [Dallas: Word Books, 1988], 213).

[31]*Mekilta de-Rabbi Ishmael*, trans. Jacob Z. Lauterback, 3 vols. (1933–35; Philadephia; Jewish Publication Society of America, 1976), 1:253.

[32]*The Apocrypha and Pseudepigrapha of the Old Testament in English*, ed. R. H. Charles, 2 vols. (New York: Oxford Univ. Press, 1963), 2:62.

[33]D. A. Carson, "Matthew," in *Expositor's Bible Commentary*, vol. 8, ed. Frank E. Gaebelein (Grand Rapids: Zondervan, 1984), 133–34.

[34]Dunn, *Romans 1–8*, 213, following Davies, *The Gospel and the Land*, 179.

[35]Davies, *The Gospel and the Land*, 49.

[36]Davies, *The Gospel and the Land*, 52–74.

[37]C. E. B. Cranfield, *A Critical and Exegetical Commentary on the Epistle to the Roman*, The International Critical Commentary (Edinburgh: T & T Clark, 1975), 240.

tant and vitally related to the restoration of Israel according to the prophets. The Old Testament already revealed a similar duality with regard to the extent of the messianic kingdom. It involved the restored kingdom of the nation of Israel at its center, but its rule was finally universal. In Genesis 49:10, one was promised to whom "the obedience of the nations" belonged (cf. Am 9:12). Frequent reference is also made to the future King's rule extending "to the ends of the earth" (cf. Ps 2:8; 72:8; Mic 5:4; Zec 9:10). In the Judean royal ideology this phrase implied "a universal empire."[38]

Finally, in relation to the land promise, there is the teaching of the writer to the Hebrews concerning the hoped for destination of Abraham and the patriarchs. Of Abraham, it is said, ". . . he was looking forward to the city with foundations, whose architect and builder is God" (Heb 11:10). Likewise, the patriarchs, as "aliens and strangers on earth, . . . were longing for a better country—a heavenly one" (11:13, 16). The divine construction of the city and the heavenly nature of the country lead many scholars to understand the goal of Abraham and the other patriarchs as heaven rather than any earthly land of the Old Testament promises. For example, F. F. Bruce states,

> The truth is, their true homeland was not on earth at all. The better country on which they had set their hearts was the heavenly country. The earthly Canaan and the earthly Jerusalem were but temporary object-lessons pointing to the saint's everlasting rest, the well-founded city of God.[39]

There is no question that the writer's description of their hope involved something more than the land of Canaan of their day. But a simple dichotomy between earthly Jerusalem and Canaan on the one hand and heaven on the other, with the implication that the literal land promise of the Abrahamic hope has been transcended in the New Testament, does not seem justified in light of the total biblical evidence.

In the first place, we should note that the immediate context refers to the literal land of Canaan, where Abraham lived "like a stranger," as "the promised land" (Heb 11:9). Isaac and Jacob are described as "heirs with him of the same promise," which can only be a reference to the same "promised land." These statements surely bear some relation to the many

---

[38]Leslie C. Allen, *The Books of Joel, Obadiah, Jonah and Micah*, NICOT (Grand Rapids: Eerdmans, 1976), 347; cf. also Kruse's statement on Ps. 72:8: ". . .'He will rule from ocean to ocean, from the sea to the end of the earth,' does not describe the 'boundaries of an ideal Palestine (BJ), but is poetical circumlocution for 'the world'" (Heinz Kruse, "David's Covenant," *Vetus Testamentum* 35 [April 1985]: 154).

[39]F. F. Bruce, *The Epistle to the Hebrews*, NIC (Grand Rapids: Eerdmans, 1964), 305; cf. also James Moffat, *A Critical and Exegetical Commentary on the Epistle to the Hebrews* (Edinburgh: T & T Clark, 1924), 170.

Old Testament promises of the land given to the patriarchs. In addition, the hoped-for destination of "a country of their own" is not contrasted to earthly Canaan, but to "the country they had left," namely, Mesopotamia. Thus it seems that we should not understand the promised destination as altogether separate from the earthly land promised in the Old Testament.

However, the language clearly portrays a situation beyond the temporal and beyond the transitory nature of the land in which Abraham and his descendants lived. The question is, was this eternal dimension somehow an aspect of the promise? Did the patriarch's hope include a final, incorruptible heavenly city and country? The answers to these questions are already suggested in the Old Testament picture of a new Jerusalem and a new earth.

As the "city of God" where he revealed his presence, the historical Jerusalem was already seen as founded by God. Thus the psalmist declared that God "built his sanctuary . . . like the earth that he established forever" (Ps 78:69). God himself "set his foundation [of Zion] on the holy mountain" (Ps 87:1; cf. Isa 14:32). But the prophets looked also to a renewed Jerusalem in the future.[40] After the divine judgment that was to come on Jerusalem because of apostasy, God would return to bring salvation to the city (Isa 49:14f.; 41:27; 46:13; Zep 3:16–17). Into a darkness reminiscent of the first day of creation, God's light would arise to shine on Zion (Isa 60:1–2).

In the Old Testament the new, eschatological Jerusalem to be created by God's saving and redeeming action is pictured as an earthly city. But, as Georg Fohrer puts it, these predictions become "the starting-point for the later idea of an upper or heavenly Jerusalem."[41] Of the "many and varied" explanations of the Jerusalem of the last days found in the apocalyptic writings, Eduard Lohse says,

> On the one hand Jerusalem at the end of the days is the city of David built again with glory and magnificence. On the other the new Jerusalem is thought of as a pre-existent city which is built by God in heaven and which comes down to earth with the dawn of a new world.[42]

---

[40]For a fuller treatment of the picture of the future Jerusalem in both the Old Testament and later Judaism, see Georg Fohrer and Eduard Lohse, "Σιών, Ἰερουσαλήμ," *Theological Dictionary of the New Testament*, vol. 7, ed. Gerhard Kittel (Grand Rapids: Eerdmans, 1971), 312–19, 325–27.

[41]Fohrer, "Σιών, Ἰερουσαλήμ," 315.

[42]Lohse, "Σιών, Ἰερουσαλήμ," 325. Some of the descriptions of that heavenly city with their sources are provided by Lohse in the following: "The clearest ref. to the heavenly Jerusalem which God built before all time is in Apc. Bar. 4:2–6. The city of which God says: 'I have graven thee upon the palms of my hands' (Is. 49:16), is not the earthly Jerusalem; it is that prepared in heaven. God built it already when He resolved to create Paradise. Adam could see it before the fall. Abraham and Moses saw its image. 'And so it is held in readiness with

Yet the description of the new Jerusalem as "heavenly" must not be hastily understood as nonearthly. When Jesus and the disciples announced the nearness of the "kingdom of heaven" (cf. Mt 4:17), they were not referring to a nonearthly entity. Rather, they were proclaiming the coming of the reign of God on the earth (cf. Mt 6:10: "Your kingdom come, your will be done on earth . . ."). The writer of Hebrews already gave a clue to his meaning of "heaven" in speaking of those "who share in the heavenly calling" (Heb 3:1) and "who have tasted the heavenly gift" (6:4). These phrases describe those who are participating in divine realities that have their origin from God in heaven, but who are locally on earth.[43]

To describe Jerusalem and the country as heavenly is simply to speak of them in their final eternal state, which is the result of God's salvation. The hope of the patriarchs and the prophets for a restored earthly Jerusalem ultimately merged into a Jerusalem of eternal, heavenly quality created anew by the final salvation of God. The final goal of such a "heavenly" land, however, does not negate the prophecies of a historical restoration of the nation of Israel to the land before that final regenerative action. Admittedly, the specific nature of the final "heavenly" fulfillment and its relation to the historical promised land is not clear. Perhaps the extension of the land promise of the Old Testament into an inheritance of the earth may be paradigmatic of a general universalization of God's blessing in the final state.

The blending by the prophets of a future restored Jerusalem and the final eternal city corresponds with their picture of the future of the entire earth and heavens. The hope of the Old Testament was ultimately for an eternal state of things, for the prophets knew that the present "heavens will vanish like smoke, the earth will wear out like a garment" (Isa 51:6). Consequently, along with their portrayal of the rule of the Messiah over a yet imperfect world (cf. Isa 2:1–4; Zec 14:16ff.),[44] they looked forward to the creation of "new heavens and a new earth" (Isa 65:17; 66:22).[45]

---

me, as Paradise also is,' v. 6. Acc. to the seer of Apc. Esr., the days will come in which the signs mentioned earlier will be seen, and then the invisible city, heavenly Jerusalem, will appear, 4 Esr. 7:26. At the end of the ages Zion will appear from heaven and be visible to all as a perfectly constructed city, 4 Esr. 13:36" (326).

[43]For a discussion of the earthly nature of the city and land in Hebrews 11:9–16, see George Wesley Buchanan, *To the Hebrews*, Anchor Bible (Garden City, N.Y.: Doubleday, 1972), 188–94.

[44]The belief in a temporary kingdom of the Messiah before the final perfect Age to Come was prevalent in the Jewish apocalyptic writings, cf. D. S. Russell, *The Method and Message of Jewish Apocalyptic* (Philadelphia: Westminster, 1964), 291–97.

[45]It is noteworthy that contexts even of the statements concerning the new heavens and earth contain references that can only refer to the yet imperfect state before eternity (cf. Isa 65:20–23). Thus the Old Testament prophetic picture does not draw as clear a line of

Even as these references to the final perfected "new heavens" and "new earth" did not cancel out the historical prophecies that were to come before the end, so the references to the final country and Jerusalem in the book of Hebrews do not negate the reality of the historical before their ultimate arrival. The writer to the Hebrews speaks of believers as already having come to the heavenly Jerusalem (Heb 12:22), but this does not negate the reality of the present earthly history of the church that is not existentially lived in the new Jerusalem. Similarly, it need not negate the reality of a future period in which the historical earthly promises about Jerusalem and the land are fulfilled in further preparation for the eternal realities.[46]

In this connection it is important to recognize that the purpose of the writer to the Hebrews is not to give us an interpretation of Old Testament prophecy. The book is rather a "word of exhortation" (13:22), which Bruce describes as a "form of sermon or homily."[47] Using material not from the prophets but primarily from the Psalms, with other materials added to elaborate the argument, the writer's goal was to establish the superiority of the gospel in contrast to all that went before, particularly the levitical system. The primary evidence of the supremacy of Christianity is presented in its *finality*. Coming to Christ means *final* access to God without any barrier.

The writer's references to heavenly realities must be understood in the context of this teaching of finality. Even as Paul's teaching of present access to God does not do away with the actual historical situation of the church (cf. Eph 2:18), so our present coming to the heavenly Jerusalem must not be seen to deny the historical reality of prophecy. Abraham's hope for eternal realities, likewise, does not negate the reality of the history that, according to God's prophecy, must intervene before the actual attaining of the perfect state.

Thus the land aspect of the Abrahamic promise retains validity in the New Testament. Its link to the nation of Israel and to the coming kingdom indicates that the fulfillment of the land promise awaits the future both in this earth and in the new "heavenly" earth to come. There is

---

chronological demarcation between the present history and the final perfect state as appears in Revelation 20–22.

[46]For a brief discussion of the debate about the earthly and heavenly realities in the early church period, see Robert L. Wilken, "Early Christian Chiliasm, Jewish Messiaism, and the Idea of the Holy Land," *Harvard Thelogical Review* 79, nos. 1–3 (1986): 298–307. An illustration of the Jewish understanding of the relationship between the earthly and the heavenly is seen in the statement by Rabbi Yohanan in the third centry. In contrast to Origen, he refused to separate the earthly and heavenly cities: "The Holy One . . . said: I will not enter the Jerusalem which is above until I enter the Jerusalem which is below" (cited by Wilken, 304).

[47]Bruce, *The Epistle to the Hebrews*, xlviii.

no evidence that the promise of the land has been either completely fulfilled historically or reinterpreted to mean a symbol of heaven or the blessing of spiritual life in general. The fact that the New Testament sees the fulfillment of the Abrahamic promise in Christ, and thus the believer's hope as being with Christ, should not lead us to the conclusion asserted by Davies, namely, that the New Testament has "substituted the holiness of the Person" for "holiness of space" and therefore "Christified space."[48] The spiritual position of being "in Christ" in no way cancels out the reality of a real material universe, which is also the inheritance of the believer with Christ.

C. The Universal Blessing

As for the third aspect of the Abrahamic promise—universal blessing—the New Testament reveals its inauguration through the redemptive work of Christ. According to the apostle Paul, "The Scripture foresaw that God would justify the Gentiles by faith, and announced the gospel in advance to Abraham: 'All nations will be blessed through you'" (Gal 3:8).

The nature of the universal blessing consists in spiritual salvation now made available to all through faith in Christ. This entails all that is involved in justification (Gal 3:8) and the gift of the Spirit (Gal 3:14). However, the presence of the Spirit in the life of the justified is only conceived as "a deposit guaranteeing our inheritance until the redemption of those who are God's possession" (Eph 1:14). So in the New Testament we find both a present and future fulfillment for the Abrahamic blessing. Spiritual salvation through justification and the working of the Spirit in sanctification are available now through faith in Christ. But there is a fullness yet to come. The final inheritance will include the complete glorification of body and spirit in the enjoyment of the fullness of God.

As for the promises concerning the land and the seed that consitute the "great nation," Israel, the New Testament views their fulfillment as belonging primarily to the future. The promise of the coming Spirit is clearly distinguished from the coming kingdom according to the teaching of Jesus. The time of the restoration of the kingdom to Israel was unknown (Ac 1:6–7). The "times or epochs" (v. 7 NASB) for establishing the kingdom are under the Father's authority, and the language here suggests that these times are a long way off.[49] The Holy Spirit, however, would come "not

---

[48]Davies, *The Gospel and the Land*, 368. According to Davies, this has been the fundamental position of Christianity. This denial of the literal spacial element, however, seems contrary to the permanence and goodness of the created universe.

[49]This post-resurrection teaching concerning the time of the kingdom is clearly reminiscent of Jesus' earlier statement on the unknown time of his return (cf. Mt 24:36; Mk 13:32).

many days from now" (v. 5 NASB). Clearly the restoration of the kingdom is not to be equated with the present spiritual work of the Spirit. Moreover, the "covenants" and the "promises," including those made with Abraham, still belong to "the people of Israel," according to the apostle Paul (Ro 9:4). God's "gifts and his call," which refer to Israel's special place in salvation history,[50] are "irrevocable" (Ro 11:29).

These blessings promised to Israel are nowhere reinterpreted as presently belonging to the church. The fact that the promises remain in force anticipates their future fulfillment. Thus, while there is in the present salvation in Christ a partial fulfillment of the spiritual blessing promised to all people through Abraham and his seed, many aspects of the promise remain to be fulfilled, especially those dealing with the "great nation" seed and the "land," but also the final inheritance of spiritual salvation.

Thus the restoration of the kingdom is associated with Christ's return (cf. Ernst Haenchen, *The Acts of the Apostles* [Philadelphia: Westminster, 1971], 143).

[50]With regard to the meaning of "gifts" and "calling," Cranfield says, "By τὰ χαρίσματα we may understand such privileges of Israel as are listed in 9.4f. . . . By ἡ κλῆσις here we may understand God's calling of Israel to be His special people, to stand in a special relation to Himself, and to fulfil a special function in history" (*A Critical and Exegetical Commentary on The Epistle to the Romans,* International Critical Commentary [Edinburgh: T & T Clark, 1979], 2:581).

Chapter 3

The Davidic Covenant

THE SECOND great covenant that expresses divine promise in the fulfillment of God's salvation program is the covenant made with David.[1]

---

[1]Because the Mosaic covenant is superseded by the new covenant and therefore does not retain force in the New Testament, we will not deal with it specifically in terms of promise and fulfillment. However, it is related to the Abrahamic covenant as its initial and partial fulfillment in the formation and function of Israel. According to William Dumbrell, the nature and purpose seen in the foundational statement of the Sinai covenant of Exodus 19:5–6 draws us back "to the intent of the Abrahamic covenant which this section restates, namely that Israel is the agent used by God to achieve the wider purposes which the Abrahamic covenant entails, purposes which involve the redemption of the whole world" (W. J. Dumbrell, *Creation and Covenant* [Nashville: Nelson, 1984], 89). This is seen in the basic theological aim of the covenant theme of the book of Deuteronomy, namely, "to unite the Sinai and Abrahamic covenants, to marry nation and land" (Dumbrell, 117).

Although the Sinai covenant, like the covenants that followed, is related to the Abrahamic promises, we should note a fundamental difference. The Davidic and new covenants, as we shall see, are basically elaborations of provisions of the Abrahamic promises and therefore partake of the perpetuity of the original Abrahamic covenant. The Sinai covenant, by contrast, being the initial fulfillment of the Abrahamic promise, was added alongside that promise to provide the structure and conditions for its temporal enjoyment before the final provision of salvation came in Christ (cf. Gal 3:19–25). The enjoyment of the blessing of the promise was conditioned on righteousness of life. But that righteousness of experiential life (i.e., "the righteous requirements of the law" through the Spirit [Ro 8:4]) was not yet fully provided to those living under the Sinai covenant as it is to those under the new covenant (cf. Eze 36:27). (This "righteousness of life," of course, is distinguished from the "righteousness of God,"

59

This covenant, in which messianic and kingdom themes are central, is especially significant to discussions about prophetic fulfillment.

I. THE DAVIDIC COVENANT IN THE OLD TESTAMENT

The central statement of the Davidic covenant is found in 2 Samuel 7 and its parallel, 1 Chronicles 17. The promise contains four elements: (1) David's name will be made great (1Sa 7:9b); (2) a "place," "a home of their own," will be provided for Israel (v. 10); (3) Israel will be given undisturbed "rest" from all her enemies (v. 10–11); and (4) a royal dynasty and kingdom will be given to David forever (vv. 11–16). The promises of a "place" and a "rest" are reminiscent of the covenants made earlier with Abraham and at Sinai. The new promise to David focuses on his great name and, most important, a permanent dynasty and kingdom.

A. The Royal Dynasty

The centrality of an enduring "house" or dynasty is evident in the frequent mention of it in the promise passage of 2 Samuel 7. Twice Nathan speaks of God's intent to build a "house" for David (vv. 11, 16), while David in his response to the Lord refers to the blessing for his "house" five more times (vv. 19, 25–27, 29). That this reference to "house" signifies physical lineage is clear from the synonymous use of "seed" (v. 12; cf. Ps 89:4, 29, 36).[2] The prediction of Abigail that "the LORD will certainly make a lasting dynasty [lit., 'house'] for my master [David]" (1Sa 25:28) and the promise to Jeroboam of "a dynasty [house] as enduring as the one I built for David" (1 Ki 11:38) also point to the importance of this aspect of the covenant.

The promise of a royal dynasty entailed a "kingdom" and "throne" (2Sa 7:16). The nation of Israel over which David ruled as king had been designated a "kingdom" from its inception (Ex 19:6; cf. Nu 24:7). Before Saul was installed as the first king of Israel, royal dominion was attributed directly to Yahweh (1Sa 8:7; 12:12; cf. Dt 33:5; Jdg 8:23). Nevertheless, the establishment of a human monarchy, although begun with the sinful request for "a king to lead us, such as all the other nations have" (1Sa 8:5), was a fulfillment of God's original intent.

Already in Genesis 49:10, the symbols of kingship were promised

---

which is reckoned through faith for justification that was fully given to those of faith under both covenants).

Because of its limitations of the experiential righteousness, the Sinai covenant could not be the means through which the Abrahamic promise was brought to perfection (cf. Heb 10:1–18). It provided only temporary and partial fulfillment of the promise.

[2]For this meaning of *house* in reference to family, cf. Ge 7:1; 35:2; Ex 2:1; Jos 7:14; 1Ki 11:38; 12:16; 13:2.

to the tribe of Judah. Likewise, Balaam, under the inspiration of the Spirit, prophesied a king for Israel (Nu 24:7). Although they do not prescribe a king, the Lord's instructions concerning the future king in Deuteronomy 17:14ff. also suggest his intent for Israel. The promise to David, therefore, carried forward the divine purpose of a human monarchy designating a permanent kingly line from the lineage of David.

The appointment of a human king did not change Yahweh's status as King over his people. Even in the prophecy announcing "his kingdom" and "throne," David was also called the "ruler over my people Israel" (2Sa 7:8). While pointing to his kingship, the term *ruler* [נגיד] was used "to emphasize the unconditional loyalty which David always showed to Yahweh."[3] In the same way, Saul had only been appointed "a leader [ruler] over his [Yahweh's] inheritance" (1Sa 10:1). Even the Messiah, who would be the climactic fulfillment of the Davidic kingly promise, was called a "prince," which shows that he "is not an autonomous Ruler. . . . He is responsible to a higher figure, and thus a kind of vizier."[4] The Chronicler viewed the Davidic king as ruling over Yahweh's kingdom (1Ch 17:14; 28:5; 29:23; 2Ch 9:8; 13:8).

B. The Everlasting Kingdom

The concept of "kingdom" in this initial statement of the Davidic promise clearly includes the meaning of the predominant use of this word in the Old Testament, namely, a "political kingdom."[5] Not only is this evident from the historical kingdom of David, but also, as noted above, it refers to the kingdom of Israel which was a political nation from its inception (Ex 19:6). In the prophecies of the messianic kingdom, Yahweh himself becomes more predominant as the ruler and the Davidic figure more subordinate (cf. Eze 34:7–24), yet there seems to be no change that would eliminate the political aspect from the meaning of the kingdom.

The national and political nature of the kingdom is seen also in the strong connection between the promised Davidic kingship and the provision of "a place for my people Israel" in which they will "have a home of their own and no longer be disturbed" (2Sa 7:10). According to A. Carlson, "The inseparable connection between the house of David, the people of Israel, and the hereditary land" is emphasized.[6] Only after David's territorial conquests had provided the "place" could the temple

---

[3]A. Carlson, "דָּוִד *davidh*, דָּוִיד *davidh*," *Theological Dictionary of the Old Testament*, vol. 3, ed. G. Johannes Botterweck and Helmer Ringgren (Grand Rapids: Eerdmans, 1978), 161.

[4]Gerhard von Rad, "Βασιλεύς," *Theological Dictionary of the New Testament*, vol. 1, ed. Gerhard Kittel (Grand Rapids: Eerdmans, 1964), 568, n.18.

[5]von Rad, *TDNT*, 1:570.

[6]Carlson, *TDOT*, 3:160.

be built by his successor. William Dumbrell notes the sequence of the provisions of promise and concludes that the bringing together of the people in a geographical place of rest with a sanctuary for God's presence "will then mark out the promised land as 'holy space' and will point to the kingship of God which undergirds the whole Davidic programme."[7]

C. The Messianic Fulfillment

The full meaning of the Davidic promise is found in numerous references that come later in Scripture, especially in the royal psalms (esp. Pss 2, 72, 89, 110, and 132) and the messianic portions of the prophets. We must note two auspicious aspects of this promise.

First, the promise of a lasting dynasty to rule over the kingdom of Yahweh signified more than a continuous line of kings. It pointed forward to a final fulfillment in one specific person. Already in Jacob's blessing it was recognized that the "scepter" and "ruler's staff" would belong to the tribe of Judah "until he comes to whom it belongs" (Ge 49:10).[8] With the Davidic covenant the kingly line was established in Judah, but it would rest finally in a particular person. The prophetic naming of the eschatological leader as "David their king" (Jer 30:9; Hos 3:5) and "my servant David" (Eze 34:23; 37:24) clearly links the ultimate hope of the Messiah to the Davidic promise. The promise of a specific Branch from David's line similarly refers to the messianic meaning found in the Davidic kingly promise (Jer 23:5; 33:15; cf. Isa 4:2; 11:2; Zec 3:8; 6:12).

Second, the Davidic promise had universal dimensions. It was not limited to a narrow nationalism that concerned only the kingdom of Israel. Rather, the blessing of the righteous rule of the promised Davidic seed was to extend to all nations. The promised king "will rule from sea to sea and from the River to the ends of the earth" (Ps 72:8; cf. vv. 9–12). God will "set his hand over the seas, his right hand over the rivers" (Ps 89:25). As Israel was promised a place above all nations, so the Davidic king would be "the most exalted of the kings of the earth" (v. 27).

According to the prophet Amos, the restoration of "David's fallen tent"—a reference to the royal dynasty—would result in the possession of "the remnant of Edom and all the nations that bear my [Yahweh's] name" (Am 9:11–12). The idea of "possession," which is taken from Balaam's prophecy in Numbers 24:17–18, here signifies the inclusion of these people under the dominion of the restored Davidic dynasty. Similar

---

[7]Dumbrell, *Covenant and Creation,* 149.

[8]Whether this difficult statement is translated as in the NIV text given here or in the NIV alternate marginal readings "until Shiloh comes" or "until he comes to whom tribute belongs," the statement that follows—"the obedience of the nations is his"—makes it evident that an individual is meant.

statements of the universal scope of the Davidic reign are found in Micah 5:4 ("his greatness will reach to the ends of the earth"); Zechariah 9:10 ("His rule will extend from sea to sea and from the River to the ends of the earth"); and Psalm 2:8 ("I will make the nations your inheritance, the ends of the earth your possession").

These statements of the universality of the final rule of the Davidic king do not deny the continuing existence of the nation of Israel in the kingdom plan of God. The fact that God has destined the whole world to come under the unifying righteous reign of his king is never seen in the Old Testament as somehow transcending the promises regarding Israel's central place in this kingdom. Rather, the promises to that nation, including the restoration to her land, are found right along with those encompassing all nations under the messianic reign. It is Israel's king who will be exalted above the other kings of the earth (Ps 89:27).

In other words, the other nations will still exist, but Israel will enjoy an exalted position. Amos's prophecies speak of the universal kingdom along with the salvation of a remnant of Israel (9:9) and their planting "in their own land" (9:15). The contexts of Micah 5:4 (5:3–9; 7:8–12) and Zechariah 9:10 (vv. 11–17) reveal similar prophecies of the restoration and centrality of the nation of Israel in the universal kingdom of the Messiah. We will see later that, far from eliminating the place of a restored nation of Israel, the prophecies give the nation a central position and service in the messianic reign.

D. The Relationship Between the Abrahamic and Davidic Covenants

Our brief survey of its key elements, especially the universal blessing, has revealed that the Davidic promise is in reality an elaboration of promises contained in the foundational Abrahamic covenant. According to Ronald E. Clements, "Yahweh's covenant with Abraham was an anticipation and a promise of his later covenant with David (2 S. 7)."[9] The similarities in the covenants are easily recognizable. Both Abraham and David are personally promised a "great name" (2Sa 7:9; cf. Ge 12:2) and the Lord's blessing (2Sa 7:29; cf. Ge 12:2). In the long range, they will have kings among their offspring (2Sa 7:12–16; cf. Ge 17:6, 16) and a land or a "place" for the nation (2Sa 7:10; cf. Ge 12:7). The aim of universal blessing, so important to the Abrahamic promise, is clearly associated later on with the Davidic promise (Ps 72:17; cf. Ge 12:3) and, as we shall see, may also be expressed in the initial promise (2Sa 7:19b).

The emphasis in the Abrahamic promise is on the future nation, with no evident connection with the promised "kings." However, the concept of a nation implies leadership, and this leadership is defined in

---

[9]Ronald E. Clements, "אַבְרָהָם *abhraham*," *TDOT*, 1:56.

the Davidic promise. Thomas McComiskey states, ". . . in the solemn moment in Israel's history when God established the Davidic dynasty by his inviolable promise to David, the reference to kings among Abraham's descendants was given greater clarity and meaning."[10]

The promise of land was also repeated in the Davidic covenant. Although God did not allow David to build the temple, it was through him that God intended to fulfill the promise of a place of rest for his people. According to Carlson, David "appears [in 2Sa 7:10ff.] in the role of a second Joshua who will finally defeat Israel's enemies and give the people rest in the promised land." This Davidic "commission to finish the work of Joshua" carries allusions to the Abrahamic traditions (2Sa 7:9; cf. Ge 12:2; 2Sa 7:12; cf. Ge 15:4), indicating "a conscious effort to connect them with David."[11] A connection to the land promise of the Abrahamic covenant is also inherent "in the assurance of national security under the aegis of the Davidic king (Isa. 11:12–16; Jer. 23:6; 33:16; Amos 9:14–15; Mic. 5:4)."[12]

Finally, the universal blessing of all nations, which was the goal of the Abrahamic promise, appears once again as the ultimate purpose of the Davidic promise. Admittedly, David's words in response to Nathan's statement of God's promise (2Sa 7:19; lit., "and this is the law [תּוֹרַת] of man") are difficult to understand, yet there is good reason to see this statement as David's expression of the universal effect of the promise just given to him.[13] Taking "this" as a reference to the content of the promise and "the torah of man" as "the decree concerning humanity in general," Walter Kaiser, followed by Dumbrell, suggests the translation, "And this is the Charter for all mankind, O Lord God."[14] A similar understanding is reflected in the translation of the New Jerusalem Bible: "Such is human destiny, Lord Yahweh." According to this interpretation, the statement has universal implications for the Davidic covenant, linking it to the final goal of the promise to Abraham. This link is expressed by McComiskey:

> Taken in its [the torah's] simplest and most literal sense, the phrase may denote that the promise that David's house would continue is the established body of teaching for mankind. There is only one body of teaching that relates the concept of the offspring to the destiny of mankind, and that is the promise given to Abraham. This understanding of 2 Samuel 7:19 emphasizes the continuity between the offspring of the Abrahamic promise and the offspring of

---

[10]Thomas E. McComiskey, *The Covenants of Promise* (Grand Rapids: Baker, 1985), 25.
[11]Carlson, *TDOT*, 3:161.
[12]McComiskey, *The Covenants of Promise*, 29.
[13]Most interpreters, by contrast, understand the "law" in the sense of custom or manner, which leads either to a question such as, "Is this your usual way of dealing with man, O Sovereign LORD?" (NIV), or a statement, "And this is the custom of man, O Lord GOD" (NASB).
[14]Walter C. Kaiser, Jr., *Toward an Old Testament Theology* (Grand Rapids: Zondervan, 1978), 154–55; Dumbrell, *Covenant and Creation*, 151–52.

David. Both are viewed as mediating the divine blessing to all mankind (cf. Gen. 22:18).[15]

Whether or not a universal blessing is present in this initial promise statement, the language that appears later regarding the Davidic king clearly expresses the Abrahamic goal: "All nations will be blessed through him, and they will call him blessed" (Ps 72:17; cf. Ge 12:3).

Being inherently related to the Abrahamic promise, the Davidic covenant shares the same promissory nature. On the relationship between the covenants, Paul S. Minear concludes that "God's one word continued to cover his dealings with 'a thousand generations'" (Ps 105:7–11). God's pledge to each of David's successors, stipulating their duty and destiny, was "oriented toward the initial vow to the patriarchs and toward all the generations yet to come (e.g., the promises given to Solomon: I Kings 2:24; 5:12; 8:15–25; 9:5; II Chr. 1:9; 6:4–20)."[16] Like the Abrahamic covenant (cf. Dt 7:12), God's covenant with David is "called הברית והחסד ['covenant of love'] (I Kings 8:23), which should be understood as 'gracious covenant.'" This is in contrast to the Sinaitic covenant, which "is defined as ברית [covenant] and never as חסד [love or loyal love]."[17]

The unconditional nature of the covenant is frequently described as "eternal" (2Sa 7:13, 16; 23:5; Ps 89:4, 28, 36–37; cf. Ps 110:4). While the Hebrew word translated "eternal" or "forever" does not by itself demand immutability or permanence, the context indicates that this is the case with God's word to David. Kyle McCarter writes that there is not only a "concern with permanence everywhere," but also "the irrevocability of the present promise . . . guaranteed by a further provision in vv. 14b–15a." According to this stipulation, disobedience will result in parental chastisement, but "the grant of kingship will remain in effect regardless of the behavior of David's sons."[18]

In addition, numerous other statements demand that the covenant be regarded as eternal. According to the psalmist, God's covenant with

---

[15]McComiskey, *The Covenants of Promise*, 23.

[16]Paul S. Minear, "Promise," in *Interpreter's Dictionary of the Bible* (Nashville: Abingdon, 1962), 3:893–94; cf. also McComiskey's statement: "A unique relationship exists between these covenants. Both are affirmations of the promise, and both lack formal stipulations of obedience" (*The Covenants of Promise*, 142).

[17]Moshe Weinfeld, "Covenant, Davidic," in *Interpreter's Dictionary of the Bible*, supp. vol. (Nashville: Abingdon, 1976), 189; cf. also G. E. Mendenhall's statement: "In every form of this tradition [the Davidic covenant] it is Yahweh alone who is bound to a promise, and it is impossible to make out of this a bilateral covenant by appealing to the traditions . . . which emphasize the king's obligations to obey the Mosaic law, for there is never any reference to a kings' oath until possibly Josiah" ("Covenant," in *Interpreter's Dictionary of the Bible*, 1:718).

[18]P. Kyle McCarter, Jr., *II Samuel*, Anchor Bible, vol. 9 (Garden City, N.Y.: Doubleday, 1984), 206, 208; cf. also Psalm 89:30–36.

David "will never fail" (Ps 89:28; cf. v. 33). The same psalm frequently expresses the eternality of the covenant parallel with statements of the endurance of the "heavens" (v. 29), "the sun" (v. 36), and "the moon" (v. 37). Similarly, the certainty and permanence of the messianic salvation, according to the prophets, was based on the eternal sureness of the promise to David (cf. Isa 9:7; Jer 33:17–22; Eze 37:25).

Given this overwhelming evidence for the eternality of the Davidic covenant promise, the statements about conditional fulfillment (cf. Ps 132:12; 1Ki 2:4; 8:25; 9:4–5) must be understood as relating only "to *personal* and *individual* invalidation of the benefits of the covenant."[19] Dumbrell writes, "In general terms the line would not fail. Yet in particular terms, benefits might be withdrawn from individuals."[20] How far the failure might go and the promise remain in force is seen in the cessation of the actual Davidic kingly reign in 587 B.C. and yet the New Testament coming of Jesus in fulfillment of this covenant (cf. Mt 1:1; Lk 1:32–33, 69).

Thus, at the close of the Old Testament period, the covenant of David, with its promise of a royal dynasty and a kingdom involving a place or land, remained intact. It was the basis for the messianic eschatological hope.

II. THE DAVIDIC COVENANT IN THE NEW TESTAMENT

The central message of the New Testament is the coming of Jesus as the Messiah, the promised descendant of David. In him the fulfillment of the Davidic covenant begins. The difficult questions that separate dispensational and non-dispensational interpreters relate to how many of the covenant promises have been fulfilled in Christ's first coming and present ministry and how many remain for the future. Two key elements of the covenant promise stand at the center of the controversy: (1) a royal dynasty or house, and (2) a kingdom with universal blessing.

We will limit our discussion here to the Scriptures that deal

---

[19]Kaiser, *Toward an Old Testament Theology*, 157.

[20]Dumbrell, *Covenants and Creation*, 150. John Bright likewise asserts the final unconditional nature of the covenant despite certain expressions of obligation: "The obligations laid on the recipient of the covenant, which in the accounts of the Abrahamic covenant are at best implicit, are in the case of the Davidic king clearly and explicitly stated. . . . Nevertheless, stress falls upon the promises, and these are unconditional and without qualification. Though the divine chastisement remains an ever-present possibility in the event of disobedience, the dynasty will nevertheless continue. The nation is therefore secure because God has so promised (II Sam. 7:15f.; Ps. 89:33–37; etc.); he may discipline both king and people, and discipline severely, but he will never remove his gracious favor from the Davidic line or be false to his promises" (*Covenant and Promise* [Philadelphia: Westminster, 1976], 70).

specifically with the Davidic dynasty and the messianic kingship. We will especially focus on the fulfillment of Psalm 110. The kingdom promise will receive more extensive treatment in the next chapter.

A. *The Royal Dynasty*

The Gospels open with a strong emphasis on Jesus' coming as the promised descendant of David. The "ancestry theme" is prominent in both of the gospels that record his birth (cf. Mt 1:1, 6, 17, 20; Lk 1:27, 32, 69; 2:4, 11; 3:31). These genealogical statements declare the writers' belief that the promise of the Davidic seed had come to fruition. This conviction is also voiced later by the apostle Paul (Ro 1:3; 2Ti 2:8).

Regarding Matthew's emphasis on Jesus as the "Son of David," D. A. Carson declares, ". . . the title was not only equivalent to saying that Jesus is the promised Christ (1:1), but that he fulfils the promises God made to David (2 Sa. 7:12–16) and reiterated through the prophets (e.g., Is. 9:6f.)."[21]

Jesus is recognized as the promised Son of David throughout his earthly ministry. Those who sought his help in healing or exorcism frequently addressed as him as "Son of David," which was an accepted messianic title at least for some Jews of Jesus' day. The prophecies had foretold miraculous works in the future messianic days (cf. Mt 11:2–6; Isa 35:4–6). The cry of the blind men, "Have mercy on us, Son of David!" (Mt 9:27), demonstrates their belief that Jesus was, in fact, the expected Messiah (cf. Mt 15:22; 20:30f. [par. Mk 10:47f.; Lk 18:38]). Similarly, all the people who witnessed the healing of the blind, mute demoniac questioned, "Could this be the Son of David?" (Mt 12:23).

The appellation "Son of David" was also used in the laudatory exclamations of the crowds at the triumphal entry of Jesus into Jerusalem (Mt 21:9; Mk 11:10) and later by the children at the temple (Mt 21:15). Although he omits the reference to the "Son of David," Luke captures the significance of the occasion in the statement, "Blessed is the king who comes in the name of the Lord!" (Lk 19:38).

Jesus himself tacitly accepts the title "Son of David" (cf. Mt 21:16). Moreover, he obviously refers to himself in his perplexing question to the Jewish authorities concerning the identity of the Christ (Mt 22:41–46; Mk 12:35–37; Lk 20:41–44). On that occasion in the temple courts, all agreed that the Christ was David's son, but David's own words in Psalm 110:1 demonstrated that the Messiah was more than a human being. He was also David's divine "Lord." The Jewish leaders had rejected Jesus' unique relationship to the Father and therefore could not respond to Jesus' query.

---

[21]D. A. Carson, "Christological Ambiguities in Matthew," in *Christ the Lord* (Downers Grove, Ill.: InterVarsity Press, 1982), 104.

As the promised Son of David Messiah, Jesus transcended their idea of that person.

The later record of the early church reveals the assurance that the crucified Jesus who had risen from the dead was indeed the fulfillment of the promised seed of David. At Pentecost, Peter proclaimed that God's promise to seat one of David's descendants on his throne had been fulfilled. "God had made this Jesus . . . both Lord and Christ" (Ac 2:36; cf. v. 30). Paul likewise declared that the "blessings promised to David" had been fulfilled in the resurrection of Jesus to an incorruptible eternal life (Ac 13:34–37). The promises of an everlasting dynasty and kingdom were bound up in him.[22] At the Jerusalem council, James speaks of Jesus' having rebuilt "David's fallen tent," a reference to the dynasty of David, which had gone into eclipse under divine judgment (Ac 15:16).

Jesus' fulfillment of the Davidic dynasty reaches a climax in the royal descriptions found in the book of Revelation. As the one "who holds the key of David" (Rev 3:7), Christ has been given full authority over the Davidic messianic kingdom.[23] The Davidic royalty appropriately appears again in the throne scene, when the seals of the scroll are broken (Rev 5:5). Because he "has triumphed" at the cross, but also because he is the "the Lion of the tribe of Judah, the Root of David,"[24] Jesus is worthy to break the seals of the scroll. In the words of G. B. Caird, the scroll represents "God's redemptive plan, foreshadowed in the Old Testament, by which he means to assert his sovereignty over a sinful world and so to achieve the

---

[22]The content of the "blessings promised to David" (v. 34; citation from Isa 55:3) is explicated in vv. 35–37; cf. Ernst Haenchen, *The Acts of the Apostles* (Philadelphia: Westminster, 1971), 412. This does not deny that the whole messianic salvation was related to the Davidic promise; cf. Wilhelm Schneemelcher, "υἱός, κτλ.," *Theological Dictionary of the New Testament,* vol. 8, ed. Gerhard Kittel (Grand Rapids: Eerdmans, 1972), 367, n. 233. Thus Paul's proclamation of forgiveness of sins in verse 38 (like Peter's in Acts 2:38) is not totally unrelated to the Davidic promise. But to see this spiritual blessing as the New Testament interpretation of "the blessings promised to David" in place of "a future Jewish kingdom," as Anthony Hoekema does, is going beyond the meaning of the apostle (see Hoekema, *The Bible and the Future* [Grand Rapids: Eerdmans, 1979], 197).

[23]The expression "key of David" is taken from the historical incident of placing Eliakim over the royal household, as related in Isaiah 22:22. "The Targum to Isa 22:22 renders the key of the house of David as a 'key to the sanctuary and dominion of the house of David'" (J. Massyngberde Ford, *Revelation,* Anchor Bible, vol. 38 [Garden City, N.Y.: Doubleday, 1975], 416). Of its application to Christ, Robert H. Mounce states, "The language of Isaiah is used to present Christ as the Davidic Messiah with absolute power to control entrance to the heavenly kingdom" (*The Book of Revelation,* NIC [Grand Rapids: Eerdmans, 1977], 116).

[24]The "root" expression stems from Isaiah's messianic prediction concerning the "Root of Jesse" (11:10; cf. v. 1). The term is used both in the sense of origin of new growth (cf. Isa 11:1) and the new growth or "shoot" itself (cf. Isa 11:10). Here the latter sense is obviously meant as the parallel "Offspring of David" demonstrates in Revelation 22:16. The reference is therefore to Isaiah 11:10 rather than to 11:1. See Christian Mauer, "ῥίζα, κτλ.," *TDNT,* 6:986–89.

purpose of creation."[25] As such it could be said to be the "title-deed" of the kingdom of God that was promised to the Davidic dynasty,[26] a demonstration of Jesus' authority as the promised seed.

A final reference to Jesus' connection to the Davidic promise is found in the last chapter of the Bible. After the disclosure of God's future victorious salvation plan for all of creation has been given to John, Jesus identifies himself to the waiting churches as the prophesied Messiah through whom God has promised to bring it all to fruition: "I am the Root and the Offspring of David" (Rev 22:16).

B. Jesus and the Messianic Kingship in Psalm 110

A key Old Testament passage used by the early apostles to support their proclamation of Christ and the gospel of the kingdom is the prediction of the messianic kingship in Psalm 110. Even as Jesus before them, these early church preachers found David's words of a future messianic king sitting at the right hand of God and ruling with divine authority useful in proving the identity of Jesus as the Messiah. For Jesus, it was simply evidence that the Messiah was more than a human son of David (cf. Mt 22:41–45). With the death, the resurrection, and especially the ascension of Jesus having occurred, the disciples moved beyond identification of the person of Jesus to see in these words the description of an event in his life.

Peter's use of Psalm 110 in his Pentecost sermon, however, the emphasis remains on proving the identity of Jesus as the promised Messiah rather than explaining any present activity. Peter's message begins with the words "Jesus of Nazareth was a man accredited by God to you by miracles" and ends with the statement "Therefore let all Israel be assured of this: God has made this Jesus, whom you crucified, both Lord and Christ" (Ac 2:22–36). To prove that Jesus is the Messiah, Peter first used Psalm 16 to show Jesus had risen from the dead (Ac 2:24–32). He then declared (Ac 2:33–35) that Jesus had been exalted to "the right hand of God," from which he gave the Spirit that was just witnessed by them. This was in fulfillment of Psalm 110:1 and proved that Jesus had been installed as the Messiah (Ac 2:36).

Peter's statement that Jesus is presently at "the right hand of God," in fulfillment of Psalm 110:1, has been a focal point of disagreement between dispensational and non-dispensational interpreters. Traditional

---

[25]G. B. Caird, *A Commentary on the Revelation of St. John the Divine* (New York: Harper & Row, 1966), 72. For other interpretations of the scroll, see Mounce, *The Book of Revelation*, 142; Ford, *Revelation*, 92–94.

[26]Cf. Alva J. McClain, *The Greatness of the Kingdom* (reprint, Winona Lake, Ind.: BMH Books, 1974), 472–73.

dispensationalists have understood this as teaching the present session of Christ in heaven before his return to fulfill the Davidic messianic kingdom promise of a literal reign on earth. They are careful to distinguish between the Davidic throne and the position that Christ presently occupies in heaven at the right hand of God (Ac 2:30).[27]

Non-dispensationalists, by contrast, see Peter's statement as a clear indication that the New Testament has reinterpreted the Davidic messianic prophecies. The messianic throne has been transferred from Jerusalem to heaven, and Jesus "has begun his messianic reign as the Davidic king."[28]

1. The Meaning of Being Seated at the Right Hand. To understand Peter's statement in Acts 2 concerning the fulfillment of the Davidic kingship in Jesus, we must see what the psalmist means of one being seated at the right hand of God (Ps 110:1b). While the psalm may have a historical reference pointing to the coronation of a particular Israelite monarch, the language clearly goes beyond any purely human being to celebrate the fulfillment of Davidic kingship in the Messiah. Such a messianic interpretation was familiar in Jewish tradition even before it was universally expressed in the New Testament and the early church.[29]

The "right hand of God," the place where the Messiah was to sit, is the position "symbolizing highest honor and closeness to Yahweh."[30] The king in this position "sits as viceroy side by side with Jahweh himself: he does not sit upon his own throne, but upon that of Jahweh [cf. 1 Chron. 28:5; 29:23; 2 Chron. 9:8; cf. also Jer. 3:17]."[31] It is significant that in the Old Testament this place of honor was earthly. As Mitchell Dahood describes it, "During the coronation ceremony the Israelite king was considered to be enthroned at the right of the invisible but nonetheless present Lord."[32] Although some Jewish messianic interpretations may have a heavenly sense, there are none that plainly express this idea.[33]

---

[27]McClain, *The Greatness of the Kingdom*, 401.

[28]George E. Ladd, *A Theology of the New Testament* (Grand Rapids: Eerdmans, 1974), 336. Oswald T. Allis likewise says, "He [Jesus] has already received and is now exercising that royal authority. This can only mean that the kingdom is now 'come.' " (*Prophecy and the Church* [Nutley, N.J.: Presbyterian and Reformed, 1945], 136).

[29]For a survey of the Jewish and early Christian interpretation, see David H. Hay, *Glory at the Right Hand* (Nashville: Abingdon, 1973), 19–51. As for a possible historical reference, John Stek in the *NIV Study Bible* (Grand Rapids: Zondervan, 1985) suggests that the psalm may have been composed by David for the coronation of his son Solomon, calling him "my lord" because of his exalted status (cf. p. 376).

[30]Hay, *Glory at the Right Hand*, 19–20. Hay suggests that there may also be a concrete meaning to the "right hand of God" in Israel, as the king's throne was to the right (south) of the temple where God was enthroned.

[31]Gerhard von Rad, *Old Testament Theology*, vol. 1 (New York: Harper & Brothers, 1962), 320.

[32]Mitchell Dahood, *Psalms III 101–150*, Anchor Bible, vol. 17B (Garden City, N.Y.: Doubleday, 1970), 114.

This earthly position corresponds with the remainder of Psalm 110 in that we find no heavenly-earthly distinction stated or implied. The psalm suggests that the enemies of the Messiah will be placed under his feet while he is at the "right hand." Also, there is no indication of a change of location from the "right hand" (v. 1) to Zion (v. 2). The apostle Paul seems to confirm this interpretation in saying that Christ "must reign until he has put all his enemies under his feet" (1Co 15:25)—language very similar to Psalm 110:1.

The entire psalm, therefore, fits the picture of the Old Testament messianic hope, the reign of the Messiah on earth. The "right hand of God" is the position of messianic authority. Taking "throne" in its metaphorical sense as a "symbol of government," the right hand of God is also the Messiah's throne.[34] It is probably in this sense that we are to understand Peter's reference to Christ as having been raised to sit on the throne of David (Ac 2:30).

But some may object that Acts 2 makes Christ's fulfillment of Psalm 110:1 dependent on his ascension to heaven (v. 34). It would appear, therefore, that either Psalm 110 is a reference to heaven or Peter was giving a new interpretation to the psalm. As we have seen, the right hand of God was not spatially thought of as being in heaven. In fact, it was not primarily a spatial concept at all, but a metaphor for the supreme position of authority next to the king. Thus Peter's teaching that Christ assumed this position through the ascension added something that was probably not recognized in earlier interpretations of the psalm.

But this should not lead to the conclusion that Peter was denying the original meaning. The outworking of the Old Testament prophetic hope necessarily involves some new aspects not clearly seen earlier. What was portrayed in the Old Testament as one single messianic movement was divided in the New Testament into two phases of fulfillment.[35] The ascension of the Messiah during the first phase was therefore not plainly evident in the Old Testament. But this reality does not cancel out a future fulfillment in the full sense of the psalm.

We must also note that although the ascension was involved, it was the resurrection that provided the primary ground for the exaltation of Jesus. Whenever he predicted his coming death, Jesus alluded to his being resurrected after three days (cf. Mk 8:31; 9:31; 10:34). This reality qualified him for the heavenly life even as the apostle states in Romans 1:4: Jesus "was declared with power to be the Son of God by his resurrection from the dead." Thus it was really the resurrection, not the

---

[33]Hay, *Glory at the Right Hand*, 31.

[34]Otto Schmitz, "θρόνος," *Theological Dictionary of the New Testament*, vol. 3, ed. Gerhard Kittel (Grand Rapids: Eerdmans, 1965), 162.

[35]See next chapter for a discussion of this point.

ascension, that was the ground of Jesus' heavenly exaltation in fulfillment of Psalm 110:1.[36]

This truth is seen further in the way the ascension is essentially linked to the resurrection as one grand event in the exaltation of Jesus. In Acts 2 Peter mentions the exaltation after the resurrection, with the ascension added later as support (cf. vv. 31–34). In Acts 5:30–31 Peter again speaks of the exaltation after the raising of Jesus from the dead, with no specific mention of the ascension. Witnesses to the resurrection are witnesses to the exaltation.[37] The ascension is therefore only an aspect joined to the primary event of the resurrection in the exaltation of Jesus to the right hand of God. Although this is not evident in Psalm 110 itself, the exaltation results from the delay in the establishment of the prophesied kingdom, which is owing to two-phased fulfillment of the messianic kingdom program revealed in the New Testament (cf. Ac 1:6–11).

The meaning of the "right hand of God" in Psalm 110:1 and Acts 2:33 is, therefore, the position of messianic authority. It is the throne of David. Although in Acts 2 it is portrayed as heavenly, it is not to be understood in spatial terms but as a symbol of authority. Its heavenly position does not preclude a reference to the messianic king on earth.

While it denotes the place of highest honor and glory, "the right hand of God" does not in itself suggest any particular function. According to David Hay, all the Jewish interpretations of Psalm 110 speak of "a person who enjoyed extraordinary favor with God. The right-hand SESSION was not, however, regularly associated with any single function or activity of that person. Sometimes it was understood to imply his inactivity."[38] It is interesting that this latter idea is applied to David. He is described as being at the right hand of God while he waits for Saul to die in order that he might reign over the kingdom.[39]

---

[36]Bernhard Weiss, *Biblical Theology of the New Testament* (Edinburgh: T & T Clark, 1885), 1:90–91. Weiss notes the lesser significance of the ascension: "Neither in the prophecy of Jesus nor in the earliest tradition is the ascension to heaven conceived of as an epoch-making event, so far was the latter from representing it as an occurrence which was perceptible to the sense. The (rightly understood) resurrection qualifies Him, of itself, for the heavenly life."

[37]On the connection of the resurrection and ascension in relation to the exaltation in these Acts passages, Hay says, "Like Acts 2.31–36, 5.30–31 implies that no sharp distinction is being drawn between Jesus' resurrection and his exaltation to the right hand. Acts 5:32 confirms this by suggesting that witnesses of the resurrection may be considered witnesses of the exaltation" (*Glory at the Right Hand*, 73).

[38]Hay, *Glory at the Right Hand*, 33, 90–91. According to Ludwig Schmidt, the psalms of enthronement (including Ps 110) emphasize the relationship of the king as adopted son of Yahweh. Their ascent is on *legitimization* of his sonship, and not on the expression of his sovereignty ("Königtum," *Theologische Realenzyklopädie* [New York: Walter de Gruyter, 1989], 19:328).

[39]Hay, *Glory at the Right Hand*, 30–31: referring to the Targum on Psalm 110:1 and Midrash Tehillim on Psalm 110, sec. 5.

The early Christians' thinking about Jesus as being at the right hand of God reveals a similar lack of focus on function. Psalm 110 is quoted or referred to indirectly some nineteen times in the New Testament. Along with the expression of his exaltation, the psalm is variously used to vindicate Jesus' messiahship (e.g., Mk 12:35–37; 14:62; Ac 2:33–36; 5:31; 7:56), to ascribe to him power and authority (e.g., Eph 1:20), and to affirm his heavenly intercession and priesthood (e.g., Ro 8:34; Heb 8:1). From this variety of uses Hay concludes that the early Christians used Psalm 110b for one basic purpose: "to articulate the supreme glory, the divine transcendence of Jesus through whom salvation was mediated." Hay adds that the statement was used primarily as a symbol of Jesus' ultimate status as Messiah and not of his saving work.[40] Significantly, it is nowhere used to express the present reign of Christ over his kingdom.[41]

Christ's triumph over all rulers and authorities, resulting in his exaltation to the right hand of God "far above all rule and authority, power and dominion" (Eph 1:20–21; cf. Col 2:10, 15), does not include the actual function of the present reign of Christ as messianic king.[42] This is evident in that believers are also said to be resurrected and enthroned with Christ in the heavenlies at present (cf. Eph 2:6; Col 3:1), yet they are never said to be reigning today in the church (cf. 1Co 4:8). Similarly, the allusion to Psalm 110 in the promise to the overcomers to sit with Christ on his throne (Rev 3:21) affirms the present exaltation of Jesus, but not a present function of ruling.

We are given two glimpses of saints as being in heaven at present (Rev 6:9–11; 7:9–17), and in neither instance are they seen as enthroned with Christ and reigning in a present kingdom. This reign remains for the future subsequent to the return of Christ (Rev 19–20). The allusion to Psalm 110:1b in 1 Corinthians 15:25—that Christ must reign until he has put all his enemies under his feet—is the only possible exception to this

---

[40]Hay, *Glory at the Right Hand*, 155.

[41]David Hay asserts, "It is a . . . serious mistake to claim that early Christian references to Ps. 110.1b regularly express convictions about Christ reigning as a royal lord in the present era" (Hay, *Glory at the Right Hand*, 91).

[42]W. R. G. Loader concurs that the first uses of Psalm 110:1 including Acts 2:32–36 were not to signify Christ's present rulership, but he argues that the apostle Paul (on the basis of these verses) later used the psalm that way, as did the writer to the Hebrews. This development is attributed to a growing awareness by the early Christians of the delay of Christ's return and their experience of power in the eschatological gifts. With this development, the idea of a present reign of Christ at the right hand eclipsed the earlier emphasis on the primacy of Jesus' intercessory activity in that position. Not only does this idea raise serious questions concerning the authority of the apostolic teaching, but as noted, these texts in the Pauline theology and Hebrews do not teach a present rulership, at least in any clear sense of a messianic kingdom reign ("Christ at the Right Hand—Ps. CX. 1 in the New Testament," *New Testament Studies* 24 [1978]: 199–217).

condition. But we will see in the next chapter that this passage is best understood as a reference to the future reign of Christ.

2. Psalm 110 and Jesus' Messianic Kingship (Ac 2:30–36). If the expression "the right hand of God" in Psalm 110ᵇ signifies the place of messianic authority, then Peter's teaching in Acts 2 states that Christ has been exalted to this position and has been installed as the Messiah (v. 36). The significance of Peter's proclamation with regard to Psalm 110 is summed up by Walter Grundmann: "The Messianic Psalm is thus fulfilled; the Messiah has entered His glory; the Messianic age has dawned. Jesus in the place of honour at the right hand of God has a share in the glory and power and deity of God which He exercises by sending the Holy Spirit."[43]

That the messianic era has indeed arrived is further indicated by Peter's deliberate insertion of "the last days" in his citation from Joel (cf. Ac 2:17). These words were a technical expression in Old Testament prophecy for the eschatological days of the Messiah (e.g., Isa 2:2). Peter's proclamation of the eschatological blessings of salvation in the forgiveness of sins and the gift of the Spirit also signaled that the time of the Old Testament hope had arrived (Ac 2:38–39).

This view—that Peter was teaching that the messianic era had arrived, in fulfillment of the prediction of Psalm 110—runs counter to the traditional dispensational interpretation, cited earlier, that both the psalmist and Peter viewed the present position of Christ as distinct from the Davidic messianic throne. The eschatological era, including promises related to the Davidic covenant, was indeed inaugurated with the work of Christ at his first coming.

But we must be careful not to read more into this inauguration than what is actually said. Is Christ's ascension into heaven to sit at God's right hand *the* fulfillment of Psalm 110 in the sense that it supersedes the original earthly meaning of that prophecy? Or is it what might be termed an additional dimension in the fulfillment that has come about in the division of the one, holistic messianic movement of the Old Testament into the two phases of the New Testament? Does Peter teach that the Christ began an *active reign* over his kingdom? As we have seen, "the right hand of God" is not a spatial term, but a symbol of authority. The fact that Christ has this position of kingly authority in heaven, therefore, in no way denies that he will have this same position when he returns to establish his kingdom on earth.

As to the nature and extent of the present fulfillment of Psalm 110 taught in Acts, we must pay close attention to exactly what Peter says and how it fits in with the entire apostolic teaching. As we have noted, Peter

---

[43]Walter Grundmann, "δεξιός," *Theological Dictionary of the New Testament*, vol. 2, ed. Gerhard Kittel (Grand Rapids: Eerdmans, 1964), 39–40.

does not cite Psalm 110 directly in support of a particular function of Jesus, but rather connects the psalm to Jesus' exaltation and identity as the Messiah. Indirectly this declaration is part of the explanation of the pouring out of the Spirit by the Messiah (Ac 2:33). Moreover, it is through him that people receive forgiveness of sin (v. 38). While these blessings are related to the Messiah and the messianic era, they are not the primary feature of the Davidic kingdom *reign* of the Messiah, nor are they part of the picture of Psalm 110. Thus they do not indicate the actual establishment of the messianic kingdom and Christ's active reign over it at present.

The evidence from the context of Peter's citation of Psalm 110, therefore, gives no support to the idea that he is teaching the inauguration of the actual kingdom *reign* of Jesus.[44] This is buttressed by the fact that Peter quotes only verse 1 of Psalm 110, in which the Messiah is pictured as essentially passive. Peter does not include verse 2, which speaks of the extension of the "mighty scepter from Zion" and his "rule" over his enemies. It is in verse 2, as Charles Briggs says, that "the enthroned lord now himself becomes active."[45] Limiting the quotation to verse 1 appears to harmonize with Peter's purpose of pointing to the status of Jesus rather than any present action of rulership; this limitation would therefore have been deliberate on Peter's part. If this is the case, then Peter's use of Psalm 110 corresponds with other instances in which only portions of the Old Testament texts are cited in support of Christ's historical ministry, with the remainder of the texts awaiting a future fulfillment (cf. Lk 4:18–19 with Isa 61:1–2; Mt 21:4–5 with Zec 9:9–10).

That Peter is not teaching the inauguration of Christ's reign over his kingdom is further supported by the general Lukan teaching of the beginning of the reign of Christ at the *parousia* (cf. Lk 19:11ff.; 21:31; 22:30; Ac 1:6–7).[46] Hans Conzelmann shows that Luke displays no concept of the development of the kingdom in the church. Rather, the "coming," or the realization, of the kingdom itself always belongs to the future.[47] Hay similarly concludes that in Luke's theological framework

---

[44]Loader, "Christ at the Right Hand," 203.

[45]Charles Augustus Briggs, *A Critical and Exegetical Commentary on the Book of Psalms* (Edinburgh: T & T Clark, 1907), 377.

[46]The statement "the kingdom is within [or 'among'] you" (Lk 17:21) does not teach that the kingdom has actually been established. It may be understood as having "appeared" in Christ, which is different from its actual coming (cf. Hans Conzelmann, *The Theology of St Luke* [New York: Harper, 1960], 120–25) or as the future eschatological coming in harmony with vv. 22–24 (cf. Herman Ridderbos, *The Coming of the Kingdom* [Philadelphia: Presbyterian and Reformed, 1962], 473–74; T. W. Manson, *The Sayings of Jesus* [Grand Rapids: Eerdmans, 1979], 303–5; Joachin Jeremias, *New Testament Theology*, vol. 1 [London: SCM Press, 1971], 100–101).

[47]Conzelmann, *The Theology of St Luke*, 119, 122.

Christ's kingdom will begin only with his coming again. Hay concludes that

> Acts represents the exalted Christ as guiding events only to a very
> limited degree; usually God the Father is represented as in control.
> Luke–Acts often applies the *kyrios* title to Jesus, but not in a
> cosmological sense. Certainly he is not a king of a sort to threaten
> Caesar's order. Probably during the interim between resurrection
> and *parousia* Luke conceived of Jesus as lord in the sense of ruling
> over the church as its recognized savior.[48]

In declaring that Jesus has been exalted to the right hand of God in fulfillment of the promise to David to seat one of his descendants on his throne, Peter was not reinterpreting the Old Testament to teach the present reign of Christ over an established kingdom. Rather, his theme was the vindication of Jesus and, secondarily, his disciples. The one who was condemned by humankind has been exalted by God to the supreme position of Messiah.[49]

This interpretation of the exaltation of Jesus to the right hand of God in fulfillment of the Davidic messianic promise therefore allows for the inaugural fulfillment of those promises in distinction from the total postponement of the Davidic promise in traditional dispensationalism. But it also denies the non-dispensational interpretation that Peter was radically reinterpreting the Old Testament promise to see its complete fulfillment in a present reign of Christ over his kingdom. To interpret Psalm 110, in regard to the kingship of Christ, as expressing a dimension of fulfillment in the present age and another dimension in the future harmonizes well with the overall picture that the eschatological prophecies of the Old Testament are fulfilled in several stages without losing their basic historical meaning.

C. The Rebuilding of the Tabernacle of David

James's citation of the prophecy of Amos to support the Gentiles in the church (Ac 15:13–18) is another crucial text in discussion between traditional dispensationalists and non-dispensationalists. Because the prophecy obviously deals with messianic times, non-dispensationalists hold that James was forthrightly declaring that the messianic kingdom has

---

[48]Hay, *Glory at the Right Hand,* 71–72.

[49]Hay remarks, "The theme of Peter's speech in Acts 2 is not the work of the exalted Christ but the vindication implied by his exaltation. In the beginning (2.22–24) and conclusion (2.36) Peter stresses that Jesus was condemned by men but glorified by God. His acquittal was revealed in the event of his resurrection-exaltation-enthronement. Ps 110 is used as a medium for describing the event (vs 33) and as an inspired text for confirming it (vss 34–36). Secondarily the exaltation of Christ (and the scriptural texts cited) constitute a vindication of Jesus' disciples (cf. 2.12–15)" (*Glory at the Right Hand,* 72).

come. This is regarded as evidence that the New Testament sees the present church fulfilling the Old Testament promises as the new Israel.[50] Dispensationalists, by contrast, contend that James was clearly portraying a future inauguration for the Davidic messianic kingdom.[51]

The traditional dispensational thinking is that James deliberately sets up a time sequence to assure the *future* fulfillment of Israel's promises despite the present work of God among the Gentiles. At present God is "taking from the Gentiles a people for himself" (v. 14). It is only "after these things" (v. 16) that God will again begin to fulfill the Old Testament promise of rebuilding David's tent.

1. The Meaning of the Amos Citation. In citing Amos 9:11–12, James diverges from both the Hebrew Masoretic text and the Greek Septuagint, although he is closer to the latter. The beginning words are significant to our discussion. Both the Hebrew and Greek texts of Amos read "in that day," whereas James says "after these things" (Ac 15:16; "after this"). Many traditional dispensationalists see this as a deliberate change made by James to set up a time sequence to assure the *future* fulfillment of Israel's promises despite the present work of God among the Gentiles. But some dispensationalists hold along with most other interpreters that James intended no essential difference in meaning from the Old Testament language "in that day." Both expressions refer to the days of the Messiah.[52] Whereas the prophecy of Amos points specifically to the time of the rebuilding ("in that day"), James seeks by his alteration to relate this act to certain prior events ("after these things").

As these time words are part of James's citation of Amos, they must find their context in the Amos passage. Thus the "things" after which God would rebuild the tabernacle are the judgments predicted in Amos 7:1– 9:10. James is not setting up a sequence for the purpose of teaching that the events predicted by Amos (cited in Acts 15:16–17) would be fulfilled only after the present age of gentile salvation in the church (v. 14).

It may be, also, that James wanted to avoid Amos's terminology, with its obvious reference to "the day of the Lord." Using the phrase "in that day" in relation to a present fulfillment would conflict with the rest of the New Testament, which uniformly sees "the day of the Lord" as future.

Another change from the Hebrew text occurs when James, following closely the Septuagint wording, views the Davidic tabernacle as being rebuilt "that the rest of mankind may seek the Lord" (Ac 15:17) instead of

---

[50]Allis, *Prophecy and the Church*, 145–50; Hoekema, *The Bible and the Future*, 209–10.

[51]Cf. W. M. Aldrich, "The Interpretation of Acts 15:13–18," *Bibliotheca Sacra* 111 (1954): 317–23; Charles C. Ryrie, *The Basis of the Premillennial Faith* (New York: Loizeaux, 1953), 101–4; John F. Walvoord, *The Millennial Kingdom* (Findlay, Ohio: Dunham, 1959), 101–4; *The New Scofield Reference Bible* (New York: Oxford Univ. Press, 1967), 1185–86.

[52]C. F. Keil, *The Twelve Minor Prophets*, Biblical Commentary on the Old Testament (Grand Rapids: Eerdmans, 1949), 1:334.

"that they may possess the remnant of Edom" (Am 9:12).[53] Despite the differences in wording, however, these statements bear essentially the same meaning. According to C. F. Keil, the concept of "possess" in relation to Edom should not be seen as a negative subjugation, but rather as a reference to the blessing of that people under the reign of the Messiah. This is borne out by the additional thought that they would be included among "all the nations that bear my name" (Am 9:12[d]).[54] The import of both statements, therefore, refers to the salvation of Gentiles.[55]

In speaking of "David's fallen tent" (NIV), Amos alludes to the Davidic dynasty or "house" (cf. 2Sa 7:11, 16), which will shortly be in a ruined state.[56] Like many others, this prophecy looks forward to the restoration of the Davidic dynasty in the Messiah after a period of abasement (cf. Mic 4:8–10; Isa 11:1; 53:2). In connection with the restoration of David's dynasty, the "ruins" of the Davidic kingdom would be restored in the days of the Messiah.[57]

2. The Application of Amos 9:11–12 by James. As noted earlier, James cites the prophecy of Amos in support of gentile salvation. That connection is seen particularly in James's statement in verse 14 that God was now taking from "the Gentiles a people for His name" and his citation from Amos in verse 17 of "all the Gentiles who are called by my name."

---

[53]For a comparison of the different Hebrew words in the Masoretic texts and those presupposed behind the Seputaguint, see F. F. Bruce, *The Acts of the Apostles: The Greek Text with Introduction and Commentary* (Grand Rapids: Eerdmans, 1990), 340–41.

[54]The phrase "that bear my name" always signifies the special possession of God (cf. Dt 28:10; 2Ch 7:14; Jer 14:9; 15:16).

[55]Keil, *The Twelve Minor Prophets*, 1:332; cf. also Thomas S. Finley, *Joel, Amos, Obadiah,* The Wycliffe Exegetical Commentary, gen. ed. Kenneth Barker (Chicago: Moody Press, 1990), 325.

[56]The Hebrew word used by Amos, according to McComiskey, "refers to a rude shelter (a 'hut') and pictures the 'house' of David that was becoming a dilapidated shack. By Amos's time the Davidic dynasty had fallen so low that it would no longer be called a house" (Thomas E. McComiskey, "Amos," in the *Expositor's Bible Commentary*, vol. 7, ed. Frank E. Gaebelein [Grand Rapids: Zondervan, 1985], 329). F. F. Bruce defines this word as "the royal house of David" (*Commentary on the Book of Acts*, 310). Brown, Driver, and Briggs explain that the use of סֻכָּה in Amos 9:11: "poet. of fallen house (dynasty) of David" (Francis Brown, S. R. Driver, and C. A. Briggs, *A Hebrew and English Lexicon of the Old Testament* (Oxford: At the Clarendon Press, 1907), 697.

The use of the active participle "fallen" by Amos looks "either to its [David's tent's] *present* state ('falling') or its impending state ('about to fall')" (see Walter C. Kaiser, "The Davidic Promise and the Inclusion of the Gentiles [Amos 9:9–15 and Acts 15:13–18]: A Test Passage for Theological Systems," *Journal of the Evangelical Theological Society* 20 [June 1977]: 101).

[57]The different pronouns used in verse 11 tie the restoration of the Davidic dynasty and kingdom together. After God would restore David's tent, "he would restore 'their' (fem. pl.) broken places. The plural pronoun apparently refers to the divided kingdom. He would restore 'his' (masc. sing.)—i.e., David's ruins and rebuilt 'it' (fem sing.), referring to 'the tent' (*sukkah,* fem.)" (McComiskey, "Amos," 329).

But the question remains as to James's intent in quoting Amos. Did James, as dispensationalists have traditionally maintained, merely want to show that the prophecy indicates that God's plan ultimately included the Gentiles and that their inclusion in the church is in harmony with this purpose? Or did James understand the present salvation of Gentiles as in some sense a fulfillment of Amos's prophecy?

A straightforward reading of the text appears to support the latter interpretation. If James were only attempting to find support for future gentile salvation, why did he not simply begin his citation with Amos 9:12 (Ac 15:17) or some other references to gentile salvation such as those cited by Paul in Romans 15:9–12? If, as we have argued, James is not dealing with a time sequence in the words "after these things" (v. 16), why did he include the rebuilding of David's fallen tent if it has no relation to the present salvation of Gentiles? It is better to believe that James used the prophecy of Amos because he viewed it as in some sense being fulfilled in the present work of God.

When we examine how the prophecy of Amos 9 is fulfilled, we must again recognize that what the Old Testament saw in one messianic movement has been divided into phases in its New Testament fulfillment. Amos looked forward to the time when God would restore the dynasty of David, reestablish the kingdom of Israel, and extend salvation to the Gentiles. Other prophecies make it evident that these blessings were to take place in the days of the Messiah, "the greater David." According to the New Testament, this prophetic picture was not completely fulfilled in the first coming of Christ. Instead, only an initial or partial fulfillment occurred, with the rest awaiting the second appearance of the Messiah.

James's application of the prophecy of Amos to the present salvation of Gentiles is best understood in this perspective. Amos looked forward to the times of the Messiah, which included the salvation of Gentiles without their becoming part of Israel. These times have arrived with Jesus, and the new work of God indicates that salvation is going out to the Gentiles apart from keeping the law. All this is evident in God's having rebuilt the fallen dynasty of David in Jesus as the Christ (Ac 2:36).

In quoting Amos, James does not put the focus on the fulfillment of the promise to restore the kingdom. Jesus had already made it clear to the disciples that this was not to take place soon (Ac 1:6–7). Rather, as Ernst Haenchen points out, it was in the Jesus event that James saw the fulfillment of prophecy.

> When he speaks of the re-erection of the ruined tabernacle of David, he does not see this as the restoration of the Davidic kingdom, nor does he even see in it an image of the true Israel. He conceives it as adumbrating the story of Jesus, culminating in the

Resurrection, in which the promise made to David has been fulfilled: the Jesus event that will cause the Gentiles to seek the Lord.[58]

Thus James did not proclaim the complete fulfillment of Amos 9:11–12. Even as the complete fulfillment of the messianic promises is still future, so there are elements of Amos's prophecy that remain to be fulfilled. The restoration of the kingdom awaits the salvation of Israel in relation to the return of Christ (cf. Ro 11:25–26).

Further evidence that we should understand the relation between Amos 9 and Acts 15 this way is seen in Paul's application of messianic kingdom passages concerning gentile salvation passages to the present salvation of Gentiles (Ro 15:9–16). Many of Paul's citations from the Old Testament have clear reference to the kingdom when Israel is in right relationship to her Messiah and he is reigning on earth (cf. Ro 15:10–12). These references cannot be interpreted as finding their complete fulfillment in the church. Nevertheless, they have an initial fulfillment because the times of the Messiah have come and his salvation is going out to the Gentiles.

That this present salvation is not the complete fulfillment of these promised blessings to the world is clear from Paul's statement that when Israel returns to her God, the riches for the Gentiles will be far more than they are even today (Ro 11:12). The Gentiles, however, are being blessed with messianic salvation at present because the Messiah has come and has accomplished salvation. This is what James meant in his reference to Amos 9 during his address recorded in Acts 15.

C. Conclusion

So far we have seen that the New Testament teaches that the fulfillment of the Davidic covenant begins in the coming of Jesus as the promised seed of David. Our study also affirms that through his victorious life, death, and resurrection Jesus has been exalted to the position of highest honor and supreme authority at the right hand of God as the Messiah, the Davidic king. While it remains for us to consider the New Testament teaching on the messianic kingdom itself, the evidence dealing with the restoration of the Davidic kingship reveals only an initial fulfillment of the covenant promises during the present age. The crucial prophecies about the reestablishment of the Davidic dynasty in Jesus and his enthronement stop short of presenting the actual reign of Christ over an established messianic kingdom. As we shall see in the next chapter, the New Testament reveals that the fulfillment of these things awaits the future.

---

[58]Ernst Haenchen, *The Acts of the Apostles* (Philadelphia: Westminster, 1971), 448.

Chapter 4

The Kingdom

THE CONCEPT of the kingdom looms large on the pages of Scripture. Its features are the dominant content of Old Testament prophecy. It is the theme of the proclamation of Jesus according to the Gospels. While mentioned far less often in the epistles, the "kingdom of God" still qualifies as the summary of the apostolic teaching (e.g., Ac 19:8; 28:23, 31). Finally, in the book of Revelation it reaches its climax and is again mentioned prominently (e.g., 1:9; 5:10; 11:15; 12:10; 20:4). All this leads to the conclusion that the kingdom of God is one of the grand themes, if not *the* theme, of Scripture.

The Davidic promise, as we observed in the last chapter, provides the central features for the kingdom in the Old Testament, especially in the aspect of the predicted messianic king. For this reason we have connected it to the Davidic covenant. However, we should note that the kingdom theme of the Bible encompasses more than these explicit promises to David. The establishment of the kingdom of God on earth is, in fact, the ultimate goal of biblical history. This event ushers in the final eternal state (cf. Rev 21–22). As the expression of God's historical work, therefore, the kingdom of God is really the end of all of his biblical covenants.[1]

---

[1]William J. Dumbrell notes "an interrelationship of divine kingship and covenant" and states that "the goal of covenant is divine rule over the world, recognized by mankind" (*Covenant and Creation* [Nashville: Nelson, 1984], 42).

I. JESUS AND THE KINGDOM

A. *The Meaning of the Kingdom*

1. The Kingdom and the Coming of Jesus. As we might expect, the gospel writers connect the promised kingdom with the coming of Jesus even as they did the promise of the royal dynasty. The angel Gabriel told Mary that God would give her son, Jesus, "the throne of his father David, and he will reign over the house of Jacob forever; his kingdom will never end" (Lk 1:32–33). The language ("throne," "house," "kingdom") is reminiscent of the original Davidic covenant promise in 2 Samuel 7:16.[2] Being familiar with the history of the Israelite monarchy and the Old Testament prophecies about the messianic kingdom, Mary could only have understood these words as announcing the coming of the prophesied kingdom. In the words of A. B. Bruce, "The Messiah is here conceived in the spirit of Jewish expectation: a son of David, and destined to restore his kingdom."[3]

The Magnificat that Mary sang (Lk 1:46–55) supports this interpretation. As with the Old Testament prophecies, Mary's hope for the kingdom included spiritual blessings for the humble (vv. 48, 52) and those who "fear him" (v. 50). But it also included God's judgment on his enemies (vv. 51–52) and the restoration of the nation of Israel. Through the coming Savior, God "helped[4] his servant Israel, remembering to be merciful to Abraham and his descendants forever, even as he said to our fathers" (vv. 54–55).

The fulfillment of the Davidic kingdom promises are also evident in the prophecy of Zechariah, the father of John the Baptist (Lk 1:67–79). God was raising up "a horn of salvation . . . in the house of his servant David" (v. 69). A description of that "salvation" follows in verses 71–75, including again both spiritual and political deliverance. In the words of I. Howard Marshall, ". . . political need and spiritual need are closely linked."[5] According to Herman Ridderbos, even the angels' proclamation

---

[2]See Raymond E. Brown, *The Birth of the Messiah* (Garden City, N.Y.: Doubleday, 1977), 310–11.

[3]A. B. Bruce, "The Synoptic Gospels," in *The Expositor's Greek Testament*, ed. W. Robertson Nicoll (Grand Rapids: Eerdmans, 1951), 1:464.

[4]According to I. Howard Marshall, the use of the aorist tense to describe the actions of God in the Magnificat "perhaps represents a 'prophetic' perfect . . . or refers to the events still future which had already begun to take place at the time of the hymn, and so could be regarded as partly realised. . . . What God has now begun to do, and Mary regards prophetically as having already come to fruition, is described in terms of what God actually did in OT times, as expressed in Israel's praise in the OT" (*The Gospel of Luke*, New International Greek Testament Commentary [Grand Rapids: Eerdmans, 1978], 84).

[5]Marshall, *The Gospel of Luke*, 92. Lloyd Gaston comments, "Vs 71 is an explication of the salvation of Vs 69, and we see clearly that it is meant in a national political sense, 'salvation

of " 'glory (*doxa*) to God in highest,' and that of the eschatological 'peace on earth' are nothing but a summary of the future bliss that will be realized in and by the coming of the kingdom."[6] Of this "peace," Lloyd Gaston says,

> *Shalom* is of course a religious concept, often equivalent to salvation in the broadest sense. Basically it means wholeness, not just in the sense of fullness of life for the individual but for the totality of human relationships within a community. Therefore *shalom* is equally a political concept. . . . A community character-ized as a perfect harmony of free persons with their Lord and with one another is a political as well as a religious goal.[7]

These anticipations of the fulfillment of the kingdom promise provide the background for the proclamation of the nearness of the kingdom first by John the Baptist (Mt 3:2) and then by Jesus himself. With Jesus opening his public ministry with the proclamation, "Repent, for the kingdom of heaven is at hand" (Mt 4:17 NASB), the message of the kingdom becomes the theme of his earthly ministry, in both teaching and action.

2. *What Jesus Meant by the "Kingdom of God."* Most scholars agree that John the Baptist had the Old Testament kingdom in mind when he spoke of the "kingdom of heaven."[8] But although Jesus used the same words, his meaning of the kingdom has been much debated.[9] Most interpreters have understood him to mean by the kingdom of God, which he announced as "at hand" something akin to the realm of spiritual

---

from our enemies and from the hand of all who hate us' " (*No Stone on Another* [Leiden: Brill, 1970], 263).

[6]Herman Ridderbos, *The Coming of the Kingdom* (Philadelphia: Presbyterian and Reformed, 1962), 28.

[7]Gaston, *No Stone on Another*, 334–35. Of the Lukan birth stories as a whole, Gaston says, "Not only is there evident a great interest in Israel as the people of the promises, but the stories rejoice confidently and positively that redemption, also in its political sense, has come to Israel in the fullest meaning of the Old Testament expectation" (275).

[8]A. B. Bruce, an amillennialist, says forthrightly, "We know what John meant when he spoke of the kingdom. He meant the people of Israel converted to righteousness, and in consequence blessed with national prosperity" (*The Kingdom of God* [Edinburgh: T & T Clark, 1904], 52). Similarly, George E. Ladd says, "John the Baptist had announced the coming of the Kingdom of God (Matt. 3:2) by which he understood the coming of the Kingdom foretold in the Old Testament" (*The Gospel of the Kingdom* [Grand Rapids: Eerdmans, 1959], 53–54).

[9]For discussion of the various opinions concerning the kingdom and Jesus, see George E. Ladd, *The Presence of the Future* (Grand Rapids: Eerdmans, 1974); and Norman Perrin, *The Kingdom of God in the Teaching of Jesus* (Philadelphia: Westminster, 1963). The confusion over Jesus' meaning of the kingdom is captured in the following statement of George Wesley Buchanan: "Scholars have internalized, de-temporalized, de-historicized, cosmologized, spiritualized, allegorized, mysticized, psychologized, philosophized, and sociologized the concept of the kingdom of God. This has all been done for the purpose of denationalizing it" (*The Consequences of the Covenant* [Leiden: Brill, 1970], 55).

salvation presently enjoyed in the church. In contrast to John's under-standing of "the apocalyptic hope of the visitation of God to inaugurate the Kingdom of God in the age to come," Jesus' meaning is said to be "no apocalyptic Kingdom but a present salvation."[10] The "nationalistic ele-ments in the Jewish concept of the kingdom" are purged away "to lay stress on the spiritual elements."[11]

It has become popular to support this spiritual meaning of the kingdom in Jesus' teaching by emphasizing the abstract dynamic meaning of the Hebrew and Greek terms for *kingdom,* namely, "the reign of a king," over against the concrete concept of a "realm."[12] While the abstract concept is primary in the biblical words for *kingdom,* in both the Old and New Testaments, the terms inevitably entail a "realm" in which this rule is exercised.

Accepting the abstract meaning of "the 'being,' 'nature,' 'state' of the king" as primary, Karl Schmidt explains, "Almost spontaneously there then intrudes a richly attested second meaning: the dignity of the king is expressed in the territory ruled by him, i.e., his 'kingdom.' . . . Both meanings are present in $\beta\alpha\sigma\iota\lambda\epsilon\iota\alpha$."[13] In the same vein, Ridderbos objects to the sole, abstract concept of "dominion," declaring it "untenable, for the reason that in the nature of the case a dominion to be effective must create or maintain a territory where it can operate. . . . The absence of any idea of a spatial kingdom would be very strange."[14]

This dual aspect of *kingdom* gains further support if, as David Wenham argues, the background for Jesus' proclamation is found in Daniel.[15] The prophecy concerning the future time when "the God of heaven will set up a kingdom" is set against the visionary image

---

[10]Ladd, *The Presence of the Future,* 110–11.

[11]I. Howard Marshal, "The Hope of a New Age: The Kingdom of God in the New Testament," *Themelios* 11 (September 1985): 9.

[12]Cf. Ladd, *The Presence of the Future,* 122–48.

[13]Karl Ludwig Schmidt, "$\beta\alpha\sigma\iota\lambda\epsilon\iota\alpha$," *Theological Dictionary of the New Testament,* vol. 1, ed. Gerhard Kittel (Grand Rapids: Eerdmans, 1964): 579–80.

[14]Ridderbos, *The Coming of the Kingdom,* 26. Although he hestitates to speak of a territory and prefers to talk of a "community," Howard Marshall likewise denies the definition of "kingdom" as simply "reign": "While it has been emphasized almost *ad nauseam* that the primary concept is that of the sovereignty or kingship or actual rule of God and not of a territory ruled by a king, it must be also emphasized that kingship cannot be exercised in the abstract but only over a people" ("Church," in *Dictionary of Christ and the Gospels,* ed. Joel B. Green and Scot McKnight [Downers Grove, Ill.: InterVarsity Press, 1992], 123). In response to the idea of kingship over a community, one might question whether we can speak of the realm of a kingdom consisting of a community without including the territory in which the people live. If every aspect of the life of the community is under the reign of a king, then surely the space that the community occupies is under the king's reign and is an aspect of his kingdom.

[15]David Wenham, "The Kingdom of God and Daniel," in *Expository Times* 98 (1987): 132–34.

representing four human "kingdoms" (cf. Da 2:36–44). These earthly kingdoms surely included both "reign" and "realm" in their meaning. B. Klappert's contention that the words *king* and *kingdom* are used in the Old Testament "first and foremost for earthly kings and their secular government, and only secondarily of Yahweh's kingship"[16] should also warn us against seeing in these terms something only abstract. While they may emphasize the rule of the king, these earthly kings did not rule apart from a kingdom.

In contrast to this view of a kingdom of spiritual salvation alone, some have taken Jesus' proclamation to be more in line with the picture of the Old Testament messianic kingdom that includes a restoration of Israel. This is the classical dispensational position,[17] but it has also found support from others.[18] J. Ramsey Michaels, for example, observes that Jesus surprises his listeners, who hold to traditional Jewish expectations, in some of his spiritual teaching; but he adds that the Gospels reveal that "Jesus' expectation is well within the framework of contemporary Jewish messianic and apocalyptic expectations." This involved a kingdom which was "*both* spiritual and national, *both* universal and ethnic."[19]

The "both/and" in relation to spiritual and national aspects of the kingdom helps explain the predominant spiritual teaching of Jesus. But his

[16]Bertold Klappert, "King, Kingdom," in *The New International Dictionary of New Testament Theology*, vol. 2, ed. Colin Brown (Grand Rapids: Zondervan, 1976), 373.

[17]For instance, Alva J. McClain, *The Greatness of the Kingdom* (Grand Rapids: Zondervan, 1959).

[18]Older advocates of this general position include H. S. Reimarus in "*Von dem Zwecke Jesu und seiner Junger*" (1895; Eng. trans., *The Goal of Jesus and His Disciples* [Leiden: Brill, 1970]); and Johannes Weiss, *Die Predigt Jesu vom Reiche Gottes* (1892; Eng. trans., *Jesus' Proclamation of the Kingdom of God* [Philadelphia: Fortress, 1971]). More recent support is found in George Wesley Buchanan, *The Consequences of the Covenant* (Leiden: Brill, 1970) and *Jesus the King and His Kingdom* (Macon, Ga.: Mercer Univ. Press, 1984); G. B. Caird, *Jesus and the Jewish Nation* (London: Athlone Press, 1965); Lloyd Gaston, *No Stone on Another* (Leiden: Brill, 1970); Richard H. Hiers, *The Historical Jesus and the Kingdom of God* (Gainesville: Univ. of Florida Press, 1973); Joachim Jeremias, *New Testament Theology*, vol. 1 (London: SCM Press, 1971), 100–102, and *Jesus' Promise to the Nations* (Naperville, Ill.: Allenson, 1958); Ben F. Meyer, *The Aims of Jesus* (London: SCM Press, 1979); J. Ramsey Michaels, "The Kingdom of God and the Historical Jesus," in *The Kingdom of God in 20th-Century Interpretation*, ed. Wendell Willis (Peabody, Mass.: Hendrickson, 1987); Christopher Rowland, *Christian Origins* (Minneapolis: Augsburg, 1985); E. P. Sanders, *Jesus and Judaism* (Philadelphia: Fortress, 1985); David Wenham, "The Kingdom of God and Daniel," in *Expository Times* 98 (1987): 132–34.

Although some of these scholars erroneously attribute a revolutionary zealotry to Jesus and others see him as misguided in his proclamation and expectation of an Old Testament kingdom, they nevertheless conclude on the basis of the New Testament that Jesus initially proclaimed a literal kingdom involving the restoration of the nation of Israel.

[19]Michaels, "The Kingdom of God and the Historical Jesus," 114, 116. Michaels acknowledges the "significant contribution" of Alva J. McClain's dispensational work *The Greatness of the Kingdom* on this final thought.

spiritual teaching cannot be used to redefine the concept of the kingdom itself. This is especially true with regard to the parables concerning the "mysteries of the kingdom." Many scholars have been led into misinterpreting the full meaning of Jesus' "kingdom" onesidedly—first, because of the tendency to use the spiritual picture of the kingdom in this teaching in an exclusive manner that ignores other data; and second, because of a failure to reckon with the rationale for this teaching in the developing situation of Jesus' ministry.[20]

Although he does not intend it, Ladd's own comment on the significance of Jesus' teaching on "the mysteries of the kingdom" appears to support the full Old Testament meaning of the *kingdom* in its initial proclamation by Jesus. Ladd explains, "In the midst of his ministry Jesus began to teach his disciples that the Old Testament prophetic ideal was not at once to be fulfilled and that the kingdom was not immediately to be manifested in the fulness of its power. This is the 'mystery' of the kingdom, a truth which God has not previously made known to man."[21]

If, in fact, the mystery teaching represents a new development in the ministry of Jesus (which it surely does, both in the nature of the teaching and in its limitation to the disciples), then what was the prior teaching? As Ladd's statement implies, the mysteries represent a *limitation* on the concept of the kingdom. The full Old Testament kingdom that had been proclaimed prior to that time was not going to be established now; the kingdom would, however, be present in the world in spiritual power during the interim. There is no expressed purging of nationalistic elements in this new teaching of the spiritual manifestation of the kingdom; these elements are only postponed until the kingdom comes in its fullness.

The entire teaching of Jesus, therefore, reveals various uses of the term *kingdom*, but these do not negate the full eschatological sense,

---

[20]While Ladd is correct in saying that "we must seek for the meaning of Jesus' proclamation of the Kingdom in terms of his entire message," it is important to note changes of emphasis in the light of historical events. McClain correctly notes, "In approaching this important body of Biblical material [the gospel records], it is possible for interpreters to forget that the stream of history never stands still, not even in the comparatively brief time-span of Christ's public ministry. His teaching about the Kingdom, therefore, cannot be read with understanding apart from the constantly changing historical situation. This principle has been rightly stressed by scholars in connection with the great expanse of Old Testament history. It is no less important in dealing with the gospel records, when the very narrowness of the time increased the swiftness of the current. Hence we shall do well, not only to heed exactly *what* the incarnate King said about His Kingdom, but also to give careful attention to the time and circumstances *when* He said what He did" (*The Greatness of the Kingdom,* 267).

[21]George E. Ladd, *Crucial Questions About the Kingdom of God* (Grand Rapids: Eerdmans, 1952), 128.

especially in the early stage of his ministry.[22] In addition to the foregoing recognition of a change in his teaching during the course of his ministry, Jesus' early proclamation of the Old Testament messianic kingdom is supported by a variety of evidence from the gospel records.[23] Among the most important evidences are these:

a. The announcement of the kingdom without explanation. John Bright notes that Jesus supplied no explanation of the kingdom when he announced it as "at hand," and from this he rightly draws the conclusion that "Jesus used the term as if assured it would be understood, and indeed it was. The kingdom of God lay within the vocabulary of every Jew. It was something they understood and longed for desperately."[24] It is inconceivable that Jesus, knowing the understanding of his hearers, would not have immediately sought to correct their thinking if he in fact had another concept of the kingdom in mind. This would especially be the case with John the Baptist, whom Jesus regarded with high esteem (cf. Mt 11:11). Jesus would not have allowed his forerunner to go on proclaiming the kingdom with an erroneous concept in mind without seeking to correct him.

b. The call for repentance in relation to the kingdom by both Jesus and John. John the Baptist proclaimed the kingdom as the potential fulfillment of Malachi's prophecy concerning Elijah.[25] Some interpreters

---

[22]Sanders offers the following explanation for the different uses of "kingdom" in the teaching of Jesus: "Those which speak of the kingdom as present, or which use it as a word to mean 'covenant relation with God,' offer little difficulty for any particular hypothesis, and certainly not for the one argued for here [Jesus' speaking of the eschatological kingdom]. One need realize only that 'kingdom' does not always carry precisely the same meaning. The kingdom in the full eschatological sense could not be present, nor could it be entirely entered into by individuals, but the meaning of the word can be stretched so that one can talk of the kingdom, in the sense of God's power, as present and as extended to individuals in the present" (*Jesus and Judaism*, 236–37).

[23]For a full discussion of the evidence for the original proclamation of the Old Testament messianic kingdom, see McClain, *The Greatness of the Kingdom*, 274–303, and the modern sources listed in note 18.

[24]John Bright, *The Kingdom of God* (New York: Abingdon, 1953), 17–18. Bright states that the "hope of the coming Kingdom of God" is a "subject as wide as the entire eschatological hope of Israel." Similarly, W. D. Davies and Dale C. Allison, Jr., commenting on the petition for the coming of the kingdom in "the Lord's Prayer" (Mt 6:10) declare, "It is also true that 'kingdom' is not here redefined, so it is natural to suppose that its connotations are pretty much those which it had in pre-Christian Judaism: see A. Mos. 10.1; Sib. Or. 3.46–8; Ps. Sol. 17.3; 1QM 6.6; 12.7; Tg. Zech. 14.9; Tg. Obad 21. One can plausibly urge that 'kingdom' is not defined or circumscribed simply because its meaning(s) can be taken for granted" (Davies and Allison, *A Critical and Exegetical Commentary on the Gospel According to Saint Matthew*, vol. 1, International Critical Commentary [Edinburgh: T & T Clark, 1988], 604).

[25]Referring to rabbinical teachings, Joachim Jeremias notes that "this prophecy of Malachi was understood to say that the forerunner would bring about the ἀποκατάστασις directly— three days, one day—before the great crisis. Mark 9.13 ['But I tell you Elijah has come . . .'] is intended to be understood against this background. . . . The forerunner has already been

contend that the kingdom John proclaimed was essentially moral and spiritual rather than in any sense material.[26] But the call for repentance and the coming of Elijah the prophet were both significant in the Old Testament prophecies related to the eschatological establishment of the messianic kingdom.[27] Repentance was a prerequisite to the physical blessings and restoration of Israel (cf. Dt 30:6–8; 2Ch 7:12–22; Eze 33:7–20). So also, Elijah's ministry would herald the advent of the "great and dreadful day of the LORD" (Mal 4:5). Jesus' preaching of repentance and his identifying John with Elijah (cf. Mt 11:11–14; Mk 9:11–13) would clearly be understood by the people as related to the coming of the prophesied kingdom. They also account fully for the primacy of the spiritual demands in the teaching of Jesus without being an indication of a change in the basic definition of the kingdom.

    c. The limitation of the proclamation of the kingdom to Israel (cf. Mt 10:5–7; 15:24). If Jesus proclaimed a kingdom consisting only of the spiritual salvation now present for all in the church, why was this message limited to the nation of Israel? Or to phrase it differently, "Why, indeed, should the reign of God have been the object of a proclamation to Israel as such unless it bore on the destiny of Israel as such?"[28] Furthermore, it might be asked, what effect would it have had on their outward bondage if the nation as a whole had responded to the call for repentance? The action of Jesus in coming first to Israel is perfectly in accord with the Old Testament picture of the restoration of Israel followed by the extension of God's kingdom blessing to the entire world. According to Ben F. Meyer,

> For him [Jesus] as for the whole of Judaic tradition, God's will and Israel's destiny were one and the same and "the reign of God" had immediate reference to it: At Yahweh's reign, no doubt, the ends of the earth would see salvation (Isa. 52.10) and Gentiles would sing to the Lord a new song of Praise (Isa. 42.10); but where and for whom, above all, would Yahweh reign? On the holy mountain and for Jerusalem (Isa. 24.23)! His reign would be his return to Zion (Isa. 52.3)![29]

The calling of twelve also had significance for the Jews of that day, suggesting a nationalistic hope as E. P. Sanders says, "His [Jesus'] use of the conception 'twelve' points toward his understanding of his own

---

here—that is how near the end is" (*New Testament Theology*, vol. 1 [London: SCM, 1971], 132).

   [26]Oswald T. Allis, *Prophecy and the Church* (Philadelphia: Presbyterian and Reformed, 1945), 70–71.

   [27]See Sanders, *Jesus and Judaism*, 92–93, 106–33.

   [28]Meyer, *The Aims of Jesus*, 133. See 133–36 for a fuller discussion of the meaning of the proclamation of the kingdom to Israel.

   [29]Meyer, *The Aims of Jesus*, 136.

mission. He was engaged in a task which would include the restoration of Israel."[30]

d. Jesus' conflict over the temple and his predictions of its destruction. Jesus' concern with the temple in Jerusalem, evidenced in both his teaching and his action, demonstrates the connection of his ministry with the Old Testament prophecies concerning Israel. McClain cogently remarks,

> Why not simply ignore this temple if . . . because of her sin God is done with the nation of Israel and the Old Testament theocratic idea? On the contrary, as the Messianic Priest-King of Israel, our Lord in His final word lays claim to the existing Jewish temple, citing an Old Testament prophecy in defense of His action: "My house shall be called a house of prayer for all the nations" (Mark 11:15–17, ASV; cf. Isa. 56:7–8).[31]

With similar thrust E. P. Sanders states that "the best explanation of Jesus' demonstrative action in the temple and his saying against the temple . . . is to be found in his eschatological expectation. The kingdom was at hand, and one of the things which that meant was that the old temple would be replaced by a new."[32]

The concern for the temple by Jesus therefore suggests that when he proclaimed the kingdom as "near" he was not talking simply about a kingdom of "spiritual" salvation. Rather his concept of the kingdom was that of the Old Testament prophecies which included spiritual, physical, and political dimensions, especially the restoration of the nation of Israel.

The understanding suggested by the evidence above that in his original announcement of the kingdom Jesus meant the full eschatological kingdom accords well with the generally agreed teaching that the Old Testament portrayed the coming of the messianic kingdom as one holistic movement. It is only with the New Testament that we learn that this involves two stages separated around two appearances of the Messiah.[33] The fact that the kingdom was announced both by John and Jesus without

---

[30]Sanders, *Jesus and Judaism*, 106, cf. also 98–106, 119; Michaels, "The Kingdom of God and the Historical Jesus," 115.

[31]McClain, *The Greatness of the Kingdom*, 294.

[32]Sanders, *Jesus and Judaism*, 77.

[33]Although he confines the messianic age to the present era in keeping with an amillennial perspective, Anthony Hoekema nevertheless correctly sees the perspective stated above: *"In the New Testament we . . . find the realization that what the Old Testament writers seemed to depict as one movement must now be recognized as involving two stages: the present Messianic age and the age of the future"* (*The Bible and the Future* [Grand Rapids: Eerdmans, 1979], 18). The position that there is one movement in the Old Testament is supported by several passages that simply portray the coming of the Messiah and his work without any real indication that this would be accomplished in separate events as indicated in the New Testament (cf. Isa 61:1–4; Zec 9:9–10).

any explanation with the apparent assumption that their hearers understood what they were talking about leads to the conclusion that this new
development was not initially part of their proclamation. The fact noted
above that it was only later in his ministry that Jesus began to teach "the
mysteries of the kingdom" that the Old Testament prophetic kingdom was
not going to be immediately manifest also supports this understanding. It
is with the new teaching concerning the kingdom in the "mysteries" that
the division of the fulfillment of the Old Testament kingdom prophecies is
introduced yielding the conclusion that prior to this time the meaning of
the kingdom still carried its full Old Testament concept. It should be
noted also that this was after his rejection by the nation was certain and
that the new teaching was now directed only toward his disciples.

This interpretation is in harmony with the fact that at the beginning
of his ministry Jesus proclaims the kingdom as "near," but at the close of
his ministry he shifts the emphasis to the kingdom's futurity. Ridderbos
recognizes this change. Noting that Jesus early on stressed the "presence
of the fulfillment" of the kingdom, Ridderbos states that ". . . at the end of
the synoptic kerygma everything is again focused upon the future. The
coming of the kingdom is then referred to in such an absolutely future
sense as if it had not yet come."[34] Such a change would seem to suggest
that the initial "kingdom" that was near did not come in its fullest sense.
Aspects of it were present, as demonstrated in the mystery parables, but
the full kingdom that was near now awaits the future.

3. The Place of the Cross. Some scholars contend that any view that
has Jesus proclaiming the "nearness" of the Old Testament prophetic
kingdom faces an insurmountable problem in placing the kingdom before
the Cross. This argument is grounded in the assumption that the very act
of proclamation to the Jewish people implied the possibility of the
kingdom's coming if the demands for spiritual repentance were met. On
this basis, Louis Berkhof asks, ". . . what would have become of the
atoning work of Jesus Christ, if He had succeeded in establishing the
Kingdom? . . . Would the establishment of the Kingdom on the basis of
repentance of the people have left any room for the sacrificial death of
Christ?"[35] Some scholars—even some avowed dispensationalists—who
hold the futuristic view of the New Testament teaching on the kingdom

---

[34]Ridderbos, *The Coming of the Kingdom*, 468. We might note that while such language
does not entail the radical postponement concept espoused in traditional dispensationalism,
it does carry some similar implications concerning the initial proclamation and postponement
of the kingdom.

[35]Louis Berkhof, *The Kingdom of God* (Grand Rapids: Eerdmans, 1951), 170. Oswald T.
Allis chides dispensationalists in similar fashion: "All this serves to show the terrible
difficulty in which Dispensationalists become involved when, in the face of plain statement
to the contrary, they insist that Christ came to set up a visible earthly kingdom and reign over
Israel" (*Prophecy and the Church*, 77).

reject the idea that Jesus was offering a restoration of the Israelite theocracy in his proclamations of the gospel.[36]

The primary tenet of dispensationalism—namely, the final fulfillment of the prophetic hope including the restoration of national Israel—does not stand or fall on the issue. However, the strong evidence supporting the idea that the kingdom concept proclaimed by Jesus included political restoration for Israel suggests that Jesus was initially referring to the kingdom in its full eschatological meaning and not just the spiritual aspects. The proclamations by the angels and prophets surrounding the birth of Jesus also support this position. The proclamation itself is not explicitly in the form of an offer of the kingdom. Rather, the issue revolves around acceptance of Jesus rather than the acceptance of the kingdom. But Jesus as the Messiah cannot be separated from the concept of the kingdom. Acceptance of the King was surely related to the coming of the kingdom. Thus the question of the possibility of a kingdom before the Cross remains.

In response to this question we should note first that this problem is not peculiar to dispensationalism. The problem exists for all who allow that any type of kingdom could be obtained or entered before the Cross. Let us suppose that Jesus was referring only to a "spiritual" kingdom in his announcement of "nearness" and the concomitant demand for repentance and the new birth for entrance into it. Surely this type of kingdom as well as the entire messianic kingdom is based only upon the Cross. Thus, no matter how the kingdom is interpreted, Jesus proclaimed it before the Cross.

We might therefore pose the question as it is used against dispensationalism: What would have happened to the Cross if Jesus had been received by the nation of Israel as well as the Gentiles before the crucifixion? It may be replied that surely some would not have received him and they could have instigated his death. But this would have lessened its importance as the sinful act done by *all humanity* represented by its leaders (cf. Ac 4:27). More important, it would have contradicted the prophecies that Jesus would in fact be rejected by Israel (cf. Isa 53:1–4; Zec 12:10). It is therefore difficult to avoid the problem posed by the facts that (1) Jesus did proclaim the nearness of the kingdom and the demand for repentance in the light of it, and (2) it was the rejection of him as the Messiah, the Son of David, the King (and thus his kingdom) that led to the Cross.

So it would seem that interpreters of all persuasions face a problem

---

[36]For example, dispensationalist Eric Sauer, *From Eternity to Eternity* (Grand Rapids: Eerdmans, 1954), 175–77; cf. also Walter C. Kaiser, Jr. "Kingdom Promises as Spiritual and National," in *Continuity and Discontinuity*, ed. John Feinberg (Westchester, Ill.: Crossway, 1988), 295–300.

in regard to Jesus' proclamation of the kingdom before the Cross. We suggest that the solution lies in the same realm as other problems related to the sovereign decree of God for history and the responsible actions of mankind. The idea that God could offer humankind a real choice and opportunity, knowing all the while that humankind would fail (and, in fact, having decreed a plan on the basis of that failure), is expressed in other passages of Scripture. In Eden, humankind was given a genuine opportunity to choose holiness, yet Scripture indicates that God's plan already included the sacrifice of Christ "from the creation of the world" (Rev 13:8; cf. Ac 2:23; 4:28). Thus in this instance, a similar unanswerable question as that related to the offer of the kingdom might be posed: What would have happened to the death of Christ if Adam and Eve had not sinned?

Aside from the final mystery of how God works his perfect will through the secondary agency of the responsible wills of personal beings, the crucial element in all these situations is the fact that the humans involved did not, when faced with the decision, know what God already knew and had already included in his plan for history.[37] Adam and Eve obviously had no knowledge of the future death of Christ that was in the plan. Nor did Jesus' disciples anticipate the death of the Messiah, even though it was disclosed in some Old Testament prophecies. The early references to the Messiah's role and work were far more concerned with his reign than with his suffering. Messiah was to come as the "king of the Jews" (Mt 2:2), the "ruler" from Bethlehem (Mt 2:6). He would receive "the throne of his father David, and . . . reign over the house of Jacob" (Lk 1:32–33); he would bring "salvation from our enemies" and rescue his people (Lk 1:71, 74).

There are, to be sure, biblical statements that Jesus would bring redemption from sin (cf. Mt 1:23; Lk 1:77; Jn 1:29), but for the most part there is no reference to his suffering and death in explaining how salvation comes. Only after his rejection was certain and the disciples had come to recognize his identity did Jesus begin clearly to teach about his impending death (cf. Mt 16:21). But even then this prediction was an enigma for his disciples and seems to have been intentionally hidden by God from their understanding (cf. Lk 9:45: 18:34). I. Howard Marshall's explanation of Luke's statements concerning the divinely purposive concealment of Christ suffering gives us some insight into the situation of the disciples' knowledge of the prophesied sufferings of Christ:

> The prediction, which is given in the briefest terms (cf. 17:25), is incomprehensible to the disciples and they make no attempt to

---

[37]The situation of the offer of the gospel to the non-elect would seem to be similar. The fact that God knows someone is non-elect (regardless of whether on Calvinistic or Arminian ground) does not preclude that person from making a responsible choice. However, if the non-elect person knew what God knew, it would definitely cloud the decision process.

understand it. Luke brings out more clearly than Mk. the thought of a divine purpose being fulfilled in the veiling of the prediction from the disciples (cf. 18:34). The predictions are understood only later after the resurrection when the risen Lord shows from the Scriptures the necessity of his path through suffering to glory. There is thus a "suffering secret" in Lk., corresponding to the so-called "Messianic secret" in Mk. Luke's purpose is evidently to show that the way of Jesus was understood only in the light of the event and of the scriptural knowledge which the disciples acquired after Easter.[38]

If we accept Marshall's explanation in seeing their lack of under-standing as divinely ordained somehow in relation to the plan of Jesus, and not simply judgmental due to hardness of heart, as some suggest,[39] then we must conclude that a clear knowledge of the place of the sufferings and death of the Messiah was not available until after the resurrection. Further support for this is that Jesus never rebuked his disciples for their unawareness until after his death and resurrection (cf. Lk 24:25). The seed which he had sown in his brief prior statments and especially the resurrection should now have alerted them to this prophetic truth and enabled them not to give up their hope in him as redeemer (cf. v. 21).[40]

If we are correct in our understanding of the situation, the disciples as godly Jews not only did not understand the prophecies of the suffering Messiah, but also such knowledge was not readily available to them from the Scriptures prior to the fact. Their responsibility in relation to Christ and the prophetic Scriptures was simply to believe in Christ as the promised Messiah without clearly understanding the outworking of his salvation. If that is so, then Christ could present himself to Israel as the fulfillment of their prophetic hope and give the Jews a sincere opportunity to receive him without their decision being confused by the knowledge that they would reject their Messiah. The fact that, according to the Gospels, not one godly Jew really understood that Jesus must die would seem to support the idea that the people were not held responsible for this knowledge prior to the resurrection.

This position also provides the rationale for the dividing of the one movement of the messianic work of the Old Testament into two phases in the New Testament. The change was related to the rejection of Jesus by his people, and not simply a new plan announced immediately in the

---

[38]Marshall, *The Gospel of Luke*, 392–93.

[39]Walter L. Liefeld, "Luke," in *The Expositor's Bible Commentary*, vol. 8, ed. Frank E. Gaebelein (Grand Rapids: Zondervan, 1984), 930.

[40]Lloyd Gaston remarks on Jesus' rebuke of the disciples: ". . . they are called foolish and slow to believe not because of the content of this hope but because they had given it up and spoke of Jesus in the past tense" (*No Stone on Another*, 292).

teaching of Jesus. As we have shown, Jesus' early teachings reveal nothing of a change of plans, but rather assume and affirm the Old Testament revelation of the kingdom.

Thus the place of the Cross in relation to the kingdom is bound up with the decree of God, which is not always known by humankind. It is at times hidden so that we can make free and responsible choices. Nevertheless, God's plan is sure. The Cross came in God's time and did provide the foundation of the kingdom—a kingdom that Jesus had announced and apparently gave people the opportunity to enter even before the crucifixion.[41]

B. The Time of the Kingdom

1. The Imminence of the Kingdom. Jesus began his proclamation of the kingdom by declaring that it was "near" (Mt 4:17; cf. John the Baptist's similar statement in 3:2). Although some scholars such as C. H. Dodd see the term ἐγγύς (i.e., "near") as signifying that the kingdom has actually arrived,[42] most see it as indicating only that the kingdom has drawn near or is imminent. To W. G. Kümmel, the term denotes "an event which is near, but has not yet taken place."[43] For Jesus to declare that "the kingdom of heaven is at hand," therefore, meant, according to David Hill, that "the decisive establishment or manifestation of the divine sovereignty has drawn so near to men that they are now confronted with the possibility and the ineluctable necessity of repentance and conversion."[44] Thus, in Jesus' preaching, the kingdom had drawn near, but its actual arrival had not yet

---

[41]Gaston relates his comments to Jesus' proclamation of an imminent kingdom and the threat of judgment upon Israel, instead of to the problem of the Cross. But he nevertheless suggests a similar conditional offer of the kingdom: ". . . he did proclaim the fulfillment of the promises of Deutero-Isaiah concerning the kingdom of God, and he did threaten something of what would happen should Israel not respond to the proclamation." Further, "There is a sense then in which Jesus' announcement of the nearness of the kingdom of God is true if people enter the kingdom but not true if they do not" (*No Stone on Another*, 426, 428).

[42]C. H. Dodd, *The Parables of the Kingdom* (London: Nisbet, 1936), 44–45.

[43]W. G. Kümmel, *Promise and Fulfillment*, Studies in Biblical Theology 23 (Naperville, Ill.: Allenson, 1957), 19; cf. Herbert Preisker, "ἐγγύς, κτλ," in *Theological Dictionary of the New Testament*, vol. 2, ed. Gerhard Kittel (Grand Rapids: Eerdmans, 1964), 330–32; Ridderbos, *The Coming of the Kingdom*, 36–42. Against both the meanings "has come" (e.g., Dodd) and "near" in the spatial sense (i.e., near in the person of Jesus; e.g., C. E. B. Cranfield, *The Gospel According to Saint Mark* [Cambridge: Cambridge Univ. Press, 1963], 68) is the fact that John the Baptist used the same word. The kingdom could not have arrived with John if he were only the forerunner of it, nor would it be near them in his person. Against viewing the nearness spatially is the fact that this term was not used on the occasion when the kingdom was clearly present in the person of Christ (Mt 12:28; Lk 11:20).

[44]David Hill, *The Gospel of Matthew*, New Century Bible Commentary (London: Oliphants, 1962), 90.

occurred. The disciples could still be taught in all sincerity to pray for its coming (Mt 6:10).

2. *The Futurity of the Kingdom.* We will see in the next section that the kingdom was in some way present in the words and deeds of Jesus. Yet his predominant teaching on the kingdom focused on the future. He taught his disciples to pray for its coming (Mt 6:10). It will be entered at the time of judgment—that is, "on that day" (Mt 7:21–22; cf. 25:34). Only "then will the righteous shine like the sun in the kingdom of their Father" (Mt 13:43). This last statement is connected with Jesus' parable of the "good seed" and the "weeds" sown in the world during this age. While the "good seed" is identified as "the sons of the kingdom," the weeds, being "sons of the evil one," are never viewed as being in the kingdom.

Some contend that the statement of the "sons" being weeded "out of his kingdom" is an indication that they exist in a present "inaugurated form of the kingdom."[45] But it is preferable to interpret the parable as teaching that the kingdom will come with Christ. As Alfred Plummer explains it, ". . . the Son of Man brings the Kingdom with Him, and at that consummation 'the sons of the evil one' may be said for the moment to be in the Kingdom; but they are immediately expelled, as having no right to be in it."[46]

Not only did Jesus promise his disciples that in the future they would sit on twelve thrones in the kingdom (Mt 19:28; cf. Lk 22:30), but he also implicitly taught the future of the kingdom in responding to James and John's petition to have places of honor in it (Mt 20:21). At the institution of the Lord's Supper, Jesus spoke of future fellowship with the disciples in "the kingdom of God" (Mk 14:25; Lk 22:18). None of these passages contains a reference to some "future" or "consummation" form of the kingdom in distinction from a "present" form. The establishment of the kingdom was still apparently regarded as future, just as it was by the spectators at the triumphal entry who shouted, "Blessed is the coming kingdom of our father David!" (Mk 11:10).

Jesus clearly expressed the futurity of the kingdom in the parable of the nobleman (Lk 19:11–26). He told the parable late in his earthly ministry, shortly before the triumphal entry into Jerusalem and his final rejection. He gave this teaching, according to the gospel writer, "because

---

[45]D. A. Carson, "Matthew," in *The Expositor's Bible Commentary*, 8:325–26.

[46]Alfred Plummer, *An Exegetical Commentary on the Gospel According to S. Matthew* (reprint, Grand Rapids: Eerdmans, 1956), 196. Similarly Willoughby C. Allen comments that this parable "must not be interpreted in such a way as to suggest that the kingdom is conceived of as a present condition of things within which tares and wheat grow together. When the Son of Man has come, then the kingdom also will have come. Hence at that future date the tares can be said to be gathered out of His kingdom" (*A Critical and Exegetical Commentary on the Gospel According to S. Matthew,* International Critical Commentary [Edinburgh: T & T Clark, 1912], 153).

he was near Jerusalem and the people thought that the kingdom of God was going to appear at once" (v.11). The parable itself tells of a nobleman who went to a distant country to receive a kingdom. After apparently a considerable interval of time, during which his servants are responsible for resources left in their charge, the nobleman returns for an accounting with his servants.

Though not included in many of the recent discussions of the presence of the kingdom, the import of this parable for the time of the kingdom and the reign of Christ is noted by several commentators. Ladd states, "If the parable of the nobleman who went into a far country to receive kingly authority (Luke 19:11f.) is applied to Jesus, we conclude that he will not exercise his kingly authority until his return in the second advent, and then the scene of the exercise of this regal authority is the same place as that from which the king departed, namely the earth."[47] Marshall likewise views the passage as teaching that "Jesus is departing, and will not be appointed as king until his return."[48] Focusing specifically on the time of Jesus' kingly reign, E. Earle Ellis writes, "Only upon his return from the 'far country' will his 'kingly power' be manifest."[49]

This parabolic teaching of the futurity of the kingdom harmonizes with Christ's statements in the Olivet Discourse. After describing the course of the age leading to his return, Jesus said, "When you see these things happening, you know that the kingdom of God is near" (Lk 21:31). The parallel passage in Matthew 24:33 reads, "When you see all these things, you know that it is near, right at the door" (cf. Mk 13:29). The word *it*, which is parallel to Luke's "kingdom of God" may also be translated "he," referring to Jesus himself. In any case, the meaning is clear that the coming of the kingdom is associated with the coming of Christ. This points to the truth expressed several times in the Gospel accounts, namely, that the kingdom is equivalent to the presence of Christ.[50] He has departed to heaven, from which the church awaits his return. It likewise awaits the arrival of the kingdom according to the parable of the nobleman.

It is noteworthy that the same term used in connection with Jesus'

---

[47]Ladd, *Crucial Questions About the Kingdom*, 71. The use of "kingdom" ("appointed king," NIV) in this parable clearly focuses on the abstract concept of the kingly rule that the nobleman would receive. Yet its understanding against the historical background of Archelaus going to Rome to be confirmed as ruler of Judea clearly shows that a realm is also involved in the reception of a "kingdom."

[48]Marshall, *The Gospel of Luke*, 700.

[49]E. Earle Ellis, *The Gospel of Luke*, New Century Bible Commentary (London: Oliphants, 1974), 222.

[50]For instance, Matthew 19:29 compared with Luke 18:29. Robert Recker aptly notes that "in the Gospels Jesus is presented as the *autobasileia*. In his person the kingdom of God has drawn near and is veritably in their midst" ("The Redemptive Focus of the Kingdom of God," *Calvin Theological Journal* 14 [November 1979]: 171).

first announcement of the kingdom is now applied to a future time. The kingdom that was "near" in the earlier teaching will now be "near" ($\dot{\epsilon}\gamma\gamma\upsilon\varsigma$) only in the future when this age has run its course and "all these things"— the events of this time leading up to the coming of Christ—are seen. This change in the emphasis of Jesus' teaching concerning the kingdom, which does not seem to be widely recognized, is clearly noted by Ridderbos. While validly calling attention to the fulfillment motif in Jesus' teaching and the truth that our age prior to the coming is a "new time of the world, viz., that of the fulfillment," Ridderbos nevertheless rightly says:

> While at the beginning of his preaching all emphasis is laid upon the presence of the fulfillment, as is seen in connection with his miracles; at the end of the synoptic kerygma everything is again focused upon the future. The coming of the kingdom is then referred to in such an absolutely future sense as if it *had not* yet come, and the *parousia* of the Son of Man—the word *parousia* means arrival and not *second coming!*—is spoken of as if he were only a person of the future.[51]

There is no question that Jesus and the early church saw something of the presence of the kingdom in their experience of new covenant salvation. But this dominant teaching of the future of the kingdom by Jesus, which as we will see is followed by the early church, should caution us in our explanation of the presence of the kingdom. Far from portraying the disciples as reigning or "building" the kingdom during this interim age, Jesus describes their position as one of suffering and danger (cf. Mt 24:9, 13; Mk 13:9–13; Lk 12:11–12; 14:26; 21:12–17, 19). Ridderbos explains, "Nowhere are the disciples or the coming church given the role of conquerors or rulers of the world." Their obedience would be "a conserving and beneficial power for temporal life (Matt. 5:13; Luke 14:34, 35; Mark 9:50); and with this prospect they may preach the gospel to the nations (Matt. 28:18). . . . [But] they are not given any promises of Christianizing the whole world nor are there any theocratic perspectives disclosed."[52]

This change of emphasis in Jesus' teaching should also make us wary in determining Jesus' meaning of the kingdom. As noted previously, this change fits well with the traditional dispensational view that the shift from Jesus' early teaching is related to his rejection by his people Israel. This change also entails differences in the kingdom concept. Unless we are to read into Jesus' first proclamation of the kingdom as "near" something different from his later teaching that the kingdom would now be "near" only in the future, we must assume that this *initially proclaimed*

[51]Ridderbos, *The Coming of the Kingdom*, 468.
[52]Ridderbos, *The Coming of the Kingdom*, 470.

kingdom did not come in its totality. Only certain dimensions of it came through the first advent of Christ and are present today.

3. The Presence of the Kingdom. There is no question that, despite a later emphasis on the futurity of the kingdom, Jesus also taught a certain presence of the kingdom initiated with his first coming.[53] In his first recorded sermon, given at Nazareth, Jesus cited a messianic prophecy from Isaiah (61:1–2) and declared this prophecy "fulfilled in your hearing" (Lk 4:21; cf. vv. 16–21). The ministries of this messianic figure, according to Isaiah, would include preaching the gospel to the poor, proclaiming freedom for prisoners, giving sight to the blind, releasing the oppressed, and proclaiming the time of God's favor. If we interpret the references to freeing the prisoners and oppressed metaphorically in the sense of the forgiveness of sins (and there is no record of prisoners' being freed literally), all these ministries were later fulfilled in the ministry of Jesus (e.g., Lk 7:22).

This passage indicates that preaching "the gospel" belonged to the new era. It was not just another promise; instead, as Ridderbos notes, Jesus' preaching of the "kingdom" was "at the same time its revelation."[54] As such, Jesus uses his preaching of the gospel as evidence to John's disciples that the promised time had arrived (Mt 11:5). The preaching of "the good news of the kingdom of God" was involved in the kingdom "forcefully advancing" (cf. Lk 16:16 with Mt 11:12). To hear "the message about the kingdom" was to receive that which "many prophets and righteous men longed to see . . . and hear" (Mt 13:17).

Along with preaching, the miraculous power of Jesus was evidence of the presence of the kingdom (cf. Mt 11:5). Expressly in relation to overcoming Satan, Jesus declared, ". . . if I drive out demons by the Spirit of God, then the kingdom of God has come upon you" (Mt 12:28; cf. Lk 11:20). In this statement the presence of the kingdom is linked to the power of the Spirit of God. This same connection is already found in the sermon at Nazareth, in which Jesus speaks of being anointed with the Spirit (Lk 4:18). This supernatural power evident in miracles and especially in the overcoming of Satan's power is a manifestation of the kingdom.

The presence of the kingdom is further indicated in that it could now be "entered." It is not always possible to determine in every case whether Jesus' statements applied to the present or the future,[55] but some

---

[53]For a full discussion of the presence of the kingdom, see Kümmel, *Promise and Fulfillment*, 105–40; Ladd, *The Presence of the Future*, 105–21, 149–242; Ridderbos, *The Coming of the Kingdom*, 61–184.

[54]Ridderbos, *The Coming of the Kingdom*, 74. Gerhard Friedrich says, "The message actualises the new time and makes possible the signs of Messianic fulfillment. The Word brings in the divine rule" ("εὐαγγελίζομαι, κτλ," in *TDNT*, 2:718).

[55]For example, Matthew 18:3; 19:23; 21:31.

of them seem clearly to be present. When he charged the scribes and Pharisees with shutting the kingdom "in men's faces," Jesus said, "You yourselves do not enter, nor will you let those enter who are trying to" (Mt 23:13). Jesus' mystery parables also describe the working of the kingdom during this age (Mt 13).

These teachings from the gospels make it clear that the kingdom was present in the words and works of Jesus and his disciples. Blessings that the prophets had foretold for eschatological times were now present. It may be questioned, however, whether the coming of aspects of kingdom salvation (primarily spiritual and individual as opposed to societal) and the manifestation of kingdom power are the same as saying that the kingdom has "come."[56] We have noted Jesus' declaration that Isaiah's prophecy of messianic activity was fulfilled in him. Nevertheless, later on he taught his disciples to pray for the kingdom to "come" (Lk 11:2). Perhaps it is best to understand this teaching in Luke 4 as similar to Jesus' announcement in Mark that "the time has come" (1:15).

While this statement clearly asserts the arrival of the eschatological era prophesied in the Old Testament, Jesus goes on to say "the kingdom of God is near. Repent and believe the good news!" The good news of the kingdom was being proclaimed, the time for it had arrived, but the kingdom itself was at that moment still only "near."

Even the miracles do not necessarily affirm the inauguration of the kingdom. In our opinion Ridderbos is correct when he says,

> These miracles are . . . only incidental and are therefore not to be looked upon as a beginning from which the whole will gradually develop, but as signs of the coming kingdom of God. For the cures and the raisings of the dead done by Jesus only have a temporary significance.[57]

Ladd similarly views Jesus' healings as "pledges of the life of the eschatological Kingdom." Pointing out that they touched only a few, he states that "the saving power of the Kingdom was not yet universally operative."[58]

Similarly, when casting out demons, Jesus taught that the strong man must *first* be overcome ("tied up," NIV) before his possessions can be

---

[56]In our opinion the statement of the presence of the kingdom deserves more careful consideration than simply saying it is here and it is coming, or some other "already/not yet" terminology. Christopher Rowland's rather forthright statement on the biblical evidence related to Jesus' teaching deserves hearing: "Despite the fact that the consensus of New Testament scholarship accepts that Jesus believed that the kingdom of God had already in some sense arrived in Jesus' words and deeds, the fact has to be faced that the evidence in support of such an assumption is not very substantial" (*Christian Origins,* 135–36).

[57]Ridderbos, *The Coming of the Kingdom,* 115.

[58]Ladd, *The Presence of the Future,* 211.

taken (Mt 12:29). George Wesley Buchanan, sees in Jesus' description of the source of his power as "the finger of God" (Lk 11:20), an analogy with the miracles performed by Moses in the Exodus, where the same terminology is used (Ex 8:19). Even as the power of "the finger of God" in the plagues was for the purpose of freeing the captive people so that the kingdom of God could then be established with them, so also the miracles of Jesus were exertions of kingdom power, but not yet the kingdom.[59]

Even in the parables that clearly teach a presence of the kingdom in the world today, the emphasis is on its future manifestation. Most contemporary interpreters of the parables of the mustard seed and the leaven—which might be viewed as showing a gradually developing kingdom—feel that the emphasis should be on the contrast between the tiny veiled beginning and the final glorious manifestation.[60] William L. Lane speaks for many when he says of the parable of the mustard seed,

> This parable is concerned with the enigmatic present manifestation of the Kingdom as embodied in Jesus' person. Its appearance may be characterized by weakness and apparent insignificance—but remember the mustard seed. The day will come when the Kingdom of God will surpass in glory the mightiest kingdoms of the earth, for it is the consequence of God's sovereign action. . . . When the glory of that manifestation breaks forth before men they will be as startled as the man who considers the tiny mustard seed and the mighty shrub.[61]

There is no doubt in these parables of some concept of an intervening process of the working of the kingdom. But the emphasis on the future is borne out by the explicit statement in the parable of the wheat and the weeds that "the righteous will shine like the sun in the kingdom" only at the end of the age (Mt 13:40–43). This does not suggest that the righteous are presently in some inaugurated kingdom on earth but not "shining." The wheat and the weeds are both growing in the same field—that is, the world, which is never identified as the kingdom. Furthermore, as we have seen, the weeds are cast out of the kingdom, but this is only with its coming at the end of the age with the return of Christ. They could not be said to be "in the kingdom" today. It is preferable, therefore, to interpret this future "shining" in the kingdom as relating to the future

---

[59]Buchanan, *Jesus, the King and His Kingdom,* 30–33.

[60]Kümmel argues that there is no emphasis on a gradually developing kingdom in the parables of the seed growing secretly (Mk 4:26ff.), the mustard seed (Mk 4:30–32; Mt 13:31f.; Lk 13:18f.), the leaven (Mt 13:33; Lk 13:20f.), the wheat and tares (Mt 13:24ff.), or the dragnet (Mt 13:47ff.).

[61]William L. Lane, *Commentary on the Gospel of Mark,* New International Commentary on the New Testament (Grand Rapids: Eerdmans, 1974), 171–72; cf. also Cranfield, *The Gospel According to Saint Mark,* 169–70; Marshall, *The Gospel of Luke,* 561.

establishment of the kingdom.[62] We concur with Kümmel that this parable does not speak of "the present growth and existence of the Kingdom of God."[63]

The statements concerning a present entrance into the kingdom also do not portray a present kingdom on earth. Rather, as Robert Recker explains, these statements teach a relationship to God through Christ. "The passages in question point not to a realm but to a relationship, and this is substantiated by many passages in their context which call for a receiving of the Christ (Mt. 7:21–22; 8:22; 10:25; 10:32–33; 38–40; 11:6), a submission to God or a stance of humility in relation to God (Mt. 5:3; 18:3–4; 20:25–28; 23:10–12), or simply of subjection to God."[64] This concept, that entering the kingdom is equivalent at present to beginning a relationship with Christ, is similar to that held in the early church, which saw its citizenship in heaven in relation to the King, whose return they awaited for the establishment of the kingdom on earth (Php 3:20).

Summary. Our survey of Jesus' teaching concerning the kingdom reveals that it was announced as "near" at the opening of his ministry. In the proclamation of the gospel of the kingdom and the supernatural power displayed in miraculous signs, the kingdom actually invaded human history. The salvation blessings prophesied of the kingdom age were now present. But the idea of a present "reign" of Christ over his kingdom on earth, whether seen in the church or in the total world, is never taught. Nor did Jesus teach that we are to be building the kingdom during this time.[65]

Although the King has received his kingdom, he is yet in the "distant country," to use the language of the parable of the nobleman (cf. Lk 19:11ff.). Jesus will commence his kingdom "reign" upon his return. The coming of the kingdom is thus still primarily future, according to Jesus. The prayer for the coming of the kingdom is still valid (Mt 6:10). The kingdom's "nearness" will be signaled by the events leading to the coming of Christ. The disciples were to go on preaching the gospel of the

---

[62]Cf. Alan Hugh McNeile, *The Gospel According to St. Matthew* (reprint, Grand Rapids: Baker, 1980). For more on interpretation of the kingdom and this verse, see p.95.

[63]Kümmel, *Promise and Fulfillment*, 136.

[64]Recker, "The Redemptive Focus of the Kingdom of God," 166.

[65]The parable of the growing seed (Mk 4:26–29) illustrates the point that the work of the kingdom rests fundamentally on sovereign divine action. The man sows the seed, and then "whether he sleeps or gets up, the seed sprouts and grows, though he does not know how." Eduard Schweizer comments on this thought: "The parable with its assurance that the harvest will come stands in opposition to any form of doubt or care which, instead of waiting for God to fulfill his promise, endeavors to force the coming of the Kingdom or to build it—by revolution like the Zealots, by exact calculations and preparation like the Apocalyptists, or by complete obedience to the law like the Pharisees" (*The Good News According to Mark* [Richmond: John Knox, 1970], 102–3). Lane concurs, declaring that the kingdom comes "mysteriously, by God's initiative and appointment, without human intervention" (*Commentary on the Gospel of Mark*, 170).

kingdom (Mt 24:14), proclaiming the salvation of "repentance and forgiveness of sins" (Lk 24:47), being good stewards of that which had been entrusted to them in the King's absence (Lk 19:11ff.), and in general living according to the principles of the coming kingdom as witnesses to the King and his coming kingdom. Jesus' teaching concerning the kingdom is well summed up by Karl Ludwig Schmidt:

> The actualisation of the rule of God is future. And this future determines man in his present. The call for conversion comes to the man who is set before God and His rule. Where man responds to this call in faith, i.e., in obedience, he is in touch with the kingdom of God which comes without his co-operation, and the Gospel is glad tidings for him.[66]

II. THE KINGDOM IN THE EARLY CHURCH

When we turn to the writings pertaining more directly to the history of the early church, we find that the references to the kingdom of God and Christ are sparse compared with the Gospels. Whereas Luke used the term "kingdom" some thirty-nine times in his Gospel, he used it only eight times in Acts. The same limited use is evident from Romans to Jude, wherein "kingdom" occurs only eighteen times. To these may be added four uses of the cognate verb "to reign" and two instances of "king." This conservative usage is in stark contrast to the total usage of 127 in the Gospels. In the book of Revelation, the frequency of the terms increases, with "kingdom" being used three times, "king" three times, and "reign" six times.

This difference between the Gospels and the writings dealing with the later church is often ignored, yet it would seem to call for some explanation. The title "lord," which appears frequently in the epistles, cannot be regarded as a substitute for "king."[67] For although both terms express authority, they also carry different meanings. "Lord," which was used broadly for anyone occupying a superior position, when used for God signified his all-encompassing sovereignty as Creator and Master over the entire universe and the personal nature of this authority.[68] In relation to

---

[66]Schmidt, "βασιλεία," in *TDNT*, 1:586–87. Bertold Klappert similarly says, "Although for Jesus the realization of God's rule is still in the future, its urgent proximity already casts its shadow over the present" ("King, Kingdom," in *The New International Dictionary of New Testament Theology*, 2:382).

[67]Cullman, for example, asserts that "the title 'King' (βασιλεύς) is . . . a variant of the *Kyrios* title. . . . Despite the subtle distinction one may make in principle between the application of the two titles to Jesus, they are interchangeable" (Oscar Cullmann, *The Christology of the New Testament*, revised edition [Philadelphia: The Westminster Press, 1963], 220–21).

[68]Werner Foerster says, "In the concept of the lord two things are conjoined in organic unity: the exercise of power as such, and the personal nature of its exercise, which reaches

Christ the term represented the divine sovereign authority that was his largely through the resurrection and exaltation. The terms "king" and "kingdom," in distinction, were generally associated with political ruler-ship, although that rulership could entail personal beneficence. [69] Thus in the Old Testament the "Lord" was also described as "King." But this appellation of "king" came into use largely after the inauguration of the monarchy.[70]

It also does not seem adequate to account for the sparseness of the use of "kingdom" terminology in the writings dealing with the later church by referring to the Old Testament where it is generally agreed that the concept is present even though the specific terminology, "the kingdom of God" is absent. The Gospels indicate that the disciples who constituted the early church were well aware of this language. The question is, why did they veer away from the use of this "kingdom" language in the writings to the later church?

It is often suggested that the early church refrained from using "king" and "kingdom" in relation to Jesus to avoid charges of sedition in the Roman Empire.[71] But two facts make this improbable. First, the frequent use of "kingdom" in the Synoptics and then again in the book of Revelation, where Jesus is openly called "King of kings" (17:14; 19:16), shows that the early Christians were not apparently avoiding this terminology for political reasons. It might also be noted in light of Pilate's recognition of Jesus' innocence that Jesus' frequent use of kingdom terminology did not apparently raise the issue of sedition against him. Second, the term "lord," ($\kappa \acute{\upsilon} \rho \iota o s$) was equally offensive to the Roman imperium which required worship of the emperor as "lord." And early church history reveals that the confession of Jesus as 'Lord' and conse-

---

beyond immediate external compulsion in the moral and legal sphere" (Werner Foerster, "$\kappa \acute{\upsilon} \rho \iota o s$, $\kappa \tau \lambda$," *Theological Dictionary of the New Testament*, vol. 3 [Grand Rapids: Eerdmans, 1965], 1040).

[69] Gerhard von Rad, "$\beta \alpha \sigma \iota \lambda \epsilon \acute{\upsilon} s$" *Theological Dictionary of the New Testament*, vol. 1 (Grand Rapids: Eerdmans, 1964), 565–71). Although I. Howard Marshall understands kingship to be involved in the title "king," he also acknowledges a certain distinction when he writes, ". . . 'Lord' tends to have a passive meaning; it signifies somebody who is to be obeyed and treated with honour, and it perhaps does not bring out sufficiently the active element of the exercise of kingship and dominion and indeed of granting salvation" (Marshall, *Jesus the Saviour: Studies in New Testment Theology* [Downers Grove, Ill.: InterVarsity Press, 1990], 210). On the political meaning of "king" see also, Per Beskow, *Rex Gloriae: The Kingship of Christ in the Early Church* (Stockholm: Almqvist & Wiksell, 1962), 39–40.

[70]Bertold Klapper, "King, Kingdom," in *The New International Dictionary of New Testament Theology*, 2:375.

[71]James D. G. Dunn, *Romans 9–16*, Word Biblical Commentary, vol. 38b (Dallas: Word Books, 1988), 822. In light of Pilate's recognition of the innocence of Jesus, his frequent use of kingdom terminology did not apparently raise the issue of sedition against him.

quent refusal to make the same confession with regard to the emperor did, in fact, lead to persecution.[72]

The best answer to the question as to why kingdom terminology is frequently found in the Gospels and Revelation but is used only very limitedly in the other writings dealing with the early church is found in the perspective of the kingdom taught in the epistles.

A. The Futurity of the Kingdom

Despite the infrequency of the terminology, the concept of the kingdom of God was clearly present in the apostolic preaching and teaching. In fact, on several occasions their message could be summarized as preaching or testifying about the kingdom of God (Ac 8:12; 19:8; 20:25; 28:23, 31). The specific theology of the kingdom is not indicated in these contexts, however. All that is clear is that the kingdom had to do with Jesus Christ. Philip preached "the good news of the kingdom of God and the name of Jesus Christ" (Ac 8:12). Paul "explained and declared to them the kingdom of God and tried to convince them about Jesus from the Law of Moses and from the Prophets" (Ac 28:23; cf. v. 31). Since the kingdom was bound up with Jesus, the kingdom message in these instances no doubt included the salvation presently available through faith in him. But the message must have also proclaimed the future coming of the kingdom. Ernst Haenchen explains that "news of the kingdom of God and the name of Jesus Christ" in Philip's message included "God's (coming) kingdom and Jesus' (all-powerful) name."[73]

We also gain insight into the apostles' meaning of the kingdom from two other passages in Acts. The question concerning restoration of the kingdom to Israel looks to the future for the arrival of the kingdom (Ac 1:6; cf. 3:21).[74] The same futurity is seen in Paul's statement that "we must go through many hardships to enter the kingdom of God" (14:22). For the most part, however, we are probably to look to the epistles for a fuller explanation of the meaning of the proclamation of the kingdom of God mentioned in Acts.

We find in the epistles that the dominant teaching concerns a future kingdom and not a present one. The idea most often expressed is that the

---

[72]Bertold Klapper writes, "The effect of the confession of *kyrios Iesous,* used by the Christians in proclaiming Jesus as the Lord, was to destroy this vital ideology of the Roman imperium [i.e., divine kingship], and the reaction it called forth was the persecution of Christians during the first three centuries" ("King, Kingdom, " in *The New International Dictionary of New Testament Theology,* 2:373); cf. also, Oscar Cullmann, *The Christology of the New Testament,* 219–20.

[73]Ernst Haenchen, *The Acts of the Apostles* (Philadelphia: Westminster, 1971), 303.

[74]For a discussion of the meaning and validity of the disciples' question in Acts 1:6, see pages 268–71. For a discussion of 3:21, see page 271.

kingdom is something to be inherited (1Co 6:9–10; 15:50; Gal 5:21; Eph 5:5; Col 1:12–13; Jas 2:5). As J. Eichler notes, this inheritance can already be recognized by faith, and believers possess "the guarantee of this inheritance in the Holy Spirit whom we have received." Nevertheless, he adds, "this kingdom [the inheritance] embraces all those promises the fulfillment of which is yet future."[75] Similarly, after analyzing all the New Testament references to "inheritance," "heirs," and "inherit," C. F. Hogg and W. E. Vine conclude that "not a present but a prospective possession is always in view in the word."[76]

The idea of the kingdom as a future inheritance is in harmony with the statement that believers will "receive a rich welcome into the eternal kingdom of our Lord and Savior Jesus Christ" (2Pe 1:11). Believers are urged "to live lives worthy of God, who calls you into his kingdom and glory" (1Th 2:12). The joining of "kingdom" and "glory" under one article in the original Greek text indicates that Paul's reference is to the future kingdom.[77] Calling this an "eschatological reference," Ernest Best comments that a "worthy walk" is "the kind of conduct appropriate to God's kingdom and glory, the kind of conduct which those who inherit the kingdom will demonstrate in the kingdom."[78] It was for this same kingdom that they were suffering (2Th 1:5) and into which Paul anticipated a safe entrance at the close of his life (2Ti 4:18).

Paul's understanding of the believers' reign supports this future concept of the kingdom. As Jesus had promised his disciples, Paul believed that he and all other believers would reign with Christ in his kingdom. But Paul made it clear that he was not reigning during this present age. Writing to the Corinthians, who were behaving as though they had already entered into the kingdom reign, Paul chided them for their radical, realized eschatology: "You have become kings [ἐβασιλεύσατε]—and that without us! How I wish that you really had become kings so that we might be kings with you!" (1Co 4:8). Paul then described the current state of the apostles as "fools for Christ," "weak," "dishonored," and "the scum of the earth, the refuse of the world" (vv. 10–13).

Although the blessings of the salvation of the kingdom are present, it is difficult to see in Paul's words any idea of a present kingdom of Christ in which believers share in his reign. For Paul, as for all believers, being

---

[75]J. Eichler, "Inheritance," in *The New International Dictionary of New Testament Theology*, vol. 2, ed. Colin Brown (Grand Rapids: Zondervan, 1976), 300.

[76]C. F. Hogg and W. E. Vine, *The Epistle to the Galatians and the Epistles to the Thessalonians* (1922; reprint, Fincastle, Va.: Scripture Truth, 1959), 147.

[77]George Milligan, *St Paul's Epistles to the Thessalonians* (reprint, Grand Rapids: Eerdmans, 1953), 27.

[78]Ernest Best, *The First and Second Epistles to the Thessalonians*, Black's New Testament Commentaries (London: Adam and Charles Black, 1972), 107.

"with Christ" (Php 1:23; 1Th 4:17) and therefore reigning with him (there is no concept of reigning without him) was always in the future (2Ti 2:12).[79]

Not only is there no reference to the present reign of believers in a kingdom; there is also no unambiguous reference in the epistles that uses the word "reign" (βασιλεύω) in relation to the present ministry of Christ.[80] Although Paul's statement that Christ "must reign until he has put all his enemies under his feet" (1Co 15:25) is often interpreted as a present "reign," there are good reasons to take it as a reference to his future reign following the *parousia*.[81] Because the term "reign" is clearly used in regard to both the Gospel predictions of Christ's reign (Lk 1:33; 19:14) and his future reign after this age (cf. 2Ti 2:12; Rev 11:15, 17), its absence in connection with the present ministry of Christ calls for explanation.[82] It would seem best to say that although Christ has been exalted to receive kingly authority over the entire universe and all its contents, he is not presently exercising that kingship in the sense of "reigning," nor are we as believers doing so.

B. The Presence of the Kingdom

Along with the primary teaching of the epistles that the kingdom is future, there are a few statements that relate it to the present experience of believers. Some passages speak of spiritual characteristics of the kingdom that are already in operation through the Spirit. Paul's teaching that "the kingdom of God is not a matter of eating and drinking, but of righteousness, peace and joy in the Holy Spirit" (Ro 14:17) is plainly attempting to

---

[79]This would also seem difficult to harmonize with any present application of Revelation 20:4–6, which teaches the believer's reign with Christ. To this we would also add the problem posed by the interpretation of 1 Corinthians 15:24 that sees Christ as giving up the kingdom at his *parousia*. If such is the case and believers are not presently reigning with him, when is the time for that coreign?

[80]Interestingly Per Beskow notes that in pre-Constantine Christian art "Christ is seldom or never portrayed as King. . . .: on Roman sarcophagi or in the catacomb paintings what we find instead is Christ the Good Shepher, Christ the Miracle worker, or Christ the Philosopher in conversation with the disciples (Per Beskow, *Rex Gloriae: The Kingship of Christ in the Early Church*, 12).

[81]For a full discussion of this verse and its teaching with reference to the millennium, see pages 280–86.

[82]The use of "reign" (βασιλεύω) with Christ and believers is found in the following references: Lk 1:33; 19:14, 27; Ro 5:17; 1Co 4:8; 15:25; Rev 5:10; 11:15, 17; 19:6; 20:4, 6; 22:5. "Reign with" (συνβασιλεύω) is found as follows: 1Co 4:8; 2Ti 2:12. For the futurity of the believer's "reign in life" in Romans 5:17, see Dunn, *Romans 9–16*, 282. Dunn remarks, ". . . they are already receiving grace, but they are not yet reigning." Similarly, noting the tenses in the original Greek, Ernst Käsemann says, ". . . the tension between the present participle ['receive'] and the future verb ['will . . . reign'] is significant" (*Commentary on Romans* [Grand Rapids: Eerdmans, 1980], 155).

encourage these traits in the present church. But applying kingdom characteristics is not necessarily the same as declaring that the kingdom has come and is presently established. According to William Sanday and Arthur C. Headlam, the "kingdom" here, in accord with Paul's normal use, is the messianic kingdom, which is "the reward and goal of the Christian life." The principles of that kingdom mentioned in this passage are, however, already exhibited in this world through the indwelling Spirit.[83] Viewing the kingdom Christologically, Cranfield, following Käsemann, says that "it is in the presence and activity of the Lord Jesus Christ, and only so, that the kingdom of God is experienced in the present."[84]

Paul's statement to the Corinthians that "the kingdom of God is not a matter of talk but of power" (1Co 4:20) is another application of the kingdom to the present. Instead of arrogant human "talking," the apostle sought the power of the kingdom—a reference, according to the context, to the power of God in the gospel that was manifest by the Spirit (cf. 1Co 1:18, 24; 2:4–5). While this teaches a present relation to the kingdom and the experience of its power, it hardly demonstrates a present established kingdom in distinction to the apostle's general teaching of a future kingdom. As C. K. Barrett says, "It is always an eschatological concept (though sometimes brought forward into the present), and the *power* with which it works is the power of the Holy Spirit (cf. Rom. xiv. 17), by which God's purpose is put into effect and the future anticipated in the present."[85]

The apostle has just chided the Corinthians for their boasting as if they had already attained the kingdom and were reigning as kings (cf. 4:8). He would hardly talk of a present kingdom just a few verses later.

The verse that most clearly expresses some kind of present position

---

[83]William Sanday and Arthur C. Headlam, *A Critical and Exegetical Commentary on the Epistle to the Romans,* International Critical Commentary (Edinburgh: T & T Clark, 1902), 391–92. Charles A. Briggs says of this verse, "It is not clear whether the kingdom of God here is the kingdom of glory, or the kingdom of the Church in this world. Paul thus far has always used it of the kingdom of glory. The presumption is that it has the same reference here. Eating and drinking are not the characteristics of that kingdom of glory. Eating and drinking are not the preparation for it. But its characteristics are righteousness, peace, and joy in the Holy Spirit. These things are to be sought for. Only those who have them will inherit the kingdom" (*The Messiah of the Apostles* [Edinburgh, T & T Clark, 1895], 172–73).

[84]C. E. B. Cranfield, *A Critical and Exegetical Commentary on the Epistle to the Romans,* International Critical Commentary, 2 vols. (Edinburgh: T & T Clark, 1979), 2:718.

[85]C. K. Barrett, *A Commentary on the First Epistle to the Corinthians* (New York: Harper & Row, 1968), 118. Compare also H. A. W. Meyer's comment on this verse: "The βασιλεία τοῦ θεοῦ, again, is not here, as it never is elsewhere . . . , and in particular never in Paul's writings (neither in this passage nor in Rom. xiv. 7; Col. 1:13, iv. 11 . . .), the *church,* or the kingdom of God in the *ethical* sense . . . , but the *Messianic kingdom*" (*Critical and Exegetical Handbook to the Epistles to the Corinthians,* 2 vols. [Edinburgh: T & T Clark, 1877–79], 104).

in the kingdom is Paul's statement that the Father "has rescued us from the dominion of darkness and brought us into the kingdom of the Son he loves" (Col 1:13). Many scholars view this "kingdom of the Son" as a present spiritual kingdom of salvation that believers enter into at the moment of conversion.[86] For example, Peter T. O'Brien, concurring with C. F. D. Moule that the kingdom is "entirely moral and spiritual . . . for the disciples of Christ," declares, "It is here an existing reality, a present possession."[87] Curtis Vaughn pointedly states, "The 'kingdom' (rule) is not to be interpreted eschatologically. It was for the Colossians a present reality (cf. John 3:3–5)."[88]

The context, however, favors an eschatological meaning for the kingdom in this verse.[89] Immediately preceding this statement, the apostle wrote that the Father "has qualified you to share in the inheritance of the saints in the kingdom of light" (Col 1:12). Several terms in this statement point to the future. Werner Foerster says that the term *inheritance* (κλῆρος) "is used to denote the eschatological portion assigned to man."[90] In addition, according to O'Brien, to describe the inheritance as belonging to "the saints in the kingdom of light" means that it is "in the realm of the light of the age to come" and is the equivalent of the "hope laid up in

---

[86]Some scholars distinguish "the kingdom of Christ" from the "kingdom of God," seeing the former as the present reign of Christ and the latter as a future event occurring after Christ hands over the kingdom to the Father (1Co 15:24; cf. F. F. Bruce, *1 and 2 Thessalonians*, Word Biblical Commentary, vol. 45 [Waco, Tex.: Word Books, 1982], 37; Eduard Lohse, *A Commentary on the Epistles to the Colossians and to Philemon* [Philadelphia: Fortress, 1971], 37–38; Gerhardus Vos, *The Pauline Eschatology* [Grand Rapids: Eerdmans, 1953], 259). Vos does acknowledge, however, that this distinction is not uniform in Paul.
Such a radical distinction does not appear to be valid. In various passages there is reference to "the kingdom of God and of Christ" (cf. Eph 5:5). Particularly telling against this distinction is the statement associated with the coming of Christ: "The kingdom of the world has become the kingdom of our Lord and of his Christ" (Rev 11:15). Even in the eternal state the throne is "of God and of the Lamb" (Rev 22:1). Bertold Klappert first shows that the "kingdom of God" is bound up with the person and work of Jesus both in the Gospels and the epistles; then he rightly concludes that "the kingdom of Jesus Christ is in the NT view the same as the kingdom of God" ("King, Kingdom," in *The New International Dictionary of New Testament Theology*, 2:386–89); cf. also Schmidt, "βασιλεία," in *TDNT*, 1:581, 588–89.
[87]Peter T. O'Brien, *Colossians, Philemon*, Word Biblical Commentary, vol. 44 (Waco, Tex.: Word Books, 1982), 28. C. F. D. Moule further adds the very questionable negative statement that "there is no trace of a nationalistic Messianism in the N. T. conception" (*The Epistle to the Colossians and to Philemon*, The Cambridge Greek Testament [Cambridge: Univ. Press, 1962], 58).
[88]Curtis Vaughn, "Colossians," in *The Expositor's Bible Commentary*, vol. 11, ed. Frank E. Gaebelein (Grand Rapids: Zondervan, 1978), 180.
[89]According to Per Beskow, all of the New Testament references to the kingdom of "the Son of Man or of Christ" are "distinctly eschatological in character" (*Rex Gloriae*, 44).
[90]Werner Foerster, "κλῆρος," in *TDNT*, 3:763.

heaven (v. 5; cf. 3:1–4)."[91] Therefore the saints are presently qualified (the Greek aorist tense) to share in the inheritance, but the reference is to a future blessing.

That this "inheritance . . . in the kingdom of light" (Col 1:12) is related to being "brought into the kingdom of the Son" (v. 13) is seen in the connection of "light" and "darkness" in these two verses. T. K. Abbott notes that the apostle spoke here of an inheritance in "light" rather than "in the heavenlies" because he wanted to represent the condition of natural mankind as "darkness" in verse 13.[92] To be qualified for "the kingdom of light" (v. 12) is therefore the equivalent of being "rescued . . . from the dominion of darkness and brought . . . into the kingdom of the Son" (v. 13).

If such is the case, then this reference to the kingdom, like many others in Paul's writings, belongs to the eschatological category of an inheritance that is already assured. It is the equivalent of the saints' having their "citizenship in heaven" (Php 3:20). This is the view of Charles A. Briggs, who acknowledges that he came to it after for many years holding the position that believers were already in a present kingdom.

> Elsewhere in the Pauline epistles the kingdom has always had an eschatological reference and has been an inheritance, a kingdom of glory. . . . My final study of it [Col. 1:13], in its connection with the Messianic conception of the Epistles of the Imprisonment, leads me to the opinion that the kingdom is eschatological here also. It is parallel with the inheritance in light. As the kingdom is elsewhere an inheritance, its parallelism with inheritance and its substitution for it in a common antithesis to authority of darkness favors that reference here. The only difficulty is in explaining how Christians may be said to be transferred into a kingdom which in its nature is eschatological. The solution of this difficulty is found in the parallelism with citizenship in heaven of the Epistle to the Philippians; and with the life hid with Christ of our Epistle [Col. 3:3].[93]

This relationship to the future kingdom, however, does carry with it a present blessing. Believers whose citizenship has been transferred into Christ's kingdom are now free from "the dominion of darkness," by which the apostle means the "satanic or demonic powers,"[94] whose slaves they had formerly been and over whom Christ had triumphed. But this

---

[91]O'Brien, *Colossians, Philemon*, 27; similarly, T. K. Abbott, *A Critical and Exegetical Commentary on the Epistles to the Ephesians and to the Colossians*, International Critical Commentary (Edinburgh: T & T Clark, n.d.), 207.

[92]Abbott, *A Critical and Exegetical Commentary on the Epistles to the Ephesians and to the Colossians*, 207.

[93]Charles A. Briggs, *The Messiah of the Apostles* (Edinburgh: T & T Clark, 1895), 211–12.

[94]Ralph Martin, "Reconciliation and Forgiveness in Colossians," in *Reconciliation and Hope*, ed. Robert Banks (Grand Rapids: Eerdmans, 1974), 107.

deliverance is not yet all-encompassing. It relates to the believer's inner personal or spiritual freedom from the domination of the evil powers, but not yet deliverance from outward evil.[95] The present effect of belonging to Christ's kingdom is elaborated in the following verse: ". . . we have redemption, the forgiveness of sins" (Col 1:14). According to Thomas Sappington, Paul in this verse, which by construction is intimately related to verse 13, "reminds his readers what they possess because of redemption 'in Christ.'"[96]

Being presently "brought into the kingdom of the Son," therefore, signifies not a kingdom reign, but spiritual salvation through a relationship with the coming King (cf. "in whom," Col 1:14), even as we saw previously concerning the present relationship to the kingdom in the teaching of Jesus. The same essential truth is expressed by Paul in relation to his commission. Christ had sent him to the Gentiles "to open their eyes and turn them from darkness to light, and from the power of Satan to God, so that they may receive forgiveness of sins and a place among those who are sanctified by faith in me" (Ac 26:18). According to the Colossians passage, that place among the sanctified means heirship in "the kingdom of light" and citizenship in "the kingdom of the Son"—which is presently in heaven but will come to earth with Christ.

The teaching of the early church, therefore, yields the same picture of the kingdom as that found in the Gospels. The establishment of the kingdom on earth is still future. The believer is related to this kingdom through faith in the King and is therefore an heir and already a citizen of the coming kingdom. The King has already bestowed some of the blessings of the kingdom on its citizens, so it is possible to speak of the presence of the kingdom now. This presence is described in terms of righteousness, peace, and joy (Rom 14:17), the forgiveness of sins (Col 1:13–14), and power (1Co 4:20), but never in terms of a present "reign."

The kingdom promised in the Old Testament, with its central features in the Davidic covenant, thus finds its fulfillment according to the New Testament teaching both in the present church age and in the future. We will see in chapter 11 that this general picture of the kingdom as "already/not yet" that is taught in the New Testament includes evidence for a temporary messianic kingdom as part of the future fulfillment of the total kingdom promise and plan for world history.

---

[95] The present limitation of freedom from the "dominion of darkness" is evident in that the apostle's language has an Old Testament–Qumranic background. Ralph P. Martin points to one Qumran reference to this evil "dominion" as that "which inflicts persecution on the children of righteousness (I QS iii.22f.)." The continuing persecution of the New Testament church thus made it evident that complete deliverance was not yet the believer's experience (Martin, *Reconciliation and Hope*).

[96] Thomas J. Sappington, *Revelation and Redemption at Colossae*, Journal for the Study of the New Testament Supplement Series 53 (Sheffield: JSOT Press, 1991), 201.

Chapter 5

The New Covenant and the Salvation of the Gentiles

ACCORDING TO the Scriptures, the salvation of God that flows from the Cross is given to all mankind through the new covenant. In both the Old and New Testaments it is the provisions of the new covenant that ultimately provide the solution to the human problem of sin and bring those in the covenant into a final perfect fellowship with God as his sons and daughters.

Some scholars reason that because the promise of the new covenant in the Old Testament is explicitly for Israel (cf. Jer 31:31), all whom it encompasses must therefore be regarded as Israel. An example of this reasoning is seen in O. Palmer Robertson, who, without denying an ethnic meaning to "Israel" in the promise of Jeremiah 31, nevertheless sees "Israel" as "a typological representation of the elect people of God." He concludes, "If the new covenant people of God are the actualized realization of typological form, and the new covenant now is in effect, those constituting the people of God in the present circumstances must be recognized as the 'Israel of God.' As a unified people, the participants of the new covenant today are 'Israel.'"[1]

Similarly, on the application of the new covenant to Christians today, Vern Poythress states, "Thus one might say that Israel and Judah

---

[1]O. Palmer Robertson, *The Christ of the Covenants* (Grand Rapids: Baker, 1980), 289.

themselves undergo a transformation at the first coming of Christ, because Christ is the final, supremely faithful Israelite. Around him all true Israel gathers."[2]

Dispensationalists deny this equating all of God's people with "Israel" on the basis that Israel retains its ethnic meaning throughout Scripture and God's salvation is provided for Gentiles without their being a part of that ethnic people. Some dispensationalists in the past have gone so far as to claim a distinct new covenant for the church different from the new covenant ascribed to Israel in Jeremiah 31.[3] But dispensationalists today generally acknowledge only one new covenant as the basis for the salvation for all of God's people, Gentiles as well as Jews. The New Scofield Bible affirms that "the new covenant . . . secures the eternal blessedness, under the Abrahamic Covenant (Gal. 3:13–29), of all who believe."[4]

Unquestionably the salvation of the new covenant provides for the ultimate unity of all God's people. But the question remains whether the Scriptures teach that this unity in salvation dissolves the distinction of Israel as a particular people among the peoples of the world and redefines "Israel" as *all* the people of God.

I. THE TEACHING OF THE OLD TESTAMENT

A. *The New Covenant*

The term "new covenant" is found only in Jeremiah 31:31 in the Old Testament and in the quotations of that passage in the New (cf. Heb 8:8–12; 10:16–17). But the concept is affirmed in other places under different terminology. Jeremiah also spoke of an "everlasting covenant" (32:40; 50:5). The prophet Ezekiel, a contemporary of Jeremiah, predicted a new covenant, which he called variously "an everlasting covenant," "my covenant," and "a covenant of peace" (16:60–62; 34:25; 37:26–27). Two centuries earlier, the prophet Isaiah had already spoken of "an everlasting covenant" that God was promising to his people—i.e., "an everlasting covenant" (Isa 55:3; 61:8), or simply "my covenant" (59:21). In addition, God's promise that he would make his Servant "to be a covenant for the people" (Isa 42:6) had in view "the salvation given in the covenant."[5]

---

[2]Vern Poythress, *Understanding Dispensationalists* (Grand Rapids: Zondervan, 1987), 106; cf. also George E. Ladd, "Historic Premillennialism," in *The Meaning of the Millennium: Four Views*, ed. Robert G. Clouse (Downers Grove, Ill.: InterVarsity, 1977), 25–27.

[3]Lewis Sperry Chafer, *Systematic Theology* (Dallas: Dallas Seminary Press, 1948), 4:325.
[4]*The New Scofield Reference Bible* (New York: Oxford Univ. Press, 1967), 1318, cf. also 804.
[5]Claus Westermann, *Isaiah 40–66* (Philadephia: Westminster, 1969), 100.

The concept of the new covenant is more pervasive in the Old Testament, however, than the rather limited use of the actual term "covenant" indicated in the references above. Although Ezekiel uses the term "covenant" infrequently, "it would not . . . be too much to claim the whole of the prophecy of Ezekiel is new covenant orientated," according to William J. Dumbrell.[6] The same new covenant theology underlies Isaiah's prophecies of chapters 40–66 and is central to the ushering in of the promised new creation.[7] Without mentioning a "covenant," Hosea's prophecy of God's final union with his people is clearly related to this concept. Hans Walter Wolff says, ". . . the new covenant announced in Jer 31:33f is prefigured in Hos 2:21f by Yahweh's new gifts and by Israel's response as well."[8] Finally, Malachi's prophecy of the coming of "the messenger of the covenant" (3:1) speaks to the same truth.

It is apparent from the above that the concept of the new covenant held a central place in the hope of the Old Testament. Not only was the concept vitally related to the final renewal of Israel, but, as indicated especially in Isaiah, it was also the promise that would ultimately provide the salvation for making all things new.

1. The Addressees of the New Covenant. As we have noted, the *locus classicus* on the subject explicitly relates the new covenant to Israel. God promised to establish the covenant "with the house of Israel and with the house of Judah" (Jer 31:31). The promise is set in the context of Jeremiah's prophecy of Israel's future suffering and final restoration. The day would come when Israel would undergo a great distress termed "a time of trouble for Jacob" (Jer 30:7). But this day, referring to the eschatological "day of the Lord," will also see the liberation of Israel from the enslavement of foreigners and her final restoration under the Messiah to serve her Lord (v. 8).

At the time Jeremiah was prophesying, the northern kingdom of Israel had long since been overthrown and the people carried off into captivity by the Assyrians (cf. 2Ki 17:5–6). By specifically mentioning both kingdoms in 31:31, Jeremiah no doubt intended to teach that both would exist in the future and would be united under the one covenant[9] (cf. Jer 50:4–5, where their union is specifically taught in relation to the covenant).

The contexts of the other passages related to prophecies about the new covenant reveal similar settings. Hosea made his prediction of God's

---

[6]William J. Dumbrell, *Covenant and Creation* (Nashville: Nelson, 1984), 185; for a good elaboration of the new covenant in Ezekiel, see Dumbrell, 185–90.

[7]Dumbrell, *Covenant and Creation*, 190–99.

[8]Hans Walter Wolff, *Hosea* (Philadelphia: Fortress, 1974), 53; cf. also Dumbrell, *Covenant and Creation*, 169.

[9]Homer A Kent, Jr., "The New Covenant and the Church," *Grace Theological Journal* 6, no. 2 (Fall 1985): 290.

future covenant relation with his people during the final tragic days of the northern kingdom. The people were experiencing God's judgment because of their failure under the Mosaic covenant, but this was not the end. God would finally give them back their land and make them his beloved people (cf. Hos 2:14–23). According to Isaiah and Ezekiel, the recipients of the new covenant would likewise be the people of Israel. In every instance, the context of the covenant promises includes the restoration of that people to their land to live in holiness and prosperity under their God (e.g., Jer 31:7–14, 35–38; 32:37–38; Eze 37:15–28).

That these promises of the new covenant mention only Israel raises the question of the participation of the Gentiles. This will be discussed more fully later, but two points may be noted in passing. First, the fact that the prophetic statements are addressed only to Israel cannot logically be understood to *exclude* others from participating even though they are not a part of Israel. The texts never say that the covenant would relate only to Israel and not to others.

Second, and perhaps more important, as we have seen, each statement of the promise of the new covenant comes to Israel in the context of the failure of the old covenant. Whether the prophetic messages came from Hosea to the northern kingdom of Israel, from Jeremiah to Judah, or from Ezekiel to the exiles, they were all intended to give hope and encouragement to a people witnessing the seeming demise of the fulfillment of their covenant hope. As the prophetic messages of impending judgment were directed toward Israel, so it is natural to see the messages of hope in the new covenant addressed to them. God had given particular promises regarding this people to the patriarchs. In the message of the new covenant, he assured this same people, Israel, that despite their sin, his grace would finally triumph to bring them to reality. The historical context thus made it natural for the new covenant promises to be given expressly to Israel.

2. *The Provisions of the New Covenant.* As the covenant that will finally bring the realization of the eschatological hope, the new covenant includes both spiritual and material blessings. The focus of the promise, however, is on the spiritual dimension since it is a new relationship with God on which all other blessings rest.

a. *The foundational provision: forgiveness of sins.* God's promise to his people that he "will forgive their wickedness and will remember their sins no more," stated as the climactic provision of the new covenant by Jeremiah (31:34; cf. also 33:8; 50:20), forms the basis for all other provisions.[10] In the words of W. Rudolph, this promise "stands at the

---

[10]Thomas E. McComiskey explains the connection of the final promise in 31:34 this way: "This gracious promise is connected to the foregoing material by the particle *ki* (for) and

conclusion not as a chance addition, but as the operative basis of the whole promise: under all that is prevailing hitherto, a line is drawn, a new life with God commences."[11] Gustave Oehler similarly asserts from Jeremiah's prophecy that "the *abolition of the old condemnation by Divine mercy*" is "the fundamental assumption in this new dispensation."[12]

The concept of forgiveness of sins can be seen also in Ezekiel's mention of cleansing in connection with receiving new life (cf. Eze 36:25–27). Most certainly it is seen in the statement of Jesus that goes to the heart of the new covenant: "This is my blood of the new covenant which is poured out for many for the forgiveness of sins" (Mt 26:28).

Forgiveness of sins was entailed in the Mosaic covenant. At the giving of the law, God proclaimed himself "the compassionate and gracious God, slow to anger, abounding in love and faithfulness . . . and forgiving wickedness, rebellion and sin" (Ex 34:6–7; cf. Nu 14:18). The sacrificial system made clear provision for forgiveness (e.g., Lev 4:20, 26; cf. 1Ki 8:30), and the people under the old covenant knew the reality of this divine grace in their lives (e.g., Pss 32:1, 5; 51:7; 86:5; 103:3).

But the provision of forgiveness under the new covenant is far more than simply a continuity of the forgiveness provided under the old covenant. First, as Robertson points out, sin under the old covenant was in actuality passed over rather than removed. The sacrifice of animals could not ultimately effect forgiveness, and the need for continual sacrifice indicated that. Thus the new factor promised in the new covenant was "the once-for-all accomplishment of that forgiveness."[13]

Several other indications of the new dimension of forgiveness follow from this basic fact of its true accomplishment.[14] The removal of punishment is an aspect of forgiveness, yet under the old covenant punishment was often mitigated rather than completely removed. Although God is a forgiving God, he also metes out punishment for the sins of his people. After revealing himself to Moses as gracious and forgiving, God declared that "he does not leave the guilty unpunished; he punishes the children and their children for the sin of the fathers to the third and fourth generation" (Ex 34:6–7; cf. 20:5–6; Nu 14:18; Dt 5:9–10). The psalmist sums up the experience of the old covenant, declaring of God,

---

establishes the basis on which God will effect the inward change of heart by which they become God's people" (*The Covenants of Promise* [Grand Rapids: Baker, 1985], 87).

[11]W. Rudolph, *Jeremia*, HAT 12 (Tübingen: J. C. B. Mohr [Paul Siebeck], 185), his emphasis. Cited by Thomas M. Raitt, *A Theology of Exile* (Philadelphia: Fortress, 1977), 193.

[12]Gustave Friedrich Oehler, *Theology of the Old Testament* (reprint, Grand Rapids: Zondervan, 1950), 458. Robertson likewise calls the provision of forgiveness "the basic substructure of the new covenant relationship" (*The Christ of the Covenants*, 282).

[13]Robertson, *The Christ of the Covenants*, 283–84.

[14]For a fuller discussion of the following points and more on the newness of forgiveness under the new covenant, see Raitt, *A Theology of Exile*, 184–94.

"you were to Israel a forgiving God, though you punished their misdeeds" (Ps 99:8). U. Cassuto says, regarding Exodus 20:6, "Sin is not completely expunged by mercy; the punishment is suspended, and if a man sins again, the Lord exacts retribution from him for both the present and the former sin."[15] The psalmist's words may also reflect the times when God forgave, but also went on to exact a certain level of punishment as at Kadesh (Nu 14:20–23).

Another indication of a different kind of forgiveness under the new covenant is seen in the fellowship with God achieved through it. As sin destroys relationships, so forgiveness restores them. While the old covenant brought a certain degree of fellowship with God, the need for mediators and the extremely limited access to his presence in the most holy place revealed that this fellowship fell far short of that promised in the new covenant. The intimacy of this new fellowship rests on this new kind of forgiveness that would finally remove the obstacle of sin completely and thus forever.

b. A new obedience by the indwelling Spirit. The removal of sin will result in a cleansed and renewed heart that will willingly obey God's righteous law in holiness of life. Instead of the law on tablets of stone that was before them, God promised to put his law "in their minds [literally 'their inward parts'] and write it on their hearts" (Jer 31:33). This amplifies the earlier statement in Jeremiah 24:7: "I will give them a heart to know me" (cf. 3:17; 32:39–40).

The significance of this changed heart becomes evident through contrast with Jeremiah's many negative statements concerning the hearts of his contemporaries. They were "rebellious" (5:23) and stubbornly evil (3:17; 7:24; 11:8; 18:12; cf. 4:14; 17:9; 22:17). But the day was coming when God would do a new thing for his people. Thomas M. Raitt says that "this is the first time that God promises to transform the heart of his whole people as part of a new and unconditional scheme of salvation."[16]

Ezekiel expressed this same transformation in declaring that God would give his people a "new heart" and a "new spirit" (Eze 36:26; cf.11:19). The "heart," according to the biblical concept, is the center of the human personality, the "wellspring" from which life proceeds (cf. Pr 23:4). While the emotions are included, the biblical focus of the heart is on the mind and the will. The new heart will be "a heart of flesh"—soft and impressionable—replacing the unresponsive "heart of stone." The "spirit" is the energizing impulse, the motivating power. By declaring that God would give "a new heart," writing his laws on it, the new covenant therefore looks to the time when the law of God would be a part of the

---

[15]U. Cassuto, *A Commentary on the Book of Exodus* (Jerusalem: Magnes Press, Hebrew University, 1967), 440.

[16]Raitt, *A Theology of Exile*, 177.

mind and will of the people "so that they obey God, not because they are supposed to, but because they want to," as W. L. Holladay puts it.[17] The "new spirit" would provide the dynamic for the actualization of the heart's new direction.

This new obedience would come about because God would give himself through his Spirit to dwell within his people. God said, "I will put my Spirit in you and move you to follow my decrees and be careful to keep my laws" (Eze 36:27). This truth of the new covenant becomes central to the gospel of the New Testament, especially in the teaching of the apostle Paul that the righteousness that belongs to salvation is by the Spirit (cf. Ro 8:4; Gal 5:16). Although it is not always linked to covenant language, the enduement of the Holy Spirit is one of the chief characteristics of the prophetic hope that would signal the eschatological days of the Messiah (cf. Isa 42:1; 44:3; 59:21; Eze 39:29; Joel 2:28).

c. A new relationship to God. The transforming work of the new covenant by the indwelling Spirit would bring about a new relationship between God and his people. The heart of the new covenant promise is expressed in the simple statement, "I will be their God, and they will be my people" (Jer 31:33; cf. 24:7; 32:38; Eze 36:28; 11:20). This goal had already been part of the Abrahamic, Mosaic, and Davidic covenants (cf. Ge 17:7; Ex 6:7; 2Sa 7:24). But the sinfulness of the people had prohibited its full realization. The promises of final forgiveness, the transformation of the heart issuing in holiness, and the indwelling of the Spirit would bring the new relationship to reality in the new covenant (cf. Rev 21:3).

The relationship promised is nothing less than a direct personal fellowship of God with humankind through his Spirit—that is, spirit to spirit and heart to heart. The result is an unmediated knowledge of God among all his people: "No longer will a man teach his neighbor . . . because they will all know me" (Jer 31:34). This knowledge is more than information; it is personal experience. The people would not only know information about God, but also have a personal relationship with him. In contrast with Hosea's complaint that there was no "knowledge of God in the land" (4:1 NASB), the "knowledge of God" promised under the new covenant would be universal among his people.[18]

The new dimension of this knowledge is that it is direct and unmediated. Under the old covenant the knowledge of God was "taught" only through the mediation of priests and prophets. But such mediation is

---

[17]W. L. Holladay, "New Covenant, the," in *Interpreter's Dictionary of the Bible,* 5 vols. (Nashville: Abingdon, 1962, 1976), supp. vol.: 624.

[18]Hosea's other uses of the "knowledge of God" make it clear that this knowledge includes the righteousness of his law (cf. 4:6; 6:6; 8:1-2), against which the people had rebelled. Thus "knowing" God through the new covenant is vitally connected with the new obedience brought about by the law's being written on the heart.

unnecessary under the new covenant. Because the goal of the covenant is unity between God and his people, he has an immediate relationship with each person. There is no need for "teachers" in the sense of mediators. (That there are still teachers in the church under the new covenant does not controvert this promise. Every believer is a priest directly taught by the Spirit [cf. 1Jn 2:20, 27]. Teachers in the church do not mediate the knowledge of God; they assist believers in their present imperfect situation to realize "the direct oneness they now experience with God through the provisions of the new covenant."[19] The new covenant, however, looks even beyond the present to the time when human natures will be perfected and no human instruction will be necessary.[20])

d. Physical blessings. The spiritual blessings that lie at the center of the new covenant are often associated with material blessings. Robertson says,

> The new covenant lays a significant stress on internal transformation. . . . Yet the context of the prophetical message concerning the new covenant resists a pure "spiritualization" of the blessings of this covenant. The language of the prophets contains far too much in terms of materially defined benedictions.[21]

Willem VanGemeren lists a number of these material blessings from the book of Jeremiah:

> . . . gathering of people to the land (31:8–11; 32:15, 37, 41), rebuilding of cities (30:18; 31:38–40), cultivation and productivity of the land (31:5, 12–14), increase in herds and flocks (33:12–13), population explosion (30:20; 31:17), resulting in expressions of joy (31:4, 7, 13; 33:11) and a state of blessing, rest, and peace (31:23–25, 27–28; 32:42–44; 33:6).[22]

Similar examples are found in the writings of other prophets, as in Ezekiel 11:16–19; 36:8–12, 24–38.[23] Ultimately the new covenant provides for the total renewal of all things in the new creation.[24]

---

[19]Robertson, *The Christ of the Covenants,* 296.

[20]Dumbrell, *Covenant and Creation,* 182.

[21]Robertson, *The Christ of the Covenants,* 297. With reference to the new covenant statement in Jeremiah 31, Walter C. Kaiser, Jr., states, "The whole context meticulously connects the new covenant strophe with a literal restoration of the Jewish nation" ("The Old Promise and the New Covenant," *Journal of the Evangelical Theological Society* 15, no. 1 [Winter 1972]: 15).

[22]William VanGemeren, "The New Covenant Before Christ?" (Unpublished paper, n.d., 4.)

[23]Robertson summarizes the material blessings of the new covenant by saying, "The return of Israel to the land, the rebuilding of the devastated cities, the reconstitution of the nation— even resurrection from the dead—play a vital role in the prophetical formulation of new covenant expectations" (*The Christ of the Covenants,* 297).

[24]See Dumbrell, *Covenant and Creation,* 197–200.

In distinction to the newness of the spiritual provisions above that would bring God's people into a final union with him, these promised material blessings were for the most part already stated in the old Mosaic covenant. But the inadequacy of the old arrangement to bring mankind to righteous perfection precluded their fulfillment. The new covenant will succeed where the old had failed. God will finally make his people perfect and bring them into the relationship with him for which they were originally created. This perfected spiritual relationship will then issue in a fullness of material blessing that befits the created spiritual-material nature of human beings and their environment.

This connection between the spiritual and material provisions of the promise makes it difficult to see any real fulfillment of these promises in the return of Israel from exile. As we shall see, Scripture clearly indicates that these spiritual elements begin with the historical work of Christ and the coming of the Spirit. To speak of a "mini-realization" after the Babylonian exile[25] would run contrary to the principle that the spiritual takes precedence over the material. We concur with Ralph Alexander's conclusions regarding the prophecy of the new covenant given in Ezekiel 36:

> This context and that of similar accounts of God's restoration of Israel to her land, along with the historical perspective, make it clear that the return mentioned in this passage does not refer to the return to Canaan under Zerubbabel but to a final and complete restoration under the Messiah in the end times. The details of Israel's reestablishment on her land set forth above simply did not occur in the returns under Zerubbabel, Ezra, and Nehemiah.[26]

3. The Relationship of the New Covenant to the Abrahamic and Davidic Covenants. The Old Testament promise to Israel of a "new" covenant is set in contrast with the old covenant enacted at Sinai. According to the writer of Hebrews, there was something "wrong with that first covenant" (8:7). The fault lay not in the essence of the covenant, for it was perfectly righteous and holy (cf. Ro 7:12). But the covenant could not bring the people to perfection and so fulfill its goal.[27] The real fault lay with the people, who did not "remain faithful to my covenant" (Heb 8:9)

---

[25]Dumbrell, *Covenant and Creation,* 298.

[26]Ralph H. Alexander, "Ezekiel," in *Expositor's Bible Commentary,* vol. 6, ed. Frank E. Gaebelein (Grand Rapids: Zondervan, 1986), 922.

[27]This limitation within the Mosaic covenant is clearly indicated by the statement of Hebrews 8:7. A textual variant in verse 8ᵃ could also be interpreted as indicating that God found fault with the covenant instead of what is usually read "with the people." For a discussion of this question, see Philip Edgcumbe Hughes, who favors the reference to the covenant (*A Commentary on the Epistle to the Hebrews* [Grand Rapids: Eerdmans, 1977], 298–99).

and consequently "broke" God's covenant (Jer 31:32).[28] In the Septuagint version of Jeremiah, which is quoted by the writer to the Hebrews, God declared that he had "turned away" from his people because of the broken covenant. The promise of a new covenant, therefore, rendered the old one "obsolete" (Heb 8:13).

Because many elements of the old covenant are also found in the new (e.g., the requirement of the law and especially the goal of fellowship with God), some scholars view the new covenant as essentially a renewal of the old Mosaic covenant[29] or its fulfillment.[30] Two factors, however, suggest that the new covenant *replaced* the Mosaic one and rendered it obsolete in salvation history: (1) the contrast with the old covenant stated in Jeremiah 31:31–34, and (2) the replacement theology expressed in the book of Hebrews.[31]

The Mosaic covenant was an administrative compact setting forth, for a limited period of history, the terms of obedience for receiving the blessings of the promise (cf. Gal 3:15–25). Its failure to secure the promised blessing because of the people's sin brought the promise of a

---

[28]Accepting the usual reading and interpretation of Hebrews 8:8ᵃ as faulting the people, Marcus Dods nevertheless cites Rendall as aptly bringing together the thought in Hebrews of the inadequacy of the covenant and the failure of the people. "There is a subtle delicacy of language in the insensible shifting of the blame from the covenant to the people. The covenant itself could hardly be said to be faultless, seeing that it failed to bind Israel to their God; but the true cause of failure lay in the character of the people, not in the law, which was holy, righteous and good." (Rendall). Dodds goes on to say: "This is the simplest construction and agrees with the ascription of blame in ver. 9. . . . He [the writer] seems not to distinguish between the covenant and the people who lived under it. The old covenant was faulty because it did not provide for enabling the people to live up to the terms or conditions of it. *It was faulty inasmuch as it did not sufficiently provide against their faultiness*" (Dods, "Hebrews," in *Expositor's Greek Testament* [Grand Rapids: Eerdmans, 1951], 4:323).

[29]VanGemeren, for example, sees the *newness* as God's "commitment to the fulfillment of the promises" related to creation and redemption. This commitment gives assurance "that all covenants, including the Mosaic and the Davidic, have a place in the *new covenant*. . . ." It "ratifies the existing covenant, especially the Sinaitic and Davidic, and enlarges the scope of all covenants" ("The New Covenant Before Christ?" 13–14). It might be noted that similar elements in the covenants need not entail continuity any more than a new mortgage contract that contains similar elements to an old contract is its renewal or fulfillment.

[30]According to Robertson, the new covenant brings to fulfillment *"all the promises of the covenants* established earlier with his people" including the obedience to God's law of the Mosaic covenant (*The Christ of the Covenants*, 275, emphasis mine). To be sure, the New Testament does teach that Christ fulfilled the righteous requirement of the law, but this is nowhere interpreted as the fulfillment of the Mosaic covenant and therefore its final establishment.

[31]The newness of the covenant in Jeremiah's promise as opposed to any concept of renewal of the old covenant is the predominant understanding of most interpreters (cf. Raitt, *A Theology of Exile*, 200). In relation to this question Gerhard von Rad rightly points out "that there is no attempt here [in Jeremiah 31]—as there was, for example, in Deuteronomy—to re-establish Israel on old bases. The new covenant is entirely new" (*Old Testament Theology*, vol. 2 [New York: Harper & Row, 1965], 212; cf. also 271–72).

new covenant in which the terms of obedience and consequently the fulfillment of the promise were guaranteed by God's sovereign grace.[32]

While the new covenant stands as a replacement for the Mosaic covenant, it bears an entirely different relationship to the covenants of promise, that is, the covenants made with Abraham and David. Nowhere does Scripture speak of the new covenant's rendering either of these covenants obsolete. Rather, the new covenant is the means through which these covenants attain final fulfillment. Walter C. Kaiser states, "The 'new' began with the 'old' promise made to Abraham and David." It is, therefore, "a continuation of the Abrahamic and Davidic covenants with the same single, promise doctrine sustained in them all."[33]

Whether we link these covenants together because of their similar nature of promise or interpret the new covenant as a vehicle to administer the promises of these earlier covenants, the result is the same. Thomas E. McComiskey, who holds the latter view, agrees that "the new covenant expresses the promise." It "differs from the preceding administrative covenants [e.g., Mosaic] in that it enables the dispensing of the promise to God's people in the context of sovereign grace."[34] Perhaps Claus Westermann states it best when he says that in the new covenant, "the covenant is included in the promise."[35]

This relationship is evident not only in the similarity of contents (a seed, land, and universal blessing through the Messiah),[36] but in the specific references to Abraham and David in the prophets' declarations of the new covenant. Jeremiah's proclamation is framed by assurances of the final restoration of Israel under the promised Davidic king (cf. 30:1–11; 33:14–26). All this is given as proof that God has not rejected "the descendants of Abraham, Isaac and Jacob" (33:26). Ezekiel likewise ties the Davidic and new covenants together when he refers to the restoration of Israel under "one shepherd, my servant David" (Eze 34:22–24), a

---

[32]In viewing the Mosaic covenant as an "administrative covenant," I am following McComiskey's excellent discussion of the biblical covenants in which he distinguishes between promise covenants (Abrahamic and Davidic) and administrative covenants (the covenant of circumcision, the Mosaic covenant, and the new covenant). Because of its gracious promissory nature, the new covenant is frequently identified with the covenants of promise.

[33]Kaiser, "The Old Promise and the New Covenant," 22–21.

[34]McComiskey, *The Covenants of Promise*, 168, 177. For a full discussion of the question of classifying the new covenant as one of promise or of administration of promise, see pages 163–77.

[35]Claus Westermann, "The Way of the Promise Through the Old Testament," in *The Old Testament and Christian Faith*, ed. Bernard W. Anderson (New York: Harper & Row, 1963), 219.

[36]For elaboration of the contents of the Abrahamic and Davidic promises, see chapters 2 and 3, pages 39–58 and 59–80.

restoration that will occur only through the gift of a new heart and spirit (cf. Eze 36:22–38).

Moreover, Isaiah's great message that all things will be made new through a new covenant (chaps. 40–66) is sprinkled with references and allusions to the Abrahamic and Davidic promises. God will protect and ultimately bring comfort to his people because they are the offspring of Abraham (41:8; 51:1–3). The promise of blessing to the nations will be the result (51:4–5). Spiritual renewal will come, not only to Israel, but to all nations because God continues his "faithful love to David" (55:1–5). Since the Davidic promise is actually grounded in the earlier promise to Abraham,[37] it can be said that Isaiah sees the final renewal of all things associated with the new covenant as the fulfillment of the foundational covenant of promise with Abraham. We will see this connection between the new covenant and the Abrahamic and Davidic promises expressed even more explicitly in the New Testament.

B. The New Covenant and the Salvation of the Gentiles

Although, as we noted at the beginning of this chapter, there is no explicit language connecting Gentiles to the new covenant, it is clear even from the Old Testament that covenant blessings were to be universal. Gentiles were to be included without becoming a part of Israel. Two lines of thought lead to this conclusion: (1) The new covenant is the elaboration and fulfillment of the Abrahamic promise, which included Gentile salvation apart from Israel, and (2) Scripture explicitly teaches that Gentiles will participate in the same eschatological salvation promised to Israel.

1. The Abrahamic Covenant and Gentile Inclusion in the New Covenant. The fact that the new covenant is vitally related to the Abrahamic covenant as its fulfillment is all important when considering the participation of the Gentiles in the new covenant. God promised Abraham that he would not only make a "great nation," but also bring blessing to "all the peoples on earth" (Gen 12:2–3). This "blessing" is not defined in the original promise, but it surely includes a personal, family relationship to God, which is the culminating goal of the new covenant. The new covenant is thus the elaboration of the original "blessing" promised to Abraham.

Consideration of the provisions of the Abrahamic promise makes it evident that this blessing for all peoples was in addition to that of making a great nation. The promise does not state that the families of the earth would be blessed by becoming part of the "great nation." Rather, that nation was destined to bring blessing to Gentiles. This distinction is borne

---

[37]See chapter 3, pages 59–80.

out in the creation and commission of Israel for God's service to all nations.[38] It remains throughout the Old Testament, where the nations are never identified with Israel but continue to retain their identity as Gentiles. Thus, if the new covenant is in reality the elaboration of the Abrahamic "blessing," then clearly the Gentiles are included in that blessing, not by becoming Israel, but as Gentiles along with Israel.

2. *The Promise of New Covenant Salvation to Gentiles.* While the prophets do not make the promise of blessing to Gentiles a stated provision of the new covenant, such blessing is included in the contexts of the new covenant. According to Ezekiel, the vindication of the name of God through the restoration of Israel under the new covenant, would bring about Gentile recognition of Israel's God (36:23).[39] Jeremiah likewise includes the salvation of the Gentiles in the context of Israel's restoration (cf. 16:14–20). Perhaps the closest connection of Gentile salvation to the new covenant is provided by Isaiah's description of the Servant himself as being the covenant. The Servant would bring "light for the Gentiles" and "salvation to the ends of the earth" (42:6; 49:6).

Beyond these references, which may be said to be broadly related to new covenant contexts, the Old Testament is replete with a variety of expressions that extend salvation to all nations. "Salvation" will be known among the nations (e.g., Pss 67:2; 117). They will "fear" and "worship" the Lord and serve him (e.g., Pss 86:9; 102:15, 22; Isa 11:10; Jer 3:17; Zep 2:9; 3:9). "Justice" (Isa 42:1, 4) and "peace" will be brought to the nations (Zec 9:9; cf. Isa 2:2–4; Mic 4:1–3). Such peace is the fruit of salvation, as H. H. Rowley explains: "Enduring peace . . . will not be achieved . . . until all nations submit themselves to the will of Jehovah, and base their life on a religious acceptance of His way. . . . The prophet held out no hope of peace save to a world whose people were united in their worship of Jehovah, and in their humble submission to the direction of this God."[40]

These descriptions of the salvation promised to the Gentiles show that it is nothing less than the salvation that God also promised to Israel.

---

[38]See chapter 12.

[39]The concept of the nations coming to know God through his dealings with Israel is frequently mentioned by Ezekiel—cf. 36:36; 37:28; 39:7. Commenting on 36:23, McComiskey says, "It is not certain that this refers to a future conversion of Gentiles, but it certainly reflects a change in their attitude toward Yahweh" (*The Covenants of Promise,* 89). In favor of its actually being a genuine saving knowledge is the fact that many of Ezekiel's predictions of coming to know Yahweh are related to his own people Israel. Walther Zimmerli says that "*this same recognition* is expected from the rest of the world's nations" (*I Am Yahweh* [Atlanta: John Knox, 1982], 88, emphasis mine).

[40]H. H. Rowley, *The Missionary Message of the Old Testament* (London: Carey Kingsgate, 1944), 40–41. Rowley similarly states concerning the promise of justice, "True justice will prevail everywhere, and a justice that rests not on human wisdom but on the knowledge and fear of Jehovah. And that knowledge and fear will not inspire the administration alone, but will be shared by all men everywhere" (43).

The salvation is the same for both. They will worship together in God's temple at Jerusalem (Isa 2:2–3; 56:7; Jer 3:17). Both are said to "know," or have a relationship with, the same God. Further confirmation is the prophecy that the Gentiles will be called by special names that in the Old Testament were reserved for the chosen people of Israel. Of Egypt, and Assyria—which, according to John N. Oswalt, "stand for all the warring nations of the earth"—Isaiah prophesied, "The LORD Almighty will bless them, saying, 'Blessed be Egypt my people, Assyria my handiwork, and Israel my inheritance'" (Isa 19:25).[41] While God called Israel "the work of my hands" (cf. Isa 60:21), she was especially related to him simply as "my people" (cf. Ex 3:10: 5:1; 6:7). Gentiles will be called by that same intimate name because through the same salvation they will have become part of the people of God along with Israel.

If the Gentiles share in the same salvation that was promised to Israel under the new covenant, what is their relation to that covenant? It is reasonable to conclude that although the particular promises of the new covenant are expressed as the hope of Israel, the Gentiles' sharing in this final salvation indicates that they are viewed as participating in its covenantal expression, i.e., the new covenant. This conclusion seems especially valid in that the final goal of the new covenant is spoken to the Gentiles (i.e., Egypt) as well as to Israel—that goal being God's familial relationship with his people expressed in the promise, "I will be their God, and they will be my people."

But another crucial question must be raised. Do the Gentiles have a share in the new covenant salvation by becoming part of a new Israel, as some scholars suggest, or are they still viewed as peoples distinct from historical Israel? Without question, the Old Testament teaching on this subject is illustrated in the salvation of Egypt and Assyria. These peoples retain a distinction within the people of God as Isaiah's words clearly indicate: "In that day Israel will be the third, along with Egypt and Assyria" (19:24).

Contrary to this conclusion, some have understood Isaiah's statement about the salvation of "all the descendants of Israel" (45:25) as indicating a new Israel composed of Jew and Gentile. Those who take this viewpoint to the proximity of this statement to Isaiah's reference to God's salvation as going to the "ends of the earth" (cf. 45:20–24).[42] The passage,

---

[41]John N. Oswalt comments on the entire passage concerning God's dealing with Egypt in Isaiah 19:19–22: "One cannot escape the impression that certain highly emotive terms, ones intimately connected wtih Hebrew religion, are consciously applied to Egypt here in an effort to show how completely Egypt will come to Israel's God." There is even indication of a covenant relationship between God and Egypt (*The Book of Isaiah Chapter 1–39* [Grand Rapids: Eerdmans, 1986], 379).

[42]According to E. J. Young, "Israel" in this reference signifies "the true Israel taken from the whole human race" (*The Book of Isaiah*, vol. 3 [Grand Rapids: Eerdmans, 1972], 218; cf.

however, does not expressly include Gentiles as part of Israel. Moreover, the extensive use of "Israel" in the context to designate the historical people in distinction to the nations makes it highly unlikely that the prophet would suddenly change the meaning of "Israel" to include Gentiles (cf. 45:4, 11, 15, 17; 46:3, 13). With Westermann, it is therefore better to understand the prophet's teaching in this passage as signifying that the Gentiles "together with Israel participate in . . . salvation (v. 25)."[43] There is a rationale for the prophet's attachment of a statement about Israel's justification and glorying to his teaching about gentile salvation. Israel was called for the universal blessing of the nations and finds her own glory in the fulfillment of that purpose. John L. McKenzie explains,

> The force of the last line [concerning Israel's justification and glory] is that the universal [i.e., Gentile] confession of Yahweh is the only victory Israel can expect, and the only legitimate boast Israel can make. Their victories and their boasts are not and never will be the victories and boasts of other nations; for they are the servant of Yahweh.[44]

Other passages speak of Gentiles joining themselves to Israel as aliens and participating in the worship of that community at Jerusalem (cf. Isa 14:1; 65:3–7). If the center of the kingdom is a glorious Jerusalem surrounded by a blessed Israel, it is not surprising that some Gentiles would join this nation and many would come to worship there. But these pictures of some Gentiles living within Israel's borders and others coming to worship there are never indicated by the Old Testament prophets as the way of *all* gentile salvation. First, there are no statements with them that gentile salvation entails becoming part of Israel. Second, these passages are far fewer in number than those that portray God's salvation going to the nations *in addition to* Israel.

We therefore conclude that the Old Testament teaches the salvation of the Gentiles alongside the nation of Israel. This is congruent with the promise in the Abrahamic covenant that the Gentiles would be blessed alongside the "great nation." So, in summary, the new covenant is the fulfillment of the promise to Abraham, and the prophets foretell a gentile salvation that is equal to and in addition to the salvation promised to Israel in the new covenant. But the Old Testament nowhere teaches that the Gentiles receive these blessings of the covenant by being incorporated into and becoming a part of Israel herself.

---

also Franz Delitzsch, *Biblical Commentary on the Prophecies of Isaiah*, vol. 2 [Grand Rapids: Eerdmans, 1960], 231).

[43]Claus Westermann, *Isaiah 40–66* (Philadelphia: Westminster, 1969), 176.

[44]John L. McKenzie, *Second Isaiah*, Anchor Bible (Garden City, N.Y.: Doubleday, 1968), 84.

II. THE TEACHING OF THE NEW TESTAMENT

A. *The New Covenant and the Gentiles*

1. The Inauguration of the New Covenant. According to the New Testament, the new covenant promise was fulfilled with the historical work of Christ. Jesus himself made this connection in the first specific reference to the new covenant in the Gospels. When he was with his disciples in the upper room at the institution of the Lord's Supper, Jesus took the cup and declared, "This cup is the new covenant in my blood, which is poured out for you" (Lk 20:22). By this Jesus meant that the new covenant would take effect through that which the contents of the cup signified, namely, his sacrificial death.[45] Although the preferred Greek texts of the parallel accounts in Matthew and Mark do not include the word "new" with "covenant,"[46] they make the same association of Jesus' death with the inauguration of the covenant (Mt 26:28; Mk 14:24; cf. also 1Co 11:25, where "new" is included).

Jesus' reference to a "new covenant" is clearly an allusion to the prophecy of Jeremiah 31, where the covenant is also called "new." Moreover, Jesus identifies the "forgiveness of sins" as the purpose of the new covenant (Mt 26:28). This blessing, as we noted earlier, was the foundational provision of the new covenant promised in Old Testament prophecy. These connections between Jesus' words and Old Testament promise of the new covenant lead to the necessary conclusion that Jesus was speaking of fulfillment of the prophesied new covenant and not some other new covenant especially for the church as some dispensationalists had previously taught. Every time the disciples observed the Lord's Supper in the church, they celebrated the reality of the new covenant that had been inaugurated through the death of Christ.

The writer of Hebrews likewise speaks of Christ as "the mediator of a new covenant" by virtue of his death (cf. Heb 9:15–18; 12:24). The twofold citation of the prophecy of Jeremiah 31 leaves no question as to the identity of the new covenant that Jesus' death initiated (cf. Heb 8:8–12; 10:16–17). Moreover, the change of priesthoods and covenants having taken place, the new covenant is in force since the sacrifice of Christ (cf. Heb 7:12; 8:13; 10:9–18).

The presence of the reality of the Old Testament promise of the new covenant is also seen in Paul's identification of himself as a minister of "a new covenant" to the church of Corinth (2Co 3:6). In addition to the language of "a new covenant," the link to the covenant prophesied in the

---

[45]I. Howard Marshall, *The Gospel of Luke*, New International Greek Testament Commentary (Grand Rapids: Eerdmans, 1978), 806.

[46]In both Matthew and Mark the word "new" is found in some Greek manuscripts.

Old Testament is seen in the description of the covenant as one "of the Spirit" (3:6) whose work is portrayed as the writing of a letter on the hearts of believers rather than tablets of stone (3:2–3). The concept of God's writing his law directly on human hearts is derived from Jeremiah 31:33; the contrast between "tablets of stone" and "tablets of hearts of flesh" is found in Ezekiel's prophecy of the new covenant (11:19; 32:26).

Along with these explicit references to the new covenant, the New Testament speaks often of the blessings of forgiveness of sins and the gift of the Spirit as the fulfillment of prophecy (e.g., Lk 24:46–47; Ac 2:38–39; 10:43). The New Testament therefore clearly teaches that the promised new covenant was inaugurated by Christ and now stands open to all who will receive it.

2. *The Inclusion of the Gentiles in the New Covenant.* As noted earlier, the fact that the new covenant, which was explicitly promised to Israel, has received fulfillment in the church has led some interpreters to conclude that the church must be conceived of as the "new Israel." The basis of this belief seems to be that all who participate in the covenant are interpreted biblically as "Israel." Or, to phrase it in negative terms, that Gentiles are not included in the new covenant as "Gentiles." Besides the fact that the New Testament never expressly calls Gentiles "Israel,"[47] there is considerable evidence to refute the notion that under the new covenant the Gentiles become a "new Israel."

a. *Jesus' teaching of the universality of the new covenant.* At the institution of the Lord's Supper, Jesus declared that his blood of the covenant was "poured out for *many* for the forgiveness of sins" (Mt 26:28, emphasis added; cf. Mk 14:24). Although some scholars limit the meaning of "many"—which in this statement is probably to be understood in its Semitic sense of "all"[48]—to the historical covenant people of Israel,[49] most give it a more universal application. Calvin wrote, "By the word *many* he [Jesus] means not a part of the world only, but the whole human race."[50] If that is the case, then Jesus was enlarging the scope of the new covenant to include Gentiles. A concept that was only implicit in the Old Testament

---

[47]See chapter 8.

[48]Compare the use of "many" in Romans 5:15–19, especially the parallel between "many" and "all" in vv. 18–19, also v. 12. Friedrich Graber says, "In the LXX it [πολλοί] often represents the Heb *rabbim*, which tends to mean 'all'" ("All, Many," in *The New International Dictionary of New Testament Theology*, vol. 1, ed. Colin Brown [Grand Rapids: Zondervan, 1975], 95. See also Joachim Jeremias, "πολλοί," *Theological Dictionary of the New Testament*, vol. 6 [Grand Rapids: Eerdmans, 1968], 543–45).

[49]C. S. Mann, *Mark*, Anchor Bible (Garden City, N.Y.: Doubleday, 1986), 418.

[50]John Calvin, *Commentary on a Harmony of the Evangelists, Matthew, Mark, and Luke* (reprint, Grand Rapids: Eerdmans, 1949), 3:214. The question of whether this statement refers to the universal community of the redeemed from all nations—i.e., the elect—or somehow to all people is beyond the purpose of our discussion and does not bear on the issue at hand.

thus became explicit in the New Testament, namely, that Gentiles are included in the new covenant.

The question remains, however, whether these Gentiles participate in the covenant as Gentiles or as part of a "new Israel." Do these words of Jesus along with other New Testament statements that explicitly apply the new covenant to Gentiles signify a change in the meaning of "Israel"? Or to put it another way, does the New Testament teach that including the Gentiles expressly fulfills the promise of the new covenant to "the house of Israel and . . . the house of Judah" (Jer 31:31), thereby requiring that these terms transcend their original Old Testament meaning? In Jeremiah these terms clearly refer to ethnic "Israel" in distinction to Gentiles. To interpret the "all" of Jesus' statement as including Gentiles as "Israel," therefore, requires that a different meaning be ascribed to that historic name.[51]

Along with the fact that the New Testament never speaks of a "new" Israel,[52] the Old Testament background of Jesus' statement supports the view that the "many" include Israel and the nations as distinct groups. According to most scholars, Jesus views himself in his death as the Suffering Servant of Isaiah 53:11–12. The entire passage of Isaiah 52:13–53:12 contains a fivefold repetition of the word "many" (cf. 52:14–15; 53:11–12 [twice]; the NIV translates the first occurrence in v. 12 as "great," but cf. marginal alternative). The identity of the "many" is undefined in all instances except 52:15; there its use as an adjective in the phrase "many nations" suggests it includes both Israel and the nations.[53]

Isaiah's words in 52:15 concerning the effect of the Servant on the "many nations" have been translated in various ways. Some take the Hebrew verb to mean "sprinkle," indicating that the Servant will cleanse many nations through his suffering. Others say the verb means "startle," which would form a parallel phrase to the latter part of the verse, "kings will shut their mouths because of him." The implication is that the nations will be astonished at the suffering and exaltation of the Servant, with the result that they will come to acknowledge the true God. As Westermann explains,

> The people who are so astonished at the Servant's exaltation and rendered dumb by it are called "nations" and "kings." This finds

---

[51]Henry Barclay Swete, for example, speaks of the new covenant's being ratified with "a greater Israel" (*The Gospel According to Mark* [Grand Rapids: Eerdmans, 1956], 336).

[52]See pages 194–207.

[53]Graber suggests that the prominent use in the Old Testament of "many" in reference to gentile nations would appear to add evidence to this conclusion: "If we omit its collective use (much water, long time, etc.), *rabbim* ['many'] in the OT is used almost always with *ammim* ['peoples'] or *goyim* ['nations'] of non-Israelite peoples. Many peoples stream to Zion to come under God's protection and enter his service (Isa. 2:2ff.); the Servant of God bears the sins of the many (Isa. 53 . . .)" ("All, Many," in *NIDNTT*, 1:96).

its explanation in the Psalms, where nations and kings are called upon to praise God for his mighty acts. The meaning is that his work which consists in the exaltation of the Servant is so stupendous that people hear of it with astonishment in far-distant places (nations) and exalted circles (kings).[54]

Both interpretations—"sprinkle" and "startle"—thus yield the same conclusion, namely, that the ministry of the Servant has a saving benefit for the "many," including nations. His work that brings this salvation is defined in 53:11–12 as his death for the "many." The "many" for whom he dies must therefore include the "many nations" of 52:15. Joachim Jeremias observes that the interpretation of Isaiah "that the atoning work of the servant of the Lord was for the nations still lived on in the 1st century A.D."[55] So the "many" for whom Christ sheds his blood of the new covenant includes Gentiles. Moreover, based on the obvious meaning of the "nations" in the Isaiah passage, they are Gentiles who are to be included *along with* but not *as* Israel.

Further evidence that Jesus distinguished between the nations and Israel lies in his explicit teaching of the salvation of the nations.[56] When he saw the faith of the gentile centurion—a "great faith" that he had not found in Israel—Jesus declared, "I say to you that many will come from the east and the west, and will take their places at the feast with Abraham, Isaac and Jacob in the kingdom of heaven. But the subjects of the kingdom will be thrown outside . . ." (Mt 8:11–12; cf. Lk 13:28–29). Because the language used here is similar to Old Testament language that refers to the regathering of Israel, some scholars see in this passage the formation of a "new Israel" that includes Gentiles.[57] But it should be noted that Jesus describes the Gentiles as joining the patriarchs at the messianic feast in "the kingdom" and not in Israel. The messianic kingdom is never equated with Israel alone, but always has a universal dimension that encompasses

---

[54]Westermann, *Isaiah 40–66*, 259; similarly, Geoffrey W. Grogan says that "kings will fall silent in his presence, astonished, over-awed, deeply respectful (cf. Job 29:7–10), and eager perhaps to see and hear rather than themselves to speak in the presence of such an unprecedented revelation" ("Isaiah," in *Expositor's Bible Commentary*, 6:301).

[55]Jeremias, "πολλοί," in *TDNT*, 6:540. This meaning would appear to be validated by the apostle Paul, who cites Isaiah 52:15 to support his ministry to the Gentiles (cf. Ro 15:21).

[56]On Jesus' teaching of gentile inclusion in salvation, see Joachim Jeremias, *Jesus' Promise to the Nations* (Naperville, Ill.: Allenson, 1958), 46–57.

[57]R. T. France, *Jesus and the Old Testament* (London: Tyndale Press, 1971), 63. The use of similar language in the Old Testament prophecies to refer to the regathering of Israel does not require identifying the Gentiles as "Israel." Not only is such language also used of Gentiles, as we have noted, but also the Scriptures frequently apply the same language to different entities. The application of the statement "Out of Egypt I called my son" to both Israel (Hos 11:1) and Christ (Mt 2:15) surely does not demand their identity.

the nations also.[58] Moreover, Jesus' language is similar to Old Testament passages that concern gentile salvation (cf. Isa 59:19; Mal 1:11).[59]

Our interpretation of Jesus' message is supported elsewhere in the Gospels. In the parable of the sheep and the goats (Mt 25:31–46), the people who are admitted into the kingdom (v. 34) come from "all the nations" (which would include Israel). Without excluding Israel as a part of the "all nations," this passage is no doubt related to the truth found earlier that the gospel must go out through the gentile mission to "all the nations" before this time comes to an end (Mt 24:14; cf. 24:9; 28:19).[60] Thus the emphasis is probably on the gentile peoples.[61]

Jesus' extension of his salvation to Gentiles is also seen in his claim of universal authority for the purpose of evangelizing "all nations" (Mt 28:18–20). Jesus' frequent self-identification as the Son of Man makes it probable that this claim to authority is a conscious allusion to Daniel 7:13–14. In that passage the Son of Man is given universal dominion so that "all peoples, nations and men of every language worshiped him." These words obviously include the Gentiles as Gentiles alongside Israel in the kingdom of the Son of Man. Nothing that Jesus said in commissioning the apostles to bring salvation to the nations would controvert this meaning.

Finally, the explicit statement of Jesus that the prophecy in Zechariah 9:9 is fulfilled in the so-called triumphal entry into Jerusalem

---

[58]See chapter 4, pages 50–53 and 62–64.

[59]Rather than being a reference to the regathering of Israel, this statement of Jesus in Matthew 8:11 and Luke 13:29, according to Jeremias, gives us "a succinct summary of the Old Testament utterances concerning the pilgrimage of the Gentiles to the Mount of God at the time of the Last Judgment" (*Jesus' Promise to the Nations*, 62).

Although Ferdinand Hahn sees significance in the fact that Jesus refers to gathering in the "kingdom" rather than Jerusalem, he likewise understands Jesus' words as refering to the Old Testament salvation of the Gentiles: "But in this passage the Old Testament promise for the Gentiles is at the same time taken up; no part is played here by Jerusalem and the temple as the goal to be reached, but rather the idea of the nations' pilgrimage is strictly related to the *basileia* proclaimed by Jesus" (*Mission in the New Testament*, Studies in Biblical Theology 47 [Naperville, Ill.: Allenson, 1965], 35).

[60]Karl Ludwig Schmidt confronts the problem of determining whether "all nations" includes the Jews. despite the addition of "all" with "nations," he says, "we sometimes have the feeling—it is hardly more—that the reference is not to all nations including Israel, but to the nations or all nations in distinction from Israel as the גוֹיִם. Thus R. 15:11, on the basis of Ps. 117:1, summons all nations to praise God. But this can hardly include Israel, since it is self-evident that Israel should praise God. Again, on the basis of another OT quotation Gl. 3:8 speaks of the blessing of all nations in Abraham. But this surely has in view the nations apart from Israel, since the blessing of Israel in Abraham as its progenitor may be assumed. This raises the possibility of similar references to the Gentiles rather than to all the nations elsewhere" ("ἔθνος," in *Theological Dictionary of the New Testament*, vol. 2 [Grand Rapids: Eerdmans, 1964], 369–70).

[61]Jeremias sees this passage as teaching the same truth as seen in John 10:16 and 11:51f., where "the scattered Gentile flock is brought to Zion by God's shepherd and united with the flock of God's people" (*Jesus' Promise to the Nations*, 65).

(cf. Mt 21:4–5) indirectly affirms his application of salvation to Gentiles. That verse in Zechariah is immediately followed by the declaration that "he will proclaim peace to the nations" under a universal rule (Zec 9:10). As with other teachings of Jesus, the New Testament record gives no reason to reinterpret the meaning of the Old Testament to include these nations in some kind of "new Israel." Thus the teachings of Jesus regarding gentile salvation support the conclusion that his application of the new covenant to the "many" includes the Gentiles as Gentiles in fulfillment of the Old Testament prophecies.

b. The new covenant as the fulfillment of the Abrahamic covenant. The New Testament makes explicit what we have already seen from the Old Testament, namely, that the new covenant is the final fulfillment of the promises to Abraham and David. In the Magnificat, Mary extolls the Lord for helping his servant Israel by "remembering to be merciful to Abraham and his descendants forever" (Lk 1:54–55).

That this "help" centers on the new covenant blessing is revealed a short time later in the prophecy of Zechariah, the father of John the Baptist. The coming Messiah would be "a horn of salvation . . . in the house of his servant David" (Lk 1:69). While this salvation would include rescue "from the hand of our enemies," it would also enable God's people "to serve him without fear in holiness and righteousness . . . all our days" (vv. 74–75). For it would "give his people the knowledge of salvation through the forgiveness of their sins" (v. 77). This spiritual redemption that would provide the basis for all latter blessings was the central provision of the new covenant. But Zechariah saw all this as the result of God's remembering "his holy covenant, the oath he swore to our father Abraham" (vv. 72–73).

The apostle Paul likewise continually connects the blessings of the new covenant with the promise to Abraham. Justification that is grounded on the new covenant provision of forgiveness of sins in Christ is the fulfillment of the promise to Abraham and belongs only to his spiritual descendants of like faith (cf. Ro 4:9–25). The gift of the Spirit, which was promised in the Old Testament as a feature of the new covenant, is also a fulfilling of the Abrahamic promise. God has redeemed us, the apostle declares, "in order that the blessing given to Abraham might come to the Gentiles . . . so that by faith we might receive the promise of the Spirit" (Gal 3:14).[62]

Last, the writer to the Hebrews, who refers to the new covenant directly more than any other New Testament writer, clearly connects that

---

[62]While the two clauses are coordinate purpose clauses, the second is an interpretation of the first, elucidating the "form" by which the "blessing of Abraham" comes on the believing Gentiles (F. F. Bruce, *The Epistle to the Galatians,* New International Greek Testament Commentary [Grand Rapids: Eerdmans, 1982], 168–69).

covenant with the Abrahamic promise. Christ's high priestly ministry of the new covenant is secured by God's promise and confirming oath to Abraham (Heb 6:13–20; cf. 8:6–7). Thus the provisions of the new covenant are equated with the promised blessing as its elaboration and explanation.

As we noted earlier, seeing the new covenant as the fulfillment of the Abrahamic and Davidic covenants leads directly to its application to Gentiles along with Israel. This is evident most in the Abrahamic covenant, which expressly included blessing for "all peoples on earth" (i.e., Gentiles) in addition to the "great nation" of Israel (Ge 12:2–3). In a context applying new covenant blessings to Gentiles, the apostle Paul writes, "The Scripture foresaw that God would justify the Gentiles by faith, and announced the gospel in advance to Abraham: 'All nations will be blessed through you'" (Gal 3:8).

Paul thus understands the new covenant blessing for the Gentiles as the fulfillment of the Abrahamic promise. In addition, he sees it as a fulfillment of the specific provision of the Abrahamic promise that refers to Gentiles and not Israel. If, as is frequently taught, the Gentiles are included only by their participation in some sort of redefined "Israel," it would seem possible for the apostle to apply the teaching of blessing for that "great nation"—now understood in the new expanded way—to the Gentiles. But nowhere does he do this. Rather, Paul sees the inclusion of Gentiles in the new covenant only in fulfillment of the provision of blessing for "all peoples," which in the Abrahamic covenant are manifestly not Israel. Both are included in the new covenant and as a result enjoy the same spiritual relation to God, but this does not entail the identification of Gentiles with Israel.

c. The new covenant and the kingdom. The inclusion of Gentiles in the new covenant may also be seen in the relation of the covenant to the kingdom. Many scholars have pointed out that the two concepts are actually two ways of expressing the same ultimate reality. According to Johannes Behm, the true religious sense of the term διαθήκη ("covenant") in the New Testament is the "'disposition' of God, the mighty declaration of the sovereign will of God in history, by which He orders the relation between Himself and men according to His own saving purpose, and which carries with it the authoritative divine ordering."[63] Similarly, C. S. Mann declares, "There is every reason to understand the term [covenant] in the New Testament as carrying with it implicitly the expression 'the Reign of God.'"[64]

---

[63]Johannes Behm, "διαθήκη," in *TDNT*, 2:134.

[64]Mann, *Mark*, 578. Noting that the New Testament concept of covenant came from the Old Testament, Mann sees the kingship idea in that "the Hebrew idea of Covenant, with its ancestry in ancient near-eastern cultures, was that of the 'suzerainty treaty' by which the

Based on this understanding of "covenant," Behm therefore concludes that "the καινὴ διαθήκη [new covenant] is a correlative of the βασιλεία τοῦ θεοῦ [kingdom of God]." The kingdom idea portrays God as the Lord of the age of salvation while the covenant expresses the divine will that sets the goal. Both concepts therefore indicate "the same goal of fulfilment," namely, "that God reigns and . . . the new divine order is valid, i.e., the order that finally determines the relation of God to man."[65]

The connection between the new covenant and the kingdom is evident in Jesus' teaching that his work, which throughout Scripture is intimately identified with the coming of the kingdom, is also the fulfillment of the new covenant. In fact, Jesus expressly tied the fulfillment of the Passover, which he celebrated with his disciples, to the coming of the kingdom of God (Lk 22:16, 18; cf. Mt 26:29; Mk 14:25). Joachim Guhrt sees an additional connection in the similarity of language in the same context. He explains that "covenant" language is used sparsely because "the underlying thought has been taken over in the sayings about the kingdom of God," and then he observes the linguistic connection in Luke 22:29, where "the phrase *diatithemai . . . basileian*, appoint a kingdom, . . . exactly expresses the formula *diatithemai diatheken* [make or establish a covenant]."[66]

The relation of the new covenant to the kingdom in the New Testament is founded on a similar thought in the Old Testament. According to VanGemeren, "For Jeremiah as for the deuteronomist, the covenant expresses God's kingdom on earth."[67]

The total biblical picture of the relationship of the new covenant and the kingdom of God is well limned by Dumbrell:

> The kingship of God sought expression through a whole web of relationships which successive covenants both pointed towards and also exercised over the people of God and their world. But this kingship presupposed a return within history to the beginning of history. As we have repeatedly noted, nothing less than a new creation—and thus a new covenant—would achieve this goal. In that sense, the notion of the kingdom of God, controlling as it does the whole of biblical thinking, was always a theological assertion pointing towards a future reality—the new covenant.[68]

---

client people bound themselves in obedience to their Lord and protector. Israel understood herself as having been chosen by God as his peculiar possession, and herself as accordingly bound to a relationship of trusting obedience."

[65]Behm, "διαθήκη," in *TDNT*, 2:134.

[66]Joachim Guhrt, "Covenant," in *New International Dictionary of New Testament Theology*, vol. 1, ed. Colin Brown (Grand Rapids: Zondervan, 1975), 369.

[67]VanGemeren, "The New Covenant Before Christ?" 2–3. In this connection VanGemeren calls attention to the parallel between the "covenant" and the "throne" in Jeremiah 14:21.

[68]Dumbrell, *Covenant and Creation*, 206.

The idea that the new covenant is correlative to the kingdom of God has clear implications for including the Gentiles under the new covenant. If the kingdom, including salvation, ultimately encompasses all the nations of the earth, then the same universality must be recognized for the new covenant. While all recognize this universality, the question remains as to whether the nations are included under their own identity or somehow included in Israel. The Old Testament evidence seems clear that God's salvation was to extend to the nations as distinct from the nation of Israel. The teaching of the New Testament on this point fulfills the Old Testament picture with nothing warranting a reinterpretation.

3. The Nature of the Present New Covenant Blessings in the Church. To determine just how the prophecy of the new covenant is fulfilled in the present, we must note the provisions of the new covenant that are expressly applied to the church. As we have seen, the heart of the new covenant is the spiritual provision for bringing sinful humankind into relationship with God. But there are material blessings that accompany the spiritual provisions.[69]

Significantly, nowhere in the New Testament are any of these material provisions of the new covenant applied to the church. From the express teaching of Jesus that his blood of the new covenant was shed for "the forgiveness of sins" to the remainder of the apostolic teaching, only the spiritual provisions are applied. Paul specifically identified his ministry of the new covenant as the ministry of the Spirit (2Co 3:6ff.). The direct citations of Jeremiah's prophecy by the writer of Hebrews are limited to the verses that speak of spiritual realities (Heb 8:8–12; 10:16–17). Along with these explicit statements, the whole course of the New Testament teaching about salvation in the church is limited to the spiritual provisions. The new covenant predictions of the restoration of Israel to the land, the rebuilding of the cities, and increased productivity of the earth are never cited in relation to the present salvation of God.

This absence of references to the material provisions of the new covenant for the present age leads us to several conclusions. First, the New Testament teachers evidently did not see the complete fulfillment of the new covenant in the church as happening during the present age. This idea seems to be shared by most interpreters, who affirm that the covenant will be completed either in a millennium or in the new heavens and earth or in both. But the reality of a temporary partial fulfillment also precludes affirming that the remaining material blessings have been either excluded or radically reinterpreted. If, in fact, there is a time of future fulfillment, the manner of the present application of the new covenant to the church in no way excludes a fulfillment of the remaining blessings according to their natural Old Testament meaning.

---

[69]See pages 118–19.

This thought leads to the further implication of the limited application of the new covenant promises to the church. If the New Testament does view the church as a new, reconstituted Israel, as is so often claimed, why are none of the new covenant blessings regarding Israel's restoration and exaltation ever applied by way of "reinterpretation" to the church? It would seem reasonable that if the church is a new "spiritual Israel" and Israel as an ethnic people or nation is outmoded, we might expect to find some of Israel's material blessings reinterpreted and applied by the apostles to the church.

The absence of any application of the material blessings—many of which were directly related to the nation Israel—leads to the conclusion that the apostles did not intend to teach that the church was fulfilling the new covenant in the place of Israel. These material blessings remained unfulfilled, and there is no teaching that precludes their future fulfillment in accord with the Old Testament meaning.

4. Conclusion. According to the New Testament, the eschatological salvation prophesied in the Old Testament under the promise of a new covenant was inaugurated through the historical work of Christ. That covenant was explicitly addressed to Israel in the Old Testament although, as we have seen, the same salvation was predicted to reach to the Gentiles. Now, in the New Testament, it is expressly associated with the saving work of God for both Jew and Gentile in the church of this age.

The application of the new covenant to the church, however, does not mean that the promise to Israel has somehow been reinterpreted so that the church is an "Israel" superseding the Israel of the original promise. Rather, the fulfillment of the covenant in the church is in perfect harmony with the Old Testament promises of eschatological salvation for both Israel and the nations. Only the spiritual provisions of the new covenant are applied at present. The material blessings particularly related to the nation of Israel are not reinterpreted and applied to the present work of God. The promise of God's future dealings with Israel (cf. Ro 9–11) indicates that the New Testament still looked forward to the time when the promises for this nation will yet be fulfilled.

B. The Fulfillment of Promises of Gentile Salvation

Our discussion of the New Testament teaching concerning the inauguration of the new covenant and its contemporary application to Jew and Gentile alike in the church has already given clear evidence that the Old Testament prophecy of eschatological salvation for the Gentiles is being fulfilled in this present age. In addition to this evidence associated directly and indirectly with the fulfillment of the new covenant, we also find specific prophecies relating to Gentile salvation applied by the New Testament teachers to the present mission of the church to the nations. It is not necessary to examine every such instance. Instead, we will use as a paradigm the apostle Paul's use of four Old Testament texts that, according to Ferdinand Hahn, give us "as in one great summary, the basic ideas of the Pauline view of the mission."[70] These passages focus on the praise and hope of the Gentiles that have resulted from the present extension of the mercy of God (Ro 15:9–12).[71]

The question is, how are we to understand the application of Old Testament prophecies about gentile salvation in relation to the present age? Do they intend to teach that the current evangelization of the nations, bringing both Jewish and gentile believers into the church, is the fulfillment of these prophecies in a way that transcends their original meaning? If that is so, the present operation of God's salvation in the church signifies the final pattern. Any future salvation for Israel will therefore be accomplished without a significance or purpose for Israel as a national entity. One proponent of this view is James D. G. Dunn, who observes that none of Paul's citations from the Old Testament recorded in Romans 15 speak of either the judgment of Gentiles in relation to the coming of the Messiah to vindicate Israel or the coming of the Gentiles to Jerusalem. From these omissions Dunn concludes that in "both cases Israel's typical covenant hope has been transformed."[72]

Hahn similarly speaks of "the great transformation by Paul of the traditional picture of the *Heilsgeschichte* and of eschatology."[73]

By contrast, might the application of these prophecies to the present time signify only an initial fulfillment that is not intended to finally reinterpret the Old Testament hope? The New Testament requires that biblical prophecies, which in the Old Testament appeared to relate to a single coming of the Messiah, must now be somehow divided in their fulfillment in relation to two comings of the Christ. Accordingly, the present fulfillment cannot be viewed as final and complete. What is going on today is only a partial fulfillment that all scholars agree was not clearly explained in the Old Testament. Since current events are not the final fulfillment, they need not cancel out a complete fulfillment of the Old Testament hope in connection with the future coming of Christ. To my mind, there are good reasons to hold this interpretation—that is, no reinterpretation is necessary to accommodate the New Testament teaching.

First—and with this advocates of the other position concur—the

---

[70]Hahn, *Mission in the New Testament*, 107.

[71]See chapter 3, pages 76–80, for a discussion of James' use of Amos 9:11–12 in support of gentile salvation in Acts 15:15–18.

[72]James D. G. Dunn, *Romans 9–16*, Word Biblical Commentary, vol. 38b (Dallas: Word Books, 1988), 850; see also 682, 692–93.

[73]Hahn, *Mission in the New Testament*, 108.

present salvific operation of God is not in strict accord with the Old Testament prophecies cited. The Old Testament passages quoted by Paul picture a gentile salvation in the context of a redeemed Israel. This is expressly indicated in Deuteronomy 32:43—"Rejoice, O nations, with his people"—and is clearly the thought in the other references in their Old Testament contexts (cf. Pss 18:49; 117:1; Isa 11:10; 52:15). If the apostle is viewing the present fulfillment as the total interpretation of God's plan of salvation, then he obviously is giving these Old Testament prophecies a considerably new twist.

Now, we must acknowledge that the apostle *does see* the fulfillment of these Old Testament texts in the present salvation of both Jews and Gentiles. He even validates the Old Testament order—"first for the Jew, then for the Gentile"—in introducing these citations in support of gentile salvation: "Christ has become a servant of the Jews . . . so that the Gentiles may glorify God" (Ro 15:8; cf. also the express teaching of this order in Ac 13:46–47; 18:6; 28:15–28). But Paul's teaching about gentile salvation in Romans 15 must be harmonized with what he writes in chapters 9–11. There he not only affirms the Old Testament covenants and promises to Israel without reinterpretation (cf. 9:4–5), but also asserts a future salvation for "all Israel" beyond the salvation of the present remnant (11:25–27). Moreover, in harmony with the Old Testament picture, he looks forward to a time of even greater blessing for the Gentiles as a result of Israel's redemption (cf. 11:12, 15).[74]

In light of the apostle's total teaching concerning the salvation of Israel and Gentiles, therefore, it is preferable to understand his use of these prophecies of gentile salvation not to "transform" totally the Old Testament hope, but simply to indicate that the eschatological age of salvation has dawned with Christ. In accordance with the Old Testament hope, that eschatological salvation does include Gentiles. Thus they along with believing Jews are forming a new people of God. But the present operation of salvation does not negate the future fulfillment of the prophecies as portrayed in the Old Testament.

A second reason to view the present fulfillment as only partial lies in the citation, from Isaiah 11:10, about "the Root of Jesse" ruling over the nations. According to Dunn, this prophecy in its context (vv. 6–10) held out "the eschatological prospect of universal peace."[75] Now, there is no universal peace among the nations today. Christ is not reigning in the sense of bringing worldwide peace, and in our understanding, such a peace will not occur until he returns. Therefore, unless Paul is radically reinterpreting this text, he cannot see in the present time of gentile salvation the complete fulfillment of this prophecy. A possible indication

---

[74]See chapter 10 for a full discussion of these issues in Romans 9–11.
[75]Dunn, *Romans 9–16*, 850.

that Paul does not intend his use of the text to be understood as the complete fulfillment of Isaiah's prophecy may be seen in the fact that his verbatim quotation from the Septuagint does not include the opening words "in that day." This phrase, which throughout the Old Testament prophecies signifies the time of eschatological fulfillment, is always reserved for the future in the apostle's writings (cf. Ro 2:5, 16; 13:12; 1Co 1:8; 3:13; 5:5, etc.). In other words, "the day of the Lord" is still to come in which this prophecy will receive its complete fulfillment.

These applications to the present age of prophecies about gentile salvation are best understood in harmony with the total picture of the New Testament teaching regarding the eschatological hope. What was viewed in the Old Testament as taking place in connection with the coming of the Messiah is now apportioned with two comings. The Old Testament predicted that in the messianic age the Gentiles would be included in the salvation of God. According to the New Testament writers, the messianic age has dawned. Thus Gentiles are being saved along with Jews. But the evangelization of the nations during this present age is not the complete fulfillment of the Old Testament hope. Nor is it the complete fulfillment of the hope of the New Testament. We find not only that there is no clear indication that the New Testament writers transformed the original picture, but also that they affirm an increased blessing for the world after the redemption of Israel and a messianic reign of peace over the nations under the Messiah.

III. CONCLUSION

A study of the teachings about the new covenant in the Old and New Testaments discloses a pattern of fulfillment similar to that of the promises to Abraham and David. And well it should, for, as we have seen, the new covenant is the culmination of these promises. All these promises pointed forward to the time of the Messiah for their ultimate fulfillment. The coming of Jesus into the world, therefore, inaugurated their realization. Ever since, the salvation of God has been connected with the fulfillment of these promises under the terms of the new covenant.

The Old Testament prophecies, the promise of salvation under the new covenant, and the promises to Abraham and David all contained provisions for the blessing of the nations along with Israel. This blessing of the nations was ascribed to the messianic era. This era has arrived, according to the New Testament, and thus the promises of the new covenant have begun to take effect and are available to all who will receive the Messiah. In accord with the promises, God's salvation is extended to both Jews and Gentiles who believe.

But as with the other promises that were to be fulfilled in the Messiah, the total new covenant fulfillment must be seen as encompassing the total work of the Messiah. What seemed in the Old Testament to be one coming has by the New Testament revelation been separated into two appearances. Thus the present operation of the new covenant in saving Jews and Gentiles in the church is not the complete fulfillment of the Old Testament prophecy. The return of Christ will bring further fulfillment. Because the New Testament clearly envisions a future for historical Israel, it seems reasonable to expect the coming of Christ to bring about the fulfillment of the salvation provisions of the new covenant that related particularly to that people as well as a richer fulfillment of blessing for all of the peoples of the world (cf. Ro 11).

PART III

THE CHURCH IN SALVATION HISTORY

Chapter 6

The Church and the Revelation of the Mysteries

A CENTRAL TENET of traditional dispensationalism holds that the church is a parenthesis in the program of biblical history. According to this view, the church occupies a place distinctly separate from the history of God's Old Testament people and from the promises prophesied for Israel and the nations in the messainic kingdom. This interpretation is supported by several arguments that are said to demonstrate the uniqueness of the character and, consequently, the time period for the church. These arguments include Paul's use of the term "mystery" in connection with the equality of Jews and Gentiles in the church (Eph 3) and Christ's indwelling the believer during this age (Col 1); the concept of the baptism with the Spirit, which forms the church; and specific terminology applied to the church such as the "body" and "bride" of Christ.

Non-dispensationalists, by contrast, argue from the same Scriptures that the church and true Israel are essentially identical and that no real distinction remains for national Israel subsequent to the founding of the New Testament church. To my mind, a study of Scripture discloses greater unity between the church and Israel than traditional dispensationalists allow, but does not eradicate all distinction for Israel as non-dispensationalists generally contend. The focus of this chapter is the use of mystery in connection with the church; we will reserve until the next chapter a discussion of the baptism with the Spirit and the body and bride terminology in relation to the place of the church.

143

I. INTRODUCTION

A. The Problem

1. Traditional Dispensationalism. While the "mystery" terminology is not applied to the church per se in Scripture, it is, according to dispensationalists, used "of the distinctive elements of the truth concerning the church as the body of Christ."[1] These elements include the composition of the body of Christ as Jews and Gentiles joined together in equality (Eph 3:4–6) and the indwelling of Christ that constitutes the church as a living organism (Col 1:27).

According to dispensationalists, the term "mystery" denotes a truth that was not previously a part of revelation. The term "revelation" in this sense means that the content of a mystery was not a part of any previous objective revelation. Lewis Sperry Chafer states this meaning clearly when he says, "The sum total of all the mysteries in the New Testament represents that entire body of added truth found in the New Testament which is unrevealed in the Old Testament."[2]

From this meaning of "mystery" and its content concerning the body of Christ and his indwelling, traditional dispensationalists draw the following conclusions: (1) The church is not found in the Old Testament.[3] Rather, it is a new unique work of God related to the coming of the Spirit and the indwelling presence of the resurrected Christ; (2) the church is not the fulfillment of any revelation found in the Old Testament.[4]

2. Non-dispensationalism. Non-dispensationalists come to quite different conclusions with respect to the mysteries related to the church. Some scholars such as Oswald T. Allis, apparently desiring to emphasize the continuity between the church and the Old Testament work of God, view the mystery revealed through Paul as only *comparatively better known now* than it was in the Old Testament.[5] Others, as we will see, regard the revelation of the mystery as something totally new, but nevertheless conclude that it is the fulfillment of the Old Testament Scriptures. Herman Ridderbos, for example, speaks of Paul's "new understanding of the prophecy that made mention of the future redemption of the gentiles together with Israel."[6] This new understanding brings

---

[1]John F. Walvoord, *The Millennial Kingdom* (Findlay, Ohio: Dunham, 1959), 231.

[2]L. S. Chafer, *Systematic Theology* (Dallas: Dallas Seminary Press, 1948), 4:76; cf. Walvoord, *The Millennial Kingdom*, 232.

[3]Charles C. Ryrie, *Dispensationalism Today* (Chicago: Moody Press, 1965), 135.

[4]Walvoord, *The Millennial Kingdom*, 240.

[5]O. T. Allis, *Prophecy and the Church* (Philadelphia: Presbyterian and Reformed, 1945), 94–95.

[6]Herman Ridderbos, *Paul: An Outline of His Theology* (Grand Rapids: Eerdmans, 1975), 339–40; cf. also 46–47.

a unification that eliminates any distinction and therefore any significance for Israel as a nation in the future. The church becomes the new Israel and heir of the promises.[7] This accords with Anthony Hoekema's words: "All thought of a separate purpose for believing Jews is here excluded."[8]

B. The Concept of Mystery in the New Testament

1. The Biblical Concept of Mystery. It is helpful at the outset to consider how the concept of "mystery" is used in the New Testament.[9] We are interested primarily whether "mystery" clearly signifies something that has not been a part of previous revelation in any sense.

In its earliest known occurrences the word "mystery" (μυστήριον) was used as a Greek religious term denoting secret rites or teachings known only to the initiates. Later it came to be used more generally among the Greeks to refer to a secret of any kind. The Jewish writings likewise used the term for human secrets of various kinds, but also with a specific theological meaning.[10] According to Günter Finkenrath, "Dan. uses the word in a very definite theological sense, that of 'eschatological secret,' the vision of what God has decreed shall take place in the future (Dan. 2:28)."[11]

This use includes the idea that the disclosure and interpretation of a divine "mystery" is reserved for God alone and for those inspired by his

---

[7]C. Leslie Mitton, *Ephesians,* New Century Bible Commentary (Grand Rapids: Eerdmans, 1973), 123.

[8]Anthony Hoekema, *The Bible and the Future* (Grand Rapids: Eerdmans, 1979), 200.

[9]See G. Bornkamm, "μυστήριον, μυέω," in *Theological Dictionary of the New Testament,* vol. 4, ed. G. W. Bromiley (Grand Rapids; Eerdmans, 1967), 802–28; Raymond E. Brown, *The Semitic Background of the Term "Mystery" in the New Testament* (Philadelphia: Fortress, 1968); G. Finkenrath, "Secret, Mystery," in *The New International Dictionary of New Testament Theology,* vol. 3, ed. Colin Brown (Grand Rapids: Zondervan, 1978), 501–11; C. F. D. Moule, "Mystery," in *The Interpreter's Dictionary of the Bible,* vol. 3 (Nashville: Abingdon, 1962), 479–81; Ridderbos, *Paul: An Outline of His Theology,* 44–53; J. Armitage Robinson, "On the Meaning of μυστήριον in the New Testament," in *St. Paul's Epistle to the Ephesians* (London: James Clarke, n.d.), 234–40. See also commentaries on the Scripture passages involved.

[10]Μυστήριον is not used in the canonical Septuagint except for eight occurrences in Daniel 2, where it translates the Aramaic word רז. The Hebrew word סוד, used for God's secret (e.g., Job 15:8; Ps 25:14; Pr 3:32; Am 3:7), is always translated by Greek words other than μυστήριον. The apocryphal writings, however, use μυστήριον for secrets of various kinds, including divine mysteries (Wisd 2:22). Later Greek versions also use it occasionally to translate the Hebrew סוד (e.g., both Symmachus and Theodotion use it in Job 15:8). It has been suggested that the earlier translations of the Old Testament avoided this term because of its pagan religious associations, but that once it passed into common use with a neutral meaning, it came to be used quite freely.

[11]Finkenrath, "Secret, Mystery," in *NIDNTT,* 3:502.

Spirit.[12] This same usage is found in the later Jewish apocalyptic writings, as to which Gunther Bornkamm explains, "The mysteries are God's counsels destined finally to be disclosed. They are the final events and states which are already truly existent in heaven and may be seen there and which will in the last days emerge from their concealment and become manifest events."[13]

The concept of "mysteries" also played an important role in the Qumran literature dated around the first century B.C. In the writings of this sectarian community the term is used in the sense of divine mysteries that are closely related to the New Testament and especially the Pauline usage (e.g., 1QH 5:36; 1QpH 7:4–5; 1Q27 1:1, 2–4).[14] Joseph Coppens describes the Qumran use of "mysteries" as "an ensemble of knowledge, of decrees, and of the riches of grace which are beyond human understanding. No one has access to them except through revelation and divine generosity."[15] According to Jewish theological usage, therefore, a divine mystery denoted a secret of God that he alone made known through revelation at the appointed time.

It is now generally agreed that this Semitic meaning, rather than the one attributed to the Greek mystery religions, provides the background for the New Testament usage.[16] Thus the basic idea of a "secret"—something which had previously been hidden, but now is made known—has come to be the generally accepted meaning of the term "mystery" in the New Testament. As a result, μυστήριον, when not translated "mystery," is frequently rendered as "secret" (NIV, NEB; cf. German *Geheimnis*). The language related to the central mystery of the New Testament—namely, Christ himself (cf. Col 2:2; 4:3)—provides clear support for this basic meaning. It was prepared before the world was created (1Co 2:7), hidden in God in the past (1Co 2:8; Eph. 3:9; Col 1:26; Ro 16:25), and now made known through revelation by the Spirit (1Co 2:2–10; Eph 3:5).[17]

---

[12]Bornkamm, "μυστήριον, μυέω," in *TDNT*, 4:815.

[13]Bornkamm, "μυστήριον, μυέω," in *TDNT*, 4:816.

[14]Cf. Joseph Coppens, "'Mystery' in the Theology of Saint Paul and Its Parallels at Qumran," in *Paul and Qumran*, ed. Jerome Murphy-O'Connor (Chicago: Priority Press, 1968), 132–58; Franz Mussner, "Contribution Made by Qumran to the Understanding of the Epistle to the Ephesians," in *Paul and Qumran*, 159–67; Brown, *Semitic Background of the Term "Mystery,"* 22–30.

[15]Coppens, "'Mystery' in the Theology of Saint Paul," 135.

[16]Chrys C. Caragounis observes that in view of recent studies in the Jewish apocryphal and pseudepigraphal writings and especially the Qumran materials, "it has become increasingly more usual to sever the ties of contact between the NT *mysterion* and the Mystery Religions, and establish them, instead, with the Jewish background" (*The Ephesian Mysterion* [Lund: CWK Gleerup, 1977], 119). Caragounis makes a good case for showing that Daniel's use in particular stands behind the use of "mystery" in Ephesians 1 and 3 (121–26).

[17]We note in passing that this simple meaning of "secret" without any connotations of something mysterious or incomprehensibleness—a meaning based largely on the authority

2. The New Testament Use of Mystery. The term μυστήριον is used a comparatively rare twenty-eight times in the New Testament, of which twenty-one occurrences are in the Pauline writings.[18] All the uses refer to divine secrets, but, following C. F. D. Moule, we may divide the nature of the mysteries into three broad categories:[19]

First, in three instances "mystery" is used for the hidden meaning found in symbols and types, such as the seven stars and seven lampstands (Rev 1:20; cf. also "mystery Babylon," 17:5, 7) and marriage (Eph 5:31–32). In these uses "mystery" probably refers both to the symbols and to their hidden meanings.

Second, "mystery" refers to various divine secrets that are conveyed to designated persons. The references to knowing and speaking "mysteries" in 1 Corinthians 13:2 and 14:2 belong in this category. Moule would also include Paul's reference to the mystery of the bodily transformation at the coming of Christ (1Co 15:51).[20]

The third use—and by far the most significant in terms of both frequency and content—entails what may be called the divine plan of salvation now revealed in Christ.

While not all the mysteries of the New Testament can be shown to be related except by the concept of mystery itself (e.g., "the mystery of lawlessness," 2Th 2:7; and the mystery of the transformation of the body at the coming of Christ, 1Co 15:51), yet there is general agreement that many of the individual references to mystery are in fact aspects of this one central mystery centered in Christ and the gospel.[21] In preaching of the crucified Christ to the Corinthians, the apostle claimed to be speaking "the

---

of J. B. Lightfoot and followed by T. K. Abbott and others—has been called into question by Caragounis (see Lightfoot, *Saint Paul's Epistles to the Colossians and to Philemon* [1879 ed.; reprint, Grand Rapids: Zondervan, 1959], 168; Abbott, *A Critical and Exegetical Commentary on the Epistles to the Ephesians and Colossians* [Edinburgh: T & T Clark, n.d.], 16).

Caragounis has amassed considerable evidence for the element of mysteriousness, or that which is unfathomable, in the original religious meaning of "mystery." He acknowledges that its meaning broadened in subsequent nonreligious usage to include mere secrets, yet he maintains that the New Testament continues the uniform meaning of "mysterious truth" from its prior religious use. It is mysterious and incomprehensible to human understanding, for only those whose minds are enlightened by the Spirit can know it. While Caragounis's thesis adds a dimension to the meaning of the term, it is not determinative for understanding the apostolic teaching about the divine mysteries.

[18]The numbers 28 and 21 include the variant reading in 1 Corinthians 2:1. In addition to the 21 in Paul's writings, the term is found three times in the Synoptic Gospels, all of which are parallel passages that concern the mysteries of the kingdom (cf. Mk 4:11 and parallels), and four times in Revelation (1:20; 10:7; 17:5, 7).

[19]Moule, "Mystery," in *IDB*, 3:480.

[20]Moule, "Mystery," in *IDB*, 3:480.

[21]Bornkamm argues also that in the New Testament the term "always has an eschatological sense" ("μυστήριον, μυέω," in *TDNT*, 4:822).

mystery of God" (1Co 2:1)[22] or "God's wisdom in mystery" (2:7, NASB). The latter expression and the context make it evident that here "mystery" is equivalent to the wisdom of God, which is nothing less than "the divine will to save fulfilled in the crucifixion of Christ (1:24)"[23] or "the gospel and . . . Christ, the content of the gospel."[24] To sum up the apostle's teaching concerning the mystery in 1 Corinthians 2, Seyoon Kim says,

> "Christ crucified" is God's wisdom ἐν μυστηρίῳ [in mystery] because he embodies "God's wise plan of redeeming the world through a crucified Messiah," "which God foreordained for our glory before the course of ages began" (1Cor 2.7), and salvation "which God prepared for those who love him" (1Cor 2.9).[25]

It is apparent that the Corinthian use is similar to the mystery related to Christ himself (Eph 3:4; Col 2:2, 4:3; 1Ti 3:16) and the gospel (Ro 16:25–26; Eph 6:19) in Paul's other letters. The mystery of God's plan of salvation would also include his purpose to bring all things together in Christ (Eph 1:9–10), including the salvation of the Gentiles and Israel (Ro 11:25; Eph 3:3–10; Col 1:26–27).

3. The Hiddenness and Revelation of a Mystery. The various New Testament uses of "mystery" suggest that there are several somewhat different senses in which a mystery may be said to have been hidden and subsequently revealed. First, as we have seen, a mystery may be hidden in symbol or language with an inner meaning (cf. Rev 1:20; Eph 5:32). In this instance the revelation of the mystery consists of the unveiling of the meaning of the symbol or language that has already been given. Second, a mystery may be hidden because its truth has never been the subject of objective revelation. The mystery of the instant change of believers at the coming of Christ (1Co 15:51) is an example of this type. Nothing concerning this phenomenon had been included in any prior revelation.

---

[22]If the reading μυστήριον is accepted over μαρτύριον: cf. the UBS text (3d ed., corrected); Markus Barth, *Ephesians 1–3*, Anchor Bible (Garden City, N.Y.: Doubleday, 1974), 125; Bornkamm, "μυστήριον, μυέω," in *TDNT*, 4:819; Brown, *Semitic Background of the Term "Mystery,"* 48–49; William F. Orr and James Arthur Walther, *1 Corinthians*, Anchor Bible (Garden City, N.Y.: Doubleday, 1976), 156; Caragounis, *The Ephesian Mysterion*, 28. For the preference of μαρτύριον, see C. K. Barrett, *A Commentary on the First Epistle to the Corinthians* (New York; Harper & Row, 1968), 62–63; Gordon Fee, *The First Epistle to the Corinthians* (Grand Rapids; Eerdmans, 1987), 91; F. W. Grosheide, *Commentary on the First Epistle to the Corinthians* (Grand Rapids: Eerdmans, 1953), 58.
[23]Bornkamm, "μυστήριον, μυέω," in *TDNT*, 4:819; cf. also Brown: "As the succeeding verses [2:9ff.] make clear, it is the economy of salvation prepared beforehand for those whom God loves, and now at last revealed. In other words *sophia en mysterio* covers much of the same conceptual territory that we shall later see covered by *mysterion* alone" (*Semitic Background of "Mystery,"* 41).
[24]Seyoon Kim, *The Origin of Paul's Gospel* (Tübingen: J. C. B. Mohr, 1981), 75.
[25]Kim, *The Origin of Paul's Gospel*, 76–77.

A third kind of hiddenness is found in relation to Christ and the divine plan of salvation in him. There is no doubt that this use of mystery involves disclosure of details concerning the person and saving work of Christ that are absent from the Old Testament prophecies; yet it is impossible to see these additional truths as constituting all that is meant in the hiddenness and revelation of this mystery.

The apostles frequently asserted that the gospel they preached and the messiahship of Jesus they taught were grounded in the Old Testament Scriptures. In Romans 1:1–2 Paul states that the "gospel of God" for which he was set apart was "promised beforehand through his prophets in the Holy Scriptures" (cf. Tit 1:1–3). This is surely the same message that later, in Ephesians 6:19, he called "the mystery of the gospel." On his first missionary journey the apostle proclaimed to those at Pisidian Antioch, "We tell you the good news: What God promised our fathers . . ." (Ac 13:32). Even the inclusion of the Gentiles in the salvation of Christ was part of the Old Testament promise that was being fulfilled through the apostle's ministry. Before Festus and Agrippa, Paul testified, "I am saying nothing beyond what the prophets and Moses said would happen—that the Christ would suffer and, as the first to rise from the dead, would proclaim light to his own people and to the Gentiles" (Ac 26:22–23).

Finally, there is the apostle's statement that his "gospel and the proclamation of Jesus Christ [is] according to the revelation of the mystery hidden for long ages past, but now revealed and made known through the prophetic writings" (Ro 16:25–26). C. E. B. Cranfield explains just how the mystery may be said to be revealed through the prophetic writings:

> . . . the manifestation, which has taken place in the gospel events and their subsequent proclamation, and is contrasted with the hiddenness of the mystery in the past, is a manifestation which is properly understood in its true significance only in the light of its OT foreshadowing and attestation. It is when the manifestation of the mystery is understood as the fulfilment of God's promises made in the OT (cf. 1.2), as attested, interpreted, clarified, by the OT (cf., e.g., 3.21; 9.33; 10.4–9, 11, 13, 16, 18–21; 11.2, 26f), that it is truly understood as the gospel of God for all mankind.[26]

---

[26]C. E. B. Cranfield, *A Critical and Exegetical Commentary on the Epistle to the Romans,* International Critical Commentary (Edinburgh: T & T Clark, 1979), 2:812. Similarly, Sanday and Headlam state, "All the ideas in this sentence are exactly in accordance with the thoughts which run through this Epistle. The unity of the Old and New Testament, the fact that Christ had come in accordance with the Scriptures (Rom. i. 1, 2), that the new method of salvation although apart from law, was witnessed to by the Law and the Prophets [cf. Rom. 3:21] . . . , the constant allusion esp. in chaps. ix–xi to the Old Testament Scriptures; all these are summed in the phrase διὰ γραφῶν προφητικῶν" (William Sanday and Arthur Headlam, *A Critical and Exegetical Commentary on the Epistle to the Romans,* ICC, 434).

If the mystery of Christ and the divine plan of salvation has already been the subject of Old Testament prophecy, then in what sense can it be said to have been hidden and only now revealed by the New Testament apostles and prophets? This question brings us to the third and perhaps primary understanding of the hiddenness and revelation of a mystery. A mystery may be hidden in the sense that its truth has not yet been realized. The corresponding revelation consists not in making the truth known in an objective or propositional sense, but in bringing it to reality or existence. In this instance the truth of the mystery may be the subject of previous prophecy, but is it said to be hidden until in God's appointed time it becomes a manifest event. Ridderbos explains this concept thus:

> "hiddenness," "mystery," etc., has, therefore, in addition to a noetic a plainly historical connotation; it is that which has not yet appeared, that which still exists in the counsel of God and has not yet been realized in history as fulfillment of that counsel. Accordingly the corresponding word "reveal" not only means the divulging of a specific truth or the giving of information as to certain events or facts, but the appearance itself, the becoming historical reality of that which until now did not exist as such, but was kept by God, hidden, held back.[27]

Similarly, F. W. Grosheide says, "Hidden does not mean 'totally unknown,' but 'not yet existing.'"[28]

This sense of hiddenness and revelation is seen in Jesus' statement concerning the Father's revelation of truth through him. To his disciples, who were recipients of his teaching of the mysteries of the kingdom, Jesus said, "Blessed are the eyes that see what you see. For I tell you that many prophets and kings wanted to see what you see but did not see it, and to hear what you hear but did not hear it" (Lk 10:23; cf. Mt 13:16–17). "Seeing" and "hearing" in this beatitude of Jesus clearly refers not to receiving new information as such, but to actualizing and experiencing prophecy given beforehand.

---

[27]Ridderbos, *Paul: An Outline of His Theology*, 46–47.

[28]Grosheide, *Commentary on the First Epistle to the Corinthians*, 64. Compare the comment by Heinrich A. Meyer on "mystery" in Ephesians 1:9: "And the mystery with which the divine will is occupied, is *the counsel of redemption accomplished through Christ*, not in so far as it is in itself incomprehensible for the understanding, but in so far as, while formed from eternity, it was until the announcement of the gospel hidden in God, and veiled and unknown to men. See Rom. xvi. 25f.; Eph. iii. 4f., 9, vi. 19; Col. i, 26. By the prophets the mystery was not disclosed, but the disclosure of it was merely *predicted*, here at the proclamation of the gospel the prophetic predictions became the *means* of it being disclosed" (*Critical and Exegetical Hand-Book to the Epistle to the Galatians and the Epistle to the Ephesians* [New York: Funk & Wagnalls, 1884], 320; cf. also Ernst Käsemann, *Commentary on Romans* [Grand Rapids; Eerdmans, 1980], 312; Bornkamm, "μυστήριον, μυέω," 4:816, 822.)

T. W. Manson explains, "The point of the saying is that what for all former generations lay still in the future is now a present reality. What was for the best men of the past only an object of faith and hope is now a matter of experience."[29] These eschatological blessings had been revealed to the prophets, at least to some extent, but they had not yet seen or heard them because they were "hidden" in the counsel of God until their becoming reality with the coming of Christ.

This teaching of Jesus entails a further significant dimension to this sense of hiddenness and revelation. The mystery is made known or revealed only through the enlightening power of the Spirit and is understood only by people of faith. According to Paul, the mystery of the wisdom of God, the message of Christ crucified, was not understood by the rulers of this age (1Co 2:7–8). They did not understand because the mystery was " 'hidden in God' and could only be grasped by a revelation of the Spirit (v. 10)."[30] This "hiddenness" continues for those whose minds are blinded by the god of this age (2Co 4:3–4). Thus, even with this proclamation the mystery "remains hidden, in so far as . . . its truth remains beyond human comprehension and can only be laid hold of by faith."[31]

This third sense of the hiddenness and revelation of the mystery may thus be summarized as entailing two dimensions. First, it is hidden and revealed with regard to its realization in God's historical plan of salvation. It may have been a part of previous prophecy, but it was hidden until the time came for its actualization. Second, it is hidden and revealed even then until the Spirit enlightens the human heart. And in this last instance, the full knowledge of the mystery awaits the final day of perfection for the believer, as Bornkamm explains:

> For the coming glorification of believers is only intimated in the μυστήριον. The riches of glory are already included in it, but they are still included in it, Christ being the "hope" of glory in whom the treasures of wisdom and knowledge are still concealed, Col. 2:3. Hence the revealed mystery still conceals the final consummation. The eschatological enactment is still only in word, the fulfilment of all things is as yet only through the Church, δόξα [glory] is only in the concealment of θλίψεις," [afflictions] Col. 1:24f.; Eph. 3:13.[32]

---

[29]T. W. Manson, *The Sayings of Jesus* (London: SCM Press, 1949), 80.
[30] Fee, *The First Epistle to the Corinthians*, 105–6; cf. Orr and Walther, *1 Corinthians*, 165–66.
[31]Hugo Rahner, *Greek Myths and Christian Mystery* (Cheshire, Conn.: Biblo and Tannen, 1971), 29.
[32]Bornkamm, "μυστήριον, μυέω," in *TDNT*, 4:822.

We note in passing that even in this third sense the contrast between the hiddenness and revelation of a mystery is best understood as absolute rather than relative. On the grounds that the Old Testament Scriptures were not silent on the mystery of Christ (Ro 16:25–26), John Murray states that in regard to the revelation, "the contrast is not absolute but . . . *relative,* and this relative contrast must not be discounted."[33]

Cranfield, however, sees in the contrasting words "but [δέ] now revealed" (Ro 16:26) a much sharper discontinuity. It is "the contrast between the ages before Christ's incarnation and the period which began with it. It was in the gospel events, the life, death, resurrection and ascension of Jesus Christ, that the mystery was manifested decisively."[34] According to Cranfield, the fact that Christ was foretold and even in a sense present in the Old Testament "must not be distorted into a denial of the utterly decisive nature of the event indicated by the statement ὁ λόγος σάρξ ἐγένετο [the Word became flesh]."[35]

The apostle's language in connection with the mystery in Ephesians 3, therefore, is best interpreted as contrastive rather than comparative. The statement that the mystery "was not made known to men in other generations as it has now been revealed" (v. 5) does not mean that it is simply better known now, but that it was not known previously and is now revealed.[36]

It is difficult to know exactly how to apply these various uses of "mystery" and revelation to particular instances in the New Testament writings. It may be possible in some uses to see them in combination, as F. F. Bruce seems to suggest in commenting on the use of mystery in the Old Testament and among the interpreters of the Qumran community.[37] The meaning of the term, he says, "need not imply that no reference at all was made to it in the OT scriptures." Then, referring directly to the principle found in the commentaries of Qumran, he adds, "According to this principle, God made known his purpose to the prophets of old, but withheld from the prophets one vital piece of information (without which the prophetic word remained a 'mystery')—namely, the time when his purpose would be fulfilled (together with the identity of the persons who would be involved, on the one side or the other, in its fulfillment)."[38]

---

[33]John Murray, *The Epistle to the Romans,* New International Commentary on the New Testament (Grand Rapids: Eerdmans, 1965), 2:242.

[34]Cranfield, *Epistle to the Romans,* 2:811

[35]Cranfield, *Epistle to the Romans,* 2:810, n.3.

[36]Heinrich Schlier, *Der Brief an die Epheser* (Düsseldorf: Patmost-Verlag, 1971), 150.

[37]It is not entirely clear from Bruce's statements whether he sees the content of the mystery only in the new details added, or whether the previous revelation that was incomplete without the added details could also be considered part of the mystery.

[38]F. F. Bruce, *The Epistles to the Colossians, to Philemon, and to the Ephesians,* New International Commentary (Grand Rapids: Eerdmans, 1984), 84–85.

It is not entirely clear from Bruce's statements whether he views the previous, incomplete revelation as part of the mystery or only the newly added details. From the application of mystery to the total program of salvation in Christ, it is difficult not to include both and thus acknowledge that a New Testament mystery can have some clear relation to previous prophetic Scripture. The question remains, therefore, as to which of these uses of mystery applies to the nature and constitution of the church in Ephesians 3 and Colossians 1. Is the truth that the apostle teaches concerning the church something totally distinct from Old Testament prophecy, or is it in some sense vitally related to prophetic truth?

II. THE MYSTERY OF THE ONENESS
OF JEW AND GENTILE IN EPHESIANS 3

This mystery is that through the gospel the Gentiles are heirs together with Israel, members together of one body, and sharers together in the promise in Christ Jesus (Eph 3:6).

The question about the historical position of the church according to the mystery of Ephesians 3 calls for a careful look at the specific statement of the mystery in Ephesians 3:6 and the discussion of the new relationship between Jew and Gentile in Christ in Ephesians 2:11ff. We must note exactly what the apostle says and what he does not say.

A. The Content of the Mystery

1. The Meaning of Ephesians 3:6. The focus of Paul's teaching about the mystery in Ephesians 3 lies in verse 6, where he describes the new relationship between Jew and Gentile in Christ. It must be noted that the word "mystery" does not occur in this verse in the Greek text.[39] Its inclusion in some English versions (cf. NIV) is only for clarification. The specific contents of the mystery in verse 6 are in reality explications of the

---

[39]In the original Greek, verse 6 begins with an infinitive (εἶναι), which is understood by most scholars as epexegetical, meaning "that is" or "namely" (Abbott, *Epistles to the Ephesians and Colossians*, 83; Meyer, *Hand-Book to the Epistle to the Galatians and Ephesians*, 410).

Although Markus Barth argues that the infinitive is not epexegetical on the ground that it would require a preceding demonstrative pronoun, his interpretation of the infinitive yields a similar meaning to the verse when he says, "the infinitive fulfills the function of a sentence that begins with 'that' and describes a perception, a belief, an utterance, or a piece of information." He prefers J. B. Phillips's paraphrase: "This secret was hidden. . . . It is simply this: that the gentiles . . . , are . . ." (vv. 5–6) (Barth, *Ephesians 1–3*, 336). Either way, the infinitive introduces the statements of verse 6, which are in focus in Paul's teaching about the mystery here.

"mystery" mentioned earlier in the context, where it is described simply as "the mystery" (v. 3) and "the mystery of Christ" (v. 4). These rather general descriptions of the mystery raise the question of the real content of the mystery.

Citing the specific contents of verse 6, some scholars limit the meaning of all the references to "mystery" in Ephesians 3 to the inclusion of Gentiles in salvation. Viewing the mystery as only "related to Christ" rather than Christ himself, T. K. Abbott defines it as "the doctrine of the free admission of the Gentiles."[40] John Eadie similarly sees it as the gentile "admission to church fellowship equally with the Jews."[41]

By contrast, the singular reference "the mystery" along with its description simply as "of Christ" leads many to understand the mystery as God's whole saving action in the person and work of Christ, but with special reference in chapter 3 to the participation of Gentiles in it. As Heinrich A. W. Meyer explains, "Christ Himself, His person and His whole work, especially His redeeming death, connecting also the Gentiles with the people of God (ver. 6), is the *concretum* of the Divine mystery."[42] This broad understanding of the mystery would connect the mystery of chapter 3 to the mystery mentioned in chapter 1. Chrys C. Caragounis says that "the mystery [Eph. 1:9–10] which deals with the universal *anakephalaiosis* ['to bring . . . together under one head'] in Christ stands hierarchically above the other μυστήριον [mystery] concepts in this Epistle and includes them as parts of a whole." The mystery dealing with the unity of the Gentiles and Jews is thus simply "a more particular facet of the general, programmatic use of the concept in ch. 1."[43]

Somewhat similarly, Bornkamm identifies the mystery in 3:4ff. as "the share of the Gentiles in the inheritance, in the body of the Church, in the promise in Christ," but then concludes that "there takes place in it already the mystery of the comprehending of the whole created world in Christ, in whom the totality receives its head and sum (Eph. 1:9, 10)"[44]

Given this general terminology—"the mystery" and "the mystery of Christ"—the broader interpretation of the content of the mystery seems

---

[40]Abbott, *Epistles to the Ephesians and to the Colossians,* 80.

[41]Eadie, *Commentary on the Epistle to the Ephesians,* 214. On the grounds that the "new revelation" composing the "mystery" is not found in the Old Testament Scriptures, Bruce identifies the mystery as the "obliteration of the old line of demarcation" in the incorporation of Gentiles and Jews into the new community of God's people. According to Bruce, gentile blessing was part of the Old Testament promises, but this total lack of discrimination was not. This latter truth is therefore the content of the mystery that has been newly revealed (Bruce, *The Epistles to the Colossians, to Philemon, and to the Ephesians,* 314).

[42]Meyer, *Hand-Book to the Epistle to the Galatians and Ephesians,* 408; similar comprehensive definitions of the mystery are held by Robinson, *St Paul's Epistle to the Ephesians,* 31, 76; Barth, *Ephesians 1–3,* 329, 331.

[43]Caragounis, *The Ephesian Mysterion,* 29, 118.

[44]Bornkamm, "μυστήριον, μυέω," in *TDNT,* 4:820.

preferable. And on that basis the specific mystery statements of verse 6 are related to the overall concept of the mystery of Christ mentioned in other parts of the New Testament. The apostle had "insight" into the entire mystery of Christ (v. 4), but desired to emphasize to the Ephesians that aspect which in particularly distinguished his apostolic ministry, namely, the new relationship of Jew and Gentile in Christ through the gospel.[45] We will return to this subject later on in our discussion.

Paul spells out the mystery of the Jew and Gentile relationship in verse 6 in three phrases: "that through the gospel the Gentiles are *heirs together* with Israel, *members together* of one body, and *sharers together* in the promise in Christ Jesus" (emphasis added).

a. "Heirs together." The word συγκληρονόμα ("heirs together") is related to the word κληρονομέω ("to inherit") and signifies those who will receive or inherit something along with others.[46] The content of the inheritance is not specified here; however, it is no doubt related to the Ephesian letter's other three references to an inheritance for believers. In the first two references (1:14, 18), as in this one, the content is not defined.[47] But in the third (5:5), Paul speaks of an "inheritance in the kingdom of Christ and of God." Other references in the New Testament— most of them in Paul's writings—reveal the content of the believer's inheritance as salvation (Heb 1:14); glory (Ro 8:17; cf. v. 23, "the redemption of our bodies"; Eph 1:18); eternal life (Lk 18:18; Tit 3:7; 1Pe 3:7); blessing (1Pe 3:9); the promises (Heb 6:12; cf. 10:36); and the kingdom of God (Mt 25:34; 1Co 6:19; 15:50; Gal 5:21; Jas 2:5).

The final scriptural reference to the inheritance (Rev 21:7) describes its content as "all this"—which the previous context describes as "the blessedness of God's people in the new creation."[48] This, Werner Foerster notes, summarizes and explains all the other descriptions of the content of the inheritance above: "This tells us what is meant by the βασιλεία τοῦ θεοῦ [kingdom of God], by ζωή [life], by σωτηρία [salvation] and εὐλογία [blessing]. In short, it tells us what the inheritance in-

---

[45]Caragounis sees the reference to mystery in verse 4 as already the narrower content of verse 6, but he defines well the relation between the broad overall mystery of God in Christ and that of verse 6: "the *mysterion* of 1:9f. is the all-comprehending eschatological purpose of God as made known to the author (among others). In 3:4 it is that *mysterion* as proclaimed by the author to the Gentiles, applying to them in its limited aspect" (*The Ephesians Mysterion*, 141).

[46]Werner Foerster, "κληρονόμος," in *Theological Dictionary of the New Testament*, vol. 3, ed. Gerhard Kittel (Grand Rapids: Eerdmans, 1965), 781. Συγκληρονόμα is found in three other instances in the New Testament (Ro 8:17; Heb 11:9; 1Pe 3:7).

[47]It is possible with the NASB and the alternative translation in the NIV to see a fourth reference to inheritance in Ephesians 1:11.

[48]G. R. Beasley-Murray, *The Book of Revelation*, New Bible Commentary (Grand Rapids; Eerdmans, 1978), 313.

cludes."[49] With the absence of limitations in 1:14, 18 and with the broad content of the "kingdom" in 5:5, it seems most likely that Paul intended the most comprehensive meaning of the inheritance of 3:6 in which the Gentiles now have a part.

To bring the Gentiles to participate in the inheritance of God's people was in a very real sense the sum of Paul's apostolic ministry. On the Damascus road, Jesus sent him to the Gentiles "to open their eyes and turn them from darkness to light, and from the power of Satan to God, so that they may receive forgiveness of sins and a place ['an inheritance,' NASB, 'a share in the inheritance,' JB] among those who are sanctified by faith in me" (Ac 26:17–18; cf. 20:32). The first aspect of the mystery—that is, that the Gentiles share in the inheritance of the saints—is thus nothing less than saying that they participate fully in the blessings of the ultimate salvation that God has prepared for all his people "in Christ" (cf. Col 1:12).

In distinction with Romans 8:17, where Paul uses the term "heirs" to teach that believers are co-heirs with Christ, the mystery of Ephesians 3 is that Gentiles have become heirs together with Israel. While there is no mention of "Israel" (as the NIV translation might suggest), the context makes it clear that it is "believing Jews" with whom the Gentiles share.[50] We must be careful here not to say more than Paul says. It is certainly biblical to say, as Markus Barth does, that according to Ephesians, "no Gentile can have communion with Christ or with God unless he also has communion with Israel." But to add, as Barth does, that the Gentiles "are grafted onto Israel"[51] goes beyond the apostle's teaching here. The relation of Gentile and Jew will be discussed in relation to Ephesians 2:11ff. Suffice it to say at this point that although they share with Jews, nothing is said about Gentiles' becoming Jews or part of Israel unless we redefine "Israel," which is difficult to justify exegetically.[52]

The inheritance of which Paul speaks here may also be viewed as "all the blessing pledged to Abraham and his descendants."[53] The true basis of the Gentiles' sharing in the inheritance with Jews is their relationship to Abraham. According to Paul, Jew and Gentile alike are "Abraham's seed" and therefore "heirs according to the promise" (Gal

[49]Foerster, "κληρονόμος," in *TDNT*, 3:783.

[50]Abbott, *Epistles to the Ephesians and Colossians*, 83; cf. Barth: ". . . together with Israel the Gentiles are now 'heirs, members, beneficiaries'" (*Ephesians 1–3*, 337).

[51]Barth, *Ephesians 1–3*, 337.

[52]Barth no doubt has such a "new" or "spiritual Israel" in mind. So also does B. F. Westcott when he says that the Gentiles are *"fellowheirs* with natural Israel of the great hopes of the spiritual Israel" (*Saint Paul's Epistle to the Ephesians* [Grand Rapids: Baker, 1979], 46). But Ephesians says nothing of such a "new" or "spiritual" Israel, nor is it clear in any other apostolic teaching (see Peter Richardson, *Israel in the Apostolic Church* [Cambridge: Cambridge Univ. Press, 1969]).

[53]Bruce, *The Epistles to the Colossians, to Philemon, and to the Ephesians*, 316.

3:29). In writing to the Romans about this same blessing of promise to Abraham and his descendants (4:9–14), Paul pointedly identifies Abraham as the father of both Gentile ("all who believe but have not been circumcised," v. 11) and Jewish believers ("the circumcised . . . who also walk in the footsteps of the faith that our father Abraham had before he was circumcised," v. 12). The mystery status of the Gentiles as co-heirs with Israel thus signifies their participation with Israel in the final inheritance that God has prepared for all his people.

b. "Members together." The second term, σύσσωμα ["members together of one body"], refers to joint incorporation of the Gentiles with believing Jews "into the body of which Christ is the Head."[54] Much of the emphasis in Paul's other teaching on the body of Christ is on the incorporation of the believer into the body and the resultant relationship with the Head and the other members (cf. Ro 12:4ff.; 1Co 12:12ff.; Eph 4:16). Here, however, the context is the reconciliation and union of Jew and Gentile in the one body (2:15–16) and the emphasis is on their joint involvement. J. Armitage Robinson explains, "In relation to the Body the members are 'incorporate': in relation to one another they are 'concorporate,' that is, sharers in the one Body."[55]

This aspect of the mystery thus informs us that the gentile believers share with believing Jews all that is involved with being in the body of Christ, that is, the blessings of spiritual union with Him and all other believers.

c. "Sharers together." The third element of the content of the mystery is that the Gentiles are "sharers together in the promise." The apostle had previously mentioned the promise in relation to the Gentiles' reception of "the promised Holy Spirit" (Eph 1:13–14) and their former existence as "foreigners to the covenants of the promise" in which Israel already participated (2:12). Now the mystery culminates in the fact that Gentiles are full partners with Israel in God's promise.

The content of "the promise" is not specified. In other places, Paul identifies the Spirit (Gal 3:14; Eph 1:13), the inheritance (Ro 4:13; Gal 3:18–19), life (Gal 3:21), righteousness (Gal 3:21), and adoption or sonship (Ro 9:8; Gal 4:22ff.). Many scholars see all these as merely different dimensions of one messianic salvation that may be said to be "the promise."[56] This explains the use of both the singular "promise" (Gal 3:17; Eph 2:12) and plural "promises" (e.g., Ro 9:4; 15:8; Gal 3:16).

---

[54]Abbott, *Epistles to the Ephesians and Colossians,* 83.

[55]Robinson, *St Paul's Epistle to the Ephesians,* 78.

[56]Julius Schniewind and Gerhard Friedrich, "ἐπαγγέλλω κτλ," in *Theological Dictionary of the New Testament,* vol. 2 (Grand Rapids: Eerdmans, 1964), 583; cf. Meyer, *Hand-Book to the Epistle to the Galatians and Ephesians,* 410; Abbott, *Epistles to the Ephesians and Colossians,* 83.

Among all these elements of the promise, the gift of the Spirit is predominant in the apostle's thinking (cf. Gal 3:14). It is the presence of the Spirit that ultimately brings to reality the other dimensions of the promised salvation. If that is the case in Ephesians 3, this third statement is the culmination of all the previous statements about the mystery, as B. F. Westcott explains:

> There is an expressive sequence in three elements of the full endowment of the Gentiles as coequal with the Jews. They had a right to all for which Israel looked. They belonged to the same Divine society. They enjoyed the gift by which the new society was distinguished from the old. And when regarded from the point of sight of the Apostolic age, the gift of the Holy Spirit, "the promise of the Father" (Lu. xxiv. 49; Acts i. 4; ii. 33; 38f.), is preeminently "the promise," to which also συμμέτοχα [sharers together] perfectly corresponds.[57]

The mystery of verse 6 may thus be summed up as the coequal participation of the Gentiles with Israel in the full messianic salvation that is realized in the crucified and risen Christ and made effective to both through the apostolic proclamation of the gospel.

2. The New Relationship of Gentiles and Jews in Ephesians 2:11ff. The equal participation of Gentiles with Jews in the mystery of Christ rests on the change in the Gentiles' plight brought about through the work of Christ. This is elaborated by Paul in 2:11ff. and provides the explanation of the summary statements of the mystery in 3:6.

a. The previous state of the Gentiles. Paul begins his discussion of the Gentiles' new relationship with five statements that recount the old one. These statements are fundamentally negative in relation to the privileges of God's people Israel (Eph 2:12).

First, the Gentiles were "separate from Christ." Although the Messiah had not yet come, there was a sense in which he was already related to Israel. Through the promises and covenant relationship established by God, Israel had enjoyed communion with the Messiah to come. He was their hope. Through the activity of God in their midst, there was a sense in which Christ was already present. Paul says that the "spiritual rock" from which they all drank in the wilderness was Christ (1Co 10:4).

---

[57]Westcott, *Saint Paul's Epistle to the Ephesians*, 47. Although Barth unduly restricts the promise to the Spirit, he holds an instructive view of the sequence of the terms: "More likely the three attributes of Eph 3:6 are so arranged as to lead to a climax. The last attribute is indeed a climax, if by 'promise' is meant the substance and earnest of the promise, the Holy Spirit. Because his presence manifests God's presence among his people, the Spirit is indeed the epitome of God's promise. The reference to inheritance emphasizes the hope for the future; the mention of the body alludes to the gift and task of an organic and social life; the endowment with the Spirit gives reason for joy and guarantees freedom. Through the Spirit the goods of the coming aeon are already tasted, cf. Heb 6:4" (*Ephesians 1–3*, 338).

Prior to their new position in Christ, the Gentiles had no such relation to this Messiah.

Second, the Gentiles were "excluded from the commonwealth of Israel" (NASB). Paul's point seems to be that they were strangers in Israel without legal or civil rights. Even if they lived in the promised land, "they were not full citizens as long as they remained Gentiles."[58] God had established Israel as his special possession among the nations of the earth, a relationship in which the Gentiles as aliens did not share.

Third, the predicament of the Gentiles before their inclusion in Christ is that they were "strangers to the covenants of promise" (NASB). The great promise of God's salvation, perhaps initially suggested in the protoevangelium of the triumph of the Seed of the woman (Ge 3:15), had been channeled through divine covenants made with Israel and the patriarchs. Paul no doubt had in mind at least the covenants with Abraham and David and the new covenant. No redemptive covenant such as these had been made with the Gentiles.

With no relation to the Messiah, excluded from the chosen nation Israel, and strangers to the promises, the Gentiles found themselves in a position "without hope and without God in the world." The last of the three statements in particular brings into focus the real issue involved in all of these distinctions between the Gentiles and Israel. The issue was soteriological and theological. Although God had a witness among the Gentiles all the time (Ac 14:17), Israel had a favored relationship and fellowship with him; the Gentiles as such had no such place.

There is no doubt an attempt in this comparison with Israel to connect the new blessings of the Gentiles in Christ with the prior redemptive activity of God in Israel. However, the emphasis is not on the nation of Israel as such and the incorporation of the Gentiles into that nation. Rather, the emphasis is on Israel's privileges compared with the place of the Gentiles: she had the covenants, the promise, hope of a coming Messiah, and knowledge of the one true God.[59]

b. The new situation of the Gentiles in Christ. It is with Paul's description of the new situation of the Gentiles in Christ that dispensationalists and non-dispensationalists part ways. Put very simply, the issue is whether that new position entails the Gentiles' being incorporated into a new, redefined Israel and the end of any distinctiveness for the Old Testament people known as Israel.

The first words that describe the Gentiles "in Christ Jesus" are that, having been "far off," they have now been "brought near" (Eph 2:13). The terms "far" and "near" are Old Testament expressions describing the

---

[58]Barth, *Ephesians 1–3,* 257.

[59]Carl B. Hoch, Jr., "The Significance of the *Syn*-compounds for Jew-Gentile Relationships in the Body of Christ," *Journal of the Evangelical Society* 25 (June 1982): 179.

relationship of Jews to the temple at Jerusalem (cf. Isa 57:19; Da 9:7).[60] But the term "far off" was ascribed to Gentiles rather than exiled Jews long before the time of Christ. Since "the sons of Israel" were a people "near" to God, as we read in Psalm 148:14, it was natural for some rabbinical scholars to associate those "far off" with Gentiles, although for them they would still have been proselytes.[61] The question is, to what or to whom does the apostle say the Gentiles were now "brought near"?

The statements about being excluded from the "commonwealth" of Israel (Eph 2:12) and becoming "fellow citizens with God's people" (v. 19) have led many interpreters to conclude that Paul was teaching a nearness to or incorporation into a redefined Israel. Charles Hodge expressed this opinion in classic terms sometime ago: "It is not, therefore, to the participation of the privileges of the old, external, visible theocracy, nor simply to the pale of the visible Christian Church, that the apostle here welcomes his Gentile brethren, but to the spiritual Israel, the communion of saints."[62] Although Markus Barth recognizes the continuing theological significance of physical Jews, he nevertheless concludes that "God's household" (v. 19), to which both Jews and Gentiles belong, is "the community of Israel."[63]

All would agree that the emphasis in the passage is on a nearness to God. We have seen that this terminology was used in the Old Testament with regard to Israel. But that nearness is transcended by the believers' new position in Christ, for peace was proclaimed both to "those who were near" and to those "who were far away" so that all might gain a new access to the Father by the Spirit (Eph 2:17–18). It is after these statements that Paul cites the new privileges of the Gentiles in contrast to their previous, deficient state. "So then," Paul says, "you are no longer strangers and aliens, but you are fellow citizens with the saints, and are of God's household" (v. 19, NASB). Whereas previously they did not have citizenship in the commonwealth of Israel and were strangers to the promise, now they are "fellow citizens."

This new citizenship, however, as we have seen, is in a new place involving a change for both Gentiles and Israel, those far and those near. Because neither this passage nor any other in the New Testament[64] identifies the Christian community or the body of Christ as a "new Israel," it seems doubtful that Paul had such an identity in mind. It makes more sense to understand this new citizenship in accordance with his teaching

---

[60]R. J. McKelvey, *The New Temple* (London: Oxford Univ. Press, 1969), 111.
[61]Barth, *Ephesians 1–3*, 276.
[62]Charles Hodge, *An Exposition of Ephesians* (Wilmington, Del.: Associated Publishers and Authors, n.d.), 52.
[63]Barth, *Ephesians 1–3*, 314; cf. Mitton, *Ephesians*, 104.
[64]See Richardson, *Israel in the Apostolic Church*.

elsewhere. Using a Greek term that is closely related to the words that are translated "commonwealth" (Eph 2:12) and "fellow citizens" (v. 19), Paul tells the believers at Philippi that their "citizenship is in heaven" (Php 3:20). In the absence of any biblical evidence that the term "Israel" had lost reference to an earthly nation, we concur with Carl B. Hoch that "It appears better, therefore, to say that Jews and Gentiles in Christ become fellow citizens in a heavenly commonwealth that is not called Israel and yet has a close historico-redemptive relationship with Israel."[65]

Because Paul speaks of believers as having been transferred "to the kingdom of the Son he loves" (Col 1:13), perhaps we do best to consider this new commonwealth the kingdom of Christ that will be established upon his return, but in which the believer may already have citizenship.

That this is not incorporation into Israel is further indicated by the statement in the passage that the Gentiles and Israel have been brought together to form a new union. Paul says that Christ has made both groups into one (Eph 2:14) and that this union is identified as "one new man" (v. 15). The nature of this union is disclosed in how it is achieved. According to Paul, this unity came about when Christ "destroyed the barrier, the dividing wall of hostility, by abolishing in his flesh the law with its commandments and regulations" (vv. 14–15). The exact grammatical relationship of the three concepts "wall," "hostility," and "law" is not certain, but it is generally agreed that they interpret one another.[66] Thus the wall and the hostility that separated Gentiles from Jew center on the law as the divisive factor.

When Paul refers to the law as a barrier and the cause of hostility between the two groups, he is obviously not thinking of the total significance of the law.[67] Surely the law as the revelation of the character and will of God was not done away with in Christ. In fact, it is the law of God that the prophets saw as the uniting principle of Israel and the Gentiles in the kingdom as the nations came to Jerusalem to learn of God (Isa 2:3; Mic 4:2). Paul's concern in this discussion, therefore, is only for those aspects of the law that stood as a dividing wall between Gentiles and Israel—most importantly, the law as the righteous standard of God that condemns humankind and augurs death. As Paul teaches, the work of Christ not only establishes a new union between Jew and Gentile but also

---

[65]Hoch, "The Significance of the *Syn*-compounds," 180.

[66]Barth, *Ephesians 1–3*, 282: cf. also Bruce, *The Epistles to the Colossians, to Philemon, and to the Ephesians*, 298.

[67]While the law was intended in its original institution to set Israel apart from other nations, the enmity that arose over this distinction was not God's intention. It came instead from human attitudes. Undoubtedly the Jews gloried in their privileges while the Gentiles resented them.

provides reconciliation for both to God through the proclamation of peace.[68]

It becomes obvious that the focus as to the means of union is on the saving work of Christ on the cross. Paul is emphasizing a newness of relationship to God for all peoples. Since this is offered equally to Jews and Gentiles, they are brought together in spiritual union. Prior to the cross, only Israel was in a covenant relationship with God, but even that was not the final salvation entailed in the new covenant. At the cross, the new covenant was inaugurated through the blood of Christ that was shed for all peoples. Now the Gentiles as well as the Jews enjoy the final, perfect covenant fellowship with God. So the union of Jew and Gentile in Christ is not described as an incorporation of Gentiles into Israel, but rather, as Meyer notes, a union that takes place by "a raising of both into a higher unity."[69] Or as Andrew T. Lincoln says: The former disadvantages of the Gentiles "have been reversed not by their being incorporated into Israel, even into a renewed Israel of Jewish Christians, but by their being made members of a new community which transcends the categories of Jew and Gentiles, an entity which is a new creation."[70]

If this is the correct understanding, then the union of Jew and Gentile is one of religious significance that does not require the dissolution of all the previous meaning of Israel and its historical distinctives. In the rest of Ephesians, Paul emphasizes the unity and oneness of believers in Christ and in the church, but nowhere does he deny the continuation of their historical differences. Markus Barth observes that the community is made up of diverse people who are given a common life of peace in Christ. This concerns "not only the Jewish or Gentile provenance of the saints but also their differences in sex, age, and socioeconomic standing."[71] Since functional differences remain in these various divisions of humanity and yet all are one sharing equally in God's salvation in Christ, it seems difficult to deny that the nation of Israel might also retain some distinction on the historical horizontal level without endangering a perfect equality and unity in Christ.

---

[68]We suggest that the barrier aspects of the law that were removed are similar to the tutorial or pedagogical aspects, which Paul said were eliminated by coming to faith in Christ (Gal 3:24–25). These may be said to consist essentially of the law of God as encompassed in the old Mosaic covenant, which was fulfilled in Christ and replaced by the law of the new covenant.

[69]Meyer, *Hand-Book to the Epistle to the Galatians and Ephesians*, 383.

[70]Andrew T. Lincoln, "The Church and Israel in Ephesians 2," *Catholic Biblical Quarterly* 49 (October 1987): 615.

[71]Barth, *Ephesians 1–3*, 311.

B. The Nature of the Mystery

The spiritual unity of Jew and Gentile in Christ raises the question of the nature of the mystery involved. Is this union a new truth of which there was no prior mention in Old Testament prophecy? Or does it belong—along with the mystery of Christ and the gospel—to the category of mystery that signifies the realization or actualization of prior prophecy perhaps also with new details? That is, is this union a fulfillment (at least partially) of Old Testament truth, or is it something completely new about which the Old Testament says nothing?

It is clear that the prophecies pointed forward to a time when God's salvation would extend to the Gentiles.[72] The prophet Isaiah spoke of a time when "with joy you will draw water from the wells of salvation." That this includes the Gentiles is evident when he adds, "Make known among the nations what he has done, and proclaim that his name is exalted" (Isa 12:3–4). Moreover, this salvation comes through the Messiah, the great Servant of the Lord whom God has appointed as "a covenant for the people and a light for the Gentiles" (Isa 42:6), so that "you may bring my salvation to the ends of the earth" (Isa 49:6).

Zechariah likewise saw the coming king as speaking peace to the nations (Zec 9:9–10).

The means through which the Messiah-king will bring salvation to the nations is furthermore related to his suffering and death (Isa 52:15; 53:12).

Finally, this salvation for the nations is predicted to come about in union with Israel. The promises pointed forward to the time when Israel and the nations would be united in the worship of the Lord (Isa 2:4; Mic 4:3) and God's house would be "called a house of prayer for all the peoples" (Isa 56:7). While the Old Testament picture of salvation for the Gentiles involves all aspects of life, including international peace, it most certainly includes the spiritual salvation that is presently enjoyed by believers in Christ. This salvation, as the New Testament reveals, is nothing less than the beginning of fulfillment of the new covenant promised in the Old Testament.[73]

When we set these Old Testament predictions alongside Paul's teaching about the union of Jew and Gentile in salvation through Christ, it seems difficult to believe that he intends no reference to these prophecies and that his use of "mystery" means previously unknown truth absolutely. We suggest, rather, that he refers to mystery in two of the senses we looked at earlier.

---

[72]For further discussion of the Old Testament teaching concerning the salvation of the Gentiles, see chapter 5.

[73]See the discussion of the gentile involvement in the new covenant in chapter 5.

First, there are undoubtedly additional dimensions of the messianic salvation now revealed than were specified in the Old Testament. There is also new truth concerning the nature of the fulfillment during this church period. The messianic predictions of the Old Testament pictured the salvation of God flowing to the Gentiles during the time when Christ was reigning over a restored Israel. But now salvation is coming to them when Israel as a people has been largely set aside. This aspect relates exactly to the mysteries of the messianic kingdom taught by Christ in the Gospels. The Old Testament pictured one coming of Christ to establish his kingdom, but Christ in the mysteries portrays a time when the kingdom would be operating on earth before his actual reign (cf. Mt 13). Thus the mystery of the union of Israel and the Gentiles in the salvation of Christ also comes during this age in a different way from that which the prophecies indicated.

Second, Paul's use of "mystery" in this passage signifies that the salvation of God in Christ, which had only been predicted, but was not yet actual at the time of the prophecies, has now been brought into reality. Thus the "mystery" of the union of Jew and Gentile in Christ that constitutes the church must be viewed as both bringing new truth to light and fulfilling Old Testament predictions pertaining to the coming of the Messiah and his ministry. In addition to the fact that the equal sharing by Jew and Gentile in the present spiritual salvation found in Christ is in accord with the Old Testament prophecies, this conclusion is supported by the fact, noted above, that the teaching of the relationship of Jews and Gentiles in Ephesians 3:6 is in reality part of the broad "mystery of Christ" that is clearly related to Old Testament prophecy.[74]

Thus we agree with the non-dispensationalists that Paul's teaching concerning the mystery of the church in the union of Jew and Gentile in Christ is a fulfillment of Old Testament predictions. But we hasten to add that such fulfillments do not require us to assert that all the prophecies related to the messianic salvation and kingdom are thereby fulfilled. Paul teaches the same basic truth of the union of Gentile and Jew by using the metaphor of the olive tree in Romans 11. There he writes that the Gentiles share in the "rich root of the olive tree" (v. 17, NASB) along with the natural branches representing Israel. But he also looks forward to a future salvation of the nation of Israel (vv. 25–26). Likewise, Paul teaches that the new union of Jew and Gentile constitutes a "holy temple in the Lord"

---

[74]Barth explains the relation of the Ephesians 3 mystery to the mystery of Christ as follows: "The one mystery is the mystery of Christ the preexistent, the revealer, the savior, the regent of church and world, the one to unite Jew and Gentiles." With regard to the inclusion of the Gentiles into God's people, Barth says that this "is not a further mystery added to the mystery of Jesus Christ. . . . Rather, to speak of the savior Messiah who includes Gentiles in his body is to speak of the one revealed secret of God" (*Ephesians 1–3*, 331).

(Eph 2:21), but also sees significance for the future temple at Jerusalem (2Th 2:4). R. J. McKelvey's caveat concerning Paul's teaching on the temple is worth taking into account whenever we study any of his teaching:

> While one may say with certainty that the apostle thought of God's dwelling in the Church in parallel fashion to his dwelling in the temple of Jerusalem, one is reluctant to deduce that (therefore) the temple of Jerusalem ceased to have religious significance for him. . . . A straightforward reading of Paul's own writings can hardly be said to bear this out. At the point where one expects the apostle to carry his teaching to its logical conclusion one finds instead a certain ambivalence.[75]

Our understanding of the term "mystery" and of Paul's teaching about it leads us, therefore, to a mediating position concerning the place of the church in God's plan and purpose in history. On the one hand, contrary to traditional dispensationalism, the church is involved in the fulfillment of the messianic promises of the Old Testament. Messianic days have dawned, albeit in a way not clearly seen in the Old Testament, but nevertheless in a way that Paul supports in various places by references to the Old Testament kingdom promises. On the other hand, as we have seen, this teaching of Paul related to the church is never said to be the complete fulfillment of these prophecies, nor does it in any way negate a fulfillment of the prophecies that speak of a future role for the nation of Israel among the nations.

C. The Mystery and the Plan of Salvation

As we have seen, nothing in the apostle Paul's teaching about the mystery of the union of Jews and Gentiles explicitly suggests that what is currently taking place is the last phase of messianic salvation. Instead, when we consider the entire teaching about the divine mystery in Ephesians, we find evidence that this is only the first step toward fulfillment of God's purpose in Christ. That goal, expressed in the revelation of "the mystery of his will," is "to bring all things in heaven and on earth together under one head, even Christ" (Eph 1:9–10).

One great obstacle to bringing all things together was the great divide in the human race exemplified in the alienation between Jew and Gentile. The focus of Ephesians 3 is on overcoming this obstacle. The realization of the mystery through the proclamation of the apostolic gospel unites humankind into a new humanity with Christ as its head. In Christ

---

[75]McKelvey, *The New Temple*, 123.

the hostility that divided Jew and Gentile is dissolved through their reconciliation to God and consequently to each other.

But removing this obstacle is not the complete fulfillment of the mystery to sum up all things in Christ. The rebellious powers present another problem. Ephesians makes it clear that Christ has been exalted above all powers whether good or evil (1:20–22). But in God's administration of the mystery the time has not yet arrived for their hostile activity to be silenced. They remain as powerful opponents of the believer in the church (6:11–12). Other letters of Paul shed light on the struggle. Colossians speaks of all things being reconciled in Christ (1:15–22, cf. 15), effected through the peace made at the cross. But the ultimate outworking of reconciliation will occur only with the final subjugation, or forced "peace" (i.e., pacification), that comes when the powers are compelled to acknowledge Jesus as Lord (Php 1:10–11).[76]

The task for the church today is not to subjugate the powers, but to be "strong in the Lord and in his mighty power" and to equip itself with divine armor so that it can "stand against the devil's schemes" and "stand" against the onslaughts "when the day of evil comes" (Eph 6:10–13). The ultimate victory will be accomplished only through the personal intervention and reign of Christ (cf. 1Co 15:24–25).

The present outworking of the mystery in the church is, therefore, not the completion of the mystery, which is to bring all things together in Christ. Rather, as Meyer puts it, it is "a voucher of the redemption which embraces all mankind, . . . the highest manifestation of divine wisdom."[77] In short, the present working of mystery in Ephesians 3 in the constitution of the church is the initial stage in the realization of the divine plan of salvation in Christ, which is the comprehensive mystery of God.

D. Conclusion

Our study of Paul's teaching about the mystery in Ephesians 3 leads to several conclusions. First, the unity of Gentile and Jew in Christ is the fulfillment of the divine salvation promised for the messianic times, during which both the nations and Israel would enjoy God's blessing. As such this reality is permanent. Jew and Gentile will from now on stand

---

[76]Peter T. O'Brien, *Colossians, Philemon*, Word Biblical Commentary, vol. 44 (Waco, Tex.: Word Books, 1982), 55–57.

[77]Meyer, *Hand-Book to the Epistle to the Galatians and the Epistle to the Ephesians*, 416. In regard to Paul's teaching that the church is God's means to make his wisdom known to "the rulers and authorities in the heavenly realms" (Eph 3:10), Meyer states, "The Christian church . . . is, in its existence and its living development, as composed of Jews and Gentiles combined in a higher unity, the medium *de facto* for the divine wisdom becoming known . . . . the church of the redeemed is therefore, as it were, the mirror, by means of which the wisdom of God exhibits itself" (415–16; cf. also Barth, *Ephesians 1–3*, 364).

together and equal in their spiritual relation to God, described as having access to the Father through the Son in the Spirit (cf. Eph 2:18). Nothing in this mystery, however, suggests more than this equality of spiritual position in Christ. The union of Jew and Gentile in the church does not rule out the possibility of *functional* distinctions between Israel and the other nations in the future—in the same way that there are functional distinctions among believers in the church today amid spiritual equality.

Second, the revelation of the mystery is a new action of God. Although it was present in the Old Testament promise, it was to this time hidden in the counsel of God and hence unknown or not yet actualized. The church that is constituted by the working of this mystery in the uniting of Gentile and Jew in Christ is, therefore, truly a new work. The church subsists in the New Testament work of Christ's first coming and the bestowal of the Spirit.

Third, although the present manifestation of the mystery may be said to be the eschatological fulfillment of the promised salvation, it does not complete the mystery of God's salvation program for the world and the universe. The rest of that plan is not disclosed in the present revelation of the mystery described in Ephesians 3. But nothing makes it disjunctive with Paul's other teaching of the divine mystery as regards a future work with Israel (Ro 11:25–26) in accord with the many promises of the Old Testament that remain as yet unfulfilled.

III. THE MYSTERY OF THE INDWELLING CHRIST IN COLOSSIANS 1

To them God has chosen to make known among the Gentiles the glorious riches of this mystery, which is Christ in you, the hope of glory (Col 1:27).

Another aspect of the mysterious nature of the church that points to its distinctive nature, according to traditional dispensationalism, is the truth of the indwelling Christ. This teaching is a prominent theme throughout the epistles, but it is Paul's reference to this as a "mystery" in Colossians 1:27 that is of special concern to dispensationalists. Regarding "mystery" as truth that has not previously been a part of any revelation, dispensationalists have traditionally taught that Christ's indwelling the members of the church is a new reality that began at Pentecost. Therefore this indwelling is something unique to the believers of the present age who make up the church, the body of Christ. Charles C. Ryrie affirms that it is the indwelling of Christ that "makes the body a living organism, and this relationship was unknown in Old Testament times."[78]

---

[78]Ryrie, *Dispensationalism Today*, 135.

The truth of the indwelling Christ which forms the body of Christ is said to belong only to the present church age. Not only was it unknown in the experience of Old Testament saints, but it was not even predicted for the future kingdom age and therefore sets the reality of the nature of the church apart as unique in the work of God. According to John F. Walvoord, the Old Testament "never once anticipates such a situation as 'Christ in you.'" He further notes the contrast between this thought and the predicted position of Christ in the kingdom age:

> Everything in this passage [Col 1:24–27] stands in contrast to the Old Testament doctrine of the millennial kingdom. There the glory of the Lord will be manifest to all the earth and His dwelling is with men. Here His glory is veiled, but His presence is the hope of future glory. It is difficult to imagine a greater contrast between the position of Christ in the believer in this age and the position of Christ in the millennial kingdom.[79]

Traditional dispensationalists therefore have used the mystery of the indwelling Christ to support the concept of the church as a unique work of God during the present age and consequently a distinct entity from Israel and the nations.

Non-dispensationalists, by contrast, reject the idea that the indwelling Christ is unique to the church and the believers of this age. They recognize it as a new spiritual reality for all the people of God for all time. Moreover, since this new reality applies to both Jews and Gentiles equally, it is viewed as uniting all believers into one people of God—often called a "new Israel." This new "Spiritual Israel" supersedes the old nationalistic form, leaving no distinctive place for that nation in the plan of God.

Before seeking to determine the proper application of the mystery of "Christ in you," it is necessary to consider the meaning of this phrase.

A. The Content of the Mystery

Scholars disagree as to the meaning of the mystery, which is formally stated as "Christ in you [ἐν ὑμῖν], the hope of glory." Eduard Lohse and others take the preposition ἐν to mean "among," thereby making the mystery the proclamation of the gospel to the Gentiles. Lohse writes, "Doubtless this does not mean the pneumatic indwelling of the Lord in the hearts of the believers, but rather the Christ preached among the nations, the Lord proclaimed in the community's midst; cf. 2 Cor. 1:19, 'Christ Jesus, whom we preached among you' (Χριστὸς Ἰησοῦς, ὁ ἐν

---

[79]Walvoord, *The Millennial Kingdom*, 238.

ὑμῖν δι ἡμῶν κηρυχθείς)."[80] Understanding the mystery in this way makes it essentially the same as that in Ephesians 3, where the Gentiles are said to be "sharers together in the promise in Christ Jesus" (v. 6).

More interpreters, however, understand the mystery as the spiritual indwelling of Christ in believers. Curtis Vaughan rejects the interpretation of the offer of redemption to the Gentiles and instead asserts that "the context requires that we understand the phrase as referring to an inner subjective experience. The mystery, therefore, long hidden but now revealed is not the diffusion of the gospel among the Gentiles but the indwelling of Christ in his people, whether Jews or Gentiles."[81] The remainder of the verse that identifies the mystery of "Christ in you" as "the hope of glory" supports this understanding of the mystery as a subjective experience and thus the personal indwelling of Christ in believers. A. S. Peake draws this conclusion: "It may refer to the indwelling of Christ in the heart, and this is rendered probable by the addition of ελπὶς τ. δόξης [hope of glory]. The indwelling Christ constitutes in Himself a pledge of future glory."[82] The same thought is suggested in Colossians 3:4, where the believer's share in the future glory of Christ is related to his present indwelling life (cf. Ro 8:10).

Although we prefer this second interpretation, it is not entirely distinct from or opposed to the first. It is the indwelling of Christ in relation to the Gentiles that is specifically noted by Paul in the context. The emphasis on the Gentiles in relation to this mystery ties it in with the mystery of Ephesians 3. According to J. B. Lightfoot, "the one special 'mystery' which absorbs St Paul's thoughts in the Epistles to the Colossians and Ephesians is the free admission of the Gentiles on equal terms to the privileges of the covenant."[83]

---

[80]Eduard Lohse, *Colossians and Philemon* (Philadelphia: Fortress, 1971), 76; see also Ralph Martin, *Colossians and Philemon* (London: Oliphants, Marshall, 1974), 72; C. F. D. Moule, *The Epistles to the Colossians and to Philemon*, Cambridge Greek Testament Commentary (Cambridge: Cambridge Univ. Press, 1962), 85.

[81]Curtis Vaughan, "Colossians," in *The Expositor's Bible Commentary*, vol. 11 (Grand Rapids: Zondervan, 1978), p192; cf. O'Brien: "Christ therefore was 'in them' (not simply 'among' them'), which is an appropriate translation of the preposition ἐν in the clause γνωρίσαι . . . ἐν τοῖς ἔθνεσιν . . . but here the ἐν ὑμῖν . . . ἐν τοῖς ἔθνεσιν . . . , having particular reference to the Colossian readers, and with the verb ἐστιν points to Christ's indwelling in them as Gentile believers" (*Colossians, Philemon*, 87; Bornkamm, "μυστήριον, μυέω," in *TDNT*, 4:820).

[82]A. S. Peake, "The Epistle to the Colossians," *The Expositor's Greek Testament*, vol. 3 (Grand Rapids: Eerdmans, 1951), 517.

[83]Lightfoot, *St. Paul's Epistle to the Colossians and to Philemon*, 168. He says this while explaining the mystery as Christ "within" instead of "among" the Gentiles (169).

B. The Nature of the Mystery

As we have seen, the teaching in Colossians 1 that Christ indwells the believing Gentiles is an inherent part of the mystery in Ephesians 3, which concerns the promised messianic salvation for the Gentiles. There is an additional element here, however—namely, that this salvation involves the union of the Messiah with his people through spiritual indwelling.

While the prophecies do not make any explicit reference to the indwelling of the Messiah, there are concepts pointing in the direction of this truth. Russell Phillip Shedd sees these in the idea of the corporate personality found in the Old Testament (e.g., corporate involvement in blessing [Ge 18:23–32] and sin [Jos 7:16–26]) and the early Jewish conception of the solidarity of Israel with the rest of humanity, based primarily on the oneness in creation (cf. *Kid* 40b, 39b; *M Aboth* 3:18) and sin (cf. *Sifra on Leviticus* 27a; *Secrets of Enoch* 41:1f.). From this evidence Shedd concludes that "the doctrine of the Body of Christ is . . . an explicit application of the Hebraic conception of corporate personality." This was not the spiritual union that is found in Christ, but it nevertheless provided the type of which "the unity of the Church is the anti-type, the real thing."[84]

The solidarity becomes more explicitly related to the Messiah in the apocalyptic writings. According to W. D. Davies,

> It is now generally accepted that the idea of a Messiah in apocalyptic did involve the idea of a community of the Messiah; and whether we trace this conception, as it is found in Jesus, to the Book of Enoch or to Dan. 7, or to Isa. 53, it is a fact that Jesus was aware that he was gathering around Himself a community of people pledged to loyalty to Him above all else.[85]

Although the apocalyptic references do not explicitly ground the community in the indwelling of the Messiah, Albert Schweitzer rightly speaks of this eschatological conception as the "union of those who are elect to the Messianic Kingdom with one another and with the Messiah."[86]

Jesus himself builds a bridge between this predicted solidarity of the Messiah and his people and the fulfillment of it in the spiritual indwelling of Christ. This bridge appears in the peculiar intimacy of Jesus' relationship with his disciples. Jesus taught that those who accept the

---

[84]Russell Phillip Shedd, *Man in Community* (Grand Rapids: Eerdmans, 1964), 165, 199; cf. also E. Earle Ellis, *The Old Testament in Early Christianity* (Tübingen: J. C. B. Mohr [Paul Siebeck], 1991), 110–12.

[85]W. D. Davies, *Paul and Rabbinic Judaism* (London: SPCK, 1965), 99–100.

[86]Albert Schweitzer, *The Mysticism of Paul the Apostle* (New York: Henry Holt, 1931), 101.

disciples accept him (Mt 10:40). To help a brother in Christ was in fact to help Christ himself (Mt 25:40). Although, as we will see, Jesus connects his indwelling with the sending of the Holy Spirit, there is already an identification that anticipates this true spiritual union.

More directly related to the mystery of the indwelling Christ is the prophetic teaching of the indwelling Spirit. At the heart of the new covenant that God promised for the messianic age is the gift of the Spirit, who was not only to be "poured out" upon his people (e.g., Joel 2:29; Isa 44:3; Eze 39:29), but would also live "within" them. According to Ezekiel, God promised to "put my Spirit in you and move you to follow my decrees" (36:27; cf. 37:14). That the indwelling Spirit would promote obedience to the law corresponds with Jeremiah's statement that under the new covenant, God would put his law within his people and write it on their hearts (Jer 31:33).

Upon turning to the New Testament we find that the indwelling of Christ is directly related to the fulfillment of this promised indwelling of the Spirit. Jesus not only foretold the coming of the Holy Spirit but also said he came to the disciples through the presence of the Spirit. Jesus told them he would ask the Father to send the Counselor, or Paraclete, then added, "I will not leave you as orphans; I will come to you." Obviously connecting his statement with the coming of the Spirit, he then said, "On that day you will realize that I am in my Father, and you are in me, and I am in you" (Jn. 14:16, 18, 20). Thus he affirmed his indwelling through the presence of the Spirit.[87]

This connection between the indwelling of Christ as a result of the indwelling of the Spirit is made elsewhere in the New Testament. The new covenant is the "ministry of the Spirit," but it is realized by receiving Christ (2Co 3:8, 14). The Spirit comes as the "Spirit of Christ" (cf. Ro 8:9; Ac 16:7) so that Paul is able to say, "Now the Lord is the Spirit," referring to their functional identity (2Co 3:17). In other words, the Lord carries on his ministry in his people through the indwelling Spirit.[88]

Nowhere is this relationship clearer than in Paul's prayer for the Ephesian believers: "that . . . he may strengthen you with power through his Spirit in your inner being, so that Christ may dwell in your hearts through faith . . . that you may be filled to the measure of all the fullness of God" (Eph 3:16–19). The link is likewise evident when Paul ties together

---

[87]See Raymond E. Brown, *The Gospel According to John XIII–XXI*, Anchor Bible (Garden City, N.Y.: Doubleday, 1970), 644–47; J. H. Bernard, *A Critical and Exegetical Commentary on the Gospel According to St. John* (Edinburgh: T & T Clark, 1928), 2:548; Henry Barclay Swete, *The Holy Spirit in the New Testament* (Grand Rapids: Baker, 1964), 300.

[88]Other references indicating a functional identity between the exalted Christ and the Spirit are Luke 12:11–12 parallel with 21:14–15 and Acts 10:13–14 parallel with 10:19. Compare also the letters to the seven churches in Revelation 2–3, where the message is from both Christ and the Spirit, e.g., 2:1, 7, etc.

the concepts of the "Spirit of God" who "dwells in you," "having the Spirit of Christ," and "Christ . . . in you" (Ro 8:9–10).

Still more evidence of this connection lies in Paul's explaining the mystery of the indwelling Christ as "the hope of glory" (Col 1:27). The terms "hope" and "glory" are both related not only to Christ but also to the presence of the Spirit. The new covenant "ministry of the Spirit" produces "hope" (2Co 3:8, 11–12; cf. Ro 8:23–24). Therefore Paul prays that believers "may overflow with hope by the power of the Holy Spirit" (Ro 15:13).[89] Similarly, while our participation in glory, whether in the present "hope of glory" or ultimately in the consummation (e.g., Ro 8:17; Col 3:4), rests on participation in Christ, it is also realized through the Spirit. The believer is presently changed into the image of Christ "with ever-increasing glory, which comes from the Lord, who is the Spirit" (2Co 3:18). The Spirit now "rests" on believers as "the Spirit of glory" (1Pe 4:14).

This functional identity of Christ and the Spirit in relation to "the hope of glory," along with the other divine ministries in the lives of believers, affirms the truth that the indwelling of Christ is inherently related to the indwelling of the Spirit promised in the new covenant.[90]

Because the indwelling of Christ is vitally related to Old Testament predictions of the Spirit's presence through the new covenant, we cannot view the mystery described in Colossians 1:27 as involving only something totally new, unrelated to prophecy, and unique to the church. The explicit concept of the indwelling Messiah had not been revealed, and therefore some aspect of the mystery must be viewed as the revelation of previously unknown truth. But the New Testament's connecting this truth to the Old Testament concepts of human solidarity, and especially the predictions of the inwardness of the final divine work in the human heart and the indwelling of God himself through the Spirit in the new covenant, also shows that this mystery is not totally unrelated to previous prophecy. As in the case of the mystery of the one body in Ephesians 3, the nature of the mystery in Colossians 1 has to do with revelation in the sense of making real or actual something that was previously foretold, but not yet fulfilled.

Not only is the *nature* of the mystery of the indwelling Christ similar to that of the union of Jew and Gentile in the body of Christ, but

---

[89]The relationship of Christ and the Spirit in Christian hope is explained thus by Rudolf Bultmann: "Thus Christian hope rests on the divine act of salvation accomplished in Christ, and, since this is eschatological, hope itself is an eschatological blessing, i.e., now is the time when we may have confidence. The waiting which is part of ἐλπίς [hope] is effected by the Spirit as the gift of the last time" ("ἐλπίς, κτλ," in *Theological Dictionary of the New Testament*, vol. 2 [Grand Rapids: Eerdmans, 1964], 532).

[90]For other parallels between the ministry of Christ and the Spirit in the life of believers, see Lewis Smedes, *All Things Made New* (Grand Rapids: Eerdmans, 1970), 62–63.

also, fundamentally, is the *content*. Both deal with the manifestation of the new messianic salvation that has come through the Christ. C. F. D. Moule captures the essence of both mysteries when he says,

> It is urged by some (e.g., Mitton, *Eph*, p. 89) that in Ephesians, though not in Colossians, a further step is taken, and the m., instead of being equated with Christ himself, is the inclusion of the Gentiles with the Jews in the Church, Eph. iii. 3–6. This is regarded as one of the points of difference between Ephesians and Colossians. But is not Col. i. 26–9 intended in this sense? The m. is "that Christ is among you (Gentiles)"—or (better still) the m. is *both* Christ himself *and* the fact that he is among them.[91]

IV. CONCLUSION

Our study of the Pauline mysteries related to the church leads to a mediating conclusion between traditional dispensationalism and non-dispensationalism. Contrary to the former, the contents of both mysteries—i.e., the equal participation of Jew and Gentile in the body of Christ (Eph 3) and his indwelling in his people (Col 1)—are best understood as fulfillments of Old Testament prophecies. Although a greater understanding of these mysteries is revealed in the New Testament, their basic substance was already contained in the Old Testament promises. The former hiddenness thus relates as much to their not being realized or actualized in history as to any new disclosure of information.

This understanding of the mysteries, however, does not lead to the non-dispensational view that any future distinction or special role for the nation of Israel is thereby eliminated. Paul's discussions of both the mystery of the composition of the body and the indwelling of Christ are concerned with spiritual salvation, i.e., a saving relationship with God. The particular truth of Ephesians 3—that Jews and Gentiles have equal standing with God—is only the fulfillment of the promise that Gentiles would one day share God's eschatological salvation along with Israel. To say that this equal standing means Israel has no future place as a nation in the service of God is to draw a conclusion that is not found in Paul's teaching about the mystery.

---

[91]Moule, *The Epistles of Paul the Apostle to the Colossians and to Philemon*, 82–83.

Chapter 7

The Baptism with the Spirit
and the Metaphors of the Church

ALONG WITH the concept of mystery, traditional dispensationalists have viewed Paul's teaching about the baptism with the Spirit and the body of Christ in 1 Corinthians 12:13 as evidence for the uniqueness of the church. The question of how to apply the metaphor of the body to the church raises the same question in regard to other metaphors that are cited to affirm that uniqueness. These concepts are central to a proper understanding of the church and therefore impinge directly on the place of the church in God's program of historical redemption.

I. THE BAPTISM OF THE SPIRIT

Like many other scholars, dispensationalists view the coming of the Holy Spirit on the day of Pentecost as the inauguration of the church.[1] To the dispensationalist, this connection is particularly related to the biblical

---

[1]For example, James D. G. Dunn: "Pentecost inaugurates the age of the Church" (*Baptism in the Holy Spirit* [Philadelphia: Westminster, 1970], 49); Eduard Schweizer: ". . . he [Luke] sees here [the coming of the Spirit at Pentecost] the beginning of the age of the Church" ("πνευμα, κτλ," *Theological Dictionary of the New Testament*, vol. 6, ed. Gerhard Friedrich [Grand Rapids: Eerdmans, 1968], 411); Emil Brunner: "The outpouring of the Holy Ghost and the existence of the *Ecclesia* are so closely connected that they may be actually identified" (*The Misunderstanding of the Church* [Philadelphia: Westminster, 1953], 161).

concept of "the baptism of the Holy Spirit." Earl D. Radmacher states, "The chief argument for the beginning of the church on the day of Pentecost relates to the baptism of the Holy Spirit."[2] This reasoning grows out of Paul's explanation that the body of Christ, which is directly identified with the church (e.g., Eph 1:22–23; Col 1:18), is formed through the baptism with the Spirit (1Co 12:13).

Since the church is a distinct work of God belonging only to the present age, traditional dispensationalists, contrary to others, contend that the Spirit baptism is applicable only to this present church era. Merrill F. Unger expresses this position clearly:

> The baptizing work of the Holy Spirit is the only ministry of the Spirit confined to this age. It is distinctive to the formation of the church, the body of Christ. When this particular group of God's elect is completed and called out of the world, there will be no longer any need for the baptizing work of the Spirit, and it will terminate.[3]

As an inherent corollary, the concept of Spirit baptism is declared to be absent from any Old Testament prophecy. It belongs to the mystery of the church, which dispensationalists have understood as involving only the revelation of totally new truth. According to Unger, its "essential nature" and "unique place in the divine program are such as to forbid it occurring, or even being predicted there (i.e., in the Old Testament)."[4]

This dispensational understanding provokes some difficult questions about the real meaning of this concept and its relation to the messianic salvation predicted in the Old Testament prophecies. It is especially problematic that the New Testament writers frequently associate the coming of the Spirit with the fulfillment of God's promise.

A. The Meaning of the Baptism with the Spirit

The terminology "baptism with the Spirit" occurs seven times in the New Testament: once in each Gospel (Mt 3:11; Mk 1:8; Lk 3:16; Jn 1:33), twice in the book of Acts (1:5; 11:16), and once in Paul's writings (1Co 12:13). In each instance the construction of the Greek phrase is identical. It is a baptism $\dot{\epsilon}\nu$ $\pi\nu\epsilon\acute{\upsilon}\mu\alpha\tau\iota$ $\dot{\alpha}\gamma\acute{\iota}\omega$ (" 'in,' 'with,' or 'by,' the Holy Spirit").[5] The context is the final determiner of the meaning in each usage,

---

[2] Earl D. Radmacher, *What the Church Is All About* (Chicago: Moody Press, 1978), 217; cf. Charles C. Ryrie, *Dispensationalism Today* (Chicago: Moody Press, 1965), 136–37.

[3] Merrill F. Unger, *The Baptism and Gifts of the Holy Spirit* (Chicago: Moody Press, 1974), 40.

[4] Unger, *The Baptism and Gifts of the Holy Spirit*, 102; cf. Ryrie, *Dispensationalism Today*, 136–37.

[5] First Corinthians 12:13 does not include $\dot{\alpha}\gamma\acute{\iota}\omega$.

but the prior uses of the same terminology must be considered, especially since most of the uses seem parallel. To understand Paul's meaning, therefore, it is necessary to trace the meaning of this concept in the Gospels and Acts.

1. Baptism with the Spirit in the Gospels. The first use of the terminology "baptism with the Spirit" comes in the preaching of John the Baptist, who contrasts that baptism with his own water baptism (Mt 3:11; Mk 1:8; Lk 3:16; Jn 1:33). John baptized "with [ἐν] water," and the Messiah will baptize "with [ἐν] the Holy Spirit." The use of the same preposition in the parallel expressions shows that "water" and "the Spirit" indicates that the Spirit is the element of the baptism performed by the Coming One even as water was the element of John's baptism. Thus in "the baptism with the Spirit" in the Gospel accounts, Christ and not the Spirit is the agent of the baptism. The Spirit is the "element" that Christ uses. To be sure, the Spirit, unlike water, is a living dynamic person who brings the effects of the life of God with his presence. But this truth does not change the basic truth of the Gospel statements, namely, that Christ is the Baptizer who baptizes people with (or "in" or "by") the Holy Spirit.

We find in the historical context of John's ministry what he meant by this expectation of the baptism of the Spirit. He made his prediction in connection with his call for repentance and his proclamation to prepare for the coming of the kingdom, which was "near" (Mt 3:2). Without any explanation to the contrary, we are probably to understand his concept of the coming kingdom as involving the establishment of the messianic kingdom predicted in Old Testament prophecy, including the reestablishment of the political theocracy of the nation Israel. George E. Ladd states, "John the Baptist had announced the coming of the Kingdom of God (Matt. 3:2) by which he understood the coming of the Kingdom foretold in the Old Testament."[6] More explicitly, A. B. Bruce wrote that John "meant the people of Israel converted to righteousness, and in consequence blessed with national prosperity."[7]

The context of John the Baptist's statement suggests, therefore, that we must look to the Old Testament prophecies for the meaning of Spirit baptism. There we find promises of the Spirit's coming upon the Messiah (Isa 11:2; cf. 42:1; 61:1) and an eschatological outpouring of the Spirit (Isa 32:15; 44:3; Eze 36:27; 37:14; 39:29; Joel 2:28; Zec 12:10). While the Old Testament prophecies depict the Spirit as coming from God and never expressly from the Messiah, there are intimations that Jewish thinking within the Qumran community was already pointing in this direction.[8]

---

[6]George E. Ladd, *The Gospel of the Kingdom* (Grand Rapids: Eerdmans, 1959), 53–54.
[7]A. B. Bruce, *The Kingdom of God* (New York: Scribner's, 1896), 62.
[8]For a good discussion of the meaning of "baptism and fire" and the possible influence of the Qumran teaching on John's statement, see James D. G. Dunn, "Spirit-and-Fire Baptism,"

Whether John was influenced by these or was simply led by the inspiration of the Holy Spirit, it is not difficult to see how John could look upon the Messiah as the means of the coming of the Spirit.

John's speaking of "fire" along with the Spirit in the accounts of Matthew (3:11) and Luke (3:16) adds to our understanding of his statements. The "fire" has been variously interpreted as "a purifying agent along with the Holy Spirit" that is applicable to the people of God[9] or the judgment fire appointed for the wicked.[10] It is probably best to see it, as James Dunn does, as "one purgative act of messianic judgment which both repentant and unrepentant would experience, the former as a blessing, the latter as destruction."[11] The concept of cleansing and judgment related to both the Spirit and fire is also prominent in the Old Testament prophecies (cf. Isa 4:4; 11:4; Zec 13:9; Mal 3:2–3).

What is significant is that John joins fire and the Spirit into one baptism.[12] It is a Spirit-fire baptism. Both its judgment and its blessing of salvation, according to John's expectations, would "take place in a single eschatological event."[13] Thus John did not foresee the coming of the kingdom in two stages, involving both present and future aspects, as that was revealed later on. Rather, his portrait is rather that of the Old Testament prophecies that do not separate the first and second comings of the Messiah, but simply associate the salvation and judgment related to the kingdom with the coming of the Messiah.[14]

John's statement of the baptism with the Spirit and fire thus anticipates the outpouring of the Spirit foretold by the prophets in connection with the messianic age. His reference to the coming of the Spirit as a "baptism," while not found in the Old Testament promises, does not indicate something different. The Old Testament frequently used

---

Novum Testamentum 14 (1972): 81–92; Joseph A. Fitzmyer, *The Gospel According to Luke I–IX*, Anchor Bible, vol. 28 (New York: Doubleday, 1981), 474.

[9]D. A. Carson, "Matthew," in *The Expositor's Bible Commentary*, vol. 8, ed. Frank E. Gaebelein (Grand Rapids: Zondervan, 1984), 105; Fitzmyer, *The Gospel According to Luke I–IX*, 474. For the Qumran expectation of the Messiah in relation to John's statement about the baptism with the Spirit, see Dunn, "Spirit-and-Fire Baptism," 87–92.

[10]George E. Ladd, *The Presence of the Future* (Grand Rapids: Eerdmans, 1974), 107.

[11]Dunn, *Baptism in the Holy Spirit*, 11; cf. also John Nolland, *Luke 1–9:20*, Word Biblical Commentary, vol. 35A (Dallas: Word Books, 1989), 153.

[12]The preposition ἐν ("with" or "in") is not repeated with "fire," thus joining both "Spirit" and "fire" under one preposition, which usually suggests a unified concept. See M. J. Harris, "Prepositions and Theology in the Greek New Testament," *New International Dictionary of the New Testament*, vol. 3, ed. Colin Brown (Grand Rapids: Zondervan, 1978), 1178.

[13]Ladd, *The Presence of the Future*, 108.

[14]The statements of Jesus that John is in some sense (at least potentially) Elijah (Mt 11:11–14; 17:9–13) also point to an expectation by John of the end-times messianic era predicted by Malachi. Dunn says, "John clearly regarded himself as a herald of the End; he probably saw himself in the role of Elijah, the precursor of 'the great and terrible day of the Lord' (Mal. 4.5)" (*Baptism in the Holy Spirit*, 13).

verbs associated with inundation in connection with the Spirit, as in "pour out" (e.g., Isa 32:15; Joel 2:28–29; Zec 12:10). This description of the bestowal of the Spirit, as Dunn notes, no doubt made it "very easy for John to speak of the messianic gift of the Spirit in a metaphor drawn from the rite which was his own hall-mark."[15]

We conclude, therefore, that the concept of "the baptism with the Spirit" in the Gospels refers not to something particular for the church, but rather to the coming of the Spirit promised for the messianic age. His coming not only marked the inauguration of the new age, but it brought his permanent presence as the Life-Giver of the new creation.

2. The Baptism with the Spirit in Acts. The "baptism with the Spirit" terminology is used twice in the book of Acts. The similarity of the first reference to the Gospel accounts makes it clear that Luke intends the same meaning when he records Jesus as saying, "For John baptized with water, but in a few days you will be baptized with the Holy Spirit" (1:5).[16] That imminent baptism was the same as that proclaimed by John the Baptist, namely the fulfillment of the Old Testament promise of the messianic bestowal of the Spirit. Although Pentecost clearly fit the Lord's prediction, the baptism terminology does not appear in Acts 2.

However, Peter did use that language later in connection with the coming of the Spirit on the Gentiles at Caesarea (Ac 10), so it is clear that Pentecost was the fulfillment of the Lord's prediction. Recounting the astounding happenings in the house of Cornelius, Peter declared that "the Holy Spirit came on them as he had come on us at the beginning. Then I remembered what the Lord had said: 'John baptized with water, but you will be baptized with the Holy Spirit'" (11:15–16). The "beginning" could only be a reference to the Pentecost event. Peter's explanation not only identifies the time of the promised fulfillment, but indicates the meaning of this event for the early church. The Spirit's coming at Pentecost was nothing less than the fulfillment of the Old Testament promise of the messianic outpouring of the Spirit.

That this is the meaning of Pentecost is confirmed in Peter's appeal to the prophecy of Joel 2:28–32 to explain the event. As the confused onlookers wondered what was going on (Ac 2:5–13)—especially with regard to the tongues-speaking—Peter asserted, "This is what was spoken

---

[15]Dunn, *Baptism in the Holy Spirit*, 12–13.

[16]While Luke's gospel account includes "fire" with the baptism with the Spirit, "fire" is absent in his Acts account, both in 1:5 and 11:16. It is also not found in the other New Testament occurrence in 1 Corinthians 12:13. Perhaps it was omitted in these later instances because the messianic work of salvation and judgment associated together in the coming of the Messiah according to Old Testament prophecy had by now clearly been separated into two comings because of the rejection of Jesus. The "fire" that spoke especially to the work of judgment was thought of by the early church as primarily associated the future coming of Christ.

by the prophet Joel: 'In the last days, God says, I will pour out my Spirit on all people. Your sons and daughters will prophesy' " (vv. 16–17). Apparently linking the tongues-speaking with the concept of prophecy, both being Spirit-inspired speech,[17] Peter affirmed that the eschatological time (i.e., "the last days") had arrived and the beginning of the fulfillment of the promised outpouring of the Spirit for all people had been inaugurated.[18]

Peter was clearly focusing on the fulfillment of Joel's prophecy, but this does not mean he was teaching that all of Joel's words, including the wonders in heaven and signs on earth (cf. vv. 19–20), were fulfilled at Pentecost. The coming of the Spirit, evidenced especially in the bestowal of the gift of inspired speech, signaled the onset of the fulfillment of the eschatological days. Like the bestowal of the Spirit, these other events belonged to those same days, but need not occur simultaneously. Peter, of course, did not know at that time that Christ's return would be delayed for many centuries, and he may have expected the other phenomena to occur soon. At any rate, he probably quoted the entire prophecy of Joel 2:28–32, according to Richard Longenecker, "because of its traditional messianic significance and because its final sentence ('And everyone who calls on the name of the Lord will be saved') leads logically to the kerygma section of his sermon."[19]

That the "baptism with the Spirit" and similar experiences of the bestowal of the Spirit are connected to the Old Testament promise of the coming Spirit is seen also in the similarity of terminology. Like other prophetic passages already cited, Joel's prophecy uses water imagery of the "pouring out" of the Spirit (cf. Ac 2:17–18). Peter used the same terminology in his Pentecost sermon in declaring that the exalted Christ had "poured out" the promised Holy Spirit (v. 33). The coming of the Spirit on Cornelius and his household is also described as a "pouring out" (10:45).[20] The use of this Old Testament terminology in Acts to describe "the baptism with the Spirit" clearly demonstrates that the baptism is understood to be the fulfillment of the Old Testament prophecy.

Further evidence that the "baptism with the Spirit" in Acts fulfilled

---

[17]On the fact that Joel speaks of prophecy whereas tongues occurred at Pentecost, Ernst Haenchen explains, "Joel does not mention speech in foreign languages, which is reason enough why Peter's discourse cannot refer to the miracle of the languages. Ecstatic utterance, on the other hand, is covered by the προφητεύειν [prophesy] of the quotation" (*The Acts of the Apostles* [Philadelphia: Westminster, 1971], 178, n. 11).

[18]Richard Longenecker views Peter's use of "last days," which gives essentially the same sense as Joel's original "afterward," as a heightening of "the note of fulfillment" ("The Acts of the Apostles," in *The Expositor's Bible Commentary*, vol. 9, ed. Frank E. Gaebelein [Grand Rapids: Zondervan, 1982], 275).

[19]Longenecker, "The Acts of the Apostles," 276.

[20]The use of the terminology "falling" or "coming on," which could be viewed as corresponding to the idea of the Spirit's being "poured out," is also frequently used in Acts (8:16; 10:44; 11:15; 19:6).

Old Testament prophecy is found in the terms "promise" and "gift." According to Peter, what was received from the Father on the day of Pentecost was "the promise of the Holy Spirit" (Ac 2:33). This marked the fulfillment, not only of the words of Jesus that he would send the Spirit from the Father (e.g., Jn 15:26), but ultimately of the promise of God to Abraham to bring blessing to all people (Gal 3:14; cf. Lk 24:49). Thus the words of Peter in his Pentecostal proclamation link the "gift of the Holy Spirit" with "the promise . . . for you and your children," words reminiscent of the Abrahamic covenant promise (Ge 17:7–10).[21] The Spirit baptism also brought the "gift" of the Spirit (Ac 2:38; 8:20; 10:45; 11:17). It is not so much a specific ministry of the Spirit that is involved in the "baptism," but the coming of the Spirit himself in fulfillment of God's promise to give the gift of his Spirit to his people in the last days.

The interrelatedness of all this terminology is well summed up by John Stott: "these penitent believers received the *gift* of the Spirit which God had *promised* before the Day of Pentecost, and were thus *baptized* with the Spirit whom God *poured out* on the Day of Pentecost."[22]

So we see that the two references in Acts to the "baptism with the Spirit" as well as terminology used to describe the same reality reveal the same basic meaning as the accounts in the Gospels. The "baptism with the Spirit" is the bestowing of the Spirit that was prophesied in the Old Testament to take place in the eschatological days of the Messiah. Although the terminology in Acts is expressed in the passive (i.e., "you will be baptized," 1:5; 11:15), it is still clear that Christ is conceived as the agent of the baptism. As Peter explained at Pentecost, it was the exalted Christ who "has received from the Father the promised Holy Spirit and poured out what you now see and hear" (2:33).

3. The Baptism with the Spirit in 1 Corinthians 12:13. The final New Testament use of the specific phrase "the baptism with [ἐν] the Spirit" occurs as Paul is teaching about the unity of believers in the body of Christ. According to Paul, that unity rests on the fact that "we were all baptized by one Spirit into one body . . . and we were all given the one Spirit to drink" (1Co 12:13). Does the phrase here mean the same thing that it does elsewhere—namely, the bestowal of the Spirit promised in the Old Testament? Or does it signify a work of the Spirit that is unique to the believers of this age, as traditional dispensationalists have taught?

Except for the addition of the word "one," the phraseology concerning the Spirit baptism in this verse is identical to the other six prior uses in the New Testament. The baptism is ἐν πνεύματι, "by ['with,' or 'in'] the Spirit." Unless the context strongly indicates otherwise, this similarity of language argues for the same meaning. In the instances where

---

[21]Cf. also the reference to the Abrahamic covenant in Peter's address in Acts 3:25.
[22]John Stott, *Baptism and Fullness* (Downers Grove, Ill.: InterVarsity Press, 1979), 25.

the act of baptism is seen more fully, the phrase clearly indicates that the baptism is enacted by Christ, with the Spirit as the element paralleling the water in John's baptism (e.g., Mt 3:11). This is also seen in the express teaching of Acts that the Spirit is "poured out" by the exalted Christ (2:33).

While acknowledging the Pauline use of the Spirit baptism as parallel to the earlier uses, traditional dispensationalists have understood the Pauline reference as teaching the Spirit as the agent of baptism. Christ is still in the remote sense the Baptizer, but the Spirit is the agent by whom Christ accomplishes the work of baptizing. Thus one frequently hears reference to the "baptizing work of the Spirit."[23] Even though the preposition ἐν can be used in the sense of agency, it never has this meaning when it is used with the word "baptism" in the New Testament. According to Dunn, when ἐν is used with "baptism," it "never designates the one who performs the baptism; . . . [rather] it always indicates the element in which the baptisand is immersed (or with which he is deluged)."[24] This holds true not only for all references to baptism with water,[25] but also for the instances where baptism with the Spirit is contrasted with water baptism (Mt 3:11; Mk 1:8; Lk 3:16; Jn 1:33; Ac 1:5; 11:16).

The use of the preposition with baptism generally—and the identity of Paul's phrase with the other six occurrences specifically— strongly argues for keeping "Spirit" parallel with the way "water" is used in ritual baptism. The agent of the baptism, although not expressed, would be understood as Christ in conformity with the express teaching of the Gospel accounts and the implied teaching of Acts. As indicated earlier, this does not mean that the Spirit must be seen as inert or without effect; it only states that Paul's statement of the baptism with or by the Spirit is the same Spirit baptism as that promised in the Gospels and Acts and inaugurated at Pentecost. It is the bestowal of the Spirit by the Messiah promised by the Old Testament prophets.

It may be argued that Paul's statement "we were all baptized by one Spirit into one body" yields a strange picture of Christ baptizing his people into himself. The idea of Christ's acting to incorporate individuals

---

[23]The Greek preposition ἐν ("by," NIV) is said to be used instrumentally in this verse in the sense of personal agency. See Lewis Sperry Chafer, *Major Bible Themes*, rev. John F. Walvoord (Grand Rapids: Zondervan, 1974), 109. Compare also the title of Merrill F. Unger's work *The Baptizing Work of the Holy Spirit* (Chicago: Scripture Press, 1953).

[24]Dunn, *Baptism in the Holy Spirit*, 128; also D. A. Carson, *Showing the Spirit* (Grand Rapids: Baker, 1987), 46–47; Gordon D. Fee, *The First Epistle to the Corinthians*, New International Commentary on the New Testament (Grand Rapids: Eerdmans, 1987), 605–6. Fee feels that the use of ἐν in this instance is locative, "expressing the 'element' in which they have all been immersed."

[25]Matthew 3:11; Mark 1:8; Luke 3:16; John 1:26, 33; Acts 1:5; 11:16; cf. also Matthew 3:6; John 3:23.

into his body is, of course, not preposterous. He surely acts in the process of salvation, which entails believers' union with him. But Paul's statement need not be seen as painting exactly this picture. The Greek preposition εἰς ("into," NIV) used in the phrase "into one body" also has the sense of movement toward or into a goal. When it is used after verbs of motion like "baptize," εἰς has "the sense of movement towards so as to be in."[26] Thus the picture is not simply that Christ immerses his people into his body, but rather that he pours out or deluges his people with the Spirit with the goal of forming one body, which is finally Christ's own body, to which as the head he provides life, leadership, and sustenance.

Gordon Fee considers the idea of "goal" most prominent here. He sums up Paul's meaning in these words: "the purpose of our common experience of the Spirit is that we be formed into one body. Hence, 'we all were immersed in the one Spirit, so as to become one body.'" Fee then shows how this statement fits Paul's emphasis on the unity of the members of the church: "How did the many of them all become one body? By their common, lavish experience of the Spirit."[27]

4. *Conclusion.* A study of the six occurrences of Spirit-baptism terminology leads to the conclusion that they all bear essentially the same meaning. There may be in some instances a particular reason for using the phrase, such as Paul's emphasis on the unity produced by the shared experience of baptism. But the meaning of the act that is termed "baptism with the Spirit" remains the same. As we have seen, it is sometimes equated with the "pouring out" of the Spirit. It is the "gift" of the Spirit and the fulfillment of the "promise." As such, the "baptism with the Spirit" is nothing less than the fulfillment of the Old Testament eschatological promises related to the new presence and ministry of the Spirit with the people of God.

B. The Application of the Baptism with the Spirit

If the phenomenon of the baptism with the Spirit is in reality the outpouring of the Spirit promised for messianic times, then its application is ultimately for all people. Joel's prophecy that the Spirit would be poured out on "all people" (2:28) signifies in its original context the coming of the Spirit upon all within the covenant nation of Israel (cf. v. 27).[28] This is in harmony with the other promises that the Spirit would

---

[26]Dunn, *Baptism in the Holy Spirit*, 128.

[27]Fee, *The First Epistle to the Corinthians*, 606. The same meaning is evident in C. K. Barrett's translation and comment: "in one Spirit we were all baptized so as to become (εἰς, not local, but describing the result of the process—so Weiss) one body, his body" (*A Commentary on the First Epistle to the Corinthians* [New York: Harper & Row, 1968], 288).

[28]Leslie C. Allen, *The Books of Joel, Obadiah, Jonah and Micah* (Grand Rapids: Eerdmans, 1976), 98; cf. also Carl Friedrich Keil, *The Twelve Minor Prophets*, Biblical Commentary on the Old Testament (reprint, Grand Rapids: Eerdmans, 1949), 1:211.

come upon Israel, as already noted (cf. Eze 39:29). In light of Peter's later amazement at the coming of the Spirit on the Gentiles (Ac 10:45), this was apparently also his understanding when he used Joel's prophecy on the day of Pentecost.

Nevertheless, Peter also spoke of the promise for "all who are far off" (Ac 2:39). By this he was no doubt thinking of the Jews of the Dispersion, but perhaps also of Gentiles who became proselytes.[29] The work of God that began with Cornelius—giving the Spirit directly to the Gentiles—along with Paul's identification of "those far off" with Gentiles (Eph 2:13, 17) shows clearly that the Spirit was not intended for Israel alone, but for all people anywhere who received Christ in faith. Although the Old Testament did not explicitly predict the coming of the Spirit on the Gentiles, it did predict the sharing of the messianic salvation with them. Inherent in this new covenant salvation, as taught in both Testaments, is the gift of the Spirit. Thus the baptism with the Spirit, as Stott says, is "a universal blessing for members of the covenant. It is part and parcel of belonging to the new age."[30]

The baptism with the Spirit is therefore not some unique ministry only for the people of the present church age, from Pentecost to the rapture, but rather is the sharing by members of the church in the Spirit's ministry of the new covenant. The baptism is at the heart of the messianic salvation that has already begun in the revelation of the mysteries that pertain to present-day believers. The fact that both Israel and the Gentiles participate in Spirit baptism points to their common identity in their spiritual relationship to God and his salvation. This common identity, however, does not remove all differences in their roles in the historical purposes of God any more than spiritual equality in the church removes all differences of function among church members.

II. THE METAPHORS OF THE CHURCH

The recognition that Spirit baptism belongs to all of the participants of the new covenant, including the nation of Israel when it turns to the Messiah, raises the question how to apply the images or metaphors associated with the present work of God in the church. This question is especially important in relation to the metaphor of the body. According to the apostle Paul, baptism with the Spirit forms the body of Christ (1Co 12:13). The body, in turn, is frequently identified with the church (e.g., Eph 1:22–23; Col 1:18). From this we could conclude that all participants in the new covenant, including the nation of Israel, are included in the church as the body of Christ and therefore any distinction between Israel

---

[29]Richard Rackham, *The Acts of the Apostles* (London: Methuen, 1901), 31.
[30]Stott, *Baptism and Fullness*, 43.

and the church—which is at the heart of the dispensationalism interpretation—is prohibited. And what can be said of the body would seem to apply
to the other images of the church also.

Dispensationalists have traditionally tended to interpret the various
images as descriptions of the church as a distinct entity rather than as
simply figurative language used to describe spiritual truth that may apply
to others besides the church. In this view, the body of Christ refers to the
church as a special group of people in distinction from other peoples of
God, that is, Israel or gentile saints of other ages. This thought is
illustrated in the note about the "Bride of Christ" found in The New
Scofield Reference Bible: " 'The marriage of the Lamb' . . . is the
consummation of the marriage of Christ and the Church as His bride. . . .
The Lamb's wife is . . . to be distinguished from Israel, the unfaithful wife
of the LORD . . . , who is to be restored in the millennium."[31]

This view of the metaphors does not seem appropriate in light of
their usage in Scripture. Nonliteral language is used by the biblical writers
to teach spiritual concepts in a way beyond the capacity of merely literal
statements. Proper interpretation of the metaphors thus involves seeking
to determine the meaning of the spiritual truth that the author seeks to
convey and its contextual application. The fact that a certain metaphor is
used in a particular context simply teaches a particular truth in that
context. It does not necessarily indicate anything with regard to the
application of that truth in another context, unless (1) it teaches an explicit
exclusivity, or (2) the truth conveyed is determined through an investigation of the rest of Scripture to have a limited applicability—that is, the
truth involved cannot apply to any others. By contrast, if the truth
conveyed through a metaphor is in fact applicable to others, then it would
seem that the metaphor would also be applicable to these. At least it would
be difficult to argue for a unique application if in fact the truth conveyed is
not unique to a specific group.

The meaning and application of the marriage-and-bride metaphor
in Scripture provides an interesting case in point. The metaphor is first
employed in the Old Testament to depict the covenant relation between
God and his people Israel both past and future (Isa 54:5–6; 62:5; Jer 2:2;
3:20; Eze 16:8; 23:4; Hos 2:2, 16, 19–20). The contexts of these Old
Testament uses indicate that the metaphor teaches the deep personal
union between God and his people involving both God's elective love and
the responsive obligation of faithful purity on the part of the people.

The apostle Paul's use of the marriage metaphor for the relation of
Christ and the church provides the second scriptural application. As might

---

[31]C. I. Scofield, ed., *The New Scofield Reference Bible* (New York: Oxford Univ. Press,
1967), 1371; cf. Lewis Sperry Chafer, *Systematic Theology* (Dallas: Dallas Theological
Seminary, 1948), 4:54ff.; 7:127–30.

be expected, the figure is used with the same meaning. Christ's giving of his life for the church is the epitome of his loving care for her (Eph 5:25–26). Likewise, the responsibility of the church as the bride is to be subject to her betrothed (Eph 5:24) and to keep herself pure in anticipation of the final consummation of the marriage union at the return of Christ (2Co 11:2). Although the church is not explicitly named in Revelation 19:7–9, it is certainly involved there also in the "wedding supper of the Lamb."

Finally, this same metaphor is applied to the great eschatological city, the "new Jerusalem," which the apostle John sees "coming down out of heaven from God, prepared as a bride beautifully dressed for her husband" (Rev 21:2; cf. v. 9). Here again the emphasis is on the perfect union (v. 3; 22:3–4), the inestimable beauty bestowed on the bride by "her husband" (21:11), and purity (21:27; 22:14–15).

This threefold biblical application of one metaphor rules out any intention toward a unique identity unless one is willing to maintain that there are, in truth, three separate brides or wives in relation to God. While some may want to argue the feasibility of this in the case of two—namely, Israel and the church—what is to be done with the new Jerusalem, which by its very description involves both the twelve tribes of Israel (Rev 21:12) and the twelve apostles (Rev 21:14), the latter no doubt related to the New Testament church?

A study of the biblical use of the bride metaphor leads to the conclusion that it is used in all three instances to convey similar truth that is applicable in each case. The Bible is not teaching that God has three different brides. Rather, the covenant people of Israel, the believers in the church, and the people related to the new Jerusalem are all in a relation to God that is beautifully symbolized by the picture of marriage.

We suggest that the metaphor of the body be understood in similar fashion. The apostle Paul finds the human body in some respects a useful analogy for explaining the nature of the church. Among the concepts that are taught through this metaphor are the living, organic relationship between Christ and his people (Eph 4:15–16; Col 1:18), the direction of the church and the supply of all its needs by its Head (Eph 5:24; Col 2:18–19), and the diversity and interrelatedness of its spiritually gifted members (Ro 12:3ff.; 1Co 12:12ff.).

The appropriateness of the body metaphor to represent the church does not itself answer the question of its total application. Does the apostle intend that the metaphor uniquely mark off the church from other peoples, or does he simply find it useful to describe the nature of the church without intending to exclude its possible application to other people? This question is answered only by analyzing the truths that are taught through this analogy and asking whether or not they are or will be true in relation to any other people.

When we consider the primary truths of the body figure, it is evident that they are vitally related to the spiritual truths of the new covenant. The vital union of Christ and his people comes through the indwelling Spirit. The indwelling Spirit likewise forms the members of the body into a union with one another and equips them for making this a living reality through loving service with spiritual gifts. If this view of what the body metaphor is teaching is correct—namely, that it is fundamentally an elaboration of new covenant realities—then it is difficult to conclude that these same realities belong only to believers living during this church age. Surely the continuation of the new covenant salvation means that other believers will be indwelt by the Spirit. Since, as we saw earlier, the indwelling Spirit involves also the indwelling Christ, it must be concluded that all new covenant believers will be "in Christ" and vitally sharing his life.

The question of spiritual gifts may not be as explicit. But given the need for ministry throughout the kingdom age and the fact there will be those serving in various capacities, it seems best to conclude that they will fulfill these roles by being spiritually enabled by the indwelling Spirit— that is, through spiritual gifts. Paul's suggestion that the spiritual gifts will cease only with the final perfection (1Co 13:10) also points to some continuation of the gifts until that time.

A study of the body metaphor therefore leads us to conclude that this image is applicable to others besides believers who are in the church. The image is not intended to be a metaphorical description of the church as an entity distinct from all others. There is, in fact, nothing in Paul's use of this image that restricts it to the church. Rather, like the metaphor of the bride, it is a useful picture applicable to the church, but also to other believers who in the course of historical redemption are similarly related to Christ and the Spirit. That the church is called the "body of Christ" at present does not preclude such a wider application, even as the use of the bride metaphor for Israel in the Old Testament did not preclude its use in reference to the church in the New Testament.

This interpretation of the metaphors of the bride and body provides a model for the other images of the church. None are explicitly limited to the church in New Testament teaching. Therefore their possible application must be found in relation to the rest of Scripture.

The teaching of the metaphors thus indicates that the members of the church share the same salvation in relation to Christ and the Spirit as other believers. This accords fully with the earlier discussion of the "mysteries" related to the church. The salvation of the messianic age has already dawned through the person and work of Christ in his first coming. The members of the church are the first to enjoy it, and the metaphors convey something of its marvelous nature. As we noted earlier, however, sharing the same spiritual realities does not preclude distinctive functions within the people in the historical outworking of God's plan of salvation.

Chapter 8

The People of God, Israel, and the Church

THE CRUCIAL distinction between dispensational and non-dispensational interpretations of Scripture centers on the meaning of Israel and the church. As indicated in chapter 1, dispensationalism has undergone considerable modification recently, moving toward greater harmony with non-dispensationalism in some areas. Even on the crucial issue, many dispensationalists see much greater unity than that taught by their forerunners. Instead of asserting a radical dichotomy of purpose and destiny, they see both Israel and the church as belonging to the one people of God and serving one historical purpose. Nevertheless, a clear distinction between dispensationalists and non-dispensationalists remains.

Non-dispensationalists have generally viewed the church as a "new Israel" or a "spiritual Israel." Herman Ridderbos expresses this in a typical way in defining the church as "the continuation of Israel": "On the one hand, in a positive sense it presupposes that the church springs from, is born out of Israel; on the other hand, the church takes the place of Israel as the historical people of God."[1] Many non-dispensationalists today still

---

[1]Herman Ridderbos, *Paul: An Outline of His Theology* (Grand Rapids: Eerdmans, 1975), 333–34. Similarly George E. Ladd says, "The church . . . is a historical manifestation of a new fellowship brought into being by Jesus as the true people of God who . . . were to take the place of the rebellious nation as the true Israel" (*The Presence of the Future* [Grand

see a future salvation for ethnic Israel, but only as a part of the new Israel, the church. The Israel of the Old Testament in the aspect of a nation distinct from the gentile nations has no special place or role to play in the future. The Old Testament prophecies that spoke of Israel's serving the nations have now been assumed by the new Israel.

By contrast, dispensationalists affirm that Israel retains its Old Testament meaning as an ethnic people throughout the New Testament. Even though the believers in the church have come to share in the present messianic salvation along with Jews and the church is now serving God's kingdom purpose, Israel in its historic meaning will yet fulfill its promised destiny.

An examination of the biblical teaching on the people of God and the identities of Israel and the church reveals both a unity and a distinction, or, as it is often stated, a continuity and a discontinuity.

I. THE CONCEPT OF "THE PEOPLE OF GOD"

The biblical idea of "the people of God" originates in reference to Israel in the Old Testament. In this use it signifies a people with whom God, through his elective love, has established a special relationship. The people become his "treasured possession" (e.g., Ex 19:5; Dt 7:6; 14:2; "own possession," NASB). This relationship is expressed and formally ratified in a covenant between God and his people (i.e., the Mosaic or Sinai covenant). The distinctive element in the concept of "the people of God" is therefore religious. H. Strathmann concludes that the term applied to the nation of Israel "expresses a sense of distinction from all other peoples on the basis of religion, an awareness that Israel stands in a special relation to Yahweh."[2]

Although the term "people of God" begins with the nation of Israel and has this predominant meaning throughout the Old Testament, there is already in the prophets the anticipation that some outside of Israel will come under its purview. Of the messianic days, Zechariah declares, "Many nations will be joined with the LORD in that day and will become my people" (2:11). Isaiah also looks forward to the day when Egypt and Assyria, traditional historical foes of Israel, will become "the third party" with her, and God will say, "Blessed be Egypt my people, Assyria my handiwork, and Israel my inheritance" (19:24–25; cf. Zec 9:7: the Philistines will be "like a clan in Judah," NASB).

Many other statements about the salvation of the nations and the

---

Rapids: Eerdmans, 1974], 261; cf. also Hans Küng, *The Church* [New York: Sheed and Ward], 108–9, 114–25).

[2]H. Strathmann, "λαός," in *Theological Dictionary of the New Testament*, vol. 4, ed. Gerhard Kittel (Grand Rapids: Eerdmans, 1967), 35.

worship of the true God relate to this same truth even though they do not explicitly use the expression "the people of God." Solomon's prayer that "all the peoples of the earth may know your name and fear you, as do your own people Israel" is prophesied as a coming reality (e.g., Isa 25:6–7; 45:18–25; 55:4–7; Jer 16:19; Zep 3:9; Ps 148:11–13). Significantly for our purposes, the concept of "God's people" is extended to the gentile nations in the Old Testament without their becoming a part of Israel. Thus, even before the New Testament was written, the concept of "the people of God" embraced both Israel and those outside of that nation.[3]

We find a similar, dual application of the "people of God" in the New Testament. One would naturally expect this terminology to carry over to the historical people of Israel before the call of the Gentiles into the church. This is, in fact, what happens frequently in the Gospels. But this usage does not cease with the inauguration of the church and the calling of the Gentiles. We will not look at all the New Testament references, but the writings of Luke, which contain more than half of the occurrences of "people" (λαός) in the New Testament, amply prove the point. Of the thirty-six uses in the Gospels and forty-four in Acts, Helmut Flender notes that "with few exceptions it is used exclusively of the Jewish people."[4] The continued use of this designation for the natural people of Israel during the church age is seen in Paul's description of Israelites as "his [God's] people" (Ro 11:1–2).

But the term also applies to those from other nations who now are included in the church. The messianic times that were anticipated in the Old Testament, when God's salvation would extend to the Gentiles, have dawned, according to apostolic teaching. God is taking from among the "Gentiles" those who can be called "a people for himself" ("for His name," NASB), even as Israel was prior to this time (Ac 15:14; cf. 18:10). Especially significant in this regard are the instances where Old Testament references to Israel as the people of God are now applied to the church that includes both Jews and Gentiles. The redeemed of the church, like Israel, are "a people that are his very own" (Tit 2:13; cf. Ex 19:5; see also Ro 9:25f.; 2Co 6:16; and esp. 1Pe 2:9–10).

As we will see, applying to the church these terms that formerly applied exclusively to Israel does not mean that the church now assumes that position exclusively for herself. However, this new usage does clearly indicate that the "people of God" has been enlarged to include those from nations other than Israel. While acknowledging that the church through

---

[3]For more on the Old Testament teaching of the salvation of the Gentiles alongside Israel, see chap. 5.

[4]Helmut Flender, *St Luke: Theologian of Redemptive History* (Philadelphia: Fortress, 1967), 132. This is clearly evident where "the people" is used for Jews in antithesis to "Gentiles" or "nations" (e.g., Ac 26:17, 23; 28:27–28).

faith in Jesus Christ has become the "people of God," H. Bietenhard warns against applying this title exclusively to the church:

> That is not, of course, to say that in the NT the church has simply taken the place of Israel as the people of God, as if Israel had lost the priority given to her by God. This is perhaps the major problem that Paul wrestles with in Rom. His conclusion is that Israel is and remains God's people, and has not been rejected by God (cf. Rom. 9–11, especially, Rom. 9:4f.; 11:1f.).[5]

Similarly, Strathmann states in relation to Acts 15:14 that

> Thus far λαός (people) and ἔθνη (Gentiles or nations) had been mutually exclusive terms. Now there rises up to God's name from the ἔθνη a λαός independent of all national preconditions. . . . The title is not herewith taken from Israel. But another λαός now takes its place along with Israel on a different basis.[6]

This summary of the biblical teaching on "the people of God" provides the fundamental outline of the relationship of Israel and the church. In the final sense it is perhaps best to say that "the people of God" are one people because all will be related to him through the same covenant salvation. But this fundamental unity in a relation to God through Christ does not remove Israel's distinction as a special nation called of God for a unique ministry in the world as a nation among nations. Nor does it define the totality of the people of God as "Israel," requiring that the church is somehow a "new Israel."

II. THE IDENTITY OF ISRAEL

To determine the relationship of the church and Israel, it is important to focus on the meaning and usage of these terms by the writers of Scripture. This is not to deny the validity of theological reasoning and even the so-called semantic field, where different terminology may be used for the same concept. Nevertheless, the express meaning of the terms as used by the biblical authors must have priority over these other considerations. Moreover, in light of the frequency of use by the biblical writers of the specific terms "Israel" and "church," it is difficult to accept that these other considerations should give these terms a different meaning from that found in their explicit use.

---

[5]H. Bietenhard, "λαός," in *The New International Dictionary of New Testament Theology*, vol. 2, ed. Colin Brown (Grand Rapids: Zondervan, 1976), 800.
[6]H. Strathmann, "λαός," in *TDNT*, 4:54.

The People of God, Israel, and the Church

A. *The Meaning of Israel in the Old Testament*

The term "Israel" (i.e., "he who strives with God," or "God strives") first appears in Scripture as a name of honor divinely bestowed on Jacob following his struggle with God at Peniel (Ge 32:28). It continued to be used as an alternate name for Jacob throughout his life and after his death (e.g., Ge 35:21; Ex 32:13). From the literal designation of Jacob's twelve sons as "the sons of Israel" (Ge 42:5), the term "Israel" came to be applied to his descendants in general (Ex 1:7) and then to the nation that was formed from them (cf. Ex 19:5).

With the division of the kingdom after Solomon's reign, "Israel" became the designation for the northern kingdom of the ten tribes centered in Ephraim in distinction to the kingdom of "Judah" (including the tribe of Benjamin) in the south (e.g., 1Sa 11:8; 1Ki 12:16). However, "Israel" was still used on occasion to refer to all the covenant people, including the southern kingdom (Isa 5:7) and to that kingdom alone after the dissolution of the northern kingdom. For Judah alone came to represent the people Israel (Mic 3:1). Thus the Old Testament usage manifests a consistent application of the term "Israel" to Jacob and his descendants that evolved into the nation of Israel.

One apparent exception to this usage is Isaiah's application of "Israel" to the Lord's servant in Isaiah 49:1–6. Although the prophet frequently applied the concept of "servant" to the people of Israel, in this passage the servant is ministering to Israel; so Israel can hardly be the servant. Scholars have rightly understood this reference to the servant "Israel" as pointing to the Messiah himself, who embodies "the ideal of what Yahweh's servant should be."[7]

Identifying "Israel" with the coming Messiah, however, cannot be made the basis of teaching that all who finally are "in Christ" are therefore equivalent to Israel. Isaiah is applying the honorific title "Israel" to the Messiah as the true Servant who will finally accomplish the task of Israel. But this does not indicate a change in the meaning of "Israel" or the rejection of the nation as the servant. Rather, the picture is that of Israel as a corporate personality in which the head first ministers to the body in order that the body may then accomplish its mission through the head. Israel was given a mission to the nations, and it is only through her Messiah, the perfect Servant of the Lord, that she can accomplish this task.

That this use of "Israel" for Christ as the head of the corporate people of Israel does not include Gentiles is seen in the fact that Christ never applied this name to himself, nor did the early church ever call Jesus "Israel."

---

[7]C. R. North, "Servant of the Lord, The," in *Interpreter's Dictionary of the Bible* (Nashville: Abingdon, 1962), 4:293.

In the Old Testament teaching, therefore, "Israel" signifies a community of people with a special relationship to God. This community is marked off from other peoples, first by its religious relationship with the true God, but also by its physical descendants. While it was possible for those who were not biological descendants from Abraham through Jacob to become part of the commonwealth of Israel as proselytes, the physical element is never discarded in favor of a purely religious definition of Israel. The "Jewish view" stated by Jakob Jocz accurately expresses the Old Testament evidence: "What divides Israel from the rest of humanity is not entirely physical, and is not entirely spiritual, but a combination of both. The physical and the spiritual are never separate entities."[8]

Of crucial significance in defining Israel according to the Old Testament is the recognition that the community of Israel constituted a "nation." God had promised Abraham that his descendants would become "a great nation" (Ge 12:2; cf. 17:5; 18:18). Deuteronomy 26:5 refers to the people as becoming "a great nation, powerful and numerous" during the Egyptian bondage. But it was through the freedom from political domination at the Exodus and the subsequent covenant at Sinai that their "nation" status was formally ratified.[9] The covenant relationship with God established them as "a kingdom of priests and a holy nation" (Ex 19:6). The terms "kingdom" and "nation" both have clear national and political significance. Although it is not nearly as common as the term "people," the term "nation" is subsequently applied to the community of Israel (cf. Ex 33:13: "this nation is your people"; Dt 4:34).

The difference in use points not only to the distinction in meanings between "people" and "nation," but also to that dimension of the term "Israel" that, at least according to its foundational Old Testament meaning, distinguishes it from the concept of "church." The lofty word "people," being a more "archaically poetical and solemn word"[10] and carrying "a strong emphasis on the element of consanguinity as the basis of union,"[11] was used to express Israel's special relation to God in distinction from all other peoples who are ordinarily called "nations."[12] In addition, the term "people" was less political and could be used for Israel following the end of the Davidic kingship in Jerusalem, when "Israel" no longer constituted an actual political entity.[13]

---

[8]Jakob Jocz, *A Theology of Election* (New York: Macmillan, 1958), 65.

[9]Strathmann, "λαός," in *TDNT*, 4:36.

[10]Strathmann, "λαός," in *TDNT*, 4:35.

[11]Ronald E. Clements, "ﬞיא goy," *Theological Dictionary of the Old Testament*, vol. 2 (Grand Rapids: Eerdmans, 1975), 427.

[12]Georg Bertram's comment on Exodus 33:13, "this nation is Thy people," sums up this distinction very well: ". . . ἔθνος [nation] is used for 'people' in general, whereas λαός [people] denotes the chosen people." ("ἔθνος," in *TDNT*, 2:366).

[13]Clements, "ﬞיא goy," in *TDOT*, 2:427, 429, 433.

Despite the less frequent use of "nation," Israel as "the people of God" was a national entity. Acknowledging that the Old Testament does not provide a precise definition of a nation, Ronald E. Clements identifies three major elements that are relevant, namely, race, government, and territory.[14]

All three elements are evident in the Old Testament picture of Israel. Even though, as previously noted, the common racial origin was expressed more in the concept of "people," Israel traced its origin as a "nation" back to Abraham (cf. Ge 12:2; 17:6; 18:18). Likewise, beginning at Sinai, Israel had a government. In the Mosaic covenant, according to Martin Buber, "YHVH unites with Israel into a political, theo-political unity."[15] The request for a king "such as all the nations have" (1Sa 8:5) demonstrates not only the normal form of government for that time, but the inherent connection of government with the concept of a nation.[16] The third main aspect of a nation involves the possession of its own territory (cf. Isa 36:18–20; Ps 105:44). The many promises about a land for the descendants of Abraham who would constitute the promised nation (cf. Ge 12:7; 17:5) and the later possession of that land under Joshua demonstrate that Israel also bore this mark of a nation.[17]

Thus, in addition to its spiritual significance as "the people of God," Israel in the Old Testament was literally a nation among the nations of the world. She was "a people who live apart" and would not "consider themselves one of the nations" (Nu 23:9). In assigning the territorial possessions of the nations of the world, God "set up boundaries for the peoples according to the number of the sons of Israel" (Dt 32:8–9). Meredith Kline confirms the reality of Israel as a national entity like other nations in saying of this action that "Yahweh took special interest in the geographical needs of Abraham's numerous seed in his providential government of all nations . . . , for Israel was his elect people."[18]

This status of a nation belongs to the very concept of Israel in terms of the Old Testament and cannot be separated from its religious meaning as "the people of God." Clements points out the force of this concept in the book of Deuteronomy: "A pervasive assumption throughout the book is that Israel is a nation, and it can scarcely be said to countenance the possibility that Israel might continue to live as Yahweh's people in some form other than that of a nation."[19] This unique blending of the religious and national dimensions continue to the present time in Jewish thought.

---

[14]Clements, "יׁוֹג goy," in *TDOT*, 2:428–29.

[15]Martin Buber, *Moses — The Revelation and the Covenant* (New York: Harper, 1958), 115.

[16]Despite the sinful request that initiated the human monarchy in Israel, there is evidence that such a monarchy was God's original intention (cf. Ge 49:10; Nu 24:7).

[17]For more discussion of the "land" in relation to Israel, see pp. 44–46..

[18]Meredith G. Kline, *Treaty of the Great King* (Grand Rapids: Eerdmans, 1963), 140.

[19]Ronald E. Clements, *Old Testament Theology* (Atlanta: John Knox, 1978), 89.

In Judaism, according to Jocz, ". . . religion and nationhood are insepar-ably welded together."[20] Buber states, "It is being a nation, but because of its own peculiar connection with the quality of being a community of faith, it is more than that."[21]

   While we do not want to understate the central religious element in the identity of Israel, we believe it is essential to recognize this national element in defining the relationship between Israel and the church. Quite clearly the national element is lacking in the concept of the church in the New Testament. It remains for us to see whether the New Testament writers strip this dimension from their understanding of "Israel" in the light of the new work of the church.

B. The Meaning of Israel in the New Testament

   1. Overview. The term "Israel" occurs sixty-eight times in the New Testament, predominantly in the writing of Matthew, Luke, and Paul.[22] Apart from a few disputed references, which we will discuss later, all the instances refer to the "national" covenant people of the Old Testament.[23] According to Reinhold Mayer, in the Synoptics "Israel stands for the people and also the land. . . . The use of the word Israel in general clearly maintains the connection with the reality and hope of Israel." John's gospel also conforms to this basic Old Testament meaning.[24] Similarly, Mark A. Elliott adds that in spite of a certain negative element in connection with Israel's rejection of Christ,

> the one consistent feature of the usage of the word [Israel] in the Gospels—in conformity with its use in the Jewish world generally—is that it retains its dignity. It continues to imply privilege associated with covenant, election and theocratic ideals. . . . Nor do the Gospels deviate from the traditional sig-nificance of the term as referring to the descendants of Abraham (through Jacob). Never, for example, is the term used either of the church or of Gentiles.[25]

---

[20]Jakob Jocz, *The Jewish People and Jesus Christ* (London: S.P.C.K., 1954), 304.

[21]Martin Buber, *Israel and the World* (New York: Schocken, 1948), 222.

[22]The specific occurrences of Israel in the New Testament number 17 in Paul's epistles (of which 11 are in Romans), 12 in Matthew, 12 in Luke, 15 in Acts, 2 in Mark, 4 in John's Gospel, 3 in Hebrews, and 3 in Revelation.

[23]For a full discussion of the term "Israel" in the New Testament church, see Peter Richardson, *Israel in the Apostolic Church* (Cambridge: Cambridge Univ. Press, 1969). Richardson argues that the first explicit use of "Israel" for the church is made by Justin Martyr in the mid-second century.

[24]R. Mayer, "Israel," in *The New International Dictionary of New Testament Theology*, vol. 2, ed. Colin Brown (Grand Rapids: Zondervan, 1976), 315.

[25]Mark A. Elliott, "Israel," in *Dictionary of Jesus and the Gospels*, ed. Joel B. Green and Scot McKnight (Downers Grove, Ill.: InterVarsity Press, 1992), 357.

Because the new work of God in the church is not the primary subject of the Gospels either historically or theologically, it is in the writings that have direct reference to the church that we expect to find any new meaning and application of the concept of Israel. These writings, however, reveal no change. In regard to Luke's writings, which include the fifteen uses of "Israel" in Acts, Jacob Jervell declares that the term "always refers to the Jewish people. At no time does it serve to characterize the church, i.e., it is never used as a technical term for the Christian gathering of Jews and Gentiles."[26] Similarly, aside from a few disputed passages, Paul's many uses of "Israel" all refer to that historic people, as do the three references in Hebrews.

Peter and John never refer to "Israel" in their epistles, which are addressed to church believers. Of the three uses of "Israel" by John in the book of Revelation, the first is clearly of Old Testament Israel (2:14). The other two refer to the twelve tribes of Israel (7:4; 21:12), but their meaning is dependent on the proper understanding of the disputed passages concerning Israel and the church in the epistles.

2. The Disputed Passages About the Meaning of "Israel." Despite this general picture that the New Testament uses of the term "Israel" refer to the ethnic nation of the Old Testament, Christian scholars for centuries have understood the New Testament to teach that the church is, in fact, the "new Israel." They have tended to base this view more on a broad reading of Scripture rather than on specific texts that use the terms "Israel" or "Jew." The primary biblical concepts underlying this view—namely, the meaning of the "seed of Abraham," the application of the new covenant, and the development of the kingdom—have already been discussed, with the conclusion that they do not compel any change of the meaning of "Israel" to include Gentiles.[27]

The general usage of the term "Israel" in the New Testament, as we have viewed it, would appear to support that conclusion. At least it must be acknowledged by all that the theological concept of the church as a "new Israel" is never clearly, let alone prominently, taught by Paul with that terminology. A few disputed texts (two using the term "Israel"; one, "Jew"), however, are often cited as evidence for giving the terms this new meaning. In addition, the concept is said to be taught by the fact that language which had previously been used for Israel is now applied to all believers in the church.

a. Texts using "Israel" or "Jew" (Ro 9:6; 2:28–29; Gal 6:16). One passage frequently cited in teaching of a "new Israel" is the apostle Paul's

---

[26]Jacob Jervell, *Luke and the People of God* (Minneapolis: Augsburg, 1972), 49.

[27]For an interpretation of these broad themes that does not entail the Gentiles' becoming Israel, see the discussion on the "seed of Abraham" in chapter 2; on the new covenant, chapter 5; and on the kingdom promises and devlopment, chapters 3 and 4.

statement in Romans 9:6: "For not all who are descended from Israel are Israel." Proponents of the "new Israel" view combine this statement of an "Israel" that is not the equivalent of the physical descendants of Israel with the subsequent reference to Abraham's "natural children" as distinguished from his "children of the promise" (vv. 8–9) and see here an explicit reference to a new "spiritual Israel" composed of believing Jews and Gentiles. Of the entire section of Romans 9:6–29, C. H. Dodd says, "If He [God] chooses to reject the Jews and to elect Gentiles, then the true 'Israel' is composed of those whom He elects. . . . Even if the entire Israelite nation is rejected, the promise has not been broken."[28]

Similarly, Rudolf Bultmann cites this passage as evidence that "the election of the People of God . . . is now being realized in the Christian Congregation . . . ," which he then designates the "Israel of God."[29]

Some acknowledge that the second "Israel" of verse 6 refers to an elect remnant within natural Israel, but still view the statement as somehow giving "Israel" a new definition that now includes Gentiles. Thus James D. G. Dunn, while denying a simple transfer of the blessings of historical Israel to the church, nevertheless concludes, " 'The Israel of God' is still God's covenant people, the character of whose covenant some Israelites . . . have misunderstood and *into whom believing Gentiles are being incorporated.*"[30]

While most interpreters today acknowledge that Paul is not going beyond natural Israel in the distinction made in Romans 9:6, it is important to recognize that the entire context of this passage deals with the problem of Israel and not Gentiles. Paul introduces this major section by declaring his concern for "my brothers, those of my own race, the people of Israel" (9:3–4); he goes on to elaborate God's elective purpose among the physical descendants of Abraham (cf. 9:7–13). Johannes Munck explains, "It is not until 9:22 ff. that Paul includes the Gentile Christians in his reflection. Here in 9:6–13 the only point he makes is that claims cannot be made on the basis of physical descent, since descendants of the patriarchs with exactly the same claims were allotted different destinies." It appears, then, that in verse 6 Paul does not "visualize 'Israelites' who do

---

[28]C. H. Dodd, *The Epistle of Paul to the Romans,* The Moffatt New Testament Commentary (London: Hodder & Stoughton, 1932), 155.

[29]Rudolf Bultmann, *Theology of the New Testament,* vol. 1 (New York: Scribner's, 1951), 97; cf. H. H. Rowley, *The Biblical Doctrine of Election* (London: Lutterworth, 1950), 144; also, Charles Hodge, *Commentary on the Epistle to the Romans* (1886; reprint, Grand Rapids: Eerdmans, 1947), 305; R. Newton Flew, *Jesus and His Church* (London: Epworth Press, 1938), 150–51.

[30]James D. G. Dunn, *Romans 9–16,* Word Biblical Commentary, vol. 38b (Dallas: Word Books, 1988), 540, emphasis added.

not belong to the physical Israel as being within the new Israel of the church."[31]

The point of this entire passage is that while the promises of God to Israel may appear to have failed in that Israel is predominantly unbelieving, there is a remnant within Israel—what John Murray aptly calls "an 'Israel' within ethnic Israel."[32] The promises to Israel, therefore, retain their validity, as William Sanday and Arthur C. Headlam assert in their explanation of the verse: "St. Paul does not mean here to distinguish a spiritual Israel (i.e., the Christian Church) from fleshly Israel, but to state that the promises made to Israel might be fulfilled even if some of his descendants were shut out from them."[33]

The following distinction between Abraham's "natural children" and those of "the promise" must be understood from the context. The terminology of "Abraham's children" and those of "promise" are applied to Gentile believers in other passages (e.g., Ro 4:9–17; Gal 3:23). But as we saw in chapter 2, the Abrahamic promise encompasses more than the great nation of Israel; it ultimately includes Gentiles as well.[34] But in this context, which deals with "Israel," the distinction with regard to Abraham's descendants is limited to ethnic Israel and is therefore not redefining "Israel" to include Gentiles. Again, Sanday and Headlam, citing the context, declare, "All of these expressions (τέκνα τοῦ θεοῦ [children of God], τέκνα τῆς ἐπαγγελίας [children of the promise] are used elsewhere of Christians, but *that is not their meaning in this passage.*"[35]

Consideration of the context also leads to the correct understanding of the identity of the real "Jew" in Romans 2:28–29. The Jews are described as those who are "circumcised in heart" by the Holy Spirit, and this description has led many scholars to conclude that all believers in Christ are "Jews" and therefore "Israel."[36] So, for example, Dunn sees the apostle's statement as a description of "the eschatological Jew [who] is Gentile as well as Jew!"[37]

Although in verse 26 Paul does speak of the obedience of Gentiles as counting for a certain "circumcision" and speaks also of the spiritual circumcision of all believers in Christ (cf. Col 2:11–12), the context of this

[31]Johannes Munck, *Christ and Israel: An Interpretation of Romans 9–11* (Philadelphia: Fortress, 1967), 36.

[32]John Murray, *The Epistle to the Romans,* vol. 2 (Grand Rapids: Eerdmans, 1965), 9; also, William Sanday and Arthur C. Headlam, *A Critical and Exegetical Commentary on the Epistle to the Romans,* International Critical Commentary (Edinburgh: T & T Clark, 1902), 240.

[33]Sanday and Headlam, *Commentary on the Epistle to the Romans,* 240.

[34]See chapter 2, pp. 46, 57–58.

[35]Ibid., 242, emphasis added.

[36]Cf. Rowley, *The Biblical Doctrine of Election,* 145.

[37]Dunn, *Romans 1–8,* WBC, 125.

statement—like that of 9:6—is concerned with ethnic Jews and not believers in general. Clearly, by verse 17 Paul is addressing those who call themselves "Jews."[38] The term "Jew," like "Israel," carried not only ethnic but also religious meaning, and the apostle was concerned to define its true meaning, which always involved faith and obedience and not simply an external covenant claim. The presence of the Spirit brought a new depth to the inward reality in accord with the promise, but neither in the Old Testament promise nor in the New Testament teaching is there any indication that this changes the meaning of "Jew." Although depth of inwardness was new under the new covenant, one could argue that Paul's notion of inwardness was not essentially different in kind from that under the old covenant, which likewise called for spiritual reality (cf. Dt 10:16; Jer 4:4).

This passage on the inner nature of a true "Jew," therefore, falls in the same category as the "Israel" of promise (9:6). In both contexts the discussion deals with the division between those who bear the name merely by ethnicity and those who also bear it with the more significant religious meaning—the latter not canceling out the former. Linking these passages together, Walter Gutbrod concludes,

> We are not told here [Ro 9:6] that Gentile Christians are the true Israel. The distinction at R. 9:6 does not go beyond what is presupposed at Jn. 1:47, and it corresponds to the distinction between Ἰουδαῖος ἐν τῷ κρυπτῷ [a Jew inwardly] and Ἰουδαῖος ἐν τῷ φανερῷ [a Jew outwardly] at R. 2:28f., which does not imply that Paul is calling Gentiles the true Jews.[39]

These two texts in Romans, therefore, provide no exegetical support for applying the term "Israel" to the church. All the many uses of "Israel" by Paul in Romans retain their historical meaning for the ethnic people of the Old Testament. To understand Paul as eliminating any national or ethnic meaning from the terms "real Jew" or the "Israel" through which the promise will be effected appears to be a reductionism that goes beyond any explicit teaching of his.

b. The "Israel of God" (Gal 6:16). The text most frequently cited in identifying the church as a "new Israel" is Galatians 6:16. After declaring that circumcision is of no value in the new creation in Christ, Paul says, "And those who will walk by this rule, peace and mercy be upon them, and upon the Israel of God" (NASB). The Greek word translated "and" can have an explicative sense of "even" (so NIV), which in this instance could render the interpretation that "those who will walk by this rule" are the

---

[38]Most probably, Paul's interlocutor should be understood as being a Jew from the beginning of the chapter.

[39]Walter Gutbrod, "Ἰσραήλ, κ.τ.λ.," in *Theological Dictionary of the New Testament*, vol. 3, ed. Gerhard Kittel (Grand Rapids: Eerdmans, 1965), 387.

equivalent of "the Israel of God." Several factors, however, make this unlikely.

First, this explicative sense is not common in the writings of Paul.[40] Unless there are strong contextual grounds, the usual copulative (i.e., "and") should be retained.[41]

Second and perhaps most important, if "the Israel of God" is a reference to the church, it would be the only instance where the apostle gives "Israel" this meaning. Ernest DeWitt Burton rightly argues that because "there is . . . no instance of his [Paul's] using Ἰσραήλ (Israel) except of the Jewish nation or a part thereof," we should view "the interpretation of the expression as applying not to the Christian community, but to Jews."[42] W. D. Davies likewise recognizes that Paul does not refer anywhere in Galatians to a "new Israel," nor does he elsewhere use "Israel" to represent the church. Davies states that if this were the meaning in Galatians 6:16, "one would have expected to find support for it in Rom. ix-xi where Paul extensively deals with 'Israel.'"[43] This is especially pertinent in that the Galatian letter was probably the first of Paul's extant writings.[44] If he did in fact believe that the church was the "Israel of God" at the time he wrote to the Galatians, why do we not find evidence of this meaning in his many subsequent uses of the term "Israel"?

Third, the purpose and message of the epistle as a whole best support the conclusion that the phrase is a reference to the Jewish people. It is generally agreed that in contrast to his other letters, Paul wrote Galatians with singleness of purpose, namely, to defend the purity of the gospel of salvation by grace through faith apart from any legal works.[45] While this is the theological theme of the epistle, in the historical situation it serves specifically as the defense of Paul's ministry. The entire book is bracketed by the beginning pronouncement of a curse on any who would preach a message contrary to what Paul preached (1:8–9) and a closing blessing on those who remained loyal to his gospel (6:16). Between those brackets Paul explains that he has a particular apostolic commission,

---

[40]On the possibility of this use in Galatians 6:16, Charles J. Ellicott says, ". . . it is doubtful whether *kai* is ever used by St. Paul in so marked an explicative force as must be assigned" (*St. Paul's Epistle to the Galatians* [London; Longman, Roberts, & Green, 1863], 139).

[41]Cf. John Eadie, who denies such contextual support and, based on the primary meaning of καί, concludes therefore that "the Israel of God are a party included in, and yet distinct from, the ὅσοι" (*Commentary on the Epistle of Paul to the Galatians* [1894; reprint, Grand Rapids: Zondervan, n.d.], 470).

[42]Ernest DeWitt Burton, *A Critical and Exegetical Commentary on the Epistle to the Galatians,* International Critical Commentary (Edinburgh: T & T Clark, 1921), 358.

[43]W. D. Davies, "Paul and the People of Israel," *New Testament Studies* 24 (1978): 10–11.

[44]F. F. Bruce, *The Epistle to the Galatians,* The New International Greek Testament Commentary (Grand Rapids: Eerdmans, 1982), 55.

[45]Bruce, *The Epistle to the Galatians,* 20–23.

namely, to take the gospel to the Gentiles. Just as others had been given grace to go to the "circumcised," so he and his colleagues were equipped by God to "go to the Gentiles" (2:7–9; cf. 1:16). His gospel was therefore "the gospel to [lit. *of*] the uncircumcised" (2:7). It was effective whether or not one was circumcised (cf. 5:6; 6:15).

Paul's doctrine of justification by faith apart from circumcision or other Jewish practices (cf. 4:10) related not only to personal soteriology, but also to the progress of salvation history. With the coming of Christ, the way had been opened for salvation to go to the Gentiles without their becoming Jews or a part of Israel. As argued later in Romans, the doctrine of justification by faith apart from the works of the law indicates that God is not the God of the Jews only, but also the God of the Gentiles (Ro 3:29–30).

Far from seeking to merge the Gentiles into some sort of "new Israel" by calling them "the Israel of God," Paul was asserting their equal participation with Jews in the new messianic salvation that came through Christ. The apostle's ministry to the Gentiles was in his mind the fulfillment of God's promise to Abraham that "all the nations shall be blessed in you" (Gal 3:8, citing Ge 12:3). That same promise included statements about Israel (cf. Ge 12:2), but Paul did not refer to these. The salvation of the Gentiles was not the fulfillment of the promises to the nation of Israel, according to the letter to the Galatians.

Paul's concept of unity involved a spiritual oneness in Christ in which there was no difference in relation to God (cf. Gal 3:29), but it was not a unity that dissolved all historical differences. Paul had no problem with Jewish believers' continuing the practice of circumcision. He had Timothy circumcised for the sake of having an effective witness to the Jews. But to require this practice of Gentiles implied that something in addition to faith was needed for salvation. This something also suggested that salvation involved living like Jews (Gal 2:14). Paul adamantly rejected both implications and affirmed that salvation comes by faith alone to both Jews and Gentiles.

George Howard asserts that Paul was concerned to establish a universal gospel, not a gospel confined to Israel. Howard also argues that Paul's concept of unity required the continued identity of both Gentile and Jew.

> Belief in Yahweh as the one universal God thus demanded mutual recognition between Jews and Gentiles that they both belonged to the same God. We may even go further and say that any attempt on either side to erase the ethnic and cultural nature of the other would be to destroy Paul's particular concept of unity between Jews and Gentiles.[46]

---

[46]George Howard, *Paul: Crisis in Galatia* (Cambridge: Cambridge Univ. Press, 1979), 79.

Paul's gospel and his ministry to the Gentiles that he defends in Galatians is in accord with what he wrote to the Romans later on. There he outlines God's future plans, which involve both the Gentiles and Israel in the service of God, for the salvation of each other so as eventually to include both within his kingdom (Ro 11:11–36). On these grounds Howard asserts that "the ultimate goal, in Paul's mind, was the mutual recognition of each under the divine rule of Jahweh, the God of Abraham."[47]

If we see the message of Galatians as a defense not only of justification by faith alone, but also of Paul's ministry of salvation to Gentiles as Gentiles, it becomes extremely unlikely that Paul would conclude his argument by calling Gentiles "the Israel of God." It is much more probable, in view of his strong condemnation of the Judaizers who sought to enslave the Gentile converts, that Paul sought to recognize also the validity of a true Israel. As Peter Richardson says, ". . . to prevent the Galatians from moving . . . to a new Christian exclusiveness and sectarianism, he adds his prayer for mercy on God's faithful people."[48]

Thus, whether the reference is to Jews in the church who were presently walking according to Paul's rule or to the "all Israel" destined for eschatological salvation (Ro 11:26), it is more in line with the apostle's language, his overall theology, and the message of Galatians to view "the Israel of God" as a reference to Jewish people. Indeed, this view appears to be gaining adherents among present-day scholars, no doubt because of increasing theological interest regarding Israel's place in God's plan.[49]

Paul's use of the term "Israel," therefore, lends no support to the idea of a continuity of Old Testament Israel with the church in the sense that the church assumes the place of a "new Israel" in God's historical plan of salvation. D. W. B Robinson writes,

> For Paul there is only one Israel. He does not speak—as do some modern theologians—of an "old Israel" and a "new Israel." He nowhere suggests that Israel has lost or changed its original character. He does not, in short, propose any new definition. Israel is the people or nation Israel, of whose identity no one had any doubt.[50]

For Paul, the historic Israel, although partially and temporarily hardened, yet had a future and therefore could not be superseded by a new people of God (cf. Ro 11:25–26). J. Christiaan Beker asserts on the basis of Romans 9–11 that Paul's present mission as "an apostle of the

---

[47]Howard, *Paul: Crisis in Galatia*, 80.

[48]Richardson, *Israel in the Apostolic Church*, 84.

[49]For a brief discussion of recent opinion, see Bruce, *The Epistle to the Galatians*, 274–75. Bruce favors the view that the "Israel of God" is the "all Israel" of Romans 11:26.

[50]D. W. B. Robinson, "The Salvation of Israel in Romans 9–11," *Reformed Theological Review* 26, no. 3 (September–December 1967): 83.

Gentiles" (11:13; cf. Gal 1:15–16) and leader in the church "does not negate Israel's historical mission to the world. . . . Israel's strategic position in salvation-history is not confined to its past, as if Israel is now absorbed by the church. Israel remains a distinct entity in the future of God's purpose. Thus . . . Paul simply refuses to equate the Gentile church with the new/true Israel."[51]

c. The application of "the circumcision" to the church. Despite the absence of explicit statements calling the church "Israel," some scholars maintain that this equation is formed in the way that the New Testament writers frequently apply to the church various terminology previously ascribed to Israel. One key example is Paul's assertion against his legalistic Jewish opponents that *all* believers in Christ constitute "the circumcision" (Php 3:3).[52] From this statement these interpreters conclude that "the church of Jesus Christ . . . is the true Israel (Gal 6:16), heir of all the rights and privileges belonging to it (Rom 9:24–26; 1 Pet 1:9–10, including the right to the title, περιτομή ('circumcision')."[53]

In response we note first of all that the apostle himself does not identify the church with Israel in this passage and context. On the contrary, he uses the term "Israel" only two verses later in the historical sense of the ethnic people; he identifies himself as being "of the people of Israel" (Php 3:5). There is no indication that this "Israel" is now an "old Israel" whose promises have somehow been transferred to a "new Israel." Beyond this, however, the strong metaphorical meaning of circumcision in both the Old and New Testaments coupled with the point of controversy between Paul and his foes in Philippi suggests that such a change in the meaning of "Israel" is in no way a necessary conclusion to this teaching on circumcision.

Paul's purpose in Philippians 3 is clearly to rebuke those who were relying on physical circumcision in their relationship to God. Their confidence for righteousness was "in the flesh" (v. 3) as opposed to the true righteousness, "which is through faith in Christ" (v. 9). In opposing a confidence in bodily circumcision, Paul was building on the teaching of the Old Testament that called for a "spiritual circumcision" in the face of a similar reliance on the physical rite. Such a spiritual circumcision is usually said to be "of the heart" (cf. Lev 26:41; Dt 10:16; 30:6; Jer 9:25–

---

[51]J. Christiaan Beker, *Paul the Apostle* (Philadelphia: Fortress, 1980), 333.

[52]For the view that Paul's statement about "the circumcision" refers only to Jewish Christians, see D. W. B. Robinson, "We Are the Circumcision," *Australian Biblical Review* 15 (1967): 30–31. The statement would appear, however, to refer to the general readers of the letter, who were mostly Gentiles.

[53]Gerald F. Hawthorne, *Philippians*, Word Biblical Commentary, vol. 43 (Waco, Tex.: Word Books, 1983), 126; also, George E. Ladd, *A Theology of the New Testament* (Grand Rapids: Eerdmans, 1974), 538; Herman Ridderbos, *Paul: An Outline of His Theology*, 335; Moises Silva, *Philippians*, Wycliffe Exegetical Commentary (Chicago: Moody, 1988), 170.

26; Eze 44:7), but it could also be applied to the ears (Jer 6:10; cf. Ac 7:51) and lips (Ex 6:12, 30). Paul's antagonists at Philippi were much like the people addressed by the prophets. The issue was one of obtaining righteousness before God—in other words, salvation.

Even under the Mosaic covenant, wherein physical circumcision was prescribed for Israel, it was not the physical rite, but the spiritual reality of humble submission to God in faith that effected justification— i.e., spiritual circumcision of the heart.

The inauguration of the new covenant and the ending of the old Mosaic covenant in Christ put circumcision in a newer light. For Paul's Jewish opponents, physical circumcision was emblematic of righteousness related to law-keeping under the old covenant (cf. Ac 15:1, 5). So Paul could argue that breaking the law was the equivalent to not being circumcised (cf. Ro 2:25). But with the coming of Christ, the righteousness of God (which could not finally be obtained under the law) was shown to come through faith in Christ. Physical circumcision, which had validity as a sign of the old covenant between God and his people, could now have no real meaning under the new covenant. Circumcision as part of the dividing wall between Jew and Gentile had been obliterated (cf. Eph 2:14–18). Now "in Christ Jesus neither circumcision nor uncircumcision has any value" (Gal 5:6; cf. 6:15; 1Co 7:19).

Paul's giving preeminence to a spiritual circumcision over a physical rite was thus linked clearly to the ultimate question of salvation by faith alone through Christ and freedom from the old covenant. This matter of "spiritual salvation," not broader questions of the meaning of "Israel" or the future of that people, is the real issue in all the contexts relating to the question of a true circumcision (see also Col 3:10).

That the apostle should use the metaphor of "spiritual circumcision" to picture the true saving faith and apply it to Gentiles as well as Israel is perfectly reasonable. First, as a concept already taught by the prophets and still present within Palestinian Judaism during the New Testament era, it could not help but be meaningful in his debate with the Jewish legalists, who tended to emphasize the outward rite.[54] But beyond its pertinence to the debate with Judaism, the Scriptures clearly affirm that "spiritual circumcision" was applicable to the saving faith of Gentiles as well as Jews.

The initial use of circumcision in Scripture—and certainly the most significant for its understanding in Paul's writings—is that of Abraham. Citing Abraham as a model of justification by faith, Paul explains that the

---

[54]Rudolf Meyer, "περιτέμνω," in *Theological Dictionary of the New Testament*, vol. 6, ed. Gerhard Friedrich (Grand Rapids: Eerdmans, 1968), 79. It is significant that in the period after the destruction of the temple, "Pharisaic-Rabbinic nomism" opposed any spiritualized meaning of circumcision, asserting only "the purely physical understanding" (Ibid.).

patriarch's circumcision was "a seal of the righteousness that he had by faith while he was still uncircumcised" (Ro 4:11). Thus the first record of circumcision did not signify membership in Israel, but a righteousness with God through faith that Abraham had *before the institution of the physical rite that was later prescribed for Old Testament covenant people.* In terms that are used later in Scripture, one could say that Abraham was "circumcised in heart" apart from and prior to any physical rite.

Moreover, Paul regarded Abraham at this point as standing in the same position as the Gentiles. Thus Abraham was both the father of the "uncircumcised"—that is, the Gentiles—who share the same faith that he had apart from circumcision and the father of the "circumcised"—that is, Israel of faith. The rite of physical circumcision that came to identify Israel thus stands secondary to a prior "spiritual circumcision" of faith that belonged to Abraham when he represented the Gentiles. So the meaning of circumcision as revealed in this initial example of Abraham is applicable to Gentiles as well as Israel, for Abraham as "circumcised in heart" is the father of both.

Paul wrote that because "there is only one God," there is finally only one method of justification for both Jew and Gentile (cf. Ro 3:28–30), namely the faith of Abraham. As a seal of the righteousness of this faith, circumcision in its deepest spiritual meaning can be applied to both. A hint that this terminology would apply to Gentiles in the future can be seen in Jeremiah's suggestion that all who will finally be saved, even among the Gentiles, must be circumcised "in heart" (Jer 9:25–26).

The applicability to Gentiles is also evident in Paul's designation of Abraham's circumcision as a "sign," or "distinguishing mark," no doubt of the covenant that God had given to him (Ro 4:11; Ge 17:10–11). Therefore, the initial use of circumcision did not pertain to the covenant with which God established his relationship with Israel at Sinai (cf. Ex 19:5). Instead, it was a sign of the Abrahamic covenant, which included the "great nation," Israel, but also "all peoples on earth" (Ge 12:2–3).

To be sure, the promise of Abraham was first administered through the Sinaitic covenant and the people of Israel, but it was never limited only to Israel. It always looked to the universal blessing of all nations. Both the Old and New Testaments looked forward to the time of a new covenant, when the salvation of God based on the promise to Abraham would go out to the Gentiles as well as Israel. Abraham's circumcision, therefore, stood for more than a sign of Israel's relationship to God. Only by somehow identifying all the participants in the Abrahamic covenant as "Israel" and making him the father of "Israel" alone, can all those related to the "sign" of the covenant—circumcision—be labeled "Israel." Many interpreters do just that, but this identification has no explicit basis in Scripture.

In summary, Paul's teaching about spiritual circumcision is always limited to the question of a spiritual relationship to God. For all in Christ there can be no distinction in this regard. But the absence of a spiritual distinction does not mean there are no distinctions at all. Nowhere in discussions of "spiritual circumcision" does Scripture explicitly specify Gentiles as "Jews" or the church as a "new Israel." Beyond this, the meaning of circumcision in its historical application to Abraham provides a basis for its spiritual application for all his descendants, Gentiles as well as Israel.

d. Similar language applied to Israel and the church. In addition to "circumcision," the New Testament applies to the church other terminology that previously referred to Israel. Peter offers a clear example in addressing the recipients of his first epistle in language that expressly applied to Israel at her inauguration as a nation. Peter's audience was "a chosen race, a royal priesthood, a holy nation, a people for God's own possession" (1Pe 2:9 NASB; cf. Ex 19:6). Obviously including Gentiles, Peter further said, in language originally spoken of Israel, "Once you were not a people, but now you are the people of God" (v. 10; cf. Hos 1:9–10; 2:23).

For many scholars, this application of Israel's terminology to the church means that the New Testament writers were identifying the church as a new Israel, hence redefining the concept of Israel. J. Ramsey Michaels, for example, says correctly that Hosea's statements that those who were not a people will become God's people mean that "these gentile Christians of Asian Minor are reenacting a chapter of Israel's own history." But does it necessarily follow from this "that the very language that identifies them as Gentiles at the same time confirms their identity (established by the metaphors of v. 9 as 'Israel')"? Is Peter really identifying the church as "simply 'Israel' as God intended her from the time of the Exodus, a holy people called to worship and praise God in the world"?[55]

That many aspects of Israel are applicable to the "people of God" in the church cannot be denied. The salvation purpose of God is presently being carried out through the church. In its witness to "the excellencies of him," it can be rightly seen as performing a priestly service to the world that belonged originally to the nation of Israel (cf. Isa 43:20–21). Because of the basic continuity in the nature of God's salvation and the consequent nature of "the people of God," many aspects of the earlier covenant people are applicable to the covenant people of the New Testament church.

Several factors, however, militate against using this transfer of

---

[55]J. Ramsey Michaels, *First Peter*, Word Biblical Commentary, vol. 49 (Waco, Tex.: Word Books, 1988), 112–13; cf. also, Peter H. Davids, *The First Epistle of Peter*, New International Commentary on the New Testament (Grand Rapids: Eerdmans, 1990), 90.

terminology as evidence to prove that the church is, in fact, a new Israel. First, the Scriptures frequently reveal different applications of similar language without implying a change in identity. The fact that the same phrase about God's son being called out of Egypt applies to both Israel and Christ does not make these objects identical (cf. Hos 11:1 and Mt 2:15). God's similar working throughout salvation history makes the use of analogous language common in the biblical revelation.

Second, while the language of Israel and its function is generally applicable to the church during this age, it is difficult to see all of the function of Israel in relation to world as taking place through the church as "new Israel," unless one holds to a generally postmillennial view of history. The Old Testament concept of the messianic kingdom with Israel at its center clearly pictures a salvation for the world including peace and prosperity among the nations that transcends the present spiritual salvation witnessed by the church.[56]

Finally, although much language about Israel is applied to the church, the name "Israel" is not used. Many aspects of Israel's old covenant experience were typical in the sense of looking forward to a final fulfillment, but Israel itself is never portrayed as a type in the strict sense of being superseded by an antitype. These facts make it preferable to conclude with Peter Richardson,

> In spite of the many attributes, characteristics, privileges and prerogatives of the latter [Israel] which are applied to the former [church], the Church is not called Israel in the NT. The continuity between Israel and the Church is partial; and the discontinuity between Israel B.C. and its continuation A.D. is partial.[57]

The New Testament writers thus give no support for a change from the Old Testament usage that defines Israel as a national people. Nor does the use of similar terminology for Israel and the church argue for a continuity of the people of God that in essence views the church as a "new Israel" taking the place of historical Israel in God's salvation plan for the world. Not only that, but the New Testament clearly affirms a future for Israel in the historic sense.[58]

---

[56]See the picture of the prophesied messianic salvation presented in chap. 9 and the function of Israel in relationship to it in chap. 12.

[57]Richardson, *Israel in the Apostolic Church*, 7. Cf. Markus Barth's comment on this matter in Ephesians: "In 1:14 as well as in 1:3–10 a terminology is used for the salvation of Jews and Gentiles which had formerly been reserved for Israel only. But expressions such as the 'new' or 'true' Israel (that seem to correspond to the 'new' covenant, the 'new' man, the 'new' Testament) are not found in this context or anywhere else in the NT" (*Ephesians 1–3*, Anchor Bible [Garden City, N.Y.: Doubleday, 1974], 97).

[58]For an excellent discussion of the Old Testament language used in relation to the church in 1 Peter 2:6–10, see W. Edward Glenny, "The Israelite Imagery of 1 Peter 2," in *Dispensationalism, Israel and the Church*, ed. Craig A. Blaising and Darrell Bock (Grand

4. Conclusion. Our study of the New Testament evidence for the identity of Israel has revealed that this term retains its basic Old Testament meaning as the national ethnic people. The rejection of Christ by the majority of the Jews led the apostles to express a division within ethnic Israel. So only a remnant "Israel" within the historic people of Israel is truly the Israel of promise. But this division was already expressed, though not as explicitly, in the prophetic writings of the Old Testament. No clear teaching of the New Testament ever goes beyond this understanding to include Gentiles in the true "Israel" by name.

The church in Christ, as we have seen, shares in the promises of God with Israel as the people of God. Moreover, with Israel's salvation still in the future (cf. Ro 11:25–26), the church performs in a partial way the function originally given to Israel as God's witness to the world. Thus many similarities can be and are expressed about the church and historic Israel. Yet, similarities do not require equating one with the other; and because the term "Israel" is not applied to the church, it seems that the New Testament writers did not draw this conclusion.

Significantly, some who regard the church as "Israel" essentially acknowledge that the New Testament never uses that name for the church. Horst Kuhli writes, "Despite the early demonstrable Christian self-understanding as the legal successor of Israel, the NT exercises extraordinary reserve in using the designation Ἰσραήλ with respect to the Church or Christians." Kuhli observes that there is not one instance that may be conclusively interpreted as evidence for applying the term "Israel" to the church.[59] More amazingly, R. T. Stamm declares, "Although he [Paul] did believe that Christians constituted the true Israel, he never called the church the Israel of God, but used the word 'Israel' to designate the Jewish nation."[60] If, as is so commonly asserted, the New Testament writers did teach that the church is a "new Israel," it would seem incumbent for the proponents of that view to explain why, with the many references to "Israel," it is not once applied unambiguously to the church.

II. THE IDENTITY OF THE CHURCH

To assert that the church is not equivalent to Israel raises the question of what distinguishes the two concepts. The discussion in the

---

Rapids: Zondervan, 1992), 156–87. Glenny views the use of Israel's language for the church as an example of "typological-prophetic hermeneutic," which is more than merely analogous language. According to this view, there is an initial fulfillment of the Old Testament typological prophecies in the church, which, however, "does not negate the future fulfillment of the national, political, and geographic promises, as well as the spiritual ones, made to Israel in these Old Testament contexts" (186–87).

[59]Horst Kuhli, "Ἰσραήλ," in *Exegetical Dictionary of the New Testament*, vol. 2, ed. Horst Balz and Gerhard Schneider (Grand Rapids: Eerdmans, 1991), 204.

[60]R. T. Stamm, *The Interpreter's Bible*, ed. George A. Buttrick (New York; Abingdon, 1953), 10:590–91.

earlier part of the chapter showing that both are "the people of God" immediately teaches that the church is not totally distinct Israel. For both to bear this appellation, they must have much in common. But if they are distinct, there must also be something that distinguished them. Our consideration of the identity of the church in relationship to Israel, therefore, will focus both on that which is common and that which is distinct.

A. *The Similarity Between the Church and Israel*

Dispensationalists traditionally have distinguished the church from Israel by many spiritual realities that were claimed to belong exclusively to the believers of the present church age. These centered on the body nature of the church and the related doctrines of the baptism with the Spirit and the indwelling Christ. We have argued in previous chapters that these spiritual realities are essentially the fulfillment of the promised new covenant salvation.[61] Since this salvation was promised to both Israel and the nations, these realities that are new with the coming of Christ and the Spirit are not unique to the church. They belong to all God's people and are, in fact, that which finally binds them together as the people of God.

The New Testament, in identifying the church, clearly puts the emphasis on its spiritual nature. The church is a spiritual organism alive with the resurrection life of Christ through the presence of the Spirit. It is the new humanity, the firstfruits after Christ of the new creation. Therefore it is possible to describe the church as the eschatological community of God's people.

If the church and Israel—indeed, all the people of God of all ages—have these definitive spiritual realities in common, then we must ask whether Israel is included in the church. As we have seen, the "body of Christ" metaphor applies to all who share in Christ's life, including future Israel. Does the fact that the body of Christ is expressly identified as "the church" (e.g., Col 1:18; Eph 5:23) mean that the salvation of Israel involves incorporation into the church as the body of Christ?

In response we note, first, that the idea of incorporating Israel into the church does not logically require that the church become a "new Israel." To say that something is a part of something else does not make the two entities identical. Israel may share that which is common to the church, but have a distinct characteristic which is not shared by all in the church. An understanding that the New Testament teaches the final inclusion of Israel in the church would, therefore, in no way necessitate

---

[61]See chap. 6 on the union of Jew and Gentile in the body of Christ, and chap. 7 on the baptism with the Spirit and the meaning of the metaphors of the Body and the Bride in relationship to the church.

the denial of the continued distinct identity of that nation and its particular place in the outworking of salvation history. The question is thus not crucial to the ultimate understanding of Israel's prophecies.

Without laboring the point, in our opinion the answer to the question rests on one's understanding of the use of the word "church." If it is the name of the body of Christ, or the final eschatological people of God throughout eternity, then it would be correct to include Israel in the church. Interestingly, however, one never finds the term "church" applied to those beyond the present age. Nowhere is the term as such, i.e., "the church" applied either to saints during the kingdom reign or in heaven either presently or in the future.

The only possible exception is the reference to the believer's coming "to the heavenly Jerusalem ... to the church of the firstborn, whose names are written in heaven" (Heb 12:22–23). Although many interpreters view this as a reference to members of the church in heaven,[62] not all do, by any means. I. Howard Marshall, for example, holds that "the allusion is to men who are still on earth but who have been enrolled by God as his people ... and who are seen as forming one company with the heavenly host and the righteous of the O.T. era."[63] Similarly, Barnabas Lindars considers this a reference to "the company of the converts on earth, 'who are enrolled in heaven' by having their names inscribed in the book of life (Rev. 21:27)."[64] Along the same lines, James Moffatt notes that the reference to their names' being written "in heaven" would be meaningless if the people were themselves already in heaven.[65]

With the single exception of this questionable reference in Hebrews, the word "church" is found only in reference to believers on earth during the present time between the first and second comings of Christ. Perhaps this usage means that the term signifies God's people during the time when they exist as a distinct "assembly" sojourning in a world that is still marked primarily by rebellion. Different terminology may be more appropriate for God's people when his rule characterizes the entire earth during the millennium and throughout eternity. Karl Ludwig

---

[62]For the various interpretations of this statement and the advocacy of the church in heaven, see William L. Lane, *Hebrews 9–13*, Word Biblical Commentary, vol. 47b (Dallas: Word Books, 1991), 467–69; F. F. Bruce, *The Epistle to the Hebrews* (Grand Rapids: Eerdmans, 1964), 376–77.

[63]I. Howard Marshall, "New Wine in Old Wine-Skins: V. The Biblical Use of the Word 'Ekklesia,'" *Expository Times* 84, no. 12 (1973): 364.

[64]Barnabas Lindars, *The Theology of the Letter to the Hebrews* (Cambridge: Cambridge Univ. Press, 1991), 115–16

[65]James Moffatt, *A Critical and Exegetical Commentary on the Epistle to the Hebrews*, International Critical Commentary (Edinburgh: T & T Clark, 1924), 217; so also, Wilhelm Michaelis, "πρῶτος, κτλ.," in *Theological Dictionary of the New Testament*, vol. 6, ed. Gerhard Friedrich (Grand Rapids: Eerdmans, 1968), 881.

Schmidt suggests such a distinction: "The Church is never triumphant. It is always militant, i.e., under pressure. Triumphant, it would be the βασιλεία τοῦ θεοῦ [kingdom of God], and no longer the ἐκκλησία [church]."[66]

In summary, the question of whether or not Israel should be considered as ultimately a part of the church rests on the biblical application of the term "church." If the church ultimately signifies all of God's people who are in Christ, then surely the saved Israel will become a part of this body. By contrast, if "church" applies only to the present age, then it would seem not to encompass that future Israel that will turn to God in faith. In either case, the church is not thereby identified with "Israel." They share a similar identity as the people of God enjoying equally the blessings of the promised eschatological salvation. But this commonality does not eliminate all distinctions between them.

B. The Distinction Between the Church and Israel

Rather than spiritual realities, it is the lack of national characteristics that distinguishes the church from Israel. As we have seen, Israel was not only the people of God but was also formed and chosen as a nation among nations. Although she did not exist as a nation for extensive periods of history and was displaced from the land, the concept of Israel never essentially changed. Ultimately, according to the prophets, she would be returned to the land and restored as a nation.

Contrariwise, the church is a spiritual entity that, despite its very real collective existence in time as the "assembly" (i.e., church), does not exist as a nation. At the Jerusalem council that confronted the issue of salvation among the Gentiles, the apostle James declared that God was "taking from the Gentiles a people for himself" (Ac 15:14). This entity was totally "independent of all national preconditions."[67] It is clear from the New Testament that this people, the church, is a community composed of both Jews and Gentiles in which neither race nor nationality nor ethnic identity has any bearing of any kind on status or function. The lack of a "national" character for the church in contrast to Israel is recongized by J. W. Flight: ". . . there is in the NT no hint of the organization of a Christian state, or any evidence of a sense of nationality on the part of the Christians as there was in Judaism."[68]

The present work of God in the church is, therefore, distinct from the previous economy of salvation history in which Israel enjoyed a

---

[66]Karl Ludwig Schmidt, "ἐκκλησία," in *TDNT*, 3:534.

[67]Strathmann, "λαός," in *TDNT*, 4:54.

[68]J. W. Flight, "Nationality," *The Interpreter's Dictionary of the Bible* (Nashville: Abingdon, 1962), 3:514.

special relation to God as a nation among the nations (cf. Ps 147:20). It is also different from the Old Testament prophetic picture of the messianic kingdom in which Israel has a preeminent position among the nations.[69] All will come to know God and share equally in his salvation, but Israel and the nations retain their identity. John Bright notes with regard to Isaiah's prophecy, ". . . the worship of foreigners will be equally acceptable (56:6–8)," but "the Jews do not lose their place of preeminence."[70]

The present nature of the church in which there is no such distinction between members of different nations is obviously distinct from these prophecies. The important question is whether the later revelation of the New Testament changes this prophetic picture. If the prophecies have been radically reinterpreted so that Israel loses its identity as a "nation," then the conclusion that the church and Israel are essentially identical is inevitable. But as we have seen, such an identity between the church and Israel is never made in the New Testament. This in itself should give some hestiation to any reinterpretation which leads to such an identity.

In addition to retaining the meaning of Israel, the New Testament does not indicate any radical reinterpretation of the Old Testament prophecies. The apostles taught the inauguration of the messianic promises of the Old Testament during the present age. But they never went to the extent of saying that the experience of the church is the complete fulfillment of the prophecies. Thus, for example, the Spirit has come in fulfillment of Joel's prophecy, but it is not necessary to see Peter as teaching that Joel 2:28ff. is completely fulfilled with Pentecost (cf. Ac 2:16–21).[71] Likewise, James viewed the salvation of Gentiles as the fulfillment of Amos 9:11–12. But we go beyond his teaching if we claim that the prophecy of Amos is receiving its complete fulfillment in what is taking place in the church today (cf. Ac 15:13–18).[72] Instead of teaching a complete fulfillment of the prophecies in the present, the New Testament often looks to the future for even greater blessing for the world, which includes a future for Israel (cf. Ro 11:11–36).[73]

The identity of the church as a "people" taken "from among [lit. 'out of'] the Gentiles" makes it distinct from Israel, which is a "nation among nations." Not only does the New Testament fail to identify the church as a "new Israel," but such an identity runs counter to the Old

---

[69]For a discussion of the relation of Israel to the nations in the messianic kingdom according to the prophets, see chaps. 9 and 12; cf. also, George N. H. Peters, *The Theocratic Kingdom* (reprint, Grand Rapids: Kregel, 1952), 2:93–101.

[70]John Bright, "Faith and Destiny," *Interpretation* 5 (1951): 22.

[71]For a more complete discussion of Acts 2, see chap. 3.

[72]For a more complete discussion of Acts 15:13–18, see chap. 3, pp. 76–80.

[73]For more discussion of the New Testament prophecies, see chap. 4, concerning the kingdom of God, and chaps. 10–11 concerning Israel.

Testament promises concerning Israel. The nations are not now coming to the church to learn the ways of God (cf. Isa 2:2–3). And how are we to understand the prophecies that Israel and the nations will both worship the same God if, in fact, all believers are "Israel" and the total "people of God" equals "Israel"? It is easier to harmonize the biblical teaching about the church and the nation of Israel if we maintain some distinctions in their identities.

III. THE POSTBIBLICAL DEVELOPMENT OF THE RELATIONSHIP OF THE CHURCH AND ISRAEL

A. The Identification of the Church as "New Israel"

What the New Testament writers did not do—namely, identify the church as "Israel"—the post-apostolic church did not long afterward. The first explicit statement to this effect is made by Justin Martyr in his *Dialogue with Trypho* around A.D. 160. But his statement was only the capstone of a developing tendency in the church to appropriate to itself the attributes and prerogatives that formerly belonged to historical Israel.[74] With Justin's statement, the developing theology of replacement was complete. There was no longer any place for historical Israel in salvation history. The prophecies addressed to this people henceforth belonged to the church.

Many scholars suggest that the trend toward seeing the church as a "new Israel" began with certain writers of the New Testament. The teaching of John especially is cited for excluding the Jews from the promises of God[75] and equating Jesus with Israel—and thus the church is part of Israel.[76] However, the negative statements of John and others about unbelieving Jews need not preclude a harmony between their teachings and those of Paul, who foretold an eventual turning of Israel to God in true faith. John, for example, recognized a true Israel (cf. Jo 1:47) while at the same time excluding unbelieving Jews from a relationship with Abraham and the promises (e.g., Jo 8:39–47) and insisting on belief in Jesus.

The post-apostolic writers, therefore, went beyond the New Testament in developing a theology about Israel and the church. At first they were cautious about applying the name "Israel" to the church. But the church increasingly assumed the prerogatives and privileges that Israel had formerly held, culminating in Justin's appropriation of the name.

---

[74]For a discussion of the tendency to usurp the prerogatives of Israel for the church in the literature prior to Justin, see Richardson, *Israel in the Apostolic Church*, 9–32; Jeffrey S. Siker, *Disinheriting the Jews: Abraham in Early Christian Controversy* (Louisville: Westminster/John Knox, 1991), 144–62.

[75]Siker, *Disinheriting the Jews*, 128–43.

[76]Richardson, *Israel in the Apostolic Church*, 180–88.

Justin's statement, besides climaxing a theology of transfer, also marks a turning point in the attitudes of the church and Israel toward each other. Richardson notes that until that time "they are able to talk together, in some places to worship together, to expect and receive converts from one to the other; but after the mid-second century these possibilities seem to disappear."[77]

B. Factors Contributing to the Theology of Replacement

The gradual development of a theology concerning the relationship of Israel and the church in the post-apostolic church did not take place in a vacuum. As the study of church history reveals, the theological enterprise is generally imposed upon the church by circumstances arising either from within the church or from outside. The church is forced to clarify its thought in relation to these new factors. The early post-apostolic Christians were not immune to this theological process. Numerous factors imposed themselves on the infant church as she attempted to come to an understanding of herself and Israel. That these were influential in her thought is evident in the literature of the period.[78]

1. The Developing Antagonism Between Judaism and Early Christianity.[79] Beginning with the Gospels, the New Testament reveals an antagonism between the early church and the Jewish establishment. Numerous references report that followers of Jesus were being put out of the synagogues (cf. Jo 9:22; 12:42; 16:2) and facing more serious persecution including execution (cf. Ac 4:1ff.; 5:17ff.; 6:12ff.; 9:1; 1Th 2:14–16; Rev 2:9). This early strife between the authorities in Jerusalem and Jewish believers was acerbated by the failure of Christians to support the Jewish revolt against the Roman authorities in A.D. 66–70, the Christians choosing instead to flee Jerusalem for the safety of Pella, across the Jordan in Decapolis.

After the war, the schism deepened with the consolidation of Judaism in a council at Yavneh (Jamnia), near the Mediterranean, around A.D. 90. One result of this council was a ban on "heretical" books that included the Septuagint, the Greek version of the Old Testament that was used largely by Christians. Although it probably had a pre-Christian origin, a revised version of the Birkat ha-Minim—the Heretic Benediction, which pronounced a curse on all who departed from the standard Jewish

---

[77]Richardson, *Israel in the Apostolic Church*, 1.

[78]Richardson speaks of historical, theological, and sociological factors "at work throughout this literature" (Ibid., 31; cf. pp. 1–8).

[79]For a survey of the deepening rift between the church and Israel, see Marvin R. Wilson, *Our Father Abraham* (Grand Rapids: Eerdmans, and Dayton, Ohio: Center for Judaic-Christian Studies, 1989), 64–96; Richardson, *Israel in the Apostolic Church*, 33–47.

faith—was also promulgated at Yavneh.[80] Although the edict was not directed specifically at Christians, it was used against them, in effect excommunicating them from the synagogue.[81] The result of this new self-definition of Judaism that took place in part as a reaction against the new Christianity caused the Christians, especially the gentile believers, increasingly to identify themselves over against Judaism.[82]

The second Jewish revolt (A.D. 132–135) led by Bar Kockhba brought the break between Judaism and the Palestinian Christians to its climax. Not only did the Christians again refuse to fight for Israel, but the Jewish support of Bar Kockhba as a messianic figure signaled its final rejection of Jesus as the Messiah. Richardson summarizes the negative effect of this second revolt: ". . . to all intents and purposes it severed the two groups, freeing later Christians from the need to assert close contact with Judaism and providing for them evidence of the full 'judgment' of God upon Israel. From this point, Christians polemize more consistently."[83]

The antagonism between Israel and the church already extended beyond Palestine, as Paul's epistles reveal. In the Roman world it was advantageous early on for the Jews to distinguish themselves from the Christians. This was probably accelerated by the indignation of the Jews at being expelled from Rome because of Christians in A.D. 49. By A.D. 64, the distinction was complete, and it is probable that Nero's persecution of the Christians at that time was due in part to denunciations by Jews.[84] After A.D. 70, some of that advantage would have been lost in the Jewish revolt. Nevertheless, the legal status of Judaism under Roman law in contrast to the illegality of Christianity until the time of Constantine in the fourth century gave it some advantage over Christianity. No doubt both Christianity and Judaism suffered from Roman persecution, but as time went on, the persecution was directed more exclusively against the church. Some evidence of the situation may be seen at the martyrdom of Polycarp sometime later (c. 165–168), when the Jews sided with the pagans.

In summary, the persecution of the early believers directly by Jews, and indirectly at times through the instigation of Roman persecution, played an important role in the break between Judaism and the church.[85]

---

[80]Steven T. Katz, "Issues in the Separation of Judaism and Christianity after 70 C.E.: A Reconsideration," *Journal of Biblical Literature* 103, no. 1 (1984): 63–76; Wilson, *Our Father Abraham*, 64–72.

[81]Birger A. Pearson, "Christians and Jews in First-Century Alexandria," *Harvard Theological Review* 79, nos.1–3 (1986): 214.

[82]Siker, *Disinheriting the Jews*, 195.

[83]Richardson, *Israel in the Apostolic Church*, 203.

[84]Father Jean Paul Lichtenberg, *From the First to the Last of the Just* (Jerusalem: IsraTypeset, 1971), 7.

[85]Richardson sums up the effect of Jewish persecution on the relationship between Israel and the church: "Jewish persecution, then, because it was original an *intro muros*

The division itself would have caused the church to consider its identity more clearly in relation to Israel. The antagonism between the two groups, however, surely influenced the thinking of the early believers in terms of how they viewed Israel.

2. *The Destruction of Jerusalem.* Along with the growing antagonism, the destructive results of the Jewish wars also had an impact on the relationship between the early church and Judaism. With the crushing defeat in the later Bar Kockhba war, which as we have see brought the break between the church and Judaism in Palestine to its climax, the early church began to speak of the hand of God's judgment on Judaism. Little reference to this idea is found in Christian writings following the first revolt in A.D. 66–70.[86] But with the beginning of a more fully developed apology against Judaism the early church now sees in both of these defeats evidence not only of God's displeasure on Judaism, but of the vindication of Chrisianity.[87] In particular the exclusion of the Jews from Jerusalem on pain of death following the second revolt made a strong impression on the early church.

The destruction of Jerusalem and the expulsion of the Jews both strengthened the Christians' position over Judaism and led them to abandon any hope for the restoration of Israel. W. H. C. Frend observes that with the second fall of Jerusalem in A.D. 135, "All hope of a restored Temple and Holy City now faded, and the Jews were thrown on to the defensive. The reference of the prophecies to an earthly restoration of the Jewish kingdom and Messiah in the form of a deliverer from Roman rule clearly had to be abandoned."[88] This position figured prominently in Justin's argument with Trypho that the land of Palestine was now to be inherited by the Patriarchs and Gentiles, not Jews.

> Justin sees the dispossession of the Jews as God's just punishment
> for their disobedience and disbelief (*Dialogue* 16.2). God foreknew
> that Jerusalem would be taken from the Jews (*Dialogue* 40.2). . . .

---

controversy, played a more creative role than did Roman opposition. The latter was concerned with Christianity only after it became separate, the former helped to make it a separate entity and see that it was recognized as such by the Roman authorities" (*Israel in the Apostolic Church*, 47).

[86]Richardson, *Israel in the Apostolic Church*, 36. The effect of the revolt in A.D. 70 on the church has often been exaggerated. Its basic effect on Christians was to teach them to completely avoid any involvement with Jewish nationalist movements, a tendency to which they were prone prior to that time (Ibid., 36; cf. also, G. W. H. Lampe, "A.D. 70 in Christian Reflection," in *Jesus and the Politics of His Day*, ed. Ernst Bammel and D. F. D. Moule [Cambridge: Cambridge Univ. Press, 1984]).

[87]Lampe, "A.D. 70 in Christian Reflection," 155ff.; Robert L. Wilken, *Judaism and the Early Christian Mind: A Study of Cyril of Alexandria's Exegesis and Theology* (New Haven: Yale Univ. Press, 1971), 228.

[88]W. H. C. Frend, "The Old Testament in the Age of the Greek Apologists A.D. 130–180," *Scottish Journal of Theology* 26 (1973): 135.

When Trypho asks whether Justin means to say that the Jews will not inherit anything "on the holy mountain of god" (*Dialogue* 25.6), Justin answers that "the Gentiles, who believe in Christ and are sorry for their sins, shall receive the inheritance along with the Patriarchs."[89]

Justin's line of reasoning persisted in the writings of the early church fathers, including Tertullian and Cyprian. G. W. H. Lampe sees in Tertullian the epitome of this view: "The Jews are scattered wanderers, excluded from their own land of Judaea; this shows how they erred and forsook their calling, and how Judaism has been, therefore, superseded by Christianity."[90]

The reasoning of these early theologians is surely understandable in light of the rivalry going on between Judaism and Christianity in their day, and especially the events of Israel's destruction before their eyes. But their exclusion of *any future for Israel* on the basis of Israel's sin clearly exceeds the theology expressed by the apostle Paul who held out hope for the future salvation of Israel despite their present judgment by God.

3. The Refusal of Jews to Accept Christ. The Pauline illustration of the olive tree in Romans 11 indicates that the early church of the New Testament era viewed itself as a participant with Israel in the promises of God. Israel's rejection of Christ had brought a temporary judgment of hardened hearts, but Israel would again turn to Christ and receive salvation (11:25–26). The incorporation of the Gentiles into the church would even help to hasten that day (11:12, 15). The anticipation of Christ's return may have raised the hope for many that the salvation of the Jews was not far off.

But as time passed, there was a growing awareness that the Jewish establishment was not going to change its mind. The formulation of Jewish tradition at Yavneh in between the two Jewish revolts—virtually the emergence of Rabbinic Judaism—was clear evidence that Judaism was insistent on having its own identity. The capstone of this developing break, however, came with the Bar Kockhba revolt, which the Jews had viewed as a messianic movement. The loyalty of Jewish Christians to Jesus as the Messiah made it impossible for them to recognize another Messiah. By contrast, as Marvin R. Wilson, observes, Judaism's "allegiance to its own messianic movement, spawned by its own charismatic leader, signaled clearly its final rejection of Jesus as Messiah."[91]

This hardened opposition of the Jews to any evangelistic efforts made itself felt in the early church. Jeffrey S. Siker explains that

---

[89]Siker, *Disinheriting the Jews*, 177.
[90]Lampe, "A.D. 70 in Christian Reflection," 171.
[91]Wilson, *Our Father Abraham*, 83.

early Christians increasingly . . . [were led] to see non-Christian Jews not as potential converts but as opponents to the gospel. As a result, whereas Paul could affirm that "as regards the gospel they are enemies of God, for your sake; but as regards election they are beloved for the sake of their forefathers" (Rom. 11:28), later generations of Christians came increasingly to affirm only the first half of Paul's statement.[92]

It is not difficult to see how this changing perspective toward unbelieving Jews contributed to the early church's appropriating the term "Israel" with its concomitant promises. Richardson explains that "as long as there was any expectation of Israel's acceptance, Christianity could not preempt the title 'Israel' without shutting the door to Judaism."[93] The loss of hope for Israel, however, together with the belief that she now stood under the irrevocable judgment of God, as evidenced by the destruction of Jerusalem and the expulsion of the Jews from that city, made this preemption not only possible, but seemingly logical. The Bible contained promises for the people of God known as "Israel." But these would now be fulfilled, not by the historical Israel, but by the "new Israel," the true believing people of God—the church.

4. *The Increasingly Gentile Composition of the Church.* The transition from a church whose first members were Jews to one dominated by people without Jewish roots led, in Siker's words, "to theological questions regarding the status of the Jews before God."[94]

The polemical tone toward the Jewish religious establishment expressed in the New Testament changed radically. As Wilson notes, quoting Longenecker, while "In the New Testament the *adversus Judaeos* polemical was 'an intra-family device used to win Jews to the Christian faith, in the second century it became anti-Semitic and was used to win Gentiles.' In the first case it was directly mainly by Jews against Jews, and in the second mainly by Gentiles against Jews."[95] Even though that polemic was expressed in strong terms in the New Testament, its origin among Jewish Christians and the abiding hope they had for the salvation of Israel kept the church from denying a place for historical Israel in the future. But the hardening of the Jews' hearts and the waning hope of Israel's conversion made it easier for the increasingly gentile church to polemicize against Judaism and to assert a replacement theology.

5. *Conclusion.* The historical circumstances impinging upon the early church, as we have recounted them, made theological thought in

---

[92]Siker, *Disinheriting the Jews*, 194.

[93]Richardson, *Israel in the Apostolic Church*, 201.

[94]Siker, *Disinheriting the Jews*, 195.

[95]Wilson, *Our Father Abraham*, 91–92; Richard N. Longenecker, *New Testament Social Ethics for Today* (Grand Rapids: Eerdmans, 1984), 40.

relation to Israel and the church inevitable. Ideally, such new theology is only a reconfiguration of canonical and biblical teaching applicable to the new situation. But history reveals that the church has at times allowed pressures to force it to unbalanced thought that no longer reflects the teaching of the Scriptures. Under assaults from both Judaism and paganism, the early church was not immune to this danger.[96] We see this, for example, in the rise of a new legalism or moralism that manifested "a lack of comprehensive understanding and profound appreciation of the gospel itself."[97] The beginnings of an excessive exaltation of the church and the doctrine of baptismal regeneration can also be traced to this period.[98] In our opinion, the theological development that denied a place for historical Israel in the prophesied kingdom salvation and gave it over to the church was also a deviation from the true meaning of Scripture.

IV. CONCLUSION

The biblical teaching about the roles of Israel and the church in history reveals that although they have much in common, they remain distinctively different. Believing Israel and the members of the church are one in their participation in the eschatological salvation of the new covenant. Because of the relationship to God that this entails, they are equally and together "the people of God."

Their difference lies not on the spiritual plane in their relationship to God, but in their specific identity and corresponding function in God's historical kingdom program. In both Testaments, the identity of "Israel" is always that historical people descended from Abraham through Jacob that became a nation. Israel was called to witness God's salvation to the other nations as a nation among nations. The church, by contrast, is identified in the New Testament as a people called out of *all* nations. In distinction to Israel in her being and witness as a "nation," the church is called to proclaim the kingdom salvation as individuals and as a community living in the midst of the nations, but not yet in the totality of a "nation."

Even in this distinction it should be noted that both the church and Israel are serving one, unified historical kingdom salvation. The emphasis in Scripture is thus on that which unifies rather than separates Israel and the church. They share in the one salvation of God and participate in the one historical plan of the kingdom to bring it to fruition. But each does so in her own way.

---

[96]For a summary of the teaching of the early post-apostolic fathers, see Reinhold Seeberg, *Text-Book of the History of Doctrines*, 2 vols. (reprint, Grand Rapids: Baker, 1977), 1:55–86.
[97]Ibid., 81.
[98]Ibid., 66–67, 78; also, J. N. D. Kelly, *Early Christian Doctrines*, rev. ed. (New York: Harper & Row, 1978), 190–91, 194–95.

PART IV

THE PLACE OF ISRAEL

Chapter 9

The Old Testament Prophecies About Israel

THE KEY DISTINCTIVE of dispensational theology, as we have seen throughout this book, is the recognition of Israel as a nation set apart from the other nations by God for the service of universal salvation for all peoples. We have already looked at some of the major promises about Israel stated in the foundational, promissory covenants with Abraham and David and in the new covenant. Now we turn our attention to the overall portrait of Israel and the nations found in the later prophetic hope that developed from those earlier promises. In chapter 10 we will examine the New Testament to see whether this picture has been radically altered by the events surrounding the first coming of Christ, or whether it remains fundamentally intact.

As in the covenants of promise, the eschatological hope of the later prophets portrays the destiny of all peoples as bound up with that of the nation of Israel. In its totality that hope was nothing less than the righting of all things by God. According to Donald E. Gowan, Old Testament eschatology expressed this hope in a basic, threefold pattern: "God must transform the human person; give a new heart and a new spirit. . . . God must transform human society; restore Israel to the promised land, rebuild cities, and make Israel's new status a witness to the nations. . . . And God must transform nature itself."[1]

The sequence of God's plan of renewal in Gowan's statement is significant. Renewal begins with the spiritual transformation of human beings. Spiritual renewal, however, is only the beginning of a total transformation. Our focus in this chapter will be primarily on the remaining dimensions of the prophetic picture, especially those dealing with Israel and her relations to the nations.

I. THE BASIC PROPHETIC THEMES[2]

A. *A Final Restoration from Exile*

Early indications of a future exile and restoration for Israel are already found in the writings of Moses.[3] A Pentateuchal collection of blessings and curses related to law keeping concludes with a curse involving the devastation of Israel by its enemies, with the result that the land would be laid waste and the people scattered among the nations (Lev 26:27–39). This divine judgment, along with the other judgments threatened for disobedience, were not God's last word to his people. Gordon Wenham observes that these judgments are described as "discipline" (vv. 18, 28): "Judgment does not prove that God has rejected his people. Rather he punishes them because they are his own (Amos 3:2)."[4]

The disciplinary purpose of God's judgment on Israel entails the promise of restoration. This restoration is conditioned on the confession and humbling of the hearts of the people, but the final outcome is assured.

---

[1]Donald E. Gowan, *Eschatology in the Old Testament* (Philadelphia: Fortress, 1986), 2.

[2]For the general picture of the eschatological hope of the Old Testament expressed through the prophets, see Ronald E. Clements, *Old Testament Theology* (Atlanta: John Knox, 1978), 144–54; Walther Eichrodt, *Theology of the Old Testament*, vol. 1 (Philadelphia: Westminster, 1961), 472–511; Ernst Jenni, "Eschatology of the Old Testament," in *The Interpreter's Dictionary of the Bible* (Nashville: Abingdon, 1962), 2:126–33; Walter C. Kaiser, Jr., *Toward an Old Testament Theology* (Grand Rapids: Zondervan, 1978), 71–261; Elmer A. Martens, *God's Design* (Grand Rapids: Baker, 1981); George N. H. Peters, *The Theocratic Kingdom*, 3 vols. (reprint, Grand Rapids: Kregel, 1952); Gerhard von Rad, *Old Testament Theology*, vol. 2 (New York: Harper & Row, 1965).

[3]Although these early statements of Moses are probably not to be regarded as primarily prophetic, they do come to be understood later as prophetic. Commenting on Deuteronomy 30, Peter C. Craigie says, "Moses, in his address, employs both the experience of the past and his notion of the potential future to force home upon the Israelites the need for obedience in the present. . . . This great vision in Moses, encompassing both past and future, does nevertheless come to be seen as prophetic over the course of time" (*The Book of Deuteronomy*, New International Commentary of the Old Testament [Grand Rapids: Eerdmans, 1976], 364).

[4]Gordon J. Wenham, *The Book of Leviticus*, New International Commentary on the Old Testament (Grand Rapids: Eerdmans, 1979), 332.

Israel "will pay for their sins because they rejected my laws and abhorred my decrees. Yet in spite of this, . . . I will not reject them or abhor them so as to destroy them completely, breaking my covenant with them. I am the LORD their God" (Lev 26:43–44).

A similar promise of restoration follows a list of blessings and cursings after the reiteration of the law in Deuteronomy. Because of the people's turning to God, Moses declares, "the LORD your God will restore your fortunes and have compassion on you and gather you again from all the nations where he scattered you" (Dt 30:3). The promise is here secured by the anticipation of the new covenant blessing of a new heart that loves God (v. 6).

The later prophets viewed the Exile as the expression of the curses laid upon Israel for her covenant disobedience. But they did not believe that the return from Babylon exhausted the blessings or the promise of restoration. Instead they looked ahead to the time of the Messiah for the final consummation of all of the blessings (cf. Eze 34–37).[5]

Numerous predictions of a final restoration of Israel are found among the later prophets, both before and after the Exile.[6] It is worth looking at several of these to grasp the importance of this theme in Israel's hope. In connection with the prophecy of a messianic "Branch" from "the stump of Jesse" (Isa 11:1–9), Isaiah declares, "In that day the Lord will reach out his hand a second time [the first being the Exodus, cf. v. 16] to reclaim the remnant that is left of his people. . . . He will . . . gather the exiles of Israel; he will assemble the scattered people of Judah from the four quarters of the earth" (Isa 11:11–12).

The messianic context of this passage makes it apparent that the reference is not to the historical return of Israel from Babylon. The rule of the "Branch," the time as "in that day" (used twice in vv. 10–11), which is an "eschatological phrase,"[7] and the declaration that the "Root of Jesse" would at that time "stand as a banner" for the nations (v. 10) all point to the eschatological times of the Messiah. The universal scope of the regathering "from the four quarters of the earth" (v. 12) also points to something more than the Babylonian return.[8] Isaiah's prophecy of a final regathering of Israel—which includes the unification of the northern and

---

[5]Wenham, *The Book of Leviticus,* 333.

[6]Of the sixteen canonical writing prophets, ten (Amos, Hosea, Isaiah, Micah, Zephaniah, Jeremiah, Ezekiel, Obadiah, Zechariah, Joel) write about a future restoration of Israel.

[7]G. W. Grogan, "Isaiah," in *The Expositor's Bible Commentary,* vol. 6, ed. Frank E. Gaebelein (Grand Rapids: Zondervan, 1986), 90.

[8]John N. Oswalt notes that the list of nations mentioned from which the remnant would be recovered—i.e., "from Assyria . . . and from the islands of the sea" (v. 11)—were not intended to be taken strictly literally, but rather were an attempt "to say that God is able to restore his people from *everywhere* (cf. v. 12)" (*The Book of Isaiah Chapters 1–39* [Grand Rapids: Eerdmans, 1986], 287).

southern kingdoms and, in the context, the subjection of their enemies (cf. vv. 13–16)—plainly refers to a future restoration of Israel under the Messiah.

In the midst of his prophecy against Babylon, Isaiah includes another statement of the restoration of Israel. Isaiah's taunting reference to Babylon in the judgments includes but goes beyond the historical empire as a symbol of the epitome of collectivized human glory and pride in opposition to the purposes of God.[9] The apostle John plays the same theme in the book of Revelation (chaps. 17–18), giving more detail of the final judgment.

To encourage and stimulate the people's faith amid the threats of foreign powers both contemporary and future, Isaiah affirmed the election and restoration of the nation of Israel. God will again "choose Israel and will settle them in their own land" (Isa 14:1). Instead of being oppressed by the nations, Israel will occupy a place of prominence among them (cf. vv. 1–2). Isaiah issued another statement of eschatological hope for Israel in a similar passage dealing with God's triumph over the nations: "In that day . . . you, O Israelites, will be gathered up one by one. . . . Those who were perishing in Assyria and those who were exiled in Egypt will come and worship the LORD on the holy mountain in Jerusalem" (27:12–13).

Several references to restoration are included among the blessings promised to Israel in the great comfort section of Isaiah's prophecy (chaps. 40–66). Along with the assurance of his love and presence, God tells his people whom he created for his glory, "I will bring your children from the east and gather you from the west. I will say to the north, 'Give them up!' and to the south, 'Do not hold them back.' Bring my sons from afar and my daughters from the ends of the earth" (43:5–6). As part of his being made a "covenant for the people," the coming messianic Servant of the LORD will restore the land, bring back the exiles, and sustain them with the fullness of divine provision (49:8–12).

Jeremiah also sounds the theme of restoration. The prophet projects a ray of hope into a message foretelling a disaster in which God would "throw" the people "out of this land." Jeremiah declares that "the days are coming" when the exodus from Egypt will no longer be viewed as the consummate expression of Israel's restoration (cf. Ex 20:2). Instead of saying "As surely as the LORD lives, who brought the Israelites up out of Egypt," the people will say, "As surely as the LORD lives, who brought the Israelites up out of the land of the north and out of the countries where he had banished them," because "I will restore them to the land I gave their forefathers" (Jer 16:14–15).

A similar analogy to the Exodus is found in Jeremiah 23:3–8, where

---

[9]For a good discussion of the meaning of Babylon in Isaiah, see Oswalt, *The Book of Isaiah Chapters 1–39,* 297–300.

God declares, using the metaphor of a shepherd, "I myself will gather the remnant of my flock out of all the countries where I have driven them and will bring them back to their pasture, where they will be fruitful and increase in number" (v. 3). These prophecies were not fulfilled in the return from Babylon, for Jews still celebrate the exodus from Egypt and not the return from Babylon as their defining moment.[10]

Other restoration promises are found in Jeremiah 30:3, 10–11 and 31:8. The regathering mentioned in 30:10 includes a proviso of permanence in the land: "Jacob will again have peace and security, and no one will make him afraid." Such a condition can only refer to the final eschatological regathering of Israel, not the historical return from Babylon, as the consummate restoration.

The so-called minor prophets of the pre-exilic time likewise offered hope of restoration. Joel declared that Judah and Jerusalem would be inhabited forever in the eschatological "that day." They would never again suffer the invasion of foreigners (3:17–21). Amos spoke of "that day" when David's fallen tent would be repaired and Israel would be planted "in their own land, never again to be uprooted" (9:11–15). "That day," according to Micah, would bring the assembling of the exiles and the rule of the Lord in Mount Zion "from that day and forever" (4:6–7). Zephaniah saw the regathering and restoration as a sign of God's blessing so that the people will have "honor and praise among all the peoples of the earth " (3:14–20).

During the exile in Babylon, Ezekiel continued to set before the people the hope of a final restoration to the land. He wrote, "the Sovereign LORD says: I will gather you from the nations and bring you back from the countries where you have been scattered, and I will give you back the land of Israel again" (11:17; cf. vv. 17–21). The addition of the new covenant promise of putting "a new spirit in them" and exchanging their stony hearts for hearts of flesh again points to a final eschatological fulfillment.

Israel must yet come into judgment, an experience the prophet likens to God's historical judgment of the people in the wilderness of the Exodus. But the outcome would be their restoration to the land of Israel, in which the nation would serve God (Eze 20:33–44). Again with the imagery of shepherding, God declared, "I myself will search for my sheep and look after them. . . . I will rescue them from all the places where they were scattered. . . . I will bring them out from the nations and gather them from the countries, and I will bring them into their own land" (34:11–13). There the Lord will pasture and tend them (vv. 14–16).

Ezekiel's well-known prophecy of the vision of dry bones speaks of the restoration of a united Israel and a final regathering to the land (chap. 37). Israel will be taken "out of the nations where they have gone" and

---

[10]Gowan, *Eschatology in the Old Testament*, 22.

will be made "one nation in the land, on the mountains of Israel" (vv. 21–22). The promise of the indwelling Spirit (v. 14), the presence of the messianic king (vv. 22–24), and the permanence of the restoration (vv. 25–27) again indicate the final regathering (cf. also 36:16–37). Add to this the promise of final restoration in connection with the destruction of Gog and Magog (39:25–29).

The message of a future eschatological restoration for Israel came from the post-exilic prophets also even as the nation was experiencing a restoration from Babylon. Zechariah still declared a future salvation for his people: "I will save my people from the countries of the east and the west. I will bring them back to live in Jerusalem" (8:7–8). The contextual evidence of a sanctified city with the very presence of God points to more than had taken place in the recent return. In chapter 10, the compassion of the Lord for his people is seen as the basis for restoration: "I will restore them because I have compassion on them. . . . I will signal for them and gather them in" (vv. 6, 8).[11]

All these messages of restoration looked beyond the historical return from Babylonian exile. Those spoken before the Babylonian return, no doubt, had significance for this nearer event. But their complete fulfillment, indicated by the extent of the promise and the presence of the new covenant and the messianic king, demanded an eschatological understanding. There are other predictions having more specific reference to the return from Babylon (e.g., Jer 24:4–7; 29:10–14; Eze 36:8–15), but even these are not totally devoid of reference to the final restoration. Ronald E. Clements observes, "The plight of those departed to Babylon has become a kind of model or symbol of the plight of all the scattered and dispossessed Jews who formed the Diaspora. . . . So the return to

---

[11]The restoration of Israel is frequently portrayed by the prophets as a certainty based solely on the grace of God. Ezekiel, for example, declares that God is going to restore Israel, not for its sake, "but for the sake of my holy name" (36:22). Of this promise, Stephen D. Ricks says, ". . . the return is strikingly certain and *sola gratia*, to use Walther Zimmerli's suggestive phrase" ("The Prophetic Literality of Tribal Reconstruction," in *Israel's Apostasy and Restoration* [Grand Rapids: Baker, 1988], 277).

Although the repentance of Israel is also often included in the restoration passages, this emphasis on God's gracious sovereign purpose indicates that the restoration promise is no longer tied to the conditional Sinaitic covenant, but is now related to the unconditional new covenant of grace (Jer 31:31ff.). It should also be noted that the land promise was already part of the unconditional promise with Abraham and therefore could not be lost in the end. All of this is in opposition to Mark W. Karlberg's thesis that Israel's blessing and prosperity in the land were always related to the conditional Mosaic covenant, under which they failed with the consequent transcendence of the material blessing by eternal spiritual blessing (see "The Significance of Israel in Biblical Typology," *Journal of the Evangelical Theological Society* 31 [Sept 1988]: 257–69).

Jerusalem and to Mount Zion became the classic image of how Israel's restoration would take place."[12]

The Israel of the prophecied restoration is described as a faithful remnant (e.g., Isa 10:20–22; 11:11, 16) in harmony with the entire biblical concept of the salvation of a remnant (cf. Ge 7:23; Mt 7:14; Rev 12:17). While the term "remnant" suggests some reduction in number from the original group, its primary meaning in relation to the people of God signifies those who escape divine judgment. The word carries both the negative idea of the judgment passed and the positive idea of merciful restraint and gracious salvation.[13] It underlines the preservation and "inherent potentiality of renewal of the remnant, no matter what its size."[14]

The prophecies do not indicate the size of the eschatological remnant, although Zechariah's statement that "there will not be room enough for them" (10:10) appears to suggest a large number. Other references to a great number are unclear as to whether they refer to the people returning or to growth subsequent to the return (cf. Isa 49:19; Eze 36:10–11).

One more significant feature of the final restoration of Israel is the help of the gentile nations. Isaiah prophesied that "nations will take them [the dispersed of Israel] and bring them to their own place" (14:2). According to Otto Kaiser, this text gives "an extravagant answer . . . to the question of how the return of the scattered Israelites is to take place: the peoples in whose midst they are forced to live will bring them back themselves into their ancestral home."[15] The dominant position of Israel over the nations, indicated in that same verse, rules out any possibility that full restoration lay in the return from Babylon under King Cyrus. Moreover, the previous context of the judgment on the whole world (13:9–13) provides the background and explanation for this reversal of relationships between Israel and the nations.[16]

Again, Isaiah prophesies that God "will beckon to the Gentiles" and "they will bring your sons in their arms and carry your daughters on their shoulders" (49:22). similar statements may be found in Isaiah 43:6;

---

[12]Clements, *Old Testament Theology*, 144–45. In noncanonical Jewish literature produced after the return from Babylon, we find the same recognition that that return was not the fulfillment of the Old Testament hope. Gowan notes that most frequently the writings from the Second Temple period reveal "a repetition of the OT pattern, which moves from exile to an eschatological restoration without attempting to account for the present state of affairs" (*Eschatology in the Old Testament*, 28).

[13]Ernst Jenni, "Remnant," in *The Interpreter's Dictionary of the Bible*, 4:32.

[14]Gerhard F. Hasel, "Remnant," in *The Interpreter's Dictionary of the Bible,* supp. vol., 735.

[15]Otto Kaiser, *Isaiah 13–39* (Philadephia: Westminster, 1974), 25.

[16]Kaiser, *Isaiah 13–39*, 25–26.

60:4–9; and 66:19–20. The latter two references especially appear to teach that the restoration is not confined to a brief time associated with the coming of the Messiah, but extends into his reign when the salvation of God flows to the nations. Jerusalem and Israel are the focal point of salvation glory during this time, and this truth moves many peoples not only to come to Jerusalem to worship and learn the ways of God (Isa 2:1–4), but also to bring back the Israelites who still dwell in distant places.

B. Israel Restored as a Nation Under a Davidic King

According to the prophets, the saved remnant of Israel was not only to be restored to the land, but also reconstituted as a nation under a king from the line of David. Prophecies of the coming Davidic king and his glorious reign in righteousness and peace are prominent. Isaiah describes a son who "will reign on David's throne and over his kingdom, establishing and upholding it with justice and righteousness from that time on and forever" (9:7). The reign of this king, called "a Branch" from "the stump of Jesse," is further described in 11:1–9.

Jeremiah records a similar promise from God: "The Days are coming ... when I will raise up to David a righteous Branch, a King who will reign wisely and do what is just and right in the land." Although this king has dominion over all the nations of the earth, his particular relation to Israel is made clear: "In his days Judah will be saved and Israel will live in safety" (Jer 23:5–6; cf. vv. 7–8). Later on, Jeremiah unites the coming king "from David's line" with the salvation and safety of Israel (33:14–17).

Ezekiel's picture of the dry bones coming together and receiving life from the Spirit culminates in "one nation" over which "my servant David will be king" (Eze 37:21–27). The mention of "one nation" recalls that restored Israel is continually portrayed as a "nation" among the other "nations" of the world. Of this eschatological assembling of the exiles, God declared through the prophet Micah, "I will make the lame a remnant, those driven away a strong nation" and "the LORD will rule over them in Mount Zion from that day and forever" (4:7). On this promise of "a strong nation," Leslie Allen says, "Israel will enjoy the status and stability of nationhood, taking bold place among the nations as a power to be reckoned with instead of a victim of powerful aggression."[17] Israel had been called and instituted as a nation (cf. Ex 9:6), had existed as a nation in

---

[17]Leslie C. Allen, *The Books of Joel, Obadiah, Jonah and Micah,* New International Commentary on the Old Testament (Grand Rapids: Eerdmans, 1976), 330. Clements likewise states that "the renewal of the monarchy would signify for Israel the return to full political independence" (*Theology of the Old Testament,* 146). For the meaning of "nation," see pp. 43–44 and 192–94.

history, and had "preserved the hope and expectation that it would again do so."[18]

This future nation would again consist of all Israel. The historical division of the two kingdoms of Israel and Judah would be healed to form the one nation. Ezekiel, symbolically joining two sticks representing Judah and Ephraim, declared, "This is what the Sovereign LORD says: I will take the Israelites out of the nations where they have gone. I will gather them from all around and bring them back into their own land. I will make them one nation in the land" (37:21–22; cf. also Jer 3:18; 23:5–6; Eze 20:42; Hos 1:11; Zec 10:6–12).

A central theme in the prophecies of restoration is the possession of the promised land. We have already noted the inherent connection between the land and the promises of descendants and nationhood given to Abraham.[19] The "land" also appeared as a place of rest for Israel undergirding the kingdom promise to David.[20] This promised possession of the land was never completely fulfilled in the history of Israel and therefore remained part of the prophetic hope.

As part of the messianic servant's task "to restore the tribes of Jacob and bring back those of Israel" (Isa 49:6), he is to "restore the land and . . . reassign its desolate inheritances" (v. 8). In this restoration, the servant, as a new "Joshua," will bring prosperity and repopulate the land with the freed captives (cf. vv. 9–12). Like shoots planted by God, the restored people of Zion "will possess the land forever" (Isa 60:21).

Undoubtedly, Israel's repossession of the land is a recurring theme for Jeremiah and Ezekiel because of the proximity of the Exile. Amid the rebellion that led to their exile under judgment, Jeremiah told the people of Israel how God longed "to give you a desireable land, the most beautiful inheritance of any nation" (Jer 3:19). The prophet foresaw the day when the people would give up their stubbornness and "the house of Judah will join the house of Israel, and together they will come . . . to the land I gave your forefathers as an inheritance" (v. 18). God promised to "bring them back to this land" (Jer 24:6; cf. also 27:22; 29:10; 30:3).

Ezekiel, probably seeking to encourage the exiles, emphasized that Israel would one day be established in the land permanently in fulfillment of the promises of God. They would go and serve idols, but afterward "on my holy mountain . . . in the land the entire house of Israel will serve me. . . . Then you will know that I am the LORD, when I bring you into the land of Israel, the land I had sworn . . . to give to your fathers" (Eze 20:39–42). Ezekiel also declared,

---

[18]Ronald E. Clements, "גוֹי goy," in *Theological Dictionary of the Old Testament*, vol. 2, ed. G. J. Botterweck and H. Ringgren (Grand Rapids: Eerdmans, 1975), 432.

[19]See pp. 44–46.

[20]See pp. 61–62.

> But you, O mountains of Israel, will produce branches and fruit for
> my people Israel, for they will soon come home. . . . I will multiply
> the number of people upon you, even the whole house of
> Israel. . . . I will settle people on you as in the past. . . . I will cause
> people, my people Israel, to walk upon you. They will possess you,
> and you will be their inheritance; you will never again deprive
> them of their children (36:8–12; cf. also v. 28).

Israel's restoration pictured by Ezekiel in the vision of the dry
bones entails their reestablishment in the land: "I am going to open your
graves and bring you up from them; I will bring you back to the land of
Israel. . . . I will put my Spirit in you and you will live, and I will settle
you in your own land" (37:12, 14; cf. also vv. 21, 22, 25). Donald E. Gowan
affirms, "For Israel to live . . . is to return to the land of Canaan."[21]

The whole concluding section of Ezekiel's prophecies (chaps. 40–
48) pictures Israel's resettlement and the redistribution of land among the
tribes (cf. 45:1; 47:13–48:35; cf. Isa 49:8). Granted that this final portrayal
merges into the eternal state, as we see from the many allusions to this
passage in Revelation 21–22 (e.g., 21:12; 22:1–2); nevertheless, the
references to sin and death (e.g., Eze 44:25, 27) make it obvious that this
restoration cannot be applied solely to the perfect, glorified state. The
combination argues for an interim period during which the promises of
Israel's restoration to the land find their fulfillment before the final age of
perfection. These times are not yet sharply distinguished by the prophets
(cf. also Isa 65–66), for they all belong to and are part of the divine work
predicted for the messianic eschatological period when all will be made
new.

The promise of the land in its earthly material reality remained
significantly central to all the promises of Israel's restoration. Clements
observes that, according to Deuteronomy, the land was "not only a gift of
God's election, but to some extent . . . an expression and confirmation of
it," and so it became "the central object of hope and eschatological
expectation" during the time of the exile. "It became impossible to think
of a restored Israel, and a cleansed and purified community, except in
relation to this land. Even more than the hope of a messiah it appeared as
an indispensable part of the life that was anticipated as the fulfilment of
Yahweh's choosing of Israel."[22]

C. Jerusalem (and Israel) as the Glorified Center
of a Universal Kingdom

The restoration of Israel to the land in prosperity is not pictured in
the Old Testament eschatological hope as a divine work involving that

---

[21]Gowan, *Eschatology in the Old Testament*, 25.
[22]Clements, *Old Testament Theology*, 94.

nation only. Rather, it is always related to the much larger, universal purpose of God for all peoples as expressed in the foundational promise to Abraham (cf. Ge 12:3). Without question, the prophets' hope entails a certain prominence for Israel among the nations. But far from being egotistically self-serving for the nation of Israel, this divine activity was designed for the blessing of all mankind. In chapter 12 we will look more closely at God's intended purpose in the call and establishment of Israel. Here we will simply survey the overall prophetic picture of Jerusalem and Israel in the Old Testament eschatological hope.

The city of Jerusalem stands at the center of the messianic kingdom that encompasses the entire world. It merits this position because the presence of God and his glory are manifest there.[23] Jeremiah declares, "At that time they will call Jerusalem The Throne of the LORD, and all nations will gather in Jerusalem to honor the name of the LORD" (3:17). According to J. A. Thompson, the city will fulfill the "function formerly played by the Ark, that is, Yahweh's throne, the symbol of Yahweh's presence ..." (cf. Eze 48:35).[24] The nations will call her "the City of the LORD, Zion of the Holy One of Israel" and "Sought After, the City No Longer Deserted" (Isa 60:14; 62:12). She will bear the name, "THE LORD IS THERE" (Eze 48:35).

The immediate cause of this adulation of Jerusalem is the presence of the Messiah himself (Mal 3:1) as the manifestation of the glory of God. In the eternal state, God himself is said to come there directly and manifest his heavenly glory among humankind on earth (Rev 21–22). For this reason, Jerusalem will be the center of life and worship. Its beauty is "the joy of the whole earth" (Ps 48:2). The city is pictured with a river flowing from it as a source of God's continual, refreshing blessings of life (cf. Ps 46:4; Eze 47:1ff.; Joel 3:18; Zec 14:8). Because the glory of the Lord has come to Zion, the nations that live in darkness will be drawn to its light (Isa 60:1-3). Because it is established as "the chief among the mountains," the nations will "stream to it" to learn the ways of the God of Israel, who dwells there (Isa 2:1–4; Mic 4:1–3).

This prophetic picture, according to Allen, affirms Jerusalem as "the focal point of humanity, and its supremacy was to be acknowledged by all.... Men are to look up to Jerusalem as superior to all other mountains, the sole place on earth where God reveals himself, the center of the world."[25]

As the focal point of the revelation of God, Jerusalem is the center

---

[23]For an informative and suggestive comment on the position of Jerusalem as the center of the world involving other than religious dimensions, see Peters, *The Theocratic Kingdom*, 3:33.

[24]J. A. Thompson, *The Book of Jeremiah*, New International Commentary on the Old Testament (Grand Rapids: Eerdmans, 1980), 203.

[25]Allen, *The Books of Joel, Obadiah, Jonah and Micah*, 324–25.

of worship. The eagerness of the nations to learn the ways of God is reminiscent of the earlier godly saints who sought instructions at the temple. Foreigners who "bind themselves to the LORD" will be brought to God's holy mountain and receive joy in the "house of prayer," which will be such "for all nations" (Isa 56:6–7). The place of the sanctuary will be adorned and glorified so that the "sons of your [Zion's] oppressors will come bowing before you . . . and will call you the City of the LORD, Zion of the Holy One of Israel" (Isa 60:13–14). Because God's glory and salvation radiate from Jerusalem to all peoples, the city will be "the praise of the earth" (Isa 62:7; cf. Jer 33:9). So also God will give the people of Israel "honor and praise among all the peoples of the earth when I restore your fortunes before your very eyes" (Zep 3:20).

Israel's being praised by the peoples of the earth reaffirms the truth taught in other Scriptures that she will have a certain prominence among the nations. Israel's restoration will result in her being "the foremost of the nations" (Jer 31:7; cf. Dt 26:19). This dominance exists because God is "Israel's father" and it is his "firstborn son" (v. 9; cf. Ex 4:22).[26]

Several prophecies of Isaiah depict the nations as being subject to Israel. The neighbors who had plundered Israel would themselves be plundered and made subject to it (Isa 11:14). So not only will the Gentiles aid in the return to the land, but Israel will "possess the nations as menservants and maidservants in the LORD's land. They will make captives of their captors and rule over their [former] oppressors" (14:2). The nations will "bow down before you . . . ; they will lick the dust at your feet" (49:23; cf. vv. 22–26). "The nation or kingdom that will not serve you will perish" (60:12).

The language in these passages does not suggest an eye-for-an-eye retribution for the earlier mistreatment of Israel by the nations. Rather, it points simply to a reversal of Israel's position in relation to them. Instead of domination and oppression, the presence of God in Israel would elevate Israel to leadership. Franz Delitzsch echoes this thought: ". . . to be ruled by the people of God is the true happiness of the nations, and to allow themselves to be so ruled is their true liberty."[27] As part of that service, the nations would enrich Israel: "the wealth on the seas will be brought to

---

[26]Although only Ephraim or the Northern Kingdom is mentioned in this text, it represents the entire nation as God's "son." Its mention before Judah (vv. 23–26) is probably owing to its having been "in exile much longer and humanly considered, were less likely to be delivered" (Charles L. Feinberg, "Jeremiah," in *The Expositor's Bible Commentary*, vol. 6, ed. Frank E. Gaebelein [Grand Rapids: Zondervan, 1986], 568).

[27]Franz Delitzsch, *Biblical Commentary on the Prophecies of Isaiah* (3d ed., 1877; reprint, Grand Rapids: Eerdmans, 1960), 307. Similarly, in relation to the concept of Israel's possessing other nations, John E. Hartley explains that "instead of defeating them in battle the nations will also become God's people (Isa. 54:3; cf. Amos 9:12)" ("ירשׁ," *Theological Wordbook of the Old Testament* [Chicago: Moody Press, 1980], 1: 410–11).

you, to you the riches of the nations will come" (Isa 60:5; cf. vv. 6–7). Restored Israel will "feed on the wealth of the nations, and in their riches ... will boast" (Isa 61:6; cf. 45:14; 66:12; Hag 2:7–9).

The concept of the supremacy of Israel in the Old Testament eschatological hope, perhaps more than any other dimension, has provoked questions of interpretation among Christians. Many scholars consider any literal understanding anachronistic in light of the melding of the nations brought about in the church of the New Testament. Otto Kaiser notes that "anyone whose starting point is the Christian universalism of salvation as found in Paul, and for whom there can be no distinctions of nation or race in the church (cf. Gal. 3.28), may regard 14.1–4a as a 'revoltingly arrogant expectation' (Duhm) or the testimony of 'the unseemly piety of a late period' (Fohrer)."[28]

The general tendency of interpreters is summarized by John N. Oswalt: "... older commentators (but also Young) have tended to spiritualize the passage [Isa. 14:2], saying that it referred to the Church and its dominion over all the earth. More recent scholars generally dismiss it as an unfortunate expression of late Jewish nationalism."[29]

Nevertheless, the fact that the same prophet portrays the final participation of the nations along with Israel in the blessings of God's gracious salvation refutes the appeal to a narrow, outmoded nationalism.[30] In the same way, viewing these prophetic statements as a "figurative expression ... that the present relationship between Israel and the nations would not always obtain,"[31] or as "metaphors for the careful protection, and the deference and attention, to be accorded to those who return home,"[32] seems to fall short of their apparent meaning. Granted that some of the language is figurative, e.g., "making captives" of the nations or their "licking dust." Yet there seems to be no ground for denying the prophets' understanding of a distinct position for Israel above the other nations of the world.

Objections appear to be based on either of two assumptions: (1) that nations have no more significance in the historical program of God, or (2) that universal salvation rules out the possibility of any distinction among peoples. The former seems to have no basis in Scripture. On the contrary, as will be seen in the next chapter, the New Testament confirms a future for Israel.[33] This in itself would appear to distinguish this nation at least to some extent. The latter assumption seems

[28]Kaiser, *Isaiah 13–39*, 26–27.
[29]Oswalt, *The Book of Isaiah*, 313.
[30]See the discussion of the Old Testament teaching of gentile salvation in chaps. 5 and 12.
[31]Oswalt, *The Book of Isaiah*, 313; cf. also 288.
[32]Claus Westermann, *Isaiah 40–66* (Philadephia: Westminster, 1969), 221.
[33]See the New Testament teaching concerning Israel in chaps. 10 and 11.

invalid because it is clearly evident that distinctions among people exist in the various functional offices of leadership in the Old Testament theocracy as well as in the church.[34] The grounds for rejecting the apparent meanings of these texts and for denying a distinction between Israel and other nations seem biblically unwarranted.

We must recognize that the purpose for Israel's prominence is not self-aggrandizement but rather the universal blessing of all peoples. On that basis the prophetic picture is not inharmonious with God's promise to "bless all the families of the earth" through Abraham and his seed (Ge 12:3).[35] The prophetic hope expressed in God's purpose to glorify himself through Israel for the salvation of all peoples is well summed up by Sigmund Mowinckel.

> The restoration of Israel and the realization of all the people's ideals were taken to be the essential factors in the kingly rule of Yahweh. It is to restore His people Israel and give it a place in the sun that Yahweh comes as king and establishes His kingdom. It is through the glorification of Israel that the glorification of Yahweh is achieved. The sight of the great miracle, which He works for His people in spite of all human probability, makes the other nations submit to Him, and come as pilgrims to His sanctuary to worship Him as the only true God, as alone worthy of the name of God. . . . The submission of the other nations to Yahweh means, in concrete terms, that when He comes and frees His people, the nations' power is crushed, and that the survivors submit to Israel. . . . Thus the kingly glory of Yahweh appears in visible and tangible form. It goes without saying that this also means that the other nations share in Israel's happiness and blessing (i.e., salvation).[36]

Far from a narrow particularism, the restoration and exaltation of Israel is destined to be the center of God's reign of peace and righteousness over all the earth. The messianic king will rule over all nations; they will all serve him (Ps 72:8–11; Zec 14:9). As a result the nations will not engage in war, and the world will live in peace (Ps 46:9; Isa 2:4; 9:5; Mic 4:3; Hos 2:18; Zec 9:10). This messianic reign of peace does not immediately involve the exclusion of all sin; that will take place only with the making of all things new. That sin is present during the Messiah's reign is evident in his settling disputes among the nations (cf. Isa 2:4) and in the possibility of punishing the disobedient (Zec 14:16–19). But that sin will never be able to thwart the righteous, powerful reign of the Messiah.

---

[34]See the discussion of the distinction of Israel on pp. 299–305.

[35]See chapter 12 for a full discussion of the divine purpose of Israel as a channel of salvation for all nations.

[36]Sigmund Mowinckel, *He That Cometh* (New York: Abingdon, 1954), 149.

D. The Spiritual Renewal of Israel

The outward transformation of Israel into a preeminent nation that provides light for the nations is based on an inward spiritual renewal. Along with a return to the land, Ezekiel prophesies a changed heart. He speaks of the inherent relationship of the outward and the inward in 11:19–20: "They will return. . . . I will give them an undivided heart and put a new spirit in them. . . . Then they will follow my decrees and be careful to keep my laws. They will be my people, and I will be their God."

Ezekiel 36:25–29 draws a similar connection: "For I will take you out of the nations. . . . I will sprinkle clean water on you, and you will be clean. . . . I will give you a new heart and put a new spirit in you" (cf. also 37:12–14, 20–27). This transformation would result from God's making with Israel "a covenant of peace . . . an everlasting covenant" (37:26). This is the same covenant prophesied earlier by Jeremiah as "a new covenant," which is associated with the physical restoration of the nation eschatologically (Jer 31:31–33; cf. vv. 27–28; 32:36–44; Zec 14:20–21; Isa 46:13). Undoubtedly, this spiritual transformation, more than material prosperity, will enable Israel to provide leadership for other nations in the service of God—even as spirituality has always been the real enablement for leadership among God's people.

E. Salvation for the Nations of the World

We spoke in chapter 5 of the salvation of the Gentiles in connection with the new covenant. Since the subject will come up again in chapter 12 in relation to the future mission of Israel, we need only highlight it here as a significant feature of the total Old Testament eschatological hope. The prophecies of God's eschatological dealings with Israel are not concerned with Israel alone. Scattered through these prophecies are references to God's concern for the nations. Through Israel, God intends to show himself "holy . . . in the sight of the nations" (Eze 20:41; 28:25) so that the nations will come to know him (36:22–23, 36; 37:28; 39:21, 23; Isa 45:14; 49:26).[37] This knowledge of God among the nations is more than a simple recognition that God exists, because the same prophetic concern relates to Israel and her spiritual restoration. Rather, it indicates "above all else the adoration that kneels because of divinely inspired recognition, an orientation toward the one who himself says 'I am Yahweh.' "[38]

Other prophetic statements testify to the effectiveness of God's

---

[37]For a full treatment of this concept especially in Ezekiel, see Walther Zimmerli, "Knowledge of God According to the Book of Ezekiel," in *I Am Yahweh* (Atlanta: John Knox, 1982), 29–98.

[38]Zimmerli, "Knowledge of God According to the Book of Ezekiel," 88.

revelation to the nations. Nations will "acknowledge" and "worship" him (cf. Isa 19:21–25; Ps 87:4). They will voluntarily come to Zion to be taught "his ways" in order to "walk in his paths" (Isa 2:3). They will "put their hope" in God's law (Isa 42:4). They will declare that they belong to the Lord and desire to associate themselves with God's people Israel (Isa 44:5; cf. Zec 8:20–22).[39] Salvation will be offered to "all you ends of the earth" and "every knee will bow,"[40] acknowledging that "in the LORD alone are righteousness and strength" (Isa 45:22–23). "All the nations will gather in Jerusalem to honor the name of the LORD," no longer following "the stubbornness of their evil hearts" (Jer 3:17).

These Scriptures indicate that the final goal of the Old Testament prophetic hope is nothing less than the establishment of the kingdom of God in which both the nations and Israel will live in peace and righteousness under God's rulership mediated through the messianic, Davidic king (cf. Zec 14:9).

F. The Return to Paradise

The prophetic picture includes not only a personal and societal restoration of humankind, but also a transformation of nature.[41] In God's original "good" creation, nature was in harmony with and was promotive of only the good of human life (cf. Ge 1:28–31). This harmony was ruined by sin (cf. Ge 3:17–19). The prophets portray a return to the pristine conditions under which the earth, including the present waste places, will be bountiful in her produce (e.g., Isa 32:15, 20; Eze 34:26–27, 29; Am 9:13–14).[42] While the focus of these statements is on the restored land of Israel, which will be "renowned for its crops" (Eze 34:29), they will

---

[39]The NIV translation of Isaiah 44:5 that a Gentile "will call himself by the name of Jacob . . . and will take the name Israel" should not be understood as teaching that these become part of the nation of Israel itself (cf. Westermann, *Isaiah 40–66*, 137–38). As the word "himself" is not in the Hebrew, the first word in the first phrase may also be translated "call on the name of Jacob" (NASB) or, as Delitzsch renders it, "solemnly name the name of Jacob," making it "the medium and object of solemn exclamation."

Likewise, to "take the name Israel" may be understood as "a name or title of honour among the heathen" (Delitzsch, *Biblical Commentary on the Prophecies of Isaiah*, 2:204–5). Because the prophetic picture as a whole views divine salvation as extending to the Gentiles without their becoming Jewish converts, it is preferable to see this text as expressing the same thought as Zechariah 8:20–22, where it is said that the Gentiles desire to associate with Israel because of the presence of God in their midst.

[40]This must not be understood as universalism or a forced submission. The context makes it clear that the reference is to those among all nations who give free assent to the salvation of God (cf. Kaiser, *Isaiah 40–66*, 146).

[41]For a brief overview of all the physical effects prophesied for the kingdom, see Alva J. McClain, *The Greatness of the Kingdom* (Grand Rapids: Zondervan, 1959), 234–41; cf. also Gowan, *Eschatology in the Old Testament*, 97–120.

[42]See also Psalm 72:16; Isaiah 29:17; Ezekiel 36:8–11, 29–30; Hosea 2:21–22.

undoubtedly also come to apply to other nations, at least to some extent, as they receive and practice the righteousness of God.

Along with the bountiful productivity, the disruption of harmony between mankind and the animal world as a result of sin will be overcome (cf. Ge 9:2). The threat of wild beasts is to be removed (cf. Isa 35:9; Eze 34:25). Animals will be restored to their original friendly relationship with mankind (Isa 11:6–9; 65:25; Hos 2:18). These physical changes culminate in what Isaiah calls the "new earth" (Isa 65:17).

These prophecies of material benefits have often been denied their natural meaning. Gowan notes that "until environmentalists began to speak [in recent times], it seemed adequate just to reaffirm these texts without interpretation, or to call them symbolic—reinterpreting them—or to call them mythological—dismissing them—or to make no comment on them whatever."[43] These interpretations indicate a tendency among many Christian scholars to discount the earthly realism of the Old Testament faith in favor of an otherworldly spirituality. To reject a literal understanding of these passages about nature seems unwarranted, however, in light of the biblical teaching of the effects of sin on the natural realm (cf. Ge 1:29–30; 3:14, 17–18; 9:2–3). If we regard the negative affects of the fall of mankind as materially evident, then it is perfectly sound to regard the positive transformations wrought by messianic salvation as empirical as well.

G. A Final State of Perfection Beyond a Millennial Kingdom

The prophetic hope concludes with a vision of a final state of perfection when all things will be made new, including the very "heavens" and "earth." Isaiah prophesied, "Behold, I will create new heavens and a new earth. The former things will not be remembered, nor will they come to mind" (Isa 65:17; cf. 66:22). This Old Testament hope provides the background for John's vision of a "new heaven and a new earth" following the passing away of the first heaven and earth (Rev 21:1). The light of the sun and moon will be replaced with the everlasting light of God's glory (Isa 60:19–20; cf. Rev 21:23; 22:5). And Isaiah's description of the beauty of Jerusalem, constructed out of jewels and precious stones (54:11–12), transcends even the glorious earthly city of the millennium and points toward the final heavenly Jerusalem of the eternal state (cf. Rev 21:18–21).

The presence of these eternal conditions reveals a tension in the prophetic picture between a millennial restoration that is not yet complete

---

[43]Gowan, *Eschatology in the Old Testament*, 108. For a discussion of material promises arguing for their literal understanding, see Antonine DeGuglielmo, "The Fertility of the Land in the Messianic Prophecies," *Catholic Biblical Quarterly* 19 (1957): 306–11.

and the final perfection of the eternal state. The messianic reign of Christ, as we have seen, is set in an as-yet-imperfect world, as indicated by the presence of continuing sin and the corresponding presence of the saving activity of God.

Several prophetic passages serve as examples illustrating these conditions. Speaking of a restored and exalted Jerusalem in the "last days," the messianic times, Isaiah describes the nations as streaming to "the mountain of the LORD's temple" in order to be taught the ways of God so that they might walk in them (2:1–3). Implied here is an imperfection that still requires what might be called the divine saving action of sanctification. Also, the Lord is said to "judge between the nations and . . . settle disputes for many peoples," and consequently the nations will "beat their swords into plowshares and their spears into pruning hooks" (v. 4).

E. J. Young, interpreting God as implementing these actions through the Messiah, explains, "God is now represented as one who in a peaceful manner intervenes in the disputes of nations, and settles them so that the nations change the implements of war into utensils of peace." As for the Messiah's "settling disputes for many peoples," Young states that this "pictures the LORD in the position of Judge and Arbiter who pronounces decisions concerning the nations and their disagreements."[44]

Allen explains the practical meaning of this picture in terms of the parallel passage in Micah 4:2–4: "Jerusalem was to become the international court whose findings would be accepted without quibble. Disputes would be settled amicably, for such would be Yahweh's prestige that even great nations in far-flung corners of the world would acknowledge his equity."[45] That there are disputes requiring the judging ministry of the Lord is evidence that sin is still present. Thus, while this activity obviously belongs to the time of the Messiah's reign, it cannot yet be assigned to the perfected state of eternity. It points therefore to what has been called a millennial reign of the Messiah before the eternal conditions have commenced.

This prophecy declared by both Isaiah and Micah poses problems for those who do not apply it to a millennial reign of Christ. Young, for example, recognized that the biblical portrayal of evil in the present age rules out any application of these prophecies to some sort of postmillennial time before the return of Christ. Nevertheless, he summarily rejected the dispensationalist application of these prophecies to the millennium. "This . . . type of interpretation," he wrote, "does violence of a serious kind to the general structure of Biblical eschatology."[46] Acknowledging that his

---

[44]Edward J. Young, *The Book of Isaiah*, New International Commentary on the Old Testament (Grand Rapids: Eerdmans, 1965), 1:107.

[45]Allen, *The Books of Joel, Obadiah, Jonah and Micah*, 325.

[46]Young, *The Book of Isaiah*, 109.

own interpretation "has difficulties, but it is all that one can do if he would be faithful to the language of the Bible," he concluded that this prophecy has begun its fulfillment during this present age and will reach its final realization at the second coming of Christ.[47]

A straightforward reading of the prophecies truly does expose the "difficulties" in both nonmillennialist and postmillennialist views. Are the nations at present streaming to the church to learn the ways of God and walk in his paths? Is Christ really "settling disputes" today for many peoples with the result that the nations are turning their weapons into plowshares? It is plain that these questions cannot be answered positively except by an unnatural bending of the text—a bending that would have been quite foreign to the original readers. Yet the texts fit well with a millennial interpretation of the Messiah's reigning from Jerusalem. We will see that this interpretation does not in fact contradict the general structure of biblical eschatology.

We obtain a further picture of millennial conditions in the prophet's description of the Messiah's reign that is given in Isaiah 11. The prophet speaks of a judgment in relation to the presence of sin: "He will not judge by what he sees with his eyes, or decide by what he hears with his ears; but with righteousness he will judge the needy, with justice he will give decision for the poor of the earth" (vv. 3–4). This judgment does not consist of simply a brief final court, but refers to the nature of the Messiah's rule. Concern for the poor was consistently part of the role expected from Israel's kings (cf. Ps 72:2; Pr 29:14; Isa 1:23) and from kings throughout the Near East.[48]

Psalm 72 also pictures the Messiah taking up the cause of the "afflicted" and "oppressed" (cf. vv. 2, 4, 12–14) and judging the "oppressor" (v. 4). Besides helping the helpless, the messianic King is pictured as bringing blessing to all nations (v. 17). Again, we have a picture of universal blessing for the nations, but not yet perfection.

Finally, Zechariah's threat of discipline for those who do not keep the proper worship of the King clearly depicts a messianic reign over an imperfect world. Zechariah describes the intervention of the Lord to defeat the invading nations of the world and rescue his people and the city of Jerusalem; then he declares, "The LORD will be king over the whole earth. On that day there will be one LORD, and his name the only name" (14:9). The reference to the personal presence of the Messiah (his feet stand on the Mount of Olives, v. 4) and the overwhelming triumph (cf. vv. 12–15) show that this passage relates to the triumphant coming (or in the light of the New Testament, the second coming) of the Messiah. This ruling over the nations does not yet signal the eternal perfect state,

---

[47]Young, *The Book of Isaiah*, 109.
[48]Oswalt, *The Book of Isaiah Chapters 1–39*, 281.

however, for the prophet goes on to warn the "survivors from all the nations that have attacked Jerusalem" that if they do not go to Jerusalem to worship the Lord, they will be punished by drought and plague (vv. 16–19).

Other evidence such as the presence of death (cf. Isa 65:20) might be added to indicate an as-yet-imperfect situation during the time of the Messiah's rule. But these are sufficient to establish the fact that the Old Testament prophetic picture saw in the future both (1) a messianic reign in righteousness over a world that still included sin and needed salvation, and (2) a final perfect state.

George E. Ladd explains this mingling by pointing out the prophetic perspective of the future. In contrast to the modern mind, which is interested in chronological sequence, he notes that

> the prophetic mind usually was not concerned with such questions but took its stand in the present and viewed the future as a great canvas of God's redemptive working in terms of height and breadth but lacking the clear dimension of depth. The prophets usually saw in the background the final eschatological visitation of God; but since they primarily concerned themselves with God's will for his people in the present, they viewed the immediate future in terms of the ultimate future without strict chronological differentiation.[49]

Thus, whereas in many instances the prophets "blended together" the historical with the eschatological so that they were "practically indistinguishable" (e.g., Joel's plague of locusts and the eschatological judgment, 1:4–12; 2:10–11; 3:11–15), so they also blended the future. What might be termed "eschatological history" was mingled with the final state.[50]

The divine plan for the restoration of all things according to the

---

[49]George E. Ladd, *The Presence of the Future* (Grand Rapids: Eerdmans, 1974), 64–65. Although he somewhat confusingly interprets the division as one between "type and antitype" or "earthly realities and eternal glory," Dirk H. Odendaal similarly portrays the prophetic admixture of these two dimensions when he says, "The return from exile, the repopulation of the country, and the rebuilding of the temple are seen ideally in their relationship to and significance for the final triumph of the kingdom of God; and thus something of that eternal glory already pervades the description of the earthly realities. The earthly restoration, on the other hand, acquires a certain transparency in the direction of the eternal and final reality. There is a degree of fluidity in the demarcation line between type and antitype" (*The Eschatological Expectation of Isaiah 40–66 with Special Reference to Israel and the Nations* [Nutley, New Jersey: Presbyterian and Reformed, 1970], 126).

[50]There is no necessity to radically distinguish the historical and apocalyptic elements of divine irruption in the eschatological hope as two irreconcilable pictures of Jewish hope, which is what many scholars have done (cf. Mowinckel, *He that Cometh*, 261–79). The Old Testament anticipated a new intrusion of God into history in a final visitation to bring his purposes to their ultimate consummation (see George E. Ladd, "Why Not Prophetic-Apocalyptic?" *Journal of Biblical Literature* 86 [1957]: 192–200).

prophets, therefore, involved two stages. One stage included a kingdom characterized by an internal spiritual salvation and the glorious reign of the Messiah over all his enemies—for the first time in human history, a rule over the whole earth by man as a representative of God's will. A certain regeneration of nature will also take place. But sin, although unable to contest the powerful rule of the Messiah, will still be present. Only after this temporary period, with the final elimination of evil from the heavens and earth and the making of all things new, will the restoration be complete. Such a sequential harmonizing of the different strains of the prophetic hope was expressed more clearly and became the dominant interpretation of later Judaism.[51]

II. SOME BASIC CHARACTERISTICS
OF THE OLD TESTAMENT PERSPECTIVE

The prophetic themes we have cited provide an overview of the prophetic hope of the Old Testament. Before looking at the New Testament teaching on these themes, it will be helpful to note some basic features of these prophecies.

A. *The Prophecies Are Comprehensive*

The Old Testament prophetic picture reveals a hope that is comprehensive and holistic. Its themes provide for the restoration of all things spiritual and material. Humankind, the focus of the original creation, is also the center of the redemptive purpose. All aspects of human life—the personal, inward, and individualistic as well as the social,

---

[51]D. S. Russell summarizes the process whereby a temporary reign of the Messiah followed by the final state became the dominant teaching in Jewish apocalyptic. "Throughout this whole process, from Daniel to II Esdras, we find evidence, then, of a tension between a this-worldly kingdom and an other-worldly kingdom. In the earlier period especially the former of these predominates and even when, in later years, the influence of the latter makes itself increasingly felt it does not oust from people's minds the earlier hope whose roots can be traced back into the ancient prophetic expectations. In their teaching concerning a millennial or a temporary kingdom to be followed, through resurrection and judgment, by 'the age to come' they were expressing a compromise which witnesses to the strength of that traditional faith which looked forward to the establishment of the ruler of God not only over his own people in their own land, but also over all people throughout the whole earth" (*The Method and Message of Jewish Apocalyptic* [Philadelphia: Westminster, 1964], 297).

George F. Moore points to the same teaching and notes the general agreement of rabbinical conceptions: "With the scheme of the later apocalypses rabbinical conceptions are in general accord. The beginning of the Messianic Age is a great crisis in the history of Israel and of the nations. As its close, the Last Things in the proper sense begin" (*Judaism in the First Centuries of the Christian Era: The Age of the Tannaim* [Cambridge: Harvard Univ. Press, 1962], 2:377).

communal, and international—are part of the total prophetic picture. It is difficult to conceive of any aspect of God's salvation portrayed in the New Testament that is not already seen in this Old Testament hope.

This comprehensive scope of Old Testament prophecy calls into question the common view that the Old Testament deals with material and earthly realities while the New Testament deals with higher, spiritual matters. To be sure, there is the *historical* progression to a more intimate relation of mankind with God.[52] This is manifest in the shadow forms of worship associated with access to God (e.g., the Mosaic sacrificial system), which give way to direct fellowship through the indwelling Spirit. But this historical reality does not constitute the whole of the Old Testament. It also includes the prediction of the spiritual reality of the new covenant, which became historical in the New Testament through the work of the Spirit.

It is often overlooked that the prophets did not see these spiritual truths as contrary to material and earthly realities. Rather, the earthly were perfectly concomitant with the spiritual. This comprehensive nature of the prophecies denies the common hermeneutical tendency to see statements dealing with material things as symbolically depicting New Testament spiritual realities. Antonine DeGuglielmo rightly sees no reason "to resort to an interpretation that understands the material to symbolize a spiritual benefit," noting "that spiritual benefits are clearly indicated in the

---

[52]This is surely the meaning of Jesus' statements concerning the worship of the Father: ". . . a time is coming when you will worship the Father neither on this mountain nor in Jerusalem. . . . true worshipers will worship the Father in spirit [probably Spirit] and truth" (Jn 4:21–23). The primary issue addressed by Jesus in this passage is the coming of a new relationship to God, not the denial of a material place in the future. In the Old Testament the Mosaic system provided a certain access to God. Jesus was declaring that such access would now be universal in that it would be direct in him through the Spirit. Thus Jerusalem, the center of Old Testament worship, would lose its significance as the place of access.

That these words did not deny any future significance for Jerusalem is seen in Jesus' concern for the temple and his citing Isaiah's prophecy of the day when the temple would be "called a house of prayer for all nations" (56:7; cf. Mt 21:13; Mk 11:17; Lk 19:46). This prophecy looked beyond the old covenant, which contributed to the "barrier" between Jew and Gentile (Eph 2:14), to the messianic days when all peoples would stand on the same religious ground and enjoy equal access to God. If Christ meant to deny any future significance to Jerusalem, why would he be concerned with the temple and cite this reference in support of his concern? For anyone who believes that Christ will reign literally on earth, there is no reason why that reign should not have a central location at which homage is given to God. This would not take away from the direct universal worship of all peoples throughout the entire world. Both Justin Martyr (*Dialogue with Trypho,* 119.5) and Tertullian (*Against Marcion,* III.24.3–4) taught the presence of the heavenly Jerusalem on earth during the millennium, indicating that they saw no conflict between Jesus' teaching in John 4 and a place in the future having religious significance.

messianic prophecies, indeed in the same passages which predict the fertility of the land, so that there is ample evidence of them."[53]

B. The Prophecies Remained Unfulfilled

As we have seen, all the main themes of the Old Testament prophetic picture—the promise of a holy nation, the possession of the land, the righteous rule of the seed of David, and a worldwide blessing of divine salvation—remain an unfulfilled hope in the Old Testament. According to Clements, "An eschatological hope of the New Israel, with a New Jerusalem, blessed by the presence of Yahweh, became a prominent feature of post-exilic Judaism."[54] Assertions of historic fulfillment such as that given by Joshua in relation to the possession of the land and rest from the enemies (Jos 21:43–45; 23:14) represent only an initial, not the final, fulfillment. Even after the return from Babylon, the promise of a final restoration to the land remained alive (e.g., Zec 8:4–8). These historical fulfillments are all part of "a great history of movement from promise toward fulfillment."[55]

But there was no final fulfillment of any of the promises in Old Testament history.[56]

C. The Prophecies Looked to a Historical Fulfillment

Although some scholars see many elements of this picture (especially those related to the nation of Israel and the promised land) as symbolic or typical of spiritual or so-called heavenly realities, the unfulfilled Old Testament prophecies looked to their fulfillment in concrete earthly reality. The prophets, according to Walther Eichrodt, made *"a real entry of God into history* the centre of their belief" so that "the hoped-for consummation and the national community in its concrete

---

[53]DeGuglielmo, "The Fertility of the Land in the Messianic Prophecies," 309–10. DeGuglielmo states that the main reason that commentators depart from the literal meaning of the material texts is their "preoccupation that the prophecies have not been fulfilled literally." He adds, "If, then, it can be shown that they have been or will be fulfilled literally, there is no longer any reason to depart from the literal meaning of these passages" (310). In our opinion, there is no further revelation in the New Testament that denies such a fulfillment and therefore there is no reason to deny the literal understanding of these prophecies.

[54]Ronald E. Clements, *Prophecy and Covenant*, Studies in Biblical Theology, no. 43 (Naperville, Ill.: Alec R. Allenson, 1965), 118.

[55]Walther Zimmerli, "Promise and Fulfillment," in *Essays on Old Testament Hermeneutics*, ed. Claus Westermann (Richmond: John Knox, 1963), 111–12.

[56]On the lack of fulfillment of the promises related to the land, see Walter C. Kaiser, Jr., *Toward Rediscovering the Old Testament* (Grand Rapids: Zondervan, 1987), 46–58.

earthly actuality" were related and "the Israelite hope remained loyal to this earth."[57]

Gerhard von Rad draws a connection between God's historical redemptive acts and his future actions as expressed in prophecy:

> Prophecy . . . is . . . merely the connecting link that binds together the witness to God and to his judgment and redemption (which . . . had already broken into Israel's history continually), and projects it into the eschatological, in that . . . it speaks of God's final work with relation to Israel. But since this is the case, can any fundamental theological distinction be made between prophetic prediction on the one hand, and witness to past history on the other?[58]

Von Rad also rejects the idea that the Old Testament is simply a "history of faith," because its promises deal with real historical blessings. The Old Testament, including its promises, he says, cannot be understood simply in terms of the "religious" and "spiritual." The redemptive benefits promised Israel are of a "material and this-worldly quality." And it is "for the sake of these things, that is, for their realization, that the *Heilsgeschichte* itself takes place.[59]

The Old Testament therefore presented a future that involved concrete earthly realities and was apparently so understood by the faithful of God's people. There are details relating to the future that were necessarily couched in the terminology of the present (e.g., weapons of future wars, perhaps also forms of worship), but these details do not negate the basic reality and concreteness of the primary prophetic elements (e.g., Israel, the land, rule of the Messiah, the peoples). Prophetic writings also use figurative language to describe God's actions, but so did historical narratives about Israel occasionally. But imagery and metaphor do not dissolve these earthly events into "spiritual truth."

For the Christian interpreter, the Old Testament does not stand alone. It must be understood in the light of the New Testament, which records not only the beginning of the fulfillment of the Old Testament promises, but prophesies of the future leading to the same consummation

---

[57]Eichrodt, *Theology of the Old Testament*, 1:490–91; cf also Mowinckel: "This national and this-worldly element remains the heart of the future hope throughout the entire Old Testament period" (*He That Cometh*, 148–49).

[58]Gerhard von Rad, "Typological Interpretation of the Old Testament," in *Essays on Old Testament Hermeneutics*, 26.

[59]von Rad, "Typological Interpretation of the Old Testament," 30–31. A. A. van Ruler similarly points to the concrete realities of the Old Testament hope: "With what is the Old Testament concerned? With concrete, secular things—possession of the land, the gift of posterity, the increase of the people, an eternal monarchy, a society based on righteousness and love. Not only the Israelites, but also the Old Testament authors and God himself, in his presence in the prophetic word and in the people of Israel, never get beyond these things" (*The Christian Church and the Old Testment* [Grand Rapids: Eerdmans, 1971], 25).

as that of the Old Testament. Granted, the inspired New Testament writers are our authoritative teachers in the understanding of the Old Testament. But the nature of the Old Testament prophecies and their prior understanding by God's people cannot be set aside as irrelevant as we seek to understand the New Testament perspective. The New Testament writers saw themselves in continuity with the Old Testament faith.

Chapter 10

The Pauline Prophecies About Israel

FOR THE CHRISTIAN, the Old and New Testaments form one holy Scripture. The early church saw itself as related to the God of Abraham, the God of Old Testament history and eschatological promise. This continuity is emphasized by the fact that the church in its beginnings and especially the normative apostolic interpreters of the new divine acts in the plan of salvation were themselves Jews who were well-acquainted with and had no doubt personally shared the prophetic hope. The latter in particular would lead us to expect to find evidence in their teaching if any radical change in this hope had occurred for them.

The themes of the Old Testament eschatological hope as reviewed in chapter 9 are not the primary content of the New Testament teaching. The New Testament writers are more taken up with explaining the new work of God in the coming of Jesus the Messiah. But when their teaching touches the Old Testament hope, including the nation of Israel, two general truths become evident. Negatively, despite a strong element of judgment upon Israel, there is no indication of a forfeiture of the promises. Positively, the main elements of the eschatological picture of the Old Testament remain intact, including a future for the nation of Israel along with the blessing of all peoples.

I. THE NONFORFEITURE OF THE PROMISE

The primary expositor of the Old Testament eschatological picture of Israel and the nations in relation to the new work of God is the apostle Paul. In his teaching, as in the Old Testament, the nation of Israel remains the primary focus. However, the various statements about the nation have implications that support the final universal hope for all nations in accord with the prophetic picture.

According to Paul, God had given the Jews an advantage by entrusting to them his "very words" (Ro 3:1–2), signifying that this people had a special place in God's revelatory activity toward the world. C. E. B. Cranfield explains, "The Jews have been given God's authentic self-revelation in trust to treasure it and to attest and declare it to all mankind. . . . They alone have been the recipients on behalf of mankind of God's message." The assertion in the next verse (v. 3) that the present unbelief of "some" in Israel does not "nullify God's faithfulness" affirms that God's covenanted purpose for Israel still stands.[1]

The firmness of God's promises to Israel undergirds the entire discussion of that nation in the major section of Romans 9–11. The hope of the believer in the church expressed in the preceding chapters of Romans rests totally on the certainty of God's word. And this puts the focus on the word that God had previously spoken to Israel (Ro 9:6). Leonhard Goppelt contends that, if that word could fail, "then the foundation upon which Christian certainty of salvation also rests would collapse, that certainty which Paul's exposition of the gospel in Romans 1–8 has led to."[2] Along that same line, Walter Gutbrod asks, "Can the new community trust God's Word when it seems to have failed the Jews (9:6)?"[3]

The apostle answers that question immediately at the beginning of his discussion of Israel with a recitation of eight privileges related to those whom he identifies as his "brothers, those of my own race, the people of

---

[1]C. E. B. Cranfield, *The Epistle to the Romans*, International Critical Commentary, vol. 1 (Edinburgh: T & T Clark, 1975), 179, 181. James D. G. Dunn also sees in 3:3 "the continuity of God's purpose in his original covenant commitment to Israel" (*Romans 1–8*, Word Biblical Commentary [Dallas: Word Books, 1988], 132).

[2]Leonhard Goppelt, "Israel and the Church in Today's Discussion and in Paul," *Lutheran World* X (October 1963): 365.

[3]Walter Gutbrod, "Ἰσραήλ," in *Theological Dictionary of the New Testament*, vol. 3, ed. Gerhard Kittel (Grand Rapids: Eerdmans, 1965), 386. Johannes Munck observes that the early church did not solve the problem by transferring Israel's promises to the Gentiles: "Israel's unbelief is a difficulty for all Christians, both Jewish and Gentile. If God has not fulfilled his promises made to Israel, then what basis has the Jewish-Gentile church for believing that the promises will be fulfilled for them? It must not be forgotten that this transference of Israel's promises to the Gentiles was not, at the time of the apostles, the simple matter that it has since become for the Gentile church" (*Christ and Israel* [Philadelphia: Fortress, 1967], 34–35).

Israel" (Ro 9:3–5). This list may be said to constitute a summary of the divinely promised prerogatives of Israel found in the Old Testament.[4] John Piper observes that even the appellation "Israelite" ("the people of Israel," NIV) is itself "redolent with a blessed antiquity and a glorious future (Is 49:3; 56:8; 66:20; Joel 2:27; 4:16 MT; Ob 20; Ps 25:22; 53:6; 130:7f.)."[5]

For our present purpose we call particular attention to the inclusion of "the covenants" and "the promises" among the possessions of the people of Israel. "Covenants" surely includes the various covenants made with Abraham, the nation at Sinai, David, and the promise of the new covenant (cf. Ro 11:26f.). In "promises," the apostle most certainly included the promises given to Abraham that are often the subject of his theology (cf. 4:13–22; Gal 3:16–29). But, according to Cranfield, Paul probably "also had in mind many other OT promises, particularly the eschatological and messianic promises."[6] Finally, it should be recognized that although "the promises" are included as one of the privileges of Israel, every item in the list (v. 4) "can be understood as promises," as C. K. Barrett points out. The "adoption as sons," "divine glory," and even "the receiving of the law" that looked forward to the gospel all pointed forward to promised eschatological blessings for Israel.[7]

That this teaching about Israel's privileges affirms the continuation of Israel's Old Testament eschatological promises is evident on two counts. First, the reference is obviously to empirical-historical Israel and not to the church as some new "spiritual Israel." Paul's mention of his own physical relationship with the Jews (v. 3) and the fact that "from them is traced the human ancestry of Christ" (v. 5) identify this as a reference to the historical people. Second, the present tense of the verb[8] shows that Paul affirms these privileges, including the covenants and promises, as the present possessions of Israel. Moreover, as the previous context regarding the apostle's longing for his countrymen indicates, they still belong to Israel in unbelief. Such is the case even after a judicial hardening has

---

[4]For a good discussion of each item demonstrating their Old Testament heritage, see John Piper, *The Justification of God* (Grand Rapids: Baker, 1983), 15–25.

[5]Piper, *The Justification of God*, 15.

[6]C. E. B. Cranfield, *The Epistle to the Romans*, International Critical Commentary, vol. 2 (Edinburgh: T & T Clark, 1979), 464.

[7]C. K. Barrett, *The Epistle to the Romans* (New York: Harper & Row, 1957), 178. See also Piper, *The Justification of God*, 15–25, for more evidence of the eschatological significance of each item listed in verse 4.

[8]The three Greek clauses that list the possessions of Israel are dependent on the initial present tense finite verb in the first clause of verse 4a, which literally reads "who are Israelites" (cf. NASB). Since the modifying clauses without verbs take their time sense from the main verb, they are to be understood likewise in the present, i.e., these various things "belong presently" to Israel.

fallen on the majority of Israelites (11:7, 25) and the church has begun with the inclusion of Gentiles.

What Paul states in chapter 9 at the outset of his discussion on the present situation of Israel is reiterated in chapter 11. Despite their obstinate unbelief, Paul asserts that God has not rejected "his people, whom he foreknew" (11:2). Paul proves this first by reminding his readers that he himself, one chosen to be an apostle of Christ, is "an Israelite . . . a descendant of Abraham, from the tribe of Benjamin" (v. 1). In addition, there continues to be a remnant of the historical, ethnic people of Israel, who have already entered into the time of fulfillment (vv. 5–7).

One might say that because this fulfillment obviously refers to the blessings attained in the church, there remains no place for the fulfillment of national promises of the Old Testament. The rest of Paul's discussion, however, rules out this conclusion by asserting the temporary nature of the present situation (cf. v. 5, "at the present time"; v. 25, "Israel has experienced a hardening . . . until"). As such, the present fulfillment cannot be understood as the complete fulfillment. The complementary teaching of a future for Israel, as we shall see, allows sufficient room for the completion of the Old Testament picture.

Paul's confidence in the continuation of Israel's hope is grounded in the sovereign elective purposes of God. Even though Israel has the status of "enemies" because of unbelief, which means that the people are under the wrath of God, it is also still "loved on account of the patriarchs" because of God's "election" (11:28). The Israel to which the election refers is not the present elect remnant mentioned in verses 6–7, but "Israel as a whole, . . . as alienated from the favour of God by unbelief. The election . . . corresponds to the 'people which he foreknew' in verse 2, the theocratic election."[9] The reference is to God's original elective love bestowed on Israel because of his promise to the fathers (cf. Dt 7:7–9).

Historical Israel remains the "beloved" of God because "God's gifts and his call are irrevocable" (v. 29). The appeal, as in 3:3 and 9:6, is to the faithfulness of God. The "gifts" refer to "such privileges of Israel as are listed in 9.4f."[10] The mention of "calling," according to Cranfield, adds the functional goal involved in the privileges, namely, "God's calling of Israel to be His special people, to stand in a special relation to Himself, and to fulfil a special function in history."[11] That these are "irrevocable" or "not repented of" is, according to John Murray, "expressly to the effect

---

[9]John Murray, *The Epistle to the Romans*, vol. 2 (Grand Rapids: Eerdmans, 1965), 101.

[10]Cranfield, *The Epistle to the Romans*, 2:581; so also James D. G. Dunn, *Romans 9–16*, Word Biblical Commentary, vol. 38 (Dallas: Word Books, 1988), 694.

[11]Cranfield, *The Epistle to the Romans*, 2:581.

that the adoption, the covenants, and the promises in their application to Israel have not been abrogated."[12]

There can be no stronger affirmation of the continuance of the Old Testament covenanted promises to the nation of Israel than this one in Romans 11, which comes at the end of a discussion of Israel's situation during the present church age. The majority of the nation have been cut off under the judgment of God, but their unbelief has not changed the purpose of God for the people. The radical rejection of God in the death of his Son and the breaking of the Old Covenant had not anulled God's plan for Israel, for it was founded on the prior "promise" of God (cf. Gal 3:17–18). Nor is there any indication that the plan has been radically reinterpreted. To be sure, the Gentiles are already entering into the experience of salvation promises that had originally been given to Israel, but the promises still belong to Israel first (Ro 1:16) and the nation will some day fulfill them because of the absolute faithfulness of God to his word.

II. THE FUTURE RESTORATION OF THE NATION OF ISRAEL

The New Testament not only affirms the continuance of the Old Testament promises to the historic people of Israel, but also teaches its future salvation in conformity with the promises. The full range of details in the eschatological picture of the Old Testament prophets is not found in the New Testament. But the New Testament writers were almost all Jews familiar with the Old Testament, so there was no need to retell the whole story. The Scriptures of the Old Testament people of God became the Scriptures of the church. Thus the New Testament affirmation of the continuance of the promises and the teaching of a future for Israel would entail the larger Old Testament picture.

The fullest statement on the future for Israel found in the New Testament is in Romans 11. Having considered the people's failure to respond to God's coming in Christ in chapters 9–10, the apostle turns to the question of their future in chapter 11. In the first section of the chapter, he asserts the continuing theological significance of Israel—i.e., God has not rejected them (vv. 1–6). This remains true even though saving grace has now gone out to the Gentiles along with believing Jews to form the new community of God that already lives in the promised eschatological salvation.

After affirming the continued significance of the people, Paul explains that present-day Israel, except for an elect remnant, is under the divine judgment of hardening (vv. 7–10). But he quickly adds that this judgment is only temporary (vv. 11–15).

[12]Murray, *The Epistle to the Romans*, 2:101.

This passage contains several statements about Israel's future. Israel has fallen, but not "beyond recovery" (v. 11). The people's disobedience had led to the coming of salvation to the Gentiles, but this is not the final act in God's plan of blessing for the world. The apostle sees a future for Israel that will bring even greater blessing to the world: "But if their transgression means riches for the world, and their loss means riches for the Gentiles, how much greater riches will their fullness bring!" (v. 12).

The term "fullness" has a variety of meanings, and its exact meaning here is uncertain. The basic thought, however, is clear, as Murray notes: "What ever might be the precise term by which to express the import here, it is obvious that the condition or state denoted is one that stands in sharp contrast with the unbelief, the trespass, and the loss characterizing Israel when the apostle wrote."[13] The reference is clearly to the restoration of Israel as a whole, which is explained by Cranfield as the "unbelieving majority's being brought up to its full numerical strength (i.e., the full strength of Israel as a whole . . .) by being reunited with the believing minority through its own (i.e., the majority's) conversion."[14]

The thought of the future restoration of Israel is reiterated in verse 15, but instead of "their fullness," it is expressed as "their acceptance." In contrast to "their rejection," which refers to the temporary casting away of unbelieving Israel by God, "their acceptance" can mean nothing less than "God's final acceptance of what is now unbelieving Israel."[15]

Paul supports his teaching of a future for Israel with two illustrations, the batch of dough (v. 16) and the olive tree (vv. 16–24). Both demonstrate that God's past and present dealings with that people are the assurance of his future work on their behalf. The "part of the dough offered as firstfruits," which makes the "whole batch . . . holy," is probably a reference to the believing Jews (cf. Paul's use of "firstfruits" in 16:5 and 1 Co 16:15 for first converts).[16] This present remnant of Jewish Christians, Paul says, represents the entire people and guarantees the final sanctification of the nation as a whole.

---

[13]Murray, *The Epistle to the Romans*, 2:78.

[14]Cranfield, *The Epistle to the Romans*, 2:558. Dunn, noting the agreement of most interpreters, similarly says that the restoration is "the broader contrast between remnant and Israel as a whole, so between the rest's failure and the prospect of all Israel being saved (v. 26)" (*Romans 9–16*, 655).

[15]Cranfield, *The Epistle to the Romans*, 2:562.

[16]This is the most probable meaning of the "part of the dough" in view of Paul's use of "firstfruits," his mention of the remnant (vv. 1–10), and the contrast with "all Israel" in verses 12 and 15 (cf. Cranfield, *The Epistle to the Romans*, 2:564, and Dunn, *Romans 9–16*, 659). However, the view of many that the "firstfruits" is a reference to the patriarchs, on the grounds that this must have the same meaning as "the root" in the same verse, would not negate the point of the illustration concerning the inclusion finally of the whole of Israel.

The picture of the root and branches makes a similar point. In this instance, the root signifies the patriarchs, especially Abraham, whom Jewish tradition held as the root of Israel.[17] The branches include all Israel, i.e., both the remnant who remain and the unbelieving people who are cut off. As the lump of dough makes the whole batch holy, so the hallowed root of the patriarchs due to the elective grace of God affects all the branches.

Paul elaborates on this second illustration. His primary point is to make clear to his gentile audience that their nourishment comes from the same root from which Israel grew and to warn them against arrogant self-complacency over against Israel (cf. vv. 17–22). The Gentiles are not only to be humble in their participation with Israel in the root, but are also to envision the possibility of fallen Israel's being brought back into the place of divine blessing (vv. 23–24).

While there is no explicit statement of Israel's future restoration in these two verses, Paul emphasizes that such a restoration is compatible with the salvation plan of God rooted in the covenant with the patriarchs. If the power and grace of God were able to graft the Gentiles, who were "wild branches," into a root that did not formerly belong to them, "how much more readily" could the "natural branches [Israel] be grafted into their own olive tree." The Gentiles should not presume that Israel's unbelief and consequent cutting off has given them superiority in relation to God's plan of salvation. It was just such an attitude that caused Israel's problem. Rather, as James D. G. Dunn says, the "gentile Christians' own experience of grace should be enough to show them that if they can be accepted by Israel's God, how much more ethnic Israel."[18]

The possibility that God's grace will bring the "natural branches" back to their root becomes a certainty in Paul's final and most explicit teaching about the future restoration of Israel. Speaking of the revelation of a "mystery"—the divine plan of redemption in Christ—Paul sums up in concise terms what he has expressed throughout chapters 9–11: "Israel has experienced a hardening in part until the full number of Gentiles has come in. And so all Israel will be saved" (11:25–26).

What might appear in the immediate context to be a rather straightforward statement of Israel's future salvation has elicited a variety of interpretations. Both the identity of "all Israel" and the time of salvation have been understood differently. Calvin and many other scholars have held to what Dunn calls "the older view,"[19] that "all Israel" refers to all

[17]Christian Mauer, "ῥίζα, " in *Theological Dictionary of the New Testament*, vol. 6, ed. Gerhard Friedrich (Grand Rapids: Eerdmans, 1968), 987–89.
[18]Dunn, *Romans 9–16*, 666.
[19]Dunn, *Romans 9–16*, 681.

the elect in history, including both Jews and Gentiles—that is, "all spiritual Israel."[20]

A second interpretation sees "all Israel" as "the total number of the elect from among the Jews" throughout history.[21] According to this view, Paul is not talking about the conversion of Israel in the end-time, but rather the total group of Jewish people who come to salvation over the course of history.

A third view regards "all Israel" as the totality of the people who will be converted in the future after "the fullness of the Gentiles" has come in. There are several variations on this general theme. Dispensationalists see the reference as signifying the salvation and restoration of Israel as a nation (though not every individual) with its centrality among the nations in accord with Old Testament prophecy.[22] Some non-dispensational premillennialists also affirm a national restoration, but apparently without taking in the whole Old Testament picture of the special status or function of Israel among the other nations. George E. Ladd refers to the future salvation of Israel as bringing "literal Israel . . . into the church" and, like Piper, suggests that "converted Israel may become for the first time in history a *truly Christian nation*."[23]

Finally, some nonmillennialists simply see a future conversion of the people of Israel to the blessing and favor of the gospel. This is the same blessing that the Gentiles experience beforehand, and therefore it has no national implications for Israel. Murray states, "There is no suggestion of any privilege or status but that which is common to Jew and Gentile in the faith of Christ."[24]

The understanding of Paul's statement concerning the salvation of all Israel entails at least three issues: (1) the meaning of "all Israel,"

[20]John Calvin, *Commentaries on the Epistle of Paul the Apostle to the Romans* (Grand Rapids: Eerdmans, 1948), 437.

[21]Anthony Hoekema, *The Bible and the Future* (Grand Rapids: Eerdmans, 1979), 140. Also, L. Berkhof, *Systematic Theology* (Grand Rapids: Eerdmans, 1941), 699; G. C. Berkouwer, *The Return of Christ* (Grand Rapids: Eerdmans, 1972), 340–49; William Hendriksen, *Israel in Prophecy* (Grand Rapids: Baker, 1968), 39–52; Herman Ridderbos, *Paul: An Outline of His Theology* (Grand Rapids: Eerdmans, 1975), 357–61.

[22]See, for example, John Walvoord, *The Millennial Kingdom* (Findlay, Ohio: Dunham, 1959), 172–73; J. Dwight Pentecost, *Things To Come* (Findlay, Ohio: Dunham, 1958), 504–6.

[23]George E. Ladd, *A Theology of the New Testament* (Grand Rapids: Eerdmans, 1974), 562–63. In discussing Romans 11:12, 15, however, Ladd does speak of "the instrumentality of Israel's conversion" in bringing blessing to "the Gentile world."

[24]Murray, *The Epistle to the Romans*, 2:99; in similar fashion, F. F. Bruce states that Paul "says nothing about the restoration of an earthly Davidic kingdom, nothing about national reinstatement in the land of Israel. What he envisaged for his people was something infinitely better" (*The Epistle to the Romans* [London: Tyndale Press, 1963], 221); cf. also Munck, *Christ and Israel*, 131–38;

(2) the time of the promised salvation, and (3) the meaning of that salvation.

A. *The Identity of "All Israel"*

On the meaning of "all Israel," most contemporary scholars reject the first interpretation—that the phrase is a reference to the elect Jews and Gentiles of all ages—and they do so because of the context. In chapters 9–11, Paul uses the term "Israel" no less than eleven times. The preceding ten indisputably denote the Jews as opposed to the Gentiles, and there is no compelling evidence to view the last use differently. Moreover, the close connection in thought between verses 25 and 26 demands ethnic Israel. Murray views these verses in the context and concludes,

> The main thesis of verse 25 is that the hardening of Israel is to terminate and that Israel is to be restored. This is but another way of affirming what had been called Israel's "fulness" in verse 12, the "receiving" in verse 15, and the grafting in again in verses 23, 24. To regard the climactic statement, "all Israel shall be saved," as having reference to anything else than this precise datum would be exegetical violence.[25]

The second interpretation, in which "all Israel" means the elect Jews of all time, is also incompatible with Paul's thinking. Even though in this view "all Israel" includes more than the remnant saved during this present age, there is still a strong emphasis on seeing the present remnant as part of, even the climactic culmination of, "all Israel." Anthony Hoekema writes, "The salvation of all Israel, therefore, does not take place exclusively at the end-time, but takes place throughout the era between Christ's first and second coming—in fact, from the time of the call of Abraham."[26] This centrality of the present salvation of the remnant in the meaning of "all Israel" is seen also in Herman Ridderbos's statement that "only under the concurrent mark of God's judgment on the unbelief of a part of Israel will Israel come to its fullness." The salvation of "all Israel" is thus complete when the full number of Gentiles has been brought in.[27]

The strong link between "all Israel" and the present remnant according to this view is evident in Paul's assertion that his own ministry to the Gentiles, which sought to make Israel "envious" (11:11, 14), was already accomplishing the salvation of "all Israel."[28] Since all the earlier

---

[25]Murray, *The Epistle to the Romans*, 2:97. See also Hendriksen, *Israel in Prophecy*, 39–43.

[26]Hoekema, *The Bible and the Future*, 145.

[27]Ridderbos, *Paul: An Outline of His Theology*, 359.

[28]Hoekema, *The Bible and the Future*, 145; Ridderbos, *Paul: An Outline of His Theology*, 358.

godly remnants of Israel historically are said to be a part of Paul's "all Israel," the reference cannot be only to the remnant of this present age. However, the emphasis given to the present remnant and to the present age as the fullest work of salvation for both Jews and Gentiles suggests that the remnant does not stand in contrast to "all Israel," but is its most important part. William Hendriksen states, "'All Israel' is 'the remnant according to the election of grace' (11:5)."[29]

Hoekema, explaining that Israel's salvation extends from the time of Abraham until the second coming, also declares, "*All Israel,* therefore, differs from the elect remnant spoken of in 11:5, but only as the sum total of all the remnants through history."[30]

This close relationship between "all Israel" and the "remnant" is rightly rejected by most interpreters. Instead of equating them, Dunn declares that "all Israel ... clearly functions in contrast to λεῖμμα ['remnant'] (11:5), and τινές ['some'] (11:17; Schlier) and indeed ἀπὸ μέρους ['in part'] (11:25), and as parallel to πλήρωμα ['fullness'] (11:12)."[31] In a similar vein, Cranfield points to the "fullness" and "acceptance" of Israel (vv. 12, 15) and the grafting in again of the broken-off branches (vv. 23–24) as indicating that the salvation of "all Israel" is unmistakably "something more than what would simply amount to the salvation of the elect remnants of Israel of all the generations."[32] Rather than the remnant alone, it includes both the remnant and the "others" of verse 7.[33]

Contrary to the views that equate "all Israel" with "spiritual Israel" composed of Jew and Gentile or as simply the elect remnant of all Jews throughout history, it is preferable to see Paul's reference to the salvation of "all Israel" as a reference to Israel as a whole, Israel as the "bearer of the promise and the recipient of its fulfillment."[34] Dunn asserts that "there is now a strong consensus that πᾶς'Ἰσραήλ must mean Israel as a whole, as a people whose corporate identity and wholeness would not be lost even if

---

[29]Hendriksen, *Israel in Prophecy,* 49.

[30]Hoekema, *The Bible and the Future,* 145.

[31]Dunn, *Romans 9–16,* 681.

[32]Cranfield, *The Epistle to the Romans,* 2:577; also, W. Sanday and A. C. Headlam, *A Critical and Exegetical Commentary on the Epistle to the Romans,* International Critical Commentary (Edinburgh: T & T Clark, 1902), 335.

[33]Ernst Käsemann, *Commentary on Romans* (Grand Rapids: Eerdmans, 1980), 313. Judith M. Gundry Volf offers some additional arguments against the idea that "all Israel" is only the "whole elect remnant from the nation of Israel"; she asserts that "this view makes Paul answer a question which he has not even raised—the future of the elect remnant—rather than the one he has raised—the future of the hardened Jews (11:1). . . . The fact that the elect remnant will be saved according to this view is no argument against Gentile Christians who prided themselves on having supposedly replaced the hardened Jews cut off from salvation" (*Paul and Perseverance* [Tübingen: J. C. B. Mohr, 1990], 182).

[34]Gutbrod, "Ἰσραήλ," 387.

in the event there were some (or indeed many) individual exceptions."[35] According to F. F. Bruce, "'all Israel' is a recurring expression in Jewish Literature, where it need not mean 'every Jew without a single exception' but 'Israel as a whole.' Thus 'all Israel has a portion in the age to come,' says the Mishnah tractate *Sanhedrin* (x. i), and proceeds immediately to name those Israelites who have no portion therein."[36]

In distinction from the present remnant of Israel, therefore, "all Israel" looks to the restoration of that people as a whole. Ferdinand Hahn aptly sums up Paul's meaning: "all Israel"

> relates to the Israelite people of actual history, who are now despising their salvation. . . . The offer of salvation will again be made to Israel, which will again be faced with a decision about belief, and as a believing Israel will attain salvation. . . . But if in the case of that first decision about belief it was only a small fraction that accepted the message, it will at some future time be the "fullness" of the Jews (cf. Rom. 11:12) who will acknowledge their Lord.[37]

B. The Time of Israel's Salvation

The meaning of the salvation of all Israel also relates to the time when this is to occur. After referring to the partial hardening of Israel and the coming in of the fullness of the Gentiles (v. 25), Paul introduces the salvation of Israel with the words, "And so [καὶ οὕτως] . . ." (v. 26). Because Paul does not use words that clearly denote sequence such as "then" or "after that," some see the salvation of Israel in verse 26 not as coming after the events of verse 25, but as occurring simultaneously.

Explaining that οὕτως ("so") describes "manner" and not temporal succession, Hoekema states, "Paul is not saying, 'Israel has experienced a hardening in part until the full number of Gentiles has come in, and *then* (after this has happened) all Israel will be saved.' But he is saying, 'Israel has experienced a hardening in part until the full number of Gentiles has come in, and in this way all Israel will be saved.'"[38] In other words, the

---

[35]Dunn, *Romans 9–16*, 681.

[36]Bruce, *The Epistle of Paul to the Romans*, 222.

[37]Ferdinand Hahn, *Mission in the New Testament* (Naperville, Ill.: Alec R. Allenson, 1965), 106–7, n.1. Similarly, H. J. Kraus says on Romans 11:25–27, "Here it is not stated simply that individual, special favored members of the Old Testament Israel will again live from the root of election and in the holy tree; the promise is that when God's invitation to join the new people of God has gone out to all nations, then 'Israel as a whole' will once again be grafted into the holy olive tree. 'For the gifts and calling of God are irrevocable' (Rom. 11:29). God will bring the work which he began in Abraham to a wonderful conclusion, and by this act he will reveal himself as the sovereign Lord of all the life of man in history" (*The People of God in the Old Testament* [New York: Association Press, 1958], 91).

[38]Hoekema, *The Bible and the Future*, 144–45; cf. Hendriksen, *Israel in Prophecy*, 34–49.

salvation of Israel is to take place during the same time as the ingathering of gentile fullness and the partial hardening of Israel.

Ridderbos makes this last parallel specific: "Only under the concurrent mark of God's judgment on the unbelief of a part of Israel will Israel come to its fullness and just then be redeemed from that judgment."[39] Exactly what Ridderbos means by "redeemed from that judgment" is not clear, but it apparently coincides with the end of the salvation of all Israel, for that salvation takes place during the hardening. Under this scheme, "all Israel" seems necessarily closely identified with the "remnant" presently being saved, for the present remnant is the correlative to the present hardening (cf. vv. 5–7). To make "all Israel" more than the "remnant" would require lifting the hardening judgment before the fullness of the Gentiles comes in. But Paul's words can hardly be interpreted this way. The hardening continues until the end of the gentile fullness.

More support for the view that Israel's salvation happens at present is alleged from Paul's statement that this people "have *now* become disobedient in order that they too may *now* receive mercy" (11:31, emphasis added). Hoekema asserts that in this summation Paul "speaks not in terms of what will happen in the future but in terms of what is happening *now*."[40] Such an immediate present action, however, is not required. The uses of "now" in verse 31, for both Israel's disobedience and their obtaining of mercy as well as the "now" for gentile salvation in verse 30b, are in contrast to the previous "at one time" (ποτέ, v. 30a). The distinction is obviously between the time before this dispensation and the present time of eschatological salvation or in Dunn's words, "the salvation-history division of epochs."

There is nothing, however, which demands that the application of this salvation to the Gentiles and "all Israel" be simultaneous within the present "now" era of eschatological salvation. As Dunn explains, it is better to see the salvation of the Gentiles and of Israel as sequential within this period of salvation: ". . . 'the now time' is subdivided into the two phases: mercy to Gentiles and Jewish disobedience; followed by mercy to Jew as well. . . . The second νῦν [now] was probably a way of highlighting the eschatological imminence of this second and final phase of 'the now time.'"[41]

We must remember that from Paul's perspective there was no way to know the duration of the "now time" of eschatological salvation— certainly not the length of the first phase. For Paul, the completion of the fullness of the Gentiles and the salvation of Israel could possibly occur

[39]Ridderbos, *Paul: An Outline of His Theology*, 359.
[40]Hoekema, *The Bible and the Future*, 146.
[41]Dunn, *Romans 9–16*, 687.

within a relatively short time, even as the coming of Christ could. But we need not conclude that he understood these events as occurring at the same time. In fact, the apostle's hope of saving only "some" of his fellow countrymen through his ministry (v. 14) suggests that he did not envision the restoration of Israel as resulting from his own efforts.

Given the total direction of Paul's teaching in Romans 11, it is better to see the salvation of "all" Israel as a subsequent action. This view is further supported by Paul's temporal statement that the hardening will last *"until* the full number of the Gentiles has come in" (italics added), which suggests that after the coming in of the Gentiles there will be a change in that the hardening will be removed. Although οὕτως ("so"), which introduces verse 26, has the basic meaning of "thus" or "in this manner," it may also include a temporal sense. Bruce comments, "To the argument that Paul does not say 'and *then* all Israel shall be saved' but 'and *so* all Israel shall be saved' (as though the ingathering of the full tale of Gentiles were in itself the salvation of all Israel), it should suffice to point out the well attested use of Gk *houtōs* ('so', 'thus') in a temporal sense."[42]

The apostle probably used this term rather than a simple adverb of sequence in order to emphasize both the manner and the sequence related to Israel's salvation. Dunn explains, "Following the ἄχρι οὗ ['until,' v. 25], some temporal weight cannot be excluded from καὶ οὕτως ['And so'] (Stuhlmann, 165); but the basic sense of οὕτως is 'thus, in this manner,' referring to Paul's conviction that conversion of the Gentiles will be the means of provoking Israel to jealousy and converting them."[43]

Paul's statement in Romans 11:26 is thus best understood as the last part of a three-part sentence: (1) the hardening of Israel, (2) the ingathering of Gentiles (which is occurring simultaneously with the hardening), and (3) the final salvation of Israel. These all elaborate the mystery of God's plan of salvation for Gentiles and Jews that Paul desires his readers to understand from his discussion throughout this passage. So the final aspect of the mystery—the salvation of "all Israel"—follows the first two with the introductory phrase "and thus," which carries the meaning "when these preconditions have been fulfilled."[44] Thus Paul regards the

---

[42]Bruce, *The Epistle of Paul to the Romans*, 222. Also, Käsemann says, "As in Acts 17:33; 20:11 it [καὶ οὕτως] has a temporal sense" (*Commentary on Romans*, 313). See also 1 Corinthians 11:28 and 14:25 for examples involving temporal sequence.

[43]Dunn, *Romans 9–16*, 681; see also Volf, who, although taking the "and thus" as logical-inferential, nevertheless acknowledges the temporal sequence: ". . . the inference is temporally determined, since the prerequisites for the salvation of all Israel are temporally specific. Israel's salvation will occur after the prerequisities for it have been met, i.e., after the fullness of the Gentiles has entered and Israel's hardening has ceased" (*Paul and Perseverance*, 180–81).

[44]Cranfield, *The Epistle to the Romans*, 2:574.

salvation of "all Israel" as happening after the present time of salvation and riches for the world (v. 11) and the ingathering of "the full number of Gentiles" (v. 25).

The relationship of Israel's salvation to the blessing of the Gentiles raises some further questions about the time of Israel's restoration. Does this sequence signify that with the salvation of Israel we have reached the end of salvation history and there is no further blessing for the world? Or does the conversion of Israel signify a period of even greater blessing for the whole world?

Scholars who hold that the salvation of Israel and the gathering of the Gentiles take place simultaneously obviously have no trouble seeing Israel's restoration as the end of salvation history. Even though they may acknowledge a sequence of the coming in of the Gentiles followed by the salvation of Israel in the apostle's language in verses 25–26, some nevertheless regard the "full number of Gentiles" as a reference to the completion of God's salvific work among the nations. Accordingly, God will bring about the salvation of Israel in connection with the completion of gentile salvation. All of this takes place in relation to Christ's coming, at which time the final resurrection will occur. It is this final fullness of resurrection life that Paul has in mind when he refers to the future blessing for the Gentiles that results from Israel's restoration (vv. 12, 15).[45]

That interpretation leaves no time for the Old Testament picture of the blessings of Gentiles *subsequent to* and *mediated through* a restored Israel. In fact, its proponents claim that Paul has inverted the Old Testament sequence.[46]

But is Paul really teaching such a radical transformation of the prophecies? It is evident that the present salvation of the Gentiles before that of Israel is not in harmony with the basic Old Testament picture. But does this represent a change in the picture or simply an addition to it? Two factors suggest to us that the latter is more in harmony with this New Testament teaching.

First, no such radical reinterpretation of the Old Testament Scriptures in relation to gentile salvation is indicated. Nowhere in the context does Paul transform the picture presented in the Old Testament of the nations streaming to Jerusalem and being blessed through restored Israel (e.g., Isa 2:1–4).[47] The present blessings of the Gentiles are related to the stumbling of Israel, but this is never explained as some kind of altering of the Old Testament hope.

Second, rather than a transformation, the passage itself gives evidence that Paul clung to the basic hope offered in the Old Testament

---

[45]Dunn, *Romans 9–16*, 680, 658. Also Cranfield, *The Epistle to the Romans*, 2:577, 563.
[46]Dunn, *Romans 9–16*, 682.
[47]See chapter 9 for a more detailed portrait of this Old Testament prophetic hope.

picture. The future "fullness" of Israel will bring "greater riches" for the Gentiles than the riches presently enjoyed during this time (v. 12). The "acceptance" of Israel will bring blessing for the world, what Paul describes as "life from the dead" (v. 16). The meaning of this last phrase is unclear. Some take it figuratively to mean the blessing of the world that far surpasses anything that has previously taken place, "an unprecedented quickening for the world in the expansion and success of the gospel."[48] Others believe it means literally the resurrection of the dead.[49]

We need not try to decide the issue here, except to point out that even if it means the resurrection, we need not take that to be the final general resurrection that issues immediately into the eternal state. Both Jewish tradition and the New Testament give evidence of two resurrections, the first for the righteous when the messianic reign begins and the second just prior to the final state (cf. Lk 14:14; Rev 20:5–6).[50] Thus time is provided for the blessing of the world through restored Israel before the eternal state. This fits both the Old Testament picture and the one that Paul presents in this passage.

To acknowledge the present salvation of Gentiles as the ingathering of their "full number" does not preclude a future time of gentile blessing. According to Murray, to take verse 25 to mean "the consummation of blessing for the Gentiles" is an "unwarranted assumption." While it denotes their "unprecedented blessing," it "does not exclude even greater

---

[48]Murray, *The Epistle to the Romans,* 2:81–84 (see for a good defense of the figurative interpretation as opposed to the literal resurrection); cf. James Denney, "St. Paul's Epistle to the Romans," in *The Expositor's Greek Testament,* vol. 2, ed. W. Robertson Nicoll (Grand Rapids: Eerdmans, 1951), 679; Everett F. Harrison, "Romans," in *The Expositor's Bible Commentary,* vol. 10, ed. Frank E. Gaebelein (Grand Rapids: Zondervan, 1976), 120–21.

[49]Cranfield, *The Epistle to the Romans,* 2:563; Dunn, *Romans 9–16,* 658; Käsemann, *Commentary on Romans,* 307.

[50]Albrecht Oepke writes of the resurrection in the New Testament, ". . . the predominant view is that of a double resurrection (Jn. 5:29: ἀνάστασις ζωῆς, κρίσεως [resurrection of life, of judgment]; cf. R. 14:9; 2 C. 5:10). Possibly in Lk. 14:14: ἡ ἀνάστασις τῶν δικαίων [the resurrection of the righteous], and certainly in Rev. 20:5, 6: ἡ ἀνάστασις ἡ πρώτη [the first resurrection], Jewish tradition is followed and the resurrection to life is seen as a prior act in time at the beginning of the millennium." Although Oepke admits that some verses (e.g., Ro 2:16) seem to indicate a different view, the verses he mentions do not require a unitary resurrection and can readily be harmonized with two resurrections ("ἀνίστημι, κτλ," in *Theological Dictionary of the New Testament,* vol. 1, ed. Gerhard Kittel [Grand Rapids: Eerdmans, 1964], 371).

Munck also notes Adolf Schlatter's argument that it cannot be the general resurrection because the expression "life from the dead" presupposes that there are still some dead who do not attain life (Munck, *Christ and Israel,* 127). We also suggest that Paul's intense desire to attain the resurrection (Phil 3:11) points to a specific resurrection, namely, that of the righteous. Everyone would participate in a general resurrection, and there would be no question or striving to be a part of that; it would be inevitable for all.

blessing to follow," in harmony with verses 11 and 15.[51] The coming in of "the full number of the Gentiles" prior to the salvation of "all Israel" is best understood as referring to the ingathering of Gentiles during the present age through the preaching of the gospel to all nations (cf. Mk 13:10; Mt 24:14). But, as Murray points out, the benefits for the Gentiles that Paul sees resulting from Israel's conversion rules out the "full number" as the culmination of all gentile salvation in the divine program. There must yet be some time following the coming in of this "fullness" that permits the even greater blessing of the world to take place. Such an understanding of the time factors in this passage harmonizes well with the Old Testament picture.

We have seen so far that Paul's teaching about the salvation of "all Israel" is in full accord with the Old Testament eschatological hope. It refers to a future salvation of Israel as a whole that follows the divine work currently affecting the nations. It remains for us to see whether the nature of the salvation of which the apostle speaks is in harmony with the Old Testament prophecies.

C. The Nature of Israel's Salvation

On the basis that Paul says nothing about a national restoration to the promised land, many interpreters maintain that the nationalistic elements are no longer part of his hope for his people. For example, Bruce says, "In all that Paul says about the restoration of Israel to God, he says nothing about the restoration of an earthly Davidic kingdom, nothing about national reinstatement in the land of Israel. What he envisaged for his people was something infinitely better."[52] But is the "argument from silence" sufficient grounds for that view? Heinrich A. W. Meyer's claim that ". . . our passage directly *controverts* the Ebionitish view, now renewed in various quarters . . . , of an actual restoration of Israel to the theocratic kingdom in Canaan, as to be expected on the ground of prophetic prediction" is surely going beyond the evidence.[53] There is nothing in the passage contrary to these additional elements.

---

[51]Murray, *The Epistle to the Romans*, 2:95–96.

[52]Bruce, *The Epistle of Paul to the Romans*, 221. Cranfield remarks, "It is also to be noted that there is here no trace of encouragement for any hopes entertained by Paul's Jewish contemporaries for the re-establishment of a national state in independence and political power, nor—incidentally—anything which could feasibly be interpreted as a scriptural endorsement of the modern nation-state of Israel" (*The Epistle to the Romans*, 2:579). The implications of this position for the Christian's thinking are apparent: The contemporary and future historical events in the Near East have no biblical significance. Recent events including the Holocaust and the establishment of the state of Israel, however, have caused many to re-evaluate this perspective in the light of Scripture. See chapter 12.

[53]Heinrich A. W. Meyer, *Critical and Exegetical Handbook to the Epistle to the Romans* (New York: Funk & Wagnalls, 1889), 452 (emphasis added).

To deal with this issue let us first look at the nature of the salvation Paul describes. With quotations from Isaiah 59:20–21; 27:9 (both closely following the Septuagint) and Jeremiah 31:34, Paul portrays Israel's future salvation in terms of the new covenant promise of the removal of their sins. This salvation will be accomplished when "the deliverer will come from Zion" (Ro 11:26). Paul substitutes "from Zion" for the Hebrew "to Zion" or "for Zion" and the Septuagint's "on behalf of Zion." But we should not take this as a deliberate attempt by Paul to reinterpret the Old Testament picture.[54] The psalmists frequently spoke of the salvation for Israel as coming "out of" or "from" Zion (Pss 14:1; 53:6; cf. 110:2). That fact may well have influenced Paul's choice of words here. He may also, as Murray notes, have wanted to focus on the relationship of the Redeemer to Israel in his choice of words.[55]

Nothing in Paul's citations, therefore, veers away from the Old Testament. According to the prophetic picture, the judgment of the Lord would go out against the enemies of Israel from Zion, but also salvation for his people Israel.[56] Although, according to Isaiah, God was the subject of the action of bringing salvation for Israel, there is rabbinic evidence that this was interpreted as the Messiah, even as Paul does here.

It is not Paul's language, however, that ultimately leads interpreters to see a transformation of the Old Testament picture of Israel's restoration. Rather, as we have already seen in Bruce's statement, it is the fact that Paul refers here only to a spiritual salvation. Now, it is difficult to see how a reference to Israel's spiritual salvation becomes positive evidence that the material aspects are no longer applicable. There is no negation of the material aspects in the passage, nor are any material or mundane promises of the Old Testament (e.g., nationhood, land) given a new, spiritualized interpretation.

Paul's reference to the salvation of Israel from sin is perfectly in

---

[54]Dunn sees in this change Paul's desire "not to rekindle the idea of Israel's national primacy in the last days" (*Romans 9–16*, 682). The picture is simply one of Christ's return from the heavenly Jerusalem to bring spiritual salvation to Israel. The psalmist's use of the same language, however, shows that the deviation from Isaiah 59:20 is still commensurate with the Old Testament eschatological hope.

[55]Murray writes, "The accent in Paul's teaching in this passage is on what the Redeemer will do *for* Zion. But in the first clause the thought is focused on the relation of the Redeemer to Zion after the pattern of 9:5. This is germane to the total emphasis of this context and underscores the relevance of the Redeemer's saving work to Israel as a people" (*The Epistle to the Romans*, 2:99, n.54).

H. P. Liddon writes, "The change of preposition is probably an intentional variation from the LXX and Heb. text of Isaiah, suggested by Ps. xiv. 7, liii. 6, in order to bring into stronger relief the promises made to the Jewish people" (*Explanatory Analysis of St. Paul's Epistle to the Romans* [reprint, Grand Rapids: Zondervan, 1961], 218).

[56]For the relation of Paul's words to the Jewish hope, see Sanday and Headlam, *A Critical and Exegetical Commentary on the Epistle to the Romans*, 337.

harmony with the Old Testament eschatological hope. The prophets always made a spiritual transformation the great priority in the restoration of Israel. Spiritual salvation was, in fact, the basis for the outward material and theocratic blessing. It is no doubt this truth, along with the fact that the focus of Paul's discussion in Romans is on the avenue of a right relationship with God, that led Paul to emphasize the spiritual dimension of the salvation of "all Israel." There is, however, no biblical or theological reason for that to preclude an additional material blessing.

Paul's affirming the irrevocableness of God's gifts and call to Israel (11:29) further indicates that he retained the full Old Testament hope for Israel. As we have seen, these gifts and call included all the covenant promises made to Israel and the purpose for which they were given. Israel's future spiritual salvation was expected because God intended to fulfill *all* his Old Testament promises including a national restoration and subsequent blessing to all nations.

Chapter 11

Other New Testament Prophecies

ALTHOUGH THE apostle Paul is the primary source of New Testament teaching about the eschatology of Israel and the nations, other writers give evidence of sharing this same hope. We will examine this evidence and note some other prophetic aspects related to this theme throughout the New Testament.

I. THE RESTORATION OF ISRAEL

According to Johannes Munck, parallels to the apostle's thought on Israel are found in the gospel accounts of Jesus' teaching.[1] Israel's primacy by divine election, her obstinancy, and her consequent judgment were all frequently asserted by Christ. In addition, the Lord's teaching also contains hints of Paul's theme of the final restoration of Israel. Matthew 23:37–39 (cf. Lk 13:34–35) records Jesus' lament over Jerusalem for killing the prophets and refusing to let him gather her under the shelter of his wings. As a result, judgment was coming: ". . . your house is left to you desolate" (v. 38).

But judgment is not the final note, for Jesus added, "For I tell you, you will not see me again until you say, 'Blessed is he who comes in the

---

[1] Johannes Munck, *Christ and Israel* (Philadelphia: Fortress, 1967), 14–22.

name of the Lord' " (v. 39). Although, according to Matthew, these last words were spoken by the people at the triumphal entry, they were clearly not fulfilled on that occasion, for only the disciples welcomed him then, not the city as a whole. So the fulfillment awaits the parousia of the Messiah.

This statement that Jerusalem will someday recognize Jesus is understood in different ways. To some it is only Israel's sad recognition of the Messiah as judge at the parousia. Joseph A. Fitzmyer, for example, explains, "The time will come when even Jerusalem will be ready to sing out, 'Blest is the one who comes in the name of the Lord,' but then it will be too late."[2] But such a negative tone is hardly compatible with the real meaning of the statement and the overall teaching of Jesus concerning his people.

The words of praise, derived from Psalm 118:26, were interpreted by the Jews as messianic. They were shouted with enthusiasm by the disciples and welcomed by Jesus on the day of his triumphal entry. In light of these facts, G. R. Beasley-Murray aptly comments, "It is difficult to believe that [here] . . . Jesus is declaring that the expression of praise . . . to be given in the end time would be rejected."[3] It is far more likely that this statement following the pronouncement of judgment is to be taken as a promise of a joyful greeting of their Messiah by the people of Jerusalem.[4]

Moreover, while Jesus teaches the participation of the Gentiles in the kingdom and warns the unrepentant Jewish sons of the kingdom that they will be excluded, he nowhere excludes all Israel. The patriarchs with whom the Gentiles will share in the kingdom, Jesus said, are more than

---

[2]Joseph A. Fitzmyer, *The Gospel According to Luke X–XXIV*, Anchor Bible, vol. 28A (Garden City, N.Y.: Doubleday, 1985), 1035–36; cf. also Norval Geldenhuys, *Commentary on the Gospel of Luke* (Grand Rapids: Eerdmans, 1951), 383, 385; T. W. Manson, *The Sayings of Jesus* (London: SCM, 1949), 128.

[3]G. R. Beasley-Murray, *Jesus and the Kingdom of God* (Grand Rapids: Eerdmans, 1986), 306.

[4]Eduard Lohse, "Σιών κτλ," in *Theological Dictionary of the New Testament*, vol. 7, ed. Gerhard Friedrich (Grand Rapids: Eerdmans, 1971), 329; on Jesus' teaching about the future of Israel and especially Luke 13:35ff., Ethelbert Stauffer says, "Would the course of salvation-history pass by the doors of the Synagogue? The answer that Jesus gave at the end of his life was 'yes.' . . . Jesus' last word on the theme of Israel [Lu. 13:35] is thus a reservation; inexorable, but nevertheless full of promise" (*New Testament Theology* [London: SCM, 1955], 189).

Commenting on the fact that Luke's reference to the welcoming of the Messiah is not in relation to Jesus' historic entrance into Jerusalem, John Koenig writes, "But this means that the prophecy recorded in Lk. 13:35 must look forward to some *other* future event. This other is probably Jesus' Parousia descent to Jerusalem as Son of Man Messiah in the Kingdom of God (Lk. 21:27; Acts 1:11). On that day Jerusalemites will repent of their blindness and welcome Jesus with blessings. Thereafter, the final restoration of Israel can proceed" (*Jews and Christians in Dialogue: New Testament Foundations* [Philadelphia: Westminster, 1979], 11–12).

individuals; they represent their descendants as well. With this in mind, Beasley-Murray rightly concludes that Jesus "anticipated his own people returning to God along with the multitudes from the nations."[5]

Another indication of Israel's restoration is found in a similar prediction of judgment. Anticipating the city's destruction by the Romans, Jesus declared that Jerusalem would be "trampled on by the Gentiles until the times of the Gentiles are fulfilled" (Lk 21:24). As in the earlier statement, the little word "until" signifies a limit to that judgment.

What was to happen after the gentile domination of Israel ended is not stated. Again, some scholars read into this silence a denial of the fulfillment of the Old Testament prophecies for Israel. Norval Geldenhuys states, "Christ nowhere implies that the 'times of the Gentiles' will be followed by Jewish dominion over the nations. The kingdom of this world is to give place to 'the kingdom of our Lord and of his Christ' (Rev. xi. 15)—not a glorified Jewish kingdom."[6] Many interpreters are content to affirm the end of the gentile domination with the coming of Christ without saying anything about a change in the fortunes of Israel.

But it might be asked, if Jesus was merely teaching that Jerusalem is to be trodden down by Gentiles until the Lord returns to conclude salvation history in the setting up of the eternal kingdom, why did he not say, "Jerusalem will be trampled . . . until I come" or something to that effect rather than "until the times of the Gentiles are fulfilled"? The times of the Gentiles will terminate with the coming of Christ. But the use of this particular language suggests the reversal of the situation for the down-trodden city as a result of the end of the gentile domination at the appearance of the Messiah. Such a scenario would be in perfect harmony with the Jewish prophecy. The motif of the treading down of Jerusalem was "a set theme in prophecy."[7] But the subsequent restoration of the nation was also a theme of that expectation. Thus, although the force of Jesus' teaching in this passage is on the coming judgment, its temporary nature makes it perfectly compatible with the rest of the Old Testament hope of the restoration of Israel.

Both Matthew 23:39 and Luke 21:24 are rightly understood only within the whole perspective of the Old Testament prophetic faith which was alive among the disciples of the New Testament. The emphasis on the judgment of Israel in these verses harmonizes with the threats of punishment for disobedience found in the Old Testament, especially

---

[5]Beasley-Murray, *Jesus and the Kingdom of God*, 307.

[6]Geldenhuys, *Commentary on the Gospel of Luke*, 536.

[7]I. Howard Marshall, *The Gospel of Luke* (Grand Rapids: Eerdmans, 1978), 773. He cites the following references in support of his statement: Zec 12:3; Da 8:10, 13; Isa 63:18; Ps 79:1; 1Macc 3:45; 51; 4:60; 2Macc 8:2; Wisd Sol 17:25; Rev 11:2.

when the general distinctions between the Old and New Testament teaching about Israel are considered. According to Berkhof,

> In the Old Testament God's faithfulness stands in the foreground, but it is stated that this is not a guarantee that the people will not sin, or that they will not be led through God's dark detours. In the New Testament, Israel's disobedience and blindness are in the foreground, but it is stated that nevertheless this cannot frustrate God's faithfulness to and salvation plans for this people.[8]

Further support for a future restoration of Israel is seen in Christ's statement that his disciples would sit on thrones judging the twelve tribes of Israel in the kingdom (Mt 19:28; Lk 22:30). The activity of judging in this instance is more than simply sitting as judge when Israel is called to give account for their response to the Messiah.[9] Although this judicial function is included, judging also conveys the idea of ruling or governing.[10] I. Howard Marshall explains that "judging . . . conveys the ideas of rule and judgment."[11] The context of Jesus' words in both Matthew and Luke suggests that the disciples are given the authority and function to judge as a reward for their sacrificial service in the present age (cf. Mt 19:27; Lk 22:28). Friedrich Büchsel points out that judging in the sense of condemning Israelites would be no real privilege for the disciples; moreover, when the saints seated on thrones in Revelation 20:4 are given authority to judge, such action is shown to have the aspect of reigning.[12]

Other contextual evidence supports the idea of reigning in the kingdom. In the chapter following this promise, Matthew records the request of James and John for the highest positions of authority in the kingdom (Mt 20:20ff.). Both the concept of rulership evident in this request and the response of Jesus would appear to demand more than some final judgment. Similarly, Jesus' statement in Luke's account about the disciples eating and drinking at his table in the kingdom point to the common Jewish metaphor of the messianic kingdom as a joyful banquet (cf. Lk 13:29; 14:15). These statements about the position of the disciples over the twelve tribes of Israel in the future reign of Christ therefore not

---

[8]Hendrikus Berkhof, *Christ, the Meaning of History* (1966; reprint, Grand Rapids: Baker, 1979), 140.

[9]This opinion is held by Beasley-Murray, *Jesus and the Kingdom of God,* 275–76; cf. also D. A. Carson, "Matthew," in *The Expositor's Bible Commentary,* vol. 8, ed. Frank E. Gaebelein (Grand Rapids: Zondervan, 1984), 426.

[10]Robert D. Culver declares that the primary sense of the Hebrew word for "judge" is to exercise the processes of government ("שָׁפַט [shapat] judge, govern," in *Theological Wordbook of the Old Testament,* vol. 2, ed. Laird R. Harris [Chicago: Moody Press, 1980], 947).

[11]Marshall, *The Gospel of Luke,* 818.

[12]Friedrich Büchsel, "κρίνω," in *Theological Dictionary of the New Testament,* vol. 3, ed. Gerhard Kittel (Grand Rapids: Eerdmans, 1965), 923.

only look to the future kingdom, but also affirm a future for the nation of Israel.

The idea that Jesus is referring to some new spiritual Israel[13] in this promise must be rejected. Matthew always makes a clear distinction between Gentiles and Jews.[14] Similarly, Luke always uses the word "Israel" to refer to Jewish people. Arthur W. Wainwright says, "Although he [Luke] believes the Church to have taken over the function of God's people, he never explicitly calls it 'Israel,' and there is not good reason to suppose that when he speaks of the restoration of Israel he is alluding to the Church. He is referring to the Jewish nation."[15] E. P. Sanders therefore concludes that Jesus' words about the disciples' judging the twelve tribes of Israel "confirms the view that Jesus looked for the restoration of Israel."[16]

Finally, Christ's teaching of a future restoration is found in Acts 1:6–7. After Jesus told them that the Spirit would come to baptize them in a "few days" (v. 5), the disciples asked, "Lord, are you at this time going to restore the kingdom to Israel?" (v. 6). In speaking of "restoration," the disciples were using an expression that had become a technical term for the messianic political restoration of Israel to its own land.[17] Jesus responded by telling them, "It is not for you to know the times or dates the Father has set by his own authority. But you will receive power when the Holy Spirit comes on you; and you will be my witnesses" (vv. 7–8).

Although many interpreters see in the disciples' question a reprehensible stubbornness to give up their Jewish materialistic hope,[18]

---

[13]Marshall, *The Gospel of Luke*, 818.

[14]Carson, "Matthew," EBC, 8:426.

[15]Arthur W. Wainwright, "Luke and the Restoration of the Kingdom to Israel," *Expository Times* 89 (December 1977): 76. This position is strengthened by the fact that "Israel" is not used by any New Testament writer for believers in general, but always for the historical people of Israel. See p. 8.

[16]E. P. Sanders, *Jesus and Judaism* (Philadelphia: Fortress, 1985), 103; cf. also Karl Ludwig Schmidt's comment on Matthew 19:28 in connection with Jesus' full view on the future of Israel: "Even where national and political hopes were not to the fore, but salvation was expected for the whole world in the last time, His contemporaries still thought it important that there should be a place of privilege for Israel. Israel was to arise with new glory, and the scattered tribes, and indeed the Gentiles, were to stream towards the new Jerusalem. Jesus shares this hope. He gives to His disciples, the twelve, as representatives of the twelve tribes of the people of God, the holy people, judicial and administrative office in the reign of God (Mt. 19:28 = Lk. 22:29 f.)" ("Βασιλεία," in *Theological Dictionary of the New Testament*, vol. 1, ed. Gerhard Kittel [Grand Rapids: Eerdmans, 1964], 586).

[17]Albrecht Oepke, "ἀποκαθίστημι, ἀποκατάστασις," in *Theological Dictionary of the New Testament*, vol. 1, ed. Gerhard Kittel (Grand Rapids: Eerdmans, 1964), 388–89.

[18]John Calvin, for example says, ". . . their blindness is remarkable, that when they had been so fully and carefully instructed over a period of three years, they betrayed no less ignorance than if they had never heard a word. There are as many errors in this question as words" (*The Acts of the Apostles, 1–13*, Calvin's Commentaries [Grand Rapids: Eerdmans,

no evidence is put forward why they should have lost hope. At the coming of Jesus, a hope for a political establishment was supported both by angelic messenger (Lk 1:32–33) and prophecy (Lk 1:68–79, cf. esp. vv. 71–75).[19] While Jesus emphasized the spiritual dimension of the messianic salvation and later taught a delay of the kingdom (cf. Lk 19:11ff.), he said nothing about removing the material political aspect. In fact, as we have seen, Jesus promised his disciples rulership over Israel in the kingdom (Mt 19:28; Lk 22:30). And shortly following the promise in Matthew's account, the nature of that kingdom in the minds of the disciples is evident in James and John's seeking the chief positions of authority in it (Mt 20:20ff.). There, as in Acts, Jesus did not deny their kingdom concept, but only their concept of greatness. He also related their request to the sovereign pleasure of the Father, even as he did the question concerning the time of the kingdom expressed in the book of Acts.

There is no question but that the disciples had difficulty with some of the spiritual teaching about the kingdom. This is evident in their failure to understand the teaching of Jesus at some points, especially with regard to the salvation of the kingdom through his death. But to charge them with a total misunderstanding of the kingdom hope of Israel based on an alleged reinterpretation of this hope is difficult to substantiate in Scripture. Just before the disciples asked about Israel and the kingdom, Luke records that Jesus had been teaching them "about the kingdom of God" (v. 3). If after all this instruction from Jesus their question had still been wrong-headed, we would certainly expect to find a rebuke and a correction in Jesus' reply. After all, he was about to leave and send them out as his witnesses. But though some disagree, we find nothing like a rebuke in Jesus' words.

The question of the disciples is therefore a legitimate one, especially in light of the announcement of the coming of the Spirit. From their own prophets they knew that the gift of the Spirit belonged to the days of messianic salvation (Joel 2:28). The words of Jesus about the Spirit signaled the new age. Consequently, it was natural for the disciples to

---

1965], 29). C. S. C. Williams likewise speaks of "the hardness of the disciples' hearts" (*A Commentary on the Acts of the Apostles* [New York: Harper Bros., 1957], 56); and G. T. Stokes calls their question "the darkened utterance of carnal and uninspired minds groping after truth" (*The Acts of the Apostles*, Expositor's Bible [New York: A. C. Armstrong and Son, 1897], 29).

[19]Robert C. Tannehill notes the general emphasis on the hope of Israel's restoration in the beginning of Luke's gospel. Considering material that "previews the course of the narrative, statements of the commission to be carried out by the main character and his followers, OT quotations or freely formulated reminders of the OT hope, and statements by characters who are presented favorably . . . — we find very strong emphasis on the view that Jesus means redemption for Israel, that is, for the Jewish people" ("Israel in Luke–Acts: A Tragic Story," *Journal of Biblical Literature* 104 [March 1985]: 72).

wonder if the restoration of Israel, which also belonged to that time, was about to take place. As R. J. Knowling says,

> such a promise as that made in ver. 5, the fulfilment of which, according to Joel ii. 28, would mark the salvation of Messianic times, might lead the disciples to ask about the restoration of the kingdom to Israel which the same prophet had foretold, to be realised by the annihilation of the enemies of God and victory and happiness for the good.[20]

Jesus replied to the disciples' question by saying that the time for the restoration of Israel was not for them to know; this knowledge belonged to the Father. His response reminds us of his earlier statement that he himself did not know the day or the hour of his coming (Mk 13:32); that, too, belonged to the Father. Jesus then focused their attention on what they could know, namely, the coming of the Spirit to empower them for their ministry as his witnesses. This was to be their immediate concern before the final fulfillment of their hope for their people Israel.

The response of Jesus, therefore, in no way denies the validity of the disciples' question or the prospect of the restoration of Israel. As Gotthard Lechler declares, "He did not deny that either their expectation of the appearance on earth of his glorious kingdom in its reality, or their hope of the glorious future which that kingdom opened to the people of Israel, was well founded; he simply subdued their eager curiosity respecting the time, and directed their attention to the practical duties which they were to perform at the present period." Far from denying the restoration of Israel, Jesus confirmed it by asserting that its time was fixed by the Father.[21]

To this we add Wainwright's comment that the occasion of Jesus' ascension, which began with the disciples' question in verse 5, ended with the promise that he "will come back in the same way you have seen him

---

[20]R. J. Knowling, "The Acts of the Apostles," in *The Expositor's Greek Testament*, vol. 2, ed. W. Robertson Nicoll (Grand Rapids: Eerdmans, 1951), 56.

[21]Gotthard Victor Lechler, "The Acts of the Apostles," in *Lange's Commentary on the Holy Scriptures*, New Testament, vol. 4 (reprint, Grand Rapids: Zondervan, 1960), 13; The Jewish writer Abraham Heschel sees the passage similarly when understood against the background of its times: ". . . the simple meaning of the entire passage has a perfect *Sitz im Leben*, and both question and answer must be understood in the spirit of their times. The Apostles were Jews and evidently shared the hope of their people of seeing the kingdom of God realized in the restoration of Israel's national independence. So now, hearing their Master speak of the new age, they asked if this was to be the occasion for restoring the kingdom to Israel. We can scarcely fail to realize or to understand the naturalness of their question. The expectation was burned into their very being by the tyranny of the Roman rule. The answer confirms the expectation that the kingdom will be restored to Israel—an expectation expressed again and again in ancient Jewish liturgy. The point in history at which that restoration will take place remains the secret of the Father" (*Israel: An Echo of Eternity* [New York: Farrar, Straus & Giroux, 1969], 166–67).

go into heaven" (v. 11). "This is the real answer to the disciples' question about the restoration of the kingdom. Jesus will return at an unknown date in the future, which will be the time for Israel's restoration."[22]

That Jesus' reply was not a rejection of Israel's hope is evident later on in Peter's invitation to the Jewish people to repent and turn to God "that times of refreshing may come from the Lord, and that he may send the Christ, who has been appointed for you—even Jesus. He must remain in heaven until the time comes for God to restore everything, as he promised long ago through his holy prophets" (Ac 3:19–21). The verb "restore" connects this statement of Peter with the earlier disciples' question about the "restoration" of the kingdom in Acts 1:5. A similar link between the two passages is seen in the terms "times" (3:20, καιροί) and "time" (3:21, χρόνων), which are the same Greek terms found in Jesus' reply to the disciples in 1:7 ("times or dates").

As we noted in relation to the disciples' question, the concept of "restoration" had specific, national implications for the Jews. These included both the physical restoration to the land (e.g., Jer 16:15; 24:6; 50:19) and the spiritual restoration promised through Elijah (cf. Mal 4:6; Mt 17:11; Mk 9:12).[23] This restoration and the "times of refreshing," which refers to the "eschatological redemption which is promised to Israel if it repents,"[24] are both linked to the future coming of Christ. All of this, according to Peter, is in fulfillment of what God had "promised long ago through his holy prophets" (v. 21). The Greek words in this last phrase are essentially identical to those used by Luke in the prophecy of Zacharias, in which the promises reveal both a physical and spiritual restoration of the nation of Israel (cf. Lk 1:71, 74–75, 77).

Even while Acts records the Jews' continued rejection of their Messiah and the apostles' turning to the Gentiles, an ultimate hope for Israel's restoration remains. On several occasions we are told of Paul's turning to the Gentiles after being rejected by Jews (e.g., Ac 13:46; 18:6). Nevertheless he continued to preach to Jews (cf. 14:1; 28:23–28) and viewed his ministry as embracing his kinsmen as well as Gentiles (Ac 9:15; 22:15; 26:17–18, 22–23). Robert C. Tannehill, after surveying both Luke and Acts, points out how Luke treats the Old Testament in regard to the hope of Israel: "This hope is important to the author of Luke–Acts, for

---

[22]Wainwright, "Luke and the Restoration of the Kingdom to Israel," 76.

[23]For a fuller discussion of the entire restoration concept, see Wainwright, "Luke and the Restoration of the Kingdom to Israel," 76–79; cf. also Oepke, "ἀποκαθίστημι, ἀποκατάστασις," *TDNT*, 1:388–89.

[24]Eduard Schweizer, "ἀνάψυξις," in *Theological Dictionary of the New Testament*, vol. 9, ed. Gerhard Friedrich (Grand Rapids: Eerdmans, 1974), 664–65. Richard B. Rackham also sees the "times of refreshing" related to the coming of Christ rather than some spiritual blessing through faith available before that time (*The Acts of the Apostles* [London: Methuen, 1947], 53).

its complete disappearance would leave him with an unresolvable theological problem. Salvation for Israel has been presented as a major aspect of God's purpose, certified by scripture, but the final outcome would be the opposite." Thus the "times of relief" and "restoration" are still affirmed.[25]

A look at the entire New Testament teaching about Israel, therefore, indicates that although the nation comes under the judgment of God for rejecting Christ, it is never said to permanently lose its position in the promises of God, including its status as a nation. As Edward H. Flannery declares, ". . . the belief the Jews could never again regain their lost nationhood did not have its origin in Scripture. . . . Hence, the existence of a Jewish state, be it the state of Israel or another, does not contradict sacred Scripture."[26] Moreover, there is positive evidence that the Old Testament hope of a restored Israel was still very much alive.

II. THE FUTURE MILLENNIAL PHASE OF THE KINGDOM

We have argued with most interpreters that the prophecies of the kingdom in the Old Testament were related to one messianic coming and in the New Testament were separated into different phases of fulfillment around two comings. These phases are usually viewed as a present manifestation and a future consummation, or as it is frequently called, the "already and not yet" of the kingdom. While this view has gained general acceptance, a substantial point of dispute remains between amillennialists and premillennialists regarding the fulfillment of the future kingdom promises.

According to amillennialist teaching, the future fulfillment of the kingdom contains essentially one phase. Christ will return to bring about the full salvation of his people and the judgment of the lost, after which the final eternal kingdom will be ushered in. For premillennialists, however, the future of the kingdom involves two phases. Christ will come and establish his kingdom on earth, which will be a glorious reign over an as-yet-imperfect world. Only after this time will he deliver the kingdom over to the Father to usher in the perfect state.

We have seen in the Old Testament prophetic hope evidence for such a temporary kingdom in which the Messiah rules from Jerusalem

---

[25]Tannehill, "Israel in Luke–Acts: A Tragic Story," 84.

[26]Edward H. Flannery, "Theological Aspects of the State of Israel," in *The Bridge*, vol. 3, ed. John M. Oesterreicher (New York: Pantheon, 1958), 312–13. Flannery traces the belief that the restoration of the nation of Israel actually contradicted Scripture to "the conviction of some Fathers of the fourth century, who unknowingly—and understandably—were impressed by an impressive practical situation: three centuries of persecution and dispersion of the Jews, and at their end a miraculous intervention, bringing an effort [under Julian the Apostate in 363] to rebuild the Temple to nought" (309; cf. 304–9).

over an imperfect world. We also noted that the dominant teaching of later Judaism agreed with this perspective.[27] Because dispensationalists consider these Old Testament prophecies—including those related to the nation of Israel—still valid, a millennium is vital and integral to their view of the future of the kingdom promises, perhaps more so than other premillennialists. But does the New Testament support this hope and include what we might call a millennial phase in the fulfillment of the kingdom? Or have the Old Testament prophecies been transformed by apostolic teaching concerning the unbelief of Israel and the establishment of the church?

A. *The Biblical Evidence*

1. The Restoration of Israel. As we have seen, the writers of the New Testament continued to believe in the restoration of the nation of Israel. Such a future restoration in itself seems to imply a millennial phase of the kingdom. The prophets portrayed Israel as a nation having a place of prominence and service among all the nations.[28] But such prominence and service cannot be part of an eternal state of perfection.

If the disciples' "judging" of the twelve tribes of Israel refers to ruling in the kingdom rather than simply participating in the final judgment, as we have argued,[29] then this future kingdom phase must also precede the eternal state. The New Testament teaching of the future restoration of the nation of Israel, therefore, not only comports with a millennial phase of the kingdom, but actually requires it.

2. Revelation 20:4–6. The apostle John's reference to a thousand-year reign of Christ and the saints no doubt contributed greatly to the millennial view that prevailed in the early church. J. Massyngberde Ford observes that during the period in which the Revelation was written, "the concept of the millennium (or an interregnum) was generally accepted, but in later years it was the occasion for some controversy."[30] Prominent proponents of millennialism in the postapostolic church were Papias, the writer of the Epistle of Barnabas, Justin Martyr, Irenaeus, Tertullian, and Hippolytus. Although such fathers as Origen and Jerome were non-chiliasts, it was not until the fourth century that a strong tide against the view was mounted with the spiritualizing interpretations of Tyconius and,

---

[27]See p. 241.
[28]For a discussion of these themes, see chap. 12.
[29]See p. 267.
[30]J. Massyngberde Ford, *Revelation*, Anchor Bible, vol. 38 (Garden City, N.Y.: Doubleday, 1975), 350.

later, Augustine.[31] After that, amillennialism became the dominant view, with periods of strong postmillennialism mixed in.

Despite those changing tides, it is not difficult to see why the early church understood John to be teaching a millennium in Revelation 20. Three arguments support this interpretation: (1) the teaching of two resurrections, (2) the binding of Satan, and (3) the ruling of the saints with Christ.

a. The teaching of two resurrections. Premillennialists usually point to John's reference to two groups who "came to life," one before the thousand-year reign and one after (vv. 4–5), as crucial to the meaning of this passage.[32] The first group is described as those who had suffered martyrdom under "the beast." Of these, John writes, "They came to life and reigned with Christ for a thousand years" (v. 4). Then he writes of a second group: "The rest of the dead [implying those who were not part of the first group] did not come to life until the thousand years were ended" (v. 5).

Many amillennialists, including Augustine, have understood this passage as applying to the present age of the church on earth or in heaven. The first "coming to life" is said to be the regeneration of these believers. Others view this as a reference to believers' entering into heavenly life with Christ at their death.[33]

The verb used by John in both verses is used elsewhere in the New Testament to mean coming to life spiritually (e.g., Jn 5:25; Eph 2:5) and physical resurrection (e.g., Mt 9:18; Ac 9:41). Nowhere else does it refer to the believer's entrance into heaven after physical death, so it is highly unlikely that that is John's meaning here.

---

[31]Ford also indicates that there are "hints of millenarism in Apollinaris of Laodicea, Lactantius, Victorinus of Petau, Sulpicius Severus, Saint Ambrose" (*Revelation*, 350). For a brief survey of the early history of the millennial question, see Hans Bietenhard, "The Millennial Hope in the Early Church," *Scottish Journal of Theology* 6, no. 1 (March 1953): 12–30. Interestingly, Bietenhard states that the attack against the Origenists by the Chiliast Nepos of Arsinoe was against their "allegorising method." Bietenhard adds that "this fact is highly significant, for it shows us that the exegetical choice was between allegorising and the rejection of the millennium on the one hand, and literalism and Chiliasm on the other" (Ibid., 22).

[32]George E. Ladd, for example, says, "The Greek behind the translation 'they come to life' is a single verb, *ezesan* [ἔζησαν], which could be translated 'they lived.' What does it mean 'to live'? The entire interpretation of the passage hinges upon the question of whether the first *ezesan* and the *ezesan* of the rest of the dead mean the same thing, namely, bodily resurrection. What is the 'first resurrection'? Is it literal, a resurrection of the body, or spiritual, a resurrection of the soul? If we can find the answer to this question, we shall have the key to the solution of the millennial question in this passage" ("Historic Premillennialism," in *The Meaning of the Millennium: Four Views*, ed. Robert G. Clouse [Downers Grove, Ill.: InterVarsity Press, 1977], 35).

[33]Anthony A. Hoekema, *The Bible and the Future* (Grand Rapids: Eerdmans, 1979), 232–34.

While the term "resurrection" is occasionally used in the spiritual sense, the context in Revelation 20 argues conclusively for physical resurrection. First, the subjects of this "coming to life" are described as souls who "had been beheaded because of their testimony for Jesus." They are thus portrayed as physically dead just before the statement "They came to life and reigned" (v. 4), which suggests that this new life is physical. Second, "coming to life" is identified with "the first resurrection" (v. 5). The New Testament writers could speak of presently living according to the resurrection life of Christ (Php 3:10 and possibly Ro 6:5)[34] and of being raised with Christ (cf. Col 2:12; 3:1). But the overwhelming use of the Greek terms for "resurrection," when not in the unrelated general sense of something rising, is for bodily resurrection.[35] Again, nowhere in the rest of the New Testament are the terms for "resurrection" in Revelation 20:4–5 used in the amillennial sense for the believer's entrance into heavenly life at death.

Finally, the use of the same verb translated "come to life" (v. 5) for those who are not part of the first resurrection indicates a bodily resurrection. The identification of the first group as believers over which the second death has no power (v. 6) clearly identifies those who have no part in the "first resurrection" as unbelievers over which the second death does have power. As such their "coming to life" could only be interpreted as bodily resurrection. Because this meaning is necessary for the second use of "coming to life," some have gone so far as to argue that John does not intend to imply a second resurrection. For example, Anthony Hoekema says,

> When he says that the rest of the dead did not live or come to life,
> he means the exact opposite of what he had just said about the

---

[34]Paul's statement in Romans 6:5 that "we will . . . be united with him in his resurrection" probably refers to the believer's future bodily resurrection (cf. James D. G. Dunn, *Romans 1–8*, Word Biblical Commentary, vol. 38A [Dallas: Word Books, 1988], 318).

[35]On the use of the noun in Revelation 20:5 (ἀνάστασις) and its corresponding verb (ἀνίστημι), see William F. Arndt and F. Wilbur Gingrich, eds., *A Greek–English Lexicon of the New Testament and Other Early Christian Literature*, 2d ed. rev., ed. F. Wilbur Gingrich and Frederick W. Danker (Chicago: Univ. of Chicago Press, 1979), 60–61, 70. As for the related verb for resurrection (ἐγείρω), L. Coenen indicates that "especially in the pass., [it] is used predominantly for what happened at Easter, i.e., the wakening of the Crucified to life, while *anhistemi* and *anastasis* refer more especially to the recall to life of people during the earthly ministry of Jesus and to the eschatological and universal resurrection. . . . Although we cannot apply it universally, we may say that the general rule in the NT is that . . . the action of God on and through Christ is expressed by *egeiro*, while *anhistemi* expresses, as it were, that which happens in the realm of human experience" ("Resurrection," in *New International Dictionary of New Testament Theology*, vol. 3, ed. Colin Brown [Grand Rapids: Zondervan, 1978], 276).

Paul uses the same term John does in speaking of the false teaching that "the resurrection has already taken place" (2Ti 2:18).

> believing dead. The unbelieving dead . . . did not live or reign
> with Christ during this thousand-year period. . . . The use of the
> word *until* does not imply that these unbelieving dead will live and
> reign with Christ after this period has ended.[36]

For most interpreters, however, the immediate identification of the
coming to life of the first group as the "first" resurrection seems clearly to
suggest a second resurrection involving those remaining.[37]

The context thus points to physical resurrection as the meaning of
"come to life" in both verses 4 and 5. The mention of two resurrections
separated by a period of a thousand years, along with the reference to the
participants in the first resurrection as reigning with Christ, clearly points
to a millennial period after the coming of Christ, when the first resurrection occurs (cf. 1Co 15:23).

b. The binding of Satan for a thousand years. More evidence for
the premillennial interpretation of Revelation 20 is found in the teaching
about the binding of Satan. During this thousand-year period Satan is said
to be "locked and sealed" in "the Abyss." The purpose of this action is "to
keep him from deceiving the nations anymore until the thousand years
were ended" (v. 3).

All attempts to apply this picture to the present period, either as a
limitation of Satan's deceptive power on believers or his inability to
prevent the spread of the gospel in the world, are difficult to harmonize
with the language of the passage and other teaching of the New
Testament. The text gives no indication that the limitation on Satan is one
of degree. Rather, as Robert H. Mounce says, "The elaborate measures
taken to insure his custody are most easily understood as implying the

---

[36]Hoekema, *The Bible and the Future*, 236. Hoekema argues that if John had meant that
they would come to life after the thousand years, he would have added a statement to that
effect, as in verse 3 where John says that the dragon will not deceive the nations any more
"until the thousand years were ended. After that he must be set free for a short time." In
response we note that the negative statement about the rest of the dead is not just the
opposite of the positive. John says that they did not come to life, but he does not say anything
about their not reigning with Christ, which would seem to be very significant if he were
attempting by this statement only to deny to them what was said about the believers in this
expression. The "first resurrection" statement that follows implies a further resurrection
supporting the idea that the statement "until the thousand years were ended" is intended to
suggest that those who did not come to life earlier would do so then. In sum, if John simply
wanted to deny the resurrection and reign to the others, he could easily have said, "The rest
of the dead did not come to life." The addition of "until the thousand years were ended"
clearly suggests subsequent action.

[37]"A second res. is presupposed by the ἀ. ἡ πρώτη [the first] of Rv 20:5f." (Arndt and
Gingrich, eds., *A Greek–English Lexicon of the New Testament and Other Early Christian
Literature*, 60).

complete cessation of his influence on earth (rather than a curbing of his activities)."[38]

Taking the rest of the New Testament teaching into account, we see not only that nothing is said of Satan's being presently bound, but also that he is extremely active on the earth during this present age. His binding, according to those who say he is presently bound, is said to have occurred with the coming of the kingdom brought by Christ (cf. Mt 12:28–29; Mk 3:23–27). But if Satan was decisively bound on earth at that time, how could he, for example, snatch the Word away from the heart of those who hear it (Mt 13:19), enter Judas for the betrayal of Christ (Lk 22:3), desire to "sift" Peter (Lk 22:31), or fill the heart of Ananias—who was probably a believer—to lie to the Holy Spirit (Ac 5:3)? How can he be prowling around "like a roaring lion looking for someone to devour" (1Pe 5:8), if he is presently imprisoned in the Abyss, "locked and sealed," as John describes him in Revelation 20?

In general, Satan is portrayed by the New Testament writers as the one who blinds the minds of unbelievers (2Co 4:3–4), seeks to deceive believers (2Co 11:3–4, 14), hinders the work of God's ministers (1Th 2:18), strongly influences all unbelievers (Eph 2:2), and is the continual antagonist of the believer (Eph 6:11–12; 1Pe 5:7–8).

In the face of this evidence for the present activity of Satan, the gospel references to the binding of "the strong man" cannot be understood as the removal of satanic activity from the earth. Rather, they are the demonstration of the superior power of Jesus, who is able to free the people enslaved by Satan. This binding occurs throughout this age each time the power of Satan and the effects of sin are overcome in a person's life. Such binding is perfectly compatible with Satan's continual presence and his antagonistic activity during this age. John's picture of Satan securely bound away from the face of the earth so as not to deceive the nations, therefore, belongs to the future and points to a millennial period prior to the final elimination of evil from the earth.

c. The reign of the saints with Christ. The mention of the participants in the first resurrection as reigning with Christ during this thousand-year period also denies a reference to the present. We note in passing that the reign of the saints runs concurrently with the binding of Satan. Because the binding clearly refers to an earthly situation, the reigning most naturally applies to the same. This raises questions about the validity of any interpretation that sees this reign as heavenly. But even beyond this, there is no biblical evidence that the saints are reigning at present either in heaven or on earth.

Contrary to Hoekema, who sees the picture of the saints in Revelation 20:4–5 as "a kind of parallel" to the saints in heaven in

---

[38]Robert H. Mounce, *The Book of Revelation* (Grand Rapids: Eerdmans, 1977), 353.

Revelation 6:9,[39] these passages appear to offer a contrast. In 6:9 the martyred saints cry out for the Lord to avenge their death upon the inhabitants of the earth (v. 10). In response they are told to "wait a little longer" until the numbers of martyrs is complete (v. 11). There is no concept here of the saints reigning. Rather, as Beasley-Murray notes, the reign of Revelation 20:4 is *the answer* to the cry of the saints in 6:9. Noting the similar description of the martyrs in the two passages, Beasley-Murray states, "In chapter 6 they are given a white robe and told to be patient a little longer. Here [20:4] their prayer is answered, and they are raised to reign with Christ in his kingdom."[40]

In addition, the continuing martyrdom of believers on earth while the saints wait in heaven is difficult to harmonize with Satan's binding, which runs concurrently with the saints' reign in 20:4. Thus the picture of the saints in 6:9 provides no support for a present reign of believers in heaven.[41]

Other references in Revelation to saints in heaven are also instructive. While the timing of these scenes in relation to world events is not always certain (e.g., 7:9ff.), John's statement in 14:13 clearly applies to saints in heaven during the present age. He writes,

> "Blessed are the dead who die in the Lord from now on."
> "Yes," says the Spirit, "they will rest from their labor, for their deeds will follow them."[42]

Again, there is no indication of any present reigning activity.

---

[39]Hoekema, *The Bible and the Future*, 231, 234–35. Hoekema does recognize that in 6:9 the saints are told to be at rest while in 20:4 they are reigning, but still he sees the descriptions as covering the same situation.

[40]G. R. Beasley-Murray, *The Book of Revelation*, New Century Bible Commentary (Grand Rapids: Eerdmans, 1974), 293.

[41]Those who hold to a present heavenly reign of the saints have a difficult time explaining the nature of that reign. Hoekema says of the saints in 20:4–5, "John sees those to whom judgment was committed sitting on thrones. The book of Revelation is much concerned about matters of justice, particularly for persecuted Christians. It is therefore highly significant that in John's vision judgment (or 'authority to judge,' NIV) is committed to those sitting on the thrones" (*The Bible and the Future*, 230). Such present judgment in relation to persecutors seems contradictory to the picture of 6:9, where the saints are told to wait for the execution of judgment.

[42]There is some question as to the time reference "from now on." We prefer to relate it to John's own time rather than the future time of the fulfillment of the vision of the 144,000 (vv. 1ff.). The exhortation to "patient endurance" preceding this (v. 12), applying to John's day, provides the background for the beatitude of blessing to those who heed it.

It might be noted in passing that if the terms "come to life" or "resurrection" in Revelation 20:4–5 meant the saints' entrance into heaven after death, we might have expected something of such terminology in this verse where we have a clear reference to the transition from earth to heaven via death.

The positive picture given of both the reign of the saints and of Christ in the book of Revelation apart from chapter 20 is that of a future reign on the earth. Of the redeemed, John says in 5:10, ". . . they will reign on the earth." The reign of God is likewise future. At the sounding of the seventh trumpet and in anticipation of the third and final woe, heavenly voices proclaim, "The kingdom of the world has become the kingdom of our Lord and of his Christ, and he will reign for ever and ever" (11:15). To this the twenty-four elders add, "We give thanks to you, Lord God Almighty, the One who is and who was, because you have taken your great power and have begun to reign" (v. 17).

In these heavenly proclamations we notice first that the kingdom reign of Christ is related to the earth. Reminiscent of Psalm 2:2, the secular power of the world is replaced by the reign of the Messiah.[43] Thus the reign is clearly on earth. Second, the reign is not present, but future, witness the future tense and the fact that the world's secular powers are still reigning. These truths provide the basis for the futuristic translation of verse 17 that only at this future time will God and his Christ have "begun to reign."[44] The pronouncement of the reign of God in 19:6 is most probably to be understood in the same way as the inauguration of the action related to the coming of Christ in 19:11ff.[45]

The picture of the reign of Christ and the saints in the rest of the book of Revelation is therefore future and earthly, providing strong evidence that 20:4–5 should be interpreted in the same way. It is neither some kind of a present spiritual reign amid secular earthly kingdoms or a present reign in heaven. Rather, as many scholars point out, the scene in Revelation 20:4–5 is an adaptation of the judgment scene in Daniel 7:9ff. There, thrones are seen (v. 9) as the setting for the judgment and inauguration of the reign of the Son of Man (vv. 13–14), which also included the saints (vv. 26–27). The establishment of this reign entailed the destruction of secular earthly powers (cf. vv. 11ff.), even as it did in the vision of the destruction of Nebuchadnezzar's image in Daniel 2 (cf. vv. 34–35, 44–45) and as we have just seen in Revelation 11:15–17.

The mention of the saints' being given "authority to judge" during their reign, as stated in Revelation 20, harmonizes with Paul's teaching of

---

[43]Noting the singular "kingdom" instead of "kingdoms," Leon Morris says, "The thought is not that of a multitude of earthly kingdoms, but of secular power considered as a unit. Perhaps, too, the beast is held to have established universal dominion" (*The Revelation of St. John* [London: Tyndale Press, 1969], 153).

[44]The aorist tense used here with "reign" is to be understood as inceptive and points to the crisis when "God has decisively dethroned evil and entered on His reign" (Morris, *The Revelation of St. John,* 153).

[45]Ladd describes this as "a proleptic statement analogous to the announcements in 14:8 of the fall of Babylon and 11:15ff of the establishment of God's reign" (*A Commentary on the Revelation of John* [Grand Rapids: Eerdmans, 1972], 246).

the future time when the saints will "judge the world" (1Co 6:2) and Jesus' reference to the disciples judging the tribes of Israel (Mt 19:28). If these passages are in fact all related, then the judging and reign in Revelation 20 is future.

On the basis of the meaning of "coming to life" as signifying bodily resurrection, the lack of a present binding of Satan with the completeness pictured in the Revelation passage, and the picture of the saints reigning seen both in the rest of Revelation and other Scriptures, we conclude that the reign in 20:4 is future and earthly. Since it cannot refer to the eternal condition because of its limitation, it must be understood as an interim future millennial aspect of the kingdom of God.

3. *Other Passages.* While Revelation 20:4–5 provides the fullest New Testament picture of a millennial kingdom, it is not the only New Testament evidence of a future temporary reign of Christ before the final state. Many see evidence of the millennium in Paul's discourse on resurrection (1Co 15, esp. vv. 20–28):

> For as in Adam all die, so in Christ all will be made alive. But each in his own turn: Christ, the firstfruits; then, when he comes, those who belong to him. Then the end will come, when he hands over the kingdom to God the Father after he has destroyed all dominion, authority and power. For he must reign until he has put all his enemies under his feet. The last enemy to be destroyed is death (vv. 22–26).

Because a millennium is not explicit in the passage, many scholars have rejected such an interpretation. They view the "end" in verse 23 as closely associated with the coming of Christ in verse 22. Thus the kingdom of Christ with the subjection of his enemies (v. 25) is complete by that time, and his kingdom is merged into the eternal kingdom of God, providing no time for a millennium.[46]

Granted that its primary purpose is not to teach a millennium, the passage has, nevertheless, several aspects that are best understood within such an eschatological framework.[47] First, the resurrection is described as

[46]See, for example, C. K. Barrett, *The First Epistle to the Corinthians* (New York: Harper & Row, 1968), 354–61; Hans Conzelmann, *1 Corinthians* (Philadelphia: Fortress, 1975); W. D. Davies, *Paul and Rabbinic Judaism* (Philadelphia: Fortress, 1980), 291–97; Gordon D. Fee, *The First Epistle to the Corinthians* (Grand Rapids: Eerdmans, 1987), 749–60.

[47]Beasley-Murray says, "Scholars differ in their understanding of 1 Corinthians 15:22–5, but there is little doubt that the whole paragraph in which those verses are set (vv. 20–8) is closely related to the theology embodied in John's vision [Rev. 20]" (*The Book of Revelation,* 290); Mathias Rissi similarly declares, " . . . it appears to be thoroughly possible that Paul here [1 Cor. 15:23–28] is thinking of the same period which the Revelation describes as the millennium. . . . 1 Corinthians certainly does not speak explicitly of this final phase. However, this does not prove in any way its nonexistence in the Pauline eschatological conceptions, and 1 Corinthians 15, as we have seen, in its extremely narrow development of

involving a sequence of events with intervals of time between them. Declaring that "in Christ all will be made alive," Paul goes on to say that they come to life "each in his own turn [Gk., τάγμα, division or group]: Christ . . . then, when he comes those who belong to him. Then the end will come" (1Co 15:22–24).

The verse division between verses 23 and 24 and especially the sentence break in the NIV tend to obscure the connectedness of this sequence. The closely related Greek words (ἔπειτα, εἶτα), which are translated "then," both introduce events that are *subsequent in time* as indicated by their use earlier in the chapter. In verses 5–7 we read that Christ "appeared to Peter, and *then* to the Twelve. After that [or *then*] to more than five hundred. . . . *Then* he appeared to James, *then* to all the apostles" (italics added). Although the durations vary, in each instance there is an interval of time expressed by these adverbs (cf. Paul's only other uses of εἶτα, v. 24; 1Ti 2:13; 3:10).

Paul's language thus signifies that the "end," when Christ delivers the kingdom to the Father, is separated from the coming of Christ even as his coming is separated from his resurrection, as we see at the beginning of the sequence. If Paul had desired to say that the "end" occurred at the coming of Christ, he could easily have used another adverb (τότε, meaning "at that time") for the second "then."[48] The presence of some interval of time between the coming of Christ and the end does not, of course, prove that we can insert a millennium here in Paul's teaching. But it offers a hint in that direction and certainly does not exclude it.

A further indication that the millennium occurs during this interval is found in other statements Paul makes about the reign of Christ (vv. 24–28). According to Paul, Christ "must reign until he has put all his enemies under his feet" (v. 26). The significant thing about this reign for our purpose is that its goal of subduing all of Christ's enemies is accomplished by the time of "the end" (v. 24). At that time he "hands over the kingdom

---

eschatology, allows room in any case for this 'mystery' " (*Time and History* [Richmond: John Knox, 1966], 121). Rissi supports his contention with the following note: "Cf. also K. L. Schmidt, *Die Polis in Kirche und Welt, Rektoratsprogramm der Universität Basel* (1939), p. 38: 'The Chiliasm clearly developed in Revelation 20 lies concealed by Paul in 1 Corinthians 15:23–28.' So also G. Schrenk, *Die Weissagung über Israel im NT* (1951), p. 71, footnote 63."

[48]With regard to the apostle's use of adverbs, F. L. Godet says, "The εἶτα, *then*, does not allow us to identify the time of the τέλος, *the end*, with that of the Advent. Paul would have required to say in that sense τότε, *at that time*, and not εἶτα, *then* or *thereafter*. The εἶτα implies, in the mind of the apostle, a longer or shorter interval between the Advent and what he calls *the end*" (*Commentary on the First Epistle of St. Paul to the Corinthians* [reprint, Grand Rapids: Zondervan, 1957], 2:357). Cf. also Christian Friedrich Kling, "The First Epistle of Paul to the Corinthians," in *Lange's Commentary on the Holy Scriptures*, New Testament, vol. 10 (reprint, Grand Rapids: Zondervan, 1960), 318.

to God the Father" and is himself "made subject to him [the Father] . . . so that God may be all in all" (vv. 24, 28).

In the reign of Christ and its transfer to the Father at the end, Paul portrays the completion of the Messiah's work of redemption.[49] F. W. Grosheide writes, ". . . the Messiah will lay down His office at the feet of the Father, when he has finished His work as such."[50] The handing over of the kingdom to the Father thus signifies nothing less than the conclusion of the messianic administration of the kingdom through which Christ brings all things back under the rule or kingdom of God.

Now, if the "end" marking the completion of Christ's reign is simultaneous with his coming, we are forced to conclude not only that his kingdom is established now and he is presently reigning, but also that this is the only age in which he will reign over the "messianic kingdom."

To my mind, this interpretation is questionable for several reasons. First, although Christ has been exalted to the messianic kingship, nowhere else in the New Testament is he said to be presently exercising that kingship in an actual "reigning" over his enemies. Not only is the language of "reign" never used for his present ministry (unless this instance is an exception), but the prevailing teaching of the futurity of the kingdom both in the teaching of Christ and the later church, and the commencement of the actual exercising of his kingship at the parousia argue against this "reign" during the present age.[51]

Second, the Scriptures frequently promise that the saints will reign with Christ in his kingdom (cf. Da 7:27; 2Ti 2:12; Rev 3:21; 5:10; 20:4–5; cf. also Mt 19:28; Lk 22:30; 1Co 6:1–3). This coreign with Christ, as Revelation 3:21 indicates, is with him on his throne ("on my throne"), which surely includes the messianic reign. Such a coreign of believers with Christ in his messianic kingdom, however, is not possible if that reign is concluded with the handing over of the kingdom to the Father at the coming of Christ. Not only does the New Testament always teach the reign

---

[49]Fee, *The First Epistle to the Corinthians*, 756.

[50]F. W. Grosheide, *Commentary on the First Epistle to the Corinthians* (Grand Rapids: Eerdmans, 1953), 369.

[51]See chapter 4 for a fuller discussion of the time of Christ's kingdom reign. The present infinitive in verse 26 points to a continuous action of Christ's reign. But it cannot be used to support a present time for that reign, since the time of the infinitive is determined by the main verb *dei* ("he must," NIV, lit., "it is necessary"). In other words, Paul says, Christ must be reigning until he has put all his enemies under his feet. The statement does not indicate when the action of reigning commences. It should also be noted that the use of the future infinitive, which would clearly indicate futurity, is greatly diminished in the New Testament and is found only in Acts and Hebrews. The present infinitive is frequently used in futuristic sense. On the meaning and use of the present and future infinitives in the New Testament, see F. Blass and A. Debrunner, *A Greek Grammar of the New Testament and Other Early Christian Literature* (Chicago: Univ. of Chicago Press, 1961), sec. 318, p. 166; sec. 338, p. 174; sec. 350, p. 178.

of believers as future, never mentioning a present reign, but Paul also states clearly in his letter to the Corinthians that this age is not the time of their reign (cf. 1Co 4:8).

The believers' coreign with Christ would, then, seem either to be placed in the eternal state or to be limited to some sort of participation in the final judgment at the coming of Christ just prior to the handing over of the kingdom to the Father. As to the latter, while judging in the sense of judicial action is an essential part of reigning, it seems inadequate for the total concept of that term and the promises that we shall "reign on the earth" (Rev 3:21) and do so for some period of time (Rev 20:4). A brief role in the final judgment hardly constitutes "reigning" with Christ in his kingdom.

So is it possible to see the promises of the coreign of believers with Christ fulfilled in eternity after his messianic reign is complete? The Scriptures do portray the saints as reigning throughout eternity, apparently with God and Christ (Rev 22:5; cf. v. 1). But this reign after the work of the Messiah is completed hardly does justice to the total biblical picture of God's historical purpose for humanity and the full redemption brought through the Messiah.

In 1 Corinthians 15:24–27, Paul pictures the reign of Christ through allusions to Psalms 8 and 110. The former declares that God has made "man" (cf. v. 6) to be "ruler" over the works of his hands and "put everything under his feet." The reference is not to a single person, but to mankind, reflecting God's original purpose for mankind to rule the earth for him (cf. Ge 1:26, 28). By citing Psalm 8:4, Paul apparently intended to show that Christ's reign is the accomplishment of this divine purpose for humankind. If that is the case, his reign in fulfillment of Psalm 8 cannot be seen apart from his people. Rather, through his redemptive work Christ has created a new humanity, of which he is the head and through which the divine purpose of human dominion over the earth is destined to be fulfilled.

Other passages in the New Testament clearly tie the fulfillment of Psalm 8 to the work of Christ. God has already placed all things under Christ's feet (Eph 1:22). But this does not completely fulfill the intent of the Psalm, for the writer of Hebrews, with reference to Psalm 8, says, "Yet at present we do not see everything subject to him. But we see Jesus . . . now crowned with glory and honor" (2:8–9). This is to say that Christ has already received the rulership of all things, but the task of bringing his people into that same position is yet incomplete. This task remains to be accomplished as part of his messianic work.

The linking of Psalm 8 with the reign of Christ in 1 Corinthians, therefore, suggests that the present reign apart from the saints is not the complete fulfillment. Even if one were to understand the "reign" of Christ as having already begun with his exaltation (which is doubtful), this reign must have a future dimension that includes his people, to fully accomplish God's purpose for mankind to rule the earth in righteousness for him. So it is impossible to see the reign of the saints with Christ as taking place only in eternity. The purpose of mankind for history, along with the promises to share in the kingdom reign of the Messiah as the head of a new humanity, argues strongly for this coreign as part of the *messianic kingdom*. As it is not occurring presently, there must be a future age before the termination of Christ's messianic work and the kingdom is handed over to the Father.[52]

When we apply this to Paul's teaching in 1 Corinthians 15, we reach the conclusion that the only possible place for this reign is during an interval between the coming of Christ and the "end."[53]

First Corinthians 15 also raises another question related to the

---

[52]The amillennial attempt to allow for a more literal fulfillment of the earthly material aspects of the Old Testament kingdom prophecies flounders on this same reasoning, in our opinion. Hoekema argues that a passage such as Isaiah 2:1–4, which refers to the beating of swords into plowshares, among other things, has its fulfillment not in a millennium but on the new earth. This interpretation does not acknowledge that this clearly places such portraits of peace among nations beyond the pale of the Messiah's redemptive work and his messianic administration of God's kingdom. If this is correct, his "messianic reign" is one of present spiritual redemption climaxing with the destruction of his enemies and their judgment. His "messianic reign" will never include a reign of manifest glory in which he takes over the government of the world to rule for God as his Anointed One in righteousness and peace in fulfillment of the historical purpose for mankind.

Aside from the difficulty of seeing everything in passages like Isaiah 2:1–4 as present in the new earth (e.g., the nations coming to learn the ways of God and the necessity of judging between them), in our opinion, such a view wrongly curtails the manifestation of Christ's glorious reign to a short period of destruction and judgment.

[53]A final comment regarding the "reign" of Christ concerns the process involved in the subjugation of Christ's enemies. Barrett says, "In the passage before us Christ appears to reign during the period in which this dispossessing takes place, one enemy after another (cf. v. 26) being overpowered" (*The First Epistle to the Corinthians*, 357). Although Barrett sees this as taking place during the present age, the New Testament does not reveal any such gradual "overpowering" or destruction (cf. NIV, Gk. καταργέω, which has the meaning here of "bring to an end") of the enemies of Christ during this age. To be sure, they are defeated every time someone is rescued for the kingdom of God or God's people choose to do his will rather than that of the enemy. But the enemies continue on in their evil works even to the coming of Christ (cf. Rev 13:7, where the beast is given power to overcome the saints).

The lack of a present, gradual subjugation of his enemies is apparent also in the description given in Hebrews of Christ now sitting at the right hand of God waiting for his enemies to be made his footstool. The term ἐκδέχεσθαι ("to wait") expresses eschatological expectation even as the farmer waits for the processes of nature (Jas 5:7) and believers wait for the coming of Christ (cf. Walter Grundmann, "δέχομαι κτλ," in *Theological Dictionary of the New Testament*, vol. 2, ed. Gerhard Kittel [Grand Rapids: Eerdmans, 1964], 56). The idea of "waiting" in each instance does not suggest a present active involvement in that which is the object of the wait—e.g., Christians are not presently involved in the coming of Christ; they can only wait for God's timing of that event. Thus Christ is not presently subjugating his enemies as he waits for their subjugation. Rather, there is presently a delay in the subjugation as the Lord prolongs the day of grace.

millennium, namely, the number of resurrections. We have already argued that the apostle John rather clearly teaches two resurrections in Revelation 20:4–6. Is there further substantiation of this teaching in the New Testament? Many interpreters find it in Paul's description of the orders of events involved in the resurrection. Admittedly, the terminology "the first resurrection" is used only by John, but Beasley-Murray says nevertheless, ". . . the doctrine may well be intended by Paul in 1 Corinthians 15:22–4."[54]

Some advocates of this interpretation see the word "end" as meaning the "rest" or "remainder" of those resurrected, i.e., the final group in the series or orders of resurrection, indicating a resurrection subsequent to Christ's coming.[55] But even if we accept the more probable meaning of "end" as "the conclusion of eschatological events,"[56] that would not exclude a further resurrection as part of that "end." It would, in fact, provide a more natural meaning of Paul's words "each in his own group," which imply more than one person (Christ) and one group (those at his coming).[57]

The resurrection was always a part of the eschatological "end." This seems to be implied even here in 1 Corinthians 15, for it is only at the "end" that the last enemy, death, is destroyed (cf. vv. 24–26). Such destruction of death is clearly attained through a final resurrection (v. 54; cf. Rev 20:11–14). If there is any time interval between the resurrection of believers at the coming of Christ and the "end" (as "then" suggests), there is valid reason to see a further resurrection indicating the final conquest of death as part of that "end."

Such a scenario gains support from the apparent limitation of the resurrection at the coming of Christ. Only "those who belong to him" (i.e., believers) are said by Paul to be resurrected at this time (v. 23). Since Paul clearly believed in the resurrection of all people, including the unrighteous (cf. Ac 24:15), the question may be asked, why are only believers mentioned as being raised at Christ's coming? One could say that Paul is talking about a general resurrection of all the dead but is only interested in

---

[54]Beasley-Murray, *The Book of Revelation,* 296.

[55]Oepke, "ἀνίστημι κτλ," *TDNT,* 1:371; Coenen, "Resurrection," *NIDNTT,* 3:277; Hans Lietzmann, *An die Korinther I/II,* 4th ed., ed. Werner G. Kümmel (Tubingen: J. C. B. Mohr [Paul Siebeck], 1949), 80–81.

[56]R. Schippers, "Goal, Near, Last, End, Complete," in *The New International Dictionary of New Testament Theology,* vol. 2, ed. Colin Brown (Grand Rapids: Zondervan, 1976), 62.

[57]Even those denying a third element recognize the problem of having only Christ and the believers at his coming mentioned. Davies says that seeing "end" as "the rest" . . . "would supply an obvious third τάγμα [division or group] of the risen which would be more natural than the enumeration of only two" (*Paul and Rabbinic Judaism,* 293). Barrett similarly says, ". . . in accord with Greek usage as a whole . . . 'each one in his own group' seems to imply more than is stated in the following words: 'Christ himself as the firstfruits, then, at his coming, those who belong to Christ'" (*The First Epistle to the Corinthians,* 355).

believers; yet it is preferable to see this passage as being in harmony with other passages that similarly appear to teach two resurrections.

While these passages are not many, they are sufficient for Albrecht Oepke to say concerning the New Testament, "the predominant view is that of a double resurrection."[58] In addition to Revelation 20:4–5, the clearest references are those that speak of the resurrection and reward of believers without any mention of the unbelievers or their judgment. One such passage is Luke 14:14, in which Jesus promises reward "at the resurrection of the righteous."[59] Another is 1 Thessalonians 4:13–18, which, like 1 Corinthians 15, speaks only of the resurrection of believers in connection with the coming of Christ. Although there is an associated judgment that will come upon the unprepared on the earth (cf. 1Th 5:1ff.), Paul makes no mention of either the resurrection or the judgment of the unsaved dead.

One of the most interesting passages about the resurrection would also appear to teach a separate, initial resurrection for those in Christ. In Philippians 3:11, Paul expresses his personal motivation to experience Christ in his life "and so, somehow, to attain to the resurrection from the dead." Two things in this statement point to a separate resurrection of the righteous. First, whereas "the resurrection *of* the dead" denotes generally the resurrection of both believers and unbelievers, the words *"from* the dead" [lit., "out of the dead ones"] are always used of believers (cf. Lk 20:35; Ac 4:2).[60]

This fact alone may not offer clear evidence that Paul has a distinct resurrection in mind in Philippians 3:11, but his expression of hope to attain this resurrection clearly warrants that conclusion. Commentators are rightly hesitant to see in the words "and so, somehow [Gk., εἴ πως] to attain . . ." an expression of strong doubt or uncertainty on Paul's part that he will participate in the hoped-for resurrection.[61] Nevertheless, these words do carry some sense of what might in this instance be termed "a *concerned* hope." This is indicated by the Greek terms involved that mean "if perhaps, if somehow."[62]

---

[58]Oepke, "ἀνίστημι κτλ," *TDNT*, 1:371; cf. also Coenen, "Resurrection," *NIDNTT*, 3:277.

[59]The mention of "sons of the resurrection" in Luke 20:36 may also be a reference to a particular resurrection of the righteous since the subjects involved are clearly limited to believers.

[60]Jac J. Müller, *The Epistles of Paul to the Philippians and to Philemon* (Grand Rapids: Eerdmans, 1955), 118, n.13.

[61]Marvin R. Vincent, for example, says, "His words here are an expression of humility and self-distrust, not of doubt." But Vincent then cites favorably Bernard Weiss's statement that "while, on the human side, the attainment of the goal may be regarded as doubtful, or at least conditioned upon humble self-estimate, on the side of the working of divine grace it appears certain" (Vincent, *A Critical and Exegetical Commentary on the Epistles to the Philippians and to Philemon*, International Critical Commentary [Edinburgh: T & T Clark, 1897], 106).

[62]Arndt and Gingrich, *A Greek–English Lexicon of the New Testament and Other Early Christian Literature*, 220. Moises Silva concurs: ". . . it seems a mistake to deny the note of

Now, if Paul believed in one general resurrection at the end in which all people, the saved and lost, would participate, it is difficult to understand his use of this language in relation to his personal participation. There would be no question of his being a part of such a resurrection. If his desire was to be part of those resurrected to life as opposed to those destined for judgment (and if the latter were raised at the same time), we would have expected Paul to add this qualifier. But he says simply that he hopes to attain to "the resurrection from the dead," apparently with reference to a distinct resurrection of the righteous—John's "first" resurrection. Only such an understanding appears to do justice to his concern to be part of it.

The explicit teaching of two resurrections in Revelation 20 and the passages that speak to a resurrection only of believers is evidence that the New Testament writers anticipated two resurrections separated by an interval. Such an interval fits in with a future, temporary millennial reign of Christ, a view that was also prominent in Jewish theology prior to the writing of the New Testament.[63]

We acknowledge that the New Testament evidence for a distinct, future millennial kingdom prior to the final state is limited. Apart from Revelation 20, which in our opinion is explicit, the evidence consists mainly of implications derived from eschatological teaching whose primary purpose does not focus on a millennial kingdom. It must be recognized, however, that this limited evidence for the millennium is provided by Jewish writers who had a broad eschatological picture drawn from the Old Testament that included a messianic kingdom (cf. Ac 1:5–6).[64] They also clearly taught a restoration for the nation of Israel and the blessing of the world as a result (cf. Ro 11:12).[65] Only a millennium would appear to provide the necessary time for this to take place. Finally, the fact that they saw the kingdom as predominantly future from their own time[66] suggests that they regarded the fulfillment of the messianic kingdom promises as still future.

The total picture of the New Testament eschatological teaching

---

doubt or uncertainty. The adverb *pos* (enclitic) serves as an indefinite modal particle; it often adds a slight nuance that cannot be easily reproduced. The specific combination *ei/ean pos* commonly designates uncertainty (cf. LSJ), and this is surely the case in the NT" (*Philippians*, in The Wycliffe Exegetical Commentary [Chicago: Moody Press, 1988], 192). To see in this language only the manner in which he will participate in the resurrection—i.e., whether in the near future through martyrdom or later through some other means (R. P. Martin, *Philippians*, New Century Bible [London: Marshall, Morgan & Scot, 1976], 135f.)—seems inadequate in the light of the meaning of the Greek terms and the other uses of these words in the New Testament (cf. Ac 27:12; Ro 1:10; 11:14).

[63]See p. 241.
[64]For a survey of the Old Testament concept of the messianic kingdom, see chaps. 4 and 9.
[65]See chap. 10.
[66]See pp. 104–6.

thus provides a supporting context for the more specific texts related to a millennium.

That the New Testament writers did not take pains to detail the distinction between the temporal messianic kingdom and the final eternal kingdom of God places them within the Old Testament framework. There the messianic kingdom is merged with the final eschatological picture of the new heaven and earth. This should caution us not to exaggerate the place of the millennium in eschatology. The millennium is only the final transition phase leading to the eternal state. But it nevertheless does have a place in the outworking of God's program of salvation.

Although New Testament evidence for a future messianic kingdom is limited, there appears to be no explicit witness to the contrary. To our knowledge there is no unambiguous evidence for a so-called general resurrection at the end of this age in which both the saved and the unsaved will participate. There are references to the resurrection of both, but none explicitly demonstrates that there is only one such resurrection or that the saved and unsaved are resurrected at the same time (e.g., Da 12:2; Jn 5:28–29). There is, therefore, nothing preventing us from viewing these as general statements about the resurrection of all people that will occur at different times in accord with the rather plain teaching of Revelation 20:4–5. There are also no explicit statements that the eternal state will commence with the coming of Christ.[67]

---

[67]Examples of statements that some say teach the eternal state following the Lord's return include the story of the goats (unbelievers) being sent into "eternal fire" or "eternal punishment" in connection with the judgment of the "nations" at the coming of Christ (Mt 25:41, 46). The reference to "eternal" here may possibly be interpreted as the Lord's simply looking at their final end in a compression of future events. Or preferably, "eternal" is to be taken as a qualitative term just as it is in the "eternal life" of believers. A person may presently enter into life that has the quality of "eternal life" and still have a fuller experience of that life in the future. So these unbelievers at the judgment of the sheep and goats may be cast into "eternal fire," a qualitative judgment of the lost, and already begin to experience that judgment in the intermediate state of Hades before Hades is cast into the final "lake of fire" (Rev 20:14). Thus they may be in a punishment during the millennium that shares the same quality ("eternal") as is found more intensively later in the lake of fire of the eternal state.

Millard J. Erickson's view of the situation seems to support this general conclusion: "We conclude that upon death believers go immediately to a place and condition of blessedness, and unbelievers to an experience of misery, torment, and punishment. Although the evidence is not clear, it is likely that these are the very places to which believers and unbelievers will go after the great judgment. . . . Yet while the place of the intermediate and final states may be the same, the experiences of paradise and Hades are doubtlessly not as intense as what will ultimately be . . ." (*Christian Theology* [Grand Rapids: Baker, 1985], 1183–84).

We may explain Peter's reference to the coming of the new earth and heavens (2Pe 3:10ff.) by noting that the "day of the Lord" of which he writes may be an extended time involving a series of events including the coming of Christ, his glorious millennial reign, the final judgment, and the creation of the new heavens and earth (cf. A. R. Fausset, "1 Corinthians– Revelation," *A Commentary Critical, Experimental and Practical on the Old and New*

B. The Rationale for a Millennium

Having looked at the biblical evidence for a millennial reign of Christ, the question might be asked, Is there any reason for such a temporary interval between the present, initial phase of the kingdom and its final consummation? The common expression "already and not yet" suggests that the kingdom promises are fulfilled in two phases, present and future. But as we have seen in both the Old and New Testaments, it is difficult to fit some of the elements of the eschatological picture into either the present age or the eternal state. Aside from this, is there any place for an intervening stage in the overall kingdom program?

It is not our purpose to enter fully into this question, but rather to indicate briefly the significance of a millennial kingdom in a premillennial understanding of biblical history. The millennial kingdom reign of Christ emphasizes the central place in history of the person and work of Christ. Few if any biblical scholars would disagree with George N. H. Peters' statement that "Jesus Christ the Son of God and the Son of David, the promised Theocratic King . . . [is] the central figure of history, both as the One to whom all history directs the heart of faith and the eye of hope, and as the One in whom history finds it fulfilment and solution."[68] John Marsh expresses a similar thought with more detail:

> Since the kingdom of God was fulfilled in Christ, then none other than that same kingdom can come at the end of history. . . . This action [Christ's fulfillment of the promises of the kingdom in himself] fulfills both what has gone before and what follows after it in history and constitutes ontologically the imposition of the divine pattern of providence and redemption upon history, and epistemologically the point at which the revelation of the divine will and purpose is fully revealed. It also means that the end of historical process can be none other than the final manifestation or revelation of the fulfillment of history that took place at its "centre."[69]

In surveying the history of the world thus far, we must acknowledge that the prominence of Christ remains hidden except to the eyes of faith. The majority of the world today, as when he walked on earth, does not recognize him. Despite the progress of the church, nothing in Scripture leads us to believe that such recognition will take place before he returns (cf. Lk 18:8; Mt 24:8–14). To be sure, the world will recognize Christ when he returns in glory. But does a short period of destruction and

Testaments, vol. 6, ed. Robert Jamieson, A. R. Fausset, and David Brown [reprint, Grand Rapids: Eerdmans, 1948], 627).

[68]George N. H. Peters, *The Theocratic Kingdom*, vol. 3 (reprint, Grand Rapids: Kregel, 1952), 429–30.

[69]John Marsh, *The Fulness of Time* (London: Nisbet, 1952), 166–67.

judgment before he turns the kingdom over to the Father for the eternal state provide an adequate explanation of the centrality of Christ and a sufficient manifestation of his glory *within history?*

In regard to the fulfillment of the kingdom promises, some amillennialists have minimized the distinction between history and eternity. Vern Poythress explains that "amillennialists like Hoekema consider that 'history' goes on through and beyond the renewal of heaven and earth."[70] But that explanation appears to negate the usual concept of history as having an "end." Just as the new heavens and earth belong to an "age" that has a beginning but no end, these amillennialists say, there would be no point or event that could be identified as "the end of history." Thus, if there is an "end of history," it must be the "end" Paul referred to as Christ's completing his messianic kingdom work and handing the kingdom over to his Father (1Co 15:24–28). After this point, when the new heavens and earth are present, there is no "end."

Taking Paul's reference to "the end" in 1 Corinthians 15:24 as the end of history, millennialists hold that to place the "end" at the time of Christ's return does not do justice to the concept that Christ is the meaning and central figure of "history." So far in history, the experience of Christ and his people has been one of oppression and nonrecognition (cf. 1Jn 3:1). If history comes to its end with the coming of Christ, there will be no significant time within history when his centrality is manifest. The millennium, however, provides just such a time when Christ's glory will pervade human history and his significance will be rightly recognized.

This need for a time when Christ will be glorified within history is central to premillennial thought. As Hendrikus Berkhof observes, there is in all millennialism "the common conviction that the period of 'refreshing' will correspond with and counterbalance the time of oppression which God's people experienced."[71]

We can affirm the same concept from the perspective of the cross and resurrection as the focal point of Christ's work, or in Peter's terms, "the sufferings of Christ and the glories that would follow" (1Pe 1:11). Up

---

[70]Vern Poythress, *Understanding Dispensationalists* (Grand Rapids: Zondervan, 1989), 50. We could find no statement in Hoekema defining "history" as going on into the time of the new earth. In fact, Hoekema sees the new heavens and earth at "the end of history" (*The Bible and the Future*, 287). Nevertheless, Hoekema does seek to place the fulfillment of many of the Old Testament promises related to the work of the Messiah in the new earth. Thus he appears to argue for much continuity between the time of the present earth and that of the new earth. We have no problem with continuity as long as the significance of Christ's giving up the kingdom, indicating the completion of his messianic work before the new heavens and earth, is recognized. If "history" has an end, then this action must signify this end. If the delivering up of the kingdom is not the end of "history," then it would appear to have no end because the "age" of the new heavens and earth is endless.

[71]Berkhof, *Christ, the Meaning of History*, 159.

to our own time and onward until his coming, suffering is the dominant experience of both Christ and his people (for he suffers with his body, the church) in world history. Berkhof says, "In the history before the consummation the resurrection is hidden more than the cross. The cross is elaborated and worked out entirely in this dispensation."[72] In the language of Martin Luther, the church lives in this age under the theology of the cross. While the resurrection is manifest to some extent in the lives of individual believers and in the church, the millennium provides a time when it will be manifest openly in world history.

This felt need for the historical manifestation of Christ's triumph has been expressed in various ways by Christian scholars. Some have framed it in liberal terms as the transformation of society through the working of the imminent divinity in mankind or in a postmillennial triumph of the kingdom. The current popularity of kingdom theology used in relation to transforming the present age physically, politically, or in other ways is an expression of this same desire. But despite the presence of the kingdom now, this age will never fulfill the desire for the manifestation of Christ's triumph within history. Only a millennium provides that. In the words of Karl Schmidt, "The millennial kingdom represents the triumph of Christ and his Church in the heart of the world and, also over the world."[73]

A millennium is needed not only for the historical display of the glory of Christ, but also for the completion of his messianic salvation.[74] The prophets pictured the saving work of the Messiah as both personal and societal renewal. The kingdom work of Christ has entered this age to bring personal salvation, but the transformation of society in terms of peace among peoples and the expression of God's righteousness in the structures of human society are never promised for this age. They await the return of the messianic King, who will destroy the evil structures of this age and institute a righteous rule over the earth for the first time in human history.

If the "end" occurs at the coming of Christ, as amillennialists claim, and the kingdom is given over to the Father, completing the Messiah's redemptive work, then the eschatological picture of peace and righteousness prevailing among the peoples of the earth is placed beyond the pale of Christ's messianic work. This does not seem to do justice to the fullness of salvation needed to restore mankind to God's original intent or that pictured in the prophets under the kingship of the Messiah. Thus, for millennialists and especially for dispensationalists, a future reign of the

---

[72]Berkhof, *Christ, the Meaning of History*, 134.

[73]Cited by Berkhof, *Christ, the Meaning of History*, 167.

[74] For a more complete discussion of the nature of the messianic salvation, see chap. 9 and pp. 311–23.

Messiah on earth is necessary for the completion of all that God has promised through the Messiah.

III. THE FUTURE OF JERUSALEM

The New Testament looks ultimately to a new Jerusalem that will come down out of heaven upon the new earth (cf. Rev 3:12; 21:2; 10ff.). This was the city to which Abraham looked in final fulfillment of the promises made to him (Heb 11:10). It is also the city presently existing in heaven to which the believer is already related (Gal 4:26; Heb 12:22). But as we observed in regard to the Abrahamic promise, the existence of a heavenly Jerusalem as the final city of God does not exclude the reality or significance of the earthly Jerusalem in the historical plan of God before the final state.[75] Thus, in harmony with this concept, we find references to a historical Jerusalem in the New Testament eschatological perspective.

Jesus' lament over the unbelief of Jerusalem also contained hope for that city in the future. It will see him again, this time in salvation when the inhabitants repent and welcome him as their Messiah, declaring, "Blessed is he who comes in the name of the Lord" (Mt 23:37–39). In discussing the future of Israel, the apostle Paul sees this city as the focal point of salvation: "The deliverer will come from Zion; he will turn godlessness away from Jacob" (Ro 11:26).

Some scholars view Paul's statement as a reference to the heavenly Zion from which the Lord will return at his coming.[76] While the Lord does have residence at present in the heavenly Jerusalem (cf. Heb 12:22–24), there is no reason to see in Paul's statement anything other than the earthly Jerusalem. This was surely the meaning of the original statement of Isaiah, whom the apostle cites (cf. Isa 59:20). Jewish eschatological tradition had long held to the salvation of God, not only coming to Jerusalem, but streaming from it to purify both that nation and the nations of the Gentiles.[77] In light of Paul's firm belief in the future salvation of Israel, evident in the context, there is no reason not to give this reference to Zion the meaning that it has in the psalmist's plea: "Oh, that salvation for Israel would come out of Zion! When the LORD restores the fortunes of his people" (Ps 14:7; cf. 53:6).

The usual ground for denying that Paul has the earthly Jerusalem in

---

[75]See pp. 53–57.

[76]William Sanday and Arthur C. Headlam, *A Critical and Exegetical Commentary on the Epistle to the Romans*, International Critical Commentary (Edinburgh: T & T Clark, 1902), 337; James D. G. Dunn, *Romans 9–16*, Word Biblical Commentary, vol. 38 (Dallas: Word Books, 1988), 682.

[77]See Georg Fohrer, "Σιών κτλ," in *Theological Dictionary of the New Testament*, vol. 7, ed. Gerhard Friedrich (Grand Rapids: Eerdmans, 1971), 312–17; Lohse, "Σιών κτλ," *TDNT*, 7:325–27.

mind is his reference to "the Jerusalem that is above" in contrast to the "present city of Jerusalem" (Gal 4:25–26). Some interpreters apparently conclude that this mention of a heavenly Jerusalem negates in Paul's mind any future significance for the earthly city. But this is not a necessary conclusion. Jewish eschatology had room for both a future, glorious earthly city and the coming of a heavenly city.

Although the Old Testament prophets did not refer explicitly to a heavenly Jerusalem, they did mingle a glorious historical future for Israel and the nations with a totally new heaven and earth. Later Jewish eschatology applied this same relationship to Jerusalem. "Alongside the concept that the earthly city would be the scene of Yahweh's victory (2 Esc. 13: 25ff.; Sib. 3:663ff.) there developed in the apocalyptic literature a belief in the heavenly, pre-existent Jerusalem (Syr. Bar. 4:2 ff.), descending to earth at the end of the age (2 Esd. 10:27, 54; 13:36)."[78]

With this Jewish background, one can readily see how Paul would speak of both a future for historical Jerusalem and a heavenly Jerusalem to which believers in Christ were already related. It is significant that "the Jerusalem that is above" is not contrasted with the "earthly" Jerusalem, but rather with "the present city of Jerusalem" (Gal 4:26). "Present Jerusalem" represented the legalistic system that Judaism had become with its adherents (i.e., "her children"), whereas the heavenly Jerusalem signified the community of believers who had gained freedom in Christ.

Thus the contrast is primarily soteriological. The heavenly Jerusalem represents the eschatological salvation that the members of the church have already received.[79] But the focus of the statement is not eschatological in the sense that Paul is teaching that the earthly Jerusalem has been superseded by a heavenly Jerusalem in the fulfillment of God's historical program. The fact that believers are presently related to the Jerusalem "that is above" in terms of the eschatological reality of their salvation in Christ in no way negates the earthly reality of the church during this present time before the coming of the heavenly Jerusalem in the eternal state (Rev 21:2). Thus it cannot be said to negate the significance of earthly Jerusalem before that time either. R. J. McKelvey rightly explains that Paul's reference to the heavenly Jerusalem says nothing about the future of earthly Jerusalem.

---

[78]H. Schultz, "Jerusalem," *The New International Dictionary of New Testament Theology*, vol. 2, ed. Colin Brown (Grand Rapids: Zondervan, 1975), 326; cf. also Lohse, "Σιών κτλ," *TDNT*, 7:325.

[79]Lohse asserts the primacy of the soteriological meaning of Paul's statement: "By setting in antithesis to present-day Jerusalem, not the future Jerusalem but that which is above, he makes it plain from his Scripture proof that eschatological salvation is not awaited in an indefinite future but has come already" ("Σιών κτλ," *TDNT*, 7:337).

> In designating the church as the Jerusalem above, the apostle is referring to its spiritual and supernatural character (cf. Phil. 3. 20). Nor does Paul's use of the image here by implication tell us anything about the destiny of the terrestrial city. . . . There is nothing in the text to permit one to say that the apostle was repudiating all eschatological hopes concerning the city.[80]

The reference to "the Jerusalem that is above," therefore, cannot be used as evidence against a future earthly Jerusalem in the eschatological hope of the apostle. Thus there is no basis for not giving to his reference to "Zion" in connection with the future salvation of Israel (Ro 11:26) the same earthly meaning that it had in both the Old Testament prophets and later Jewish thought. Christ will descend from heaven, but then go out from Zion for the salvation or sanctification of Israel. The latter action is what Paul refers to in Romans.[81]

Such a scenario harmonizes well with Paul's reference to the destruction of the "man of lawlessness," or the Antichrist, who has set himself up as God in the future temple (2Th 2:3–4). The postapostolic church interpreted this as a reference to the historical temple. But from the fourth century on, the predominant view has been to see it as the church into which some heresy has penetrated.[82] Against the latter, McKelvey points out that "the whole section (2 Thess. 2.1–12) is so demonstrably apocalyptic in tone and so clearly based on the prophecies of Daniel concerning the temple of Jerusalem that it can only be the latter, or possibly the temple in heaven."[83] The heavenly temple, however, seems improbable in view of Paul's assumption that people on earth would be aware of these events.

There is also no evidence in the context for taking F. F. Bruce's view that the earthly Jerusalem temple is meant in "a metaphorical sense."[84] So it is best to see this as a reference to future Jerusalem, which

---

[80]R. J. McKelvey, *The New Temple* (London: Oxford Univ. Press, 1969), 143.

[81]Although Sanday and Headlam view Paul's reference to Zion in Romans 11:26 as the heavenly Jerusalem, they nevertheless cite several passages from Jewish literature that portray the Jewish expectation of the restoration and purification of Israel with Jerusalem serving as the center of the kingdom. They then add that Paul was very likely influenced by these conceptions and for this reason "inserts 'there' and reads ἐκ Σιών [out of Zion]" (337).

[82]O. Michel, "ναός," in *Theological Dictionary of the New Testament*, vol. 4, ed. Gerhard Kittel (Grand Rapids: Eerdmans, 1967), 887.

[83]McKelvey, *The New Temple*, 136.

[84]F. F. Bruce, *1 and 2 Thessalonians*, Word Biblical Commentary, vol. 45 (Waco, Tex.: Word Books, 1982), 169.

for Johannes Munck fits well into Paul's picture of the second coming: "Christ descends in Jerusalem, destroys Antichrist on Zion [2 Thess. 2:8], and from thence appears to Israel to save it."[85]

Finally, the book of Revelation clearly retains significance for the historical city of Jerusalem in the eschatological understanding of the early church (cf. 11:2; 20:9). Again, many have preferred symbolic interpretations to a literal city. But they appear to be based more on theological conclusions derived from elsewhere than on exegetical considerations of the passages themselves. In Revelation 11:2, "the holy city" is given over to the Gentiles to be trampled for forty-two months. The name "holy city," probably derived from Daniel 9:24, is used several other times in Scripture to denote the earthly city of Jerusalem (Ne 11:1; Isa 48:2; 52:1; Mt 4:5; 27:53).[86]

Further evidence that earthly Jerusalem is in view comes in the mention of Jerusalem in verse 8 as the "great city" where Christ was crucified. Also, the distinction of the outer court from the temple proper, which corresponds to the earthly temple prior to A.D. 70, and the future temple of Ezekiel points to a literal earthly scene.[87]

The city's being the site of the witnesses martyrdom (vv. 7–8) is clearly related to God's permitting it to be trampled by the Gentiles (cf. Lk 21:24). Moreover, the time period of this trampling (forty-two months) is the same as that given in 13:5 for the eschatological beast to exercise authority. We conclude, therefore, that the evidence points to "the holy city" in Revelation 11:2 as the future earthly Jerusalem.

John's picture of the Lamb and the 144,000 standing on "Mount Zion" in Revelation 14:1 is probably also a reference to earthly Jerusalem.[88] And finally, John's depiction of the final revolt against "the city he loves" after the thousand-year reign (20:9) clearly places the future city of Jerusalem in the center of the eschatological picture.

These references to future Jerusalem by the New Testament writers are more than a recognition of the important place that the city had in the early history of the church. They indicate a continual religious significance for that city as shown by its designation as the holy city.[89] This theological importance of Jerusalem gives evidence of an abiding belief in the future fulfillment of the Old Testament prophetic hope in which this

---

[85]Munck, *Christ and Israel*, 137.

[86]Hermann Strathmann says that "simply calling Jerusalem the holy city without any name . . . corresponds to the widespread practice of later Judaism and of a tradition which reaches well back into OT history" ("πόλις κτλ," in *Theological Dictionary of the New Testament*, vol. 6, ed. Gerhard Friedrich [Grand Rapids: Eerdmans, 1968], 530).

[87]Michel, "ναός," *TDNT*, 4:887–88.

[88]Lohse, "Σιών κτλ," *TDNT*, 7:336.

[89]Strathmann, "πόλις κτλ," *TDNT*, 6:531.

city played a central role.[90] A future for Jerusalem thus comports well with a future millennial reign of Christ in which Israel as a nation plays a central role.

We might add that such a picture of a future earthly Jerusalem was also part of a theology that viewed the believer in Christ as already related to the eternal pre-existent heavenly Jerusalem in terms of having reached the eschatological salvation in Christ. But this salvation was not yet fully realized in history. Thus the earthly realities, including the city of Jerusalem, still had meaning and significance in the outworking of the eschatological promises.

IV. CONCLUSION

We have seen in chapters 10 and 11 that the New Testament writers paint a future eschatological picture that has the same essential elements as the Old Testament. On this basis dispensationalists affirm the continued validity of the prophetic hope for world history that was set forth so fully by the prophets.

The new outworking of this hope in relation to the two comings of the Messiah is revealed in the New Testament. But this new outworking, according to dispensationalists, does not radically alter the meaning of the prophecies. The salvation of God through the preaching of the gospel to all nations today is obviously not the complete fulfillment of the prophecies. There remains yet the work of the Messiah in bringing God's righteousness to human societies in an outward reign of peace—a theme of great importance to the prophets.

In light of the New Testament teaching, this dimension of the eschatological hope is still to be realized in the manner of the prediction. Christ will reign over the nations with a restored Israel fulfilling its assigned God-given role in the service of this salvation for the world.

---

[90]J. Massyngberde Ford places the reference to "Zion" in Revelation 14:1 in the context of the importance of Jerusalem in the Old Testament and specifically the prophecies of the future: "Zion is the 'city of Yahweh' (Isa 60:14; cf. Ps 48:2), His sanctuary (Ps 20:2), His holy mountain (Joel 2:1). It is used especially for 'the city of the eschatological age of salvation (Is 1–39, Jer. Dt, 3rd Is. Joel, Mic 4 and Zech 1–9) . . . the seat and city of God . . . for the royal residence and capital, the symbol of the people or community esp. Dt Is, Ps and Lam,' (TWNT, VII, 300), and the cultic site and temple city (esp. Pss., e.g., 77:68–72, and Lam). It is from Zion that God as a warrior roaring from heaven comes to judge (Jer 25:30) and to inaugurate his eschatological reign; Isa 24:23; 52:7; Obad 21; Mich 4:7; Zeph 3:16; Zech 14:9; Pss 146:10; 149:2. It is here that the Anointed One is established (Ps 2:6) and receives the scepter as an investiture of power (Ps 90:2). On this mountain God swears to preserve the dynasty of David; Ps 132:11–12. God chooses it for his resting place; Ps 132:13–18. From here will come material blessings (vs. 15), blessings for the righteous (vs. 16), permanence for the monarchy (vs. 17). This will be the place of entry for the messianic ruler (Zech 9:9) and the rallying point of the remnant—the nucleus of the messianic restoration—cf. II Kings 19:30–31, Obad 17, 21" (*Revelation*, 240).

Chapter 12

The Future Purpose of Israel

THE OLD TESTAMENT prophecies picture Israel as having a central role in the eschatological plan of God's salvation, a subject we considered in chapter 9. The New Testament does not contain as much detail about Israel's place in the future. Nevertheless, we have sought to show that it retains the Old Testament picture by affirming the continuity of Israel's promises and covenants and the restoration of Israel in accordance with the prophetic hope.

This understanding of Scripture immediately raises strong questions, if not objections, in the light of the present position of the church in the salvation program. Why should God again distinguish one nation among all the nations of the world when these distinctions are not present in the church? Anthony Hoekema undoubtedly speaks for many when he sees this as a retrogression in salvation history.

> To suggest that God has in mind a separate future for Israel, in distinction from the future he has planned for Gentiles, actually goes contrary to God's purpose. It is like putting the scaffolding back up after the building has been finished. It is like turning the clock of history back to Old Testament times. It is imposing Old Testament separateness upon the New Testament, and ignoring the progress of revelation. God's present purpose with Israel is that Israel should believe in Christ as its Messiah, and thus become part

of the one fellowship of God's redeemed people which is the church.[1]

This objection to a future distinction of Israel is obviously aimed particularly against the traditional dispensational position that the union of Jews and Gentiles in the body of Christ (Eph 2:11–3:6) is applicable only to the present church age. On this point we agree with the objector. Paul's teaching of the unity of Jews and Gentiles in Christ, as we have seen in chapter 6, signifies that both groups share in the salvation of the New Covenant and this is permanent. The future distinction of Israel, therefore, cannot be the same as the distinctiveness it held during Old Testament history.

That is not to say, however, that there is *no* future distinction for Israel. The Old Testament prophets looked forward to a time when the Gentiles would participate in God's salvation on the same basis as Israel. But in their view, this did not eliminate a particular place for Israel. The New Testament continuity of the promises and covenants undergirding Israel's role in God's program also suggests that the soteriological unity of Jew and Gentile in Christ does not negate a special place for Israel in the future.

But if there is such a place of prominence in Israel's future, the question may be rightly asked, why? What purpose does the restoration and elevation of Israel to a distinct position among the nations serve in salvation history? A crucial issue in the answer is the nature of that distinction. Does God's particular work with one nation give that people a closer relationship with God and thus deny the spiritual unity of Jews and Gentiles?

These kinds of questions lay dormant for much of church history. The majority of the church had little concern for Israel as a nation in the future plan of salvation history. Hans Küng says, "For long centuries the Church simply dismissed Israel."[2] Having concluded that the church had replaced national Israel as a new "spiritual Israel," Christian theology had no place for the restoration of that nation, let alone a future ministry for it. H. H. Rowley speaks for many Christian thinkers throughout church history when he argues that with the crucifixion of Christ Judaism rejected its mission and "missed the greater glory it might have known." Consequently the church is "the heir of the world task of Judaism."[3]

---

[1]Anthony Hoekema, *The Bible and the Future* (Grand Rapids: Eerdmans, 1979), 201.

[2]Hans Küng, *The Church* (Garden City, N.Y.: Doubleday/Image Books, 1976), 178.

[3]H. H. Rowley, *The Missionary Message of the Old Testament* (London: Carey Kingsgate, 1944), 79, 81. Hans Urs von Balthasar similarly explains, "The Christian attitude, generally speaking, can be summed up approximately as follows: the Jews forfeited their mission when they failed to recognise Christ as their Messiah; they had, in consequence, to hand over the

That position, however, is being strongly challenged today. Two events of recent history in particular have called attention to the continued historical existence of the Jews and have sparked renewed theological inquiry, namely, the Holocaust and the establishment of the state of Israel.[4] Many would concur with Karl Rengstorf: "The fact that the Jewish people still exists after so many centuries and has outlived most of its foes makes it one of the greatest riddles for the historian. But even more than for the historian it is a cause of wonder for the Christian observer."[5]

Does Israel as a national people still have meaning in the plan and purpose of God? If so, then Israel still bears some distinction from the other nations of the world. What is the nature of that distinction, and what is its purpose?

I. THE DISTINCTION OF ISRAEL

A. *The Unique Status of Israel*

Basic to Israel's identity was her unique relationship with God based on his sovereign election. Thoughout history, the people of Israel were constantly reminded that they had been redeemed out of the bondage of Egypt and given a land of their own because Yahweh had chosen them "out of all the peoples on the face of the earth . . . to be his treasured possession" (Dt 7:6; 14:2; cf. 4:37). It was a nation that was elected and not just individuals, for Israel was chosen "above all the nations" (Dt 10:15; cf. Lev 20:26). This is confirmed in the repeated biblical references to Israel as a "nation" (e.g., Ex 19:6).[6]

God's election of Israel to a special status among the nations is central to the subsequent history recounted in the Old Testament (cf. 1Ki

---

books which belonged to them up to that time to be administered by those who had become the people of God" (*Martin Buber and Christianity* [New York: Macmillan, 1961], 15).

[4]On the significance of the reestablishment of the state of Israel, Küng asserts, ". . . this is an event which ranks as the most important in Jewish history since the destruction of Jerusalem and of the temple and one with religious consequences" (*The Church*, 186–87).

In addition to the two events Küng mentions, Jürgen Moltmann adds another reason for the present questioning concerning Israel. Contrary to the triumphalism that has caused the church to see itself as the kingdom of God on earth, the church is now beginning to recognize this as an impossible claim and to rediscover "Christianity's own provisional nature in the framework of the still unfulfilled hope of the messianic kingdom," the fulfilment of which entails Israel (*The Church in the Power of the Spirit* [New York: Harper & Row, 1977], 136–37).

[5]Karl Heinrich Rengstorf, "The Jewish Problem and the Church's Understanding of Its Own Mission," in *The Church and the Jewish People*, ed. Gote Hedenquist (London: Edinburgh House, 1954), 27. For a list of the recent literature dealing with the question of Israel and the church, see Küng, *The Church*, 178–79.

[6]For the meaning of Israel as a "nation," see pp. 43–44 and 192–94.

3:8; Pss 33:12; 105:6; 135:4; Eze 20:5). God's choosing of priests, kings, and even Zion, the place of his dwelling, always fulfilled the purpose of serving the elect community of Israel.[7] So also was the selection of those outside of Israel. Whether as instruments of divine judgment (e.g., Nebuchadnezzar, Jer 25:9; Assyria, Isa 7:18–20) or of blessing (e.g., Cyrus, Isa 45:1–3), their role always had significance "only in so far as its purpose touches Israel."[8]

Israel's election not only was foundational to her historical identity, but also undergirded her future. Looking forward to messianic times, Israel was assured of restoration and the fulfillment of her mission because she was God's "chosen people" (cf. Isa 41:8–9; 43:20–21; 44:1–2; 45:4). The same picture of Israel as the elect nation of God is carried over to the New Testament, where Paul not only recalls their choice historically, but affirms their continued elective status (Ro 11:28).

Scripture is clear and emphatic that this election and consequent distinction rest solely upon God's sovereign love and no inherent righteousness or greatness of Israel (cf. Dt 4:37; 7:6–8; 9:4–6; 23:5). Therefore that elective status must ultimately be unconditional. This did not mean that every individual Israelite would share in the fulfillment of the promises made to the nation. Obedience by faith was necessary to obtain the goal of divine election. But the promises for that nation based on the sovereign love of God will finally reach their goal. Despite Israel's repeated historical failures, the prophets looked forward to the time when the grace of the new covenant would bring about the necessary obedience. God would put his Spirit in the people and move them to keep his ways (Eze 36:27; cf. Jer 31:33).

According to the prophets, this elective distinction of Israel was destined to bring a certain prominence to that nation among the other nations of the world in the eschatological times. Israel and the city of Jerusalem were to have a central place in the messianic kingdom. God was to dwell there in a special way. Because the nations, too, would come to recognize and worship the God of Israel as the true God, they would serve and enrich God's peculiar treasure, Israel.[9]

This Old Testament picture of an Israel distinguished among the nations in the messianic kingdom raises the question whether it has harmony with the New Testament teaching of the equality of Jews and

---

[7]Specifically in relation to the king, G. Quell states, "Personally elected by God, the ruler of the people of Yahweh guarantees the divine direction of its destiny in virtue of the religious basis of his position. . . . It was for the sake of His people Israel that Yahweh established the disputed kingship of David" ("λέγω κτλ," in *Theological Dictionary of the New Testament*, vol. 4, ed. Gerhard Kittel (Grand Rapids: Eerdmans, 1967), 155.

[8]H. H. Rowley, *The Biblical Doctrine of Election* (London: Lutterworth Press, 1950), 138.

[9]See chapter 9 for the fuller teaching of the Old Testament prophets on the prominence of Israel and an explanation of some of the verses concerning her dominance among the nations.

Gentiles in Christ. To pose the question more broadly, does the development of salvation history, including the rejection of the Messiah by Israel, require us to reinterpret these prophecies in such as way as to negate a national distinction? To find the answer we must first examine the real nature of Israel's prophetic distinctiveness.

B. The Nature of Israel's Distinction

1. A Distinction for Service. Israel's election was first of all an election for service. Concerning the term used for the choosing of Israel, Horst Seebass explains: "everywhere that *bhr* [בָּחַר, to choose] occurs in relationship to persons, it denotes choice out of a group . . . , so that the chosen one discharges a function in relationship to the group."[10] T. C. Vriezen similarly declares that "in the OT the choice is always the action of God, of his grace, and always contains a mission for man; and only out of this mission can man comprehend the choice of God."[11] This significance of God's choice is clear, for example, in regard to Abraham, who was chosen for the ultimate blessing of the whole world, and David, who was chosen for service to the nation.

But service is also the meaning of God's choice of the nation Israel. According to the covenant that defines its election, Israel is designated "a kingdom of priests," an appellation that signifies ministry. Her status as "a holy nation," with strict requirements for separation from the religious practices of the nations around her, served the purpose of distinguishing Yahweh as the true God and making this plain to the nations (cf. Dt 14:1ff.). Even the command to destroy the Canaanite peoples was ultimately for the good of the nations, as it would prevent the demise of the knowledge of the true God through accommodation with the false gods of the nations (cf. De 7:1–6).[12]

---

[10]Horst Seebass, "בָּחַר," in *Theological Dictionary of the Old Testament*, vol. 2 (Grand Rapids: Eerdmans, 1975), 82–83.

[11]Th. C. Vriezen, *Die Erwählung Israels nach dem AT: vol. 24, Abhandlungen zur Theologie des Alten und Neuen Testaments* (Zurich: n.p., 1953), 109, cited by Seebass, "בָּחַר," in *TDOT*, 2:87. Similarly, Quell says, "From one standpoint, it is a useful instrument to show the particular status of the elect, and Dt. is obviously concerned to define this correctly as a task. . . . Election establishes an authority which must be regarded by the people of God and which will bring its moral powers into play: 'Thou art a people, holy for Yahweh, thy God.' To be apprehended by God, to be drawn into His sphere, can only mean to be at the service of His purposes" ("λέγω κτλ," in *TDNT*, 4:164).

[12]Seebass says of the Canaanite religion, "As the people that is distinguished by the unique unalterability of its God, Israel has it role in the circle of nations. . . . If Israel does not take an inflexible stand against this religion she can never be the people of Yahweh, because he can never be understood as he really is as long as Canaanitism is connected with him. But in this case *bhr* ['to choose'] means that in her struggle against the Canaanite spirit Israel is the people chosen with reference to all peoples, in that all religions have to take

Although Israel frequently acted to the contrary, the true meaning of her distinction both in the past and in the future messianic era was always service, according to the prophets. It was first and foremost service to God, who through his election and redemption had a claim upon the nation that issued in a call to the service of his universal saving love for all peoples.[13] Robert Martin-Achard concludes, "The choice of Israel . . . belongs to the realm of means not ends; . . . Israel has to serve God before the world and its worship of Yahweh contributes to the good of all the peoples."[14] According to Psalm 117, it is the great love of God toward his chosen people Israel that calls for praise from all nations.

2. No Distinction of Superiority. God's election of Israel brought distinction among the nations, but not superiority. Despite Israel's frequent perversion of her elective privilege through national pride, Scripture declares that apart from God's grace she was not different from other nations. God reminded the people of this through the prophet Amos: "Are not you Israelites the same to me as the Cushites? . . . Did I not bring Israel up from Egypt, the Philistines from Caphtor and the Arameans from Kir?" (Am 9:7). Israel was no different in herself from the far-off Cushites or the nearby Philistines and Arameans. If Israel was led to the land by the sovereign God, so were the latter two nations.

Israel should have recognized this equality among the nations. Hans Walter Wolff notes, "The interrogative form of the sentence [in Amos 9:7] presupposes that it was part of Israel's tradition to know that its relationship to Yahweh did not rest upon any special qualities or accomplishments of its own."[15]

We see that being chosen by God did not mean preferential treatment above the other nations because Israel was called to be a witness to the uniqueness of Yahweh before all nations at exactly the time when she was being delivered over to destruction under Babylon (Isa 43:8–13). Yahweh proved that he alone is God in his being willing to judge his own people for the sake of truth. In their judgment, according to Seebass, Israel was to see the uniqueness of God in that he did "not renounce his deity for the sake of saving his people." They were therefore instructed to "proclaim to the nations that Yahweh is the only God because he shows no respect of persons (43:10)."[16]

Moritz Güdemann sums up well the relation of Israel and the other

---

their stand in the struggle Israel undertakes paradigmatically and in the final analysis inflexibly" ("בָּחַר," in *TDOT*, 2:84).

[13]For a good study of the corollary of service in the election of Israel, see Rowley, *The Biblical Doctrine of Election*, 45–68.

[14]Robert Martin-Achard, *A Light to the Nations* (Edinburgh: Oliver and Boyd, 1962), 40–41.

[15]Hans Walter Wolff, *Joel and Amos* (Philadelphia: Fortress, 1977), 347.

[16]Seebass, "בָּחַר," in *TDOT*, 2:85.

nations in the Old Testament: "The character of Israel as the chosen people does not involve the inferiority of other nations. The universality of Israel's God is sufficient proof against such an assumption."[17]

We observe this same equality of Israel and the nations in Paul's statement that "God does not show favoritism" (Ro 2:11; cf. Ac 10:34). Yet Paul could refer to Israel's advantages without being contradictory (3:1). The advantages did not signify favoritism, but rather privileges with a corresponding responsibility for the good of others, namely, the entrustment of the oracles of God for the sake of all peoples. Israel's position as the chosen people thus places them on absolutely level ground with Gentiles in relation to salvation through faith (cf. Ro 3:22; 10:12). Any privileges the people enjoyed beyond the nations were related solely to their responsibility of service.

3. *A Distinction of Exaltation Because of Service.* Israel's distinction for service entails not only certain privileges and responsibilities, but also a place of honor and preeminence among the nations of the world. As a "kingdom of priests," according to Charles A. Briggs, Israel had "a sacred ministry of priesthhood, *as well as sovereignty* with reference to the nations of the world."[18] What God had promised Israel under the old covenant is pictured in the prophets as fulfilled through an obedient Israel under the new covenant. Israel would be "set ... in praise, fame and honor high above all the nations" (Dt 26:19).

We have already seen something of Israel's exaltation in the Old Testament picture of her future. The nations not only aid in the return of the Israelites to their land, but also continue to serve and enrich them. As we have seen, these pictures of Israel's dominance over the other nations do not mean the reversal of the harsh experiences suffered at the hands of the nations. Rather, they mark the way to happiness and freedom that comes from submitting to Israel's God and the people chosen to be a blessing to the world.[19] Israel's renown among the nations would come because she reflected to them the glory of God in her national life.[20]

---

[17]Cited by Kaufmann Kohler, "Chosen People," in *The Jewish Encyclopedia*, ed. Isidore Singer (New York: KTAV, n.d.), 4:46.

[18]Charles A. Briggs, *Messianic Prophecy* (New York: Scribner's, 1889), 102 (emphasis added).

[19]See chapter 9 for a discussion of many texts related to the prominence of Israel among the nations. We add to those ideas the rulership of Israel over the nations due to God's blessing of prosperity predicted in Deuteronomy 15:6: "For the LORD your God will bless you as he promised, and you will lend to many nations but will borrow from none. You will rule over many nations but none will rule over you" (cf. Dt 28:12–13).

Peter C. Craigie says of this anticipated rulership that "the sense of the words is that Israel would become a major mercantile state, wealthy enough to lend to other nations and therefore ruling over them in a sense, but not needing to borrow from them and therefore not being subject to them. . . . The prosperity in external affairs described in v. 6b would be a result of the blessing of God, but God's blessing would be contingent upon the inner health

In an excellent discussion of particularism and universalism in the so-called Second Isaiah, Robert Davidson shows that far from being opposed to the universalism of God's salvation, Israel's distinction and exaltation promotes the salvation of the nations.

> For Second Isaiah, it is the consolidation of Israel, the renewal of the covenant bond between Yahweh and His people, which is the covenantal means of grace for others; it is Yahweh's exaltation of Israel involving a political decision against other peoples which is the means of extending Yahweh's truth to the nations; it is the far seen triumph of Yahweh in the life of Israel which is the light drawing others to true faith.[21]

The exaltation of the servant who brings blessing is expressed throughout Scripture as well as in our present experience. As chosen vessels for service, Abraham, Moses, and David were highly exalted by others. Similarly, leaders in the church are to be esteemed by the people they serve. This seems to include some practical expression of service along with verbal honor (cf. 1Th 5:12–13). True service to God, as exemplified in Christ, entails suffering—often at the very hands to whom the service is rendered. When that kind of service is recognized for what it truly is—i.e., the channel of the blessing and grace of God's salvation—we readily see how those who receive the service desire to exalt the servant and in so doing receive great blessing for themselves.

The prophets looked forward to the day when Israel would fulfill her function as a truly holy nation in priestly service to the nations. In recognition of God and his servant people, the nations will honor that people because of God's grace, grace at work both in that nation and through her to them. Is it too much to say that even Israel's suffering at the hands of the nations has somehow served the salvation of the nations and will someday be recognized as such and thus contribute to Israel's grateful exaltation (cf. Ro 11:12, 15)?[22]

This recognition and exaltation for service does not entail any greater distinction *before God* than was true for Moses and David within Israel or the apostles and leaders in the early church.

Finally, even as the exaltation of human leadership in the church

---

of the nation" (*The Book of Deuteronomy*, New International Commentary of the Old Testament [Grand Rapids: Eerdmans, 1976], 237).

[20]Craigie, *The Book of Deuteronomy*, 325.

[21]Robert Davidson, "Universalism in Second Isaiah," *Scottish Journal of Theology* 16 (1963): 181.

[22]While Israel's suffering is different from that of Christ in that Israel suffers in disobedience, there is some aspect of the suffering of Israel among the nations (in terms of anti-Semitism) that results from their claim to a special relationship to God—a claim that more than anything else has kept them from losing their identity and has enabled them to maintain a distinction among the nations.

does not compromise and rob the glory of the unique serivce of the Supreme Servant of the Lord, the ministry of Israel in the future must also be seen as not only subservient to, but wholly dependent upon the ministry of the Messiah. The true perspective of Israel's distinction of exaltation is well summed up by Rowley:

> Nations shall honour her because she is His people, and therefore in honouring her they will really honour Him. This is not the climax of Old Testament teaching, which is concerned only with the honour of God, and which thinks of Israel not so much as destined to receive honour from men as called to fulfil the purpose of her election in the service of men.[23]

II. THE FUTURE ROLE OF ISRAEL

The idea that Israel has some role in the outworking of divine salvation for the world is gaining increasing recognition. Somehow these "chosen people" are related to the future blessing of all peoples. Ernst Käsemann writes, "Israel is the bearer of the blessing both in the present and in the future. . . . Israel is an integral part of the end of history. . . . both the begining and the end of the drama of salvation are determined by the destiny of Israel."[24]

With more positive emphasis, John Murray comments on Romans 11:15: "This restoration of Israel will have a marked beneficial effect, described as 'life from the dead.' Whatever this result may be it must denote a blessing far surpassing in its proportions anything that previously obtained in the unfolding of God's counsel." Murray explains this effect as "an unprecedented quickening for the world in the expansion and success of the gospel."[25]

---

[23]Rowley, *The Biblical Doctrine of Election*, 19.

[24]Ernst Käsemann, *Commentary on Romans* (Grand Rapids: Eerdmans, 1980), 305, 307.

[25]John Murray, *The Epistle to the Romans*, vol. 2 (Grand Rapids: Eerdmans, 1965), 81, 84. George E. Ladd likewise says that through Israel's salvation, "a new wave of life will come to the whole world" (*A Theology of the New Testament* [Grand Rapids: Eerdmans, 1974], 562).

A similar thought has been expressed by Richard De Ridder: "The blessing God is ready to reign on Jew and Gentile has not been seen in Israel's history or in the history of the Christian church. It will come when Israel knows her Messiah and King. . . . God's purposes of love, like deep, restless rivers, flow out from Israel to an ocean beyond all comprehension. When He showed His mercy to Israel first, God planned to use this people to bring His blessing to mankind." Although he affirms a continuing identity as Jews for Jews who place faith in Jesus Christ and a future function for Israel, De Ridder does not seem to think these entail a literal existence for Israel as a nation. He believes that the central role that Israel holds in prophecy as a nation among the nations is replaced and filled by Christ. See De Ridder, *My Heart's Desire for Israel* (Nutley, N.J.: Presbyterian & Reformed, 1974), 13, 77, 82.

Some Roman Catholic interpreters also see a future blessing of the world through Israel's conversion.[26]

Although these statements affirm some kind of a future role for Israel, they make no clear reference to the establishment of that people as a distinct and central nation among the nations of the world as seen in the Old Testament prophecies. Some who hold to the general position of a future mission of Israel do go so far as to see Israel's role as involving the transformation of real historical societal structures in accordance with millennial conditions. But for the most part Israel's future role is viewed as simply bringing an increase of the blessings of the new covenant among the nations as part of the church without any national distinction. Murray, for example, asserts that "there is no suggestion of any privilege or status but that which is common to Jew and Gentile in the faith of Christ."[27]

George E. Ladd does appear to envision a national entity: ". . . it may be that in the millennium, for the first time in human history, we will witness a truly Christian nation." But on the hermeneutical grounds that the New Testament reinterprets the Old Testament prophecies, Ladd refuses to affirm any further details about Israel's future. "A nondispensational eschatology," he says, "simply affirms the future salvation of Israel and remains open to God's future as to the details."[28] While dispensationalists welcome these affirmations of Israel's future role in bringing God's blessing to the world, they go beyond them and assert that Israel fulfills this mission as a distinct national entity among the nations of the world in accordance with the prophetic picture.

A. The Statement of Israel's Mission

It is generally recognized that God's original creation and election of the nation of Israel had cosmic significance entailing a mission toward all nations. In speaking of the promise of blessing "to all the families of the earth"[29] given in the divine call to Abraham, Rowley says,

> From this faint gleam we may trace the growing light through [various Old Testament passages] . . . , to the full perception of

---

[26]For example, Charles Journet writes, "For Israel must one day come back to its Messiah, so that the nations, enlivened and enriched by its return, may at that moment enter the second state of their conversion. . . . Israel holds back the supreme outpouring of grace on the world and thus the course of redemptive history" ("The Mysterious Destinies of Israel," in *The Bridge,* vol. 2 [New York: Pantheon, 1956], 69).

[27]Murray, *The Epistle to the Romans,* 2:99.

[28]George E. Ladd, "Historic Premillennialism," in *The Meaning of the Millennium: Four Views,* ed. Robert G. Clouse (Downers Grove, Ill.: InterVarsity Press, 1977), 28.

[29]For a discussion of the grammatical connection arguing that this universal promise is the result of the previous statement concerning the making of a "great nation," i.e., Israel, see p. 42.

Deutero-Isaiah that by her election Israel is called to a conscious mission to the world, and that she can only fulfil the purpose of her election in the execution of the mission.[30]

At her founding as a nation Israel was given a mediatorial role on behalf of God: "You will be for me a kingdom of priests and a holy nation" (Ex 19:5). The two expressions "kingdom of priests"[31] and "a holy nation" both convey mediatorial significance. Martin Noth interprets the word "kingdom" as meaning " 'state' in just the same way as the nations on the earth are usually organized into states." Then he explains the meaning of the phrase "kingdom of priests" for Israel's purpose: "Israel is to have the role of the priestly member in the number of earthly states. Israel is to do 'service' for all the world (cf. also Isa. 65:5f.); this is the purpose for which Israel has been chosen."[32] Similarly, Brevard S. Childs states, "Israel as a people is also dedicated to God's service among the nations as priests function with a society."[33]

The description of Israel as a "holy nation" also denotes a ministry to the world. As a " 'holy people' . . . they are to be a people set apart, different from all other people by what they are and are becoming—a display-people, a showcase to the world of how being in covenant with Yahweh changes a people."[34] Noting that the term "nation" is used rather than "people," William J. Dumbrell sees in this Sinai statement an advance in the Abrahamic promise concerning the "great nation" of Genesis 12:2.

> No longer does she [Israel] belong merely to a general community of peoples from whom she can only with difficulty be differentiated. She has now been elevated into a distinct entity and endowed with special privileges. Probably then we are here . . . thinking of Israel as offering in her constitution a societary model for the world. She will provide, under the direct divine rule which the covenant contemplates, the paradigm of the theocratic rule which is to be the biblical aim for the whole world.[35]

---

[30]Rowley, *The Biblical Doctrine of Election*, p. 67.

[31]Although scholars disagree on how to translate מַמְלֶכֶת כֹּהֲנִים, the generally accepted rendering of "kingdom of priests" is probably to be preferred (cf. NIV, NASB, NEB, JB). William J. Dumbrell explains, "As related in the verse the two terms stand in a genitive relationship. Normally in such a relationship the second Hebrew word functions as a modifier of the first. 'Priests' would thus be the expected qualifier, in an adjectival sense, of 'kingdom.' We should therefore seek some such translation as 'priestly kingdom,' 'priestly royalty' or the like" (*Covenant and Creation* [Nashville: Nelson, 1984], 86). For a brief listing of some present-day options, see John I. Durham, *Exodus*, Word Biblical Commentary, vol. 3 (Waco, Tex.: Word Books, 1987), 263.

[32]Martin Noth, *Exodus* (Philadephia: Westminster, 1962), 157.

[33]Brevard S. Childs, *The Book of Exodus* (Philadelphia: Westminster, 1974), 367.

[34]Durham, *Exodus*, 263.

[35]Dumbrell, *Covenant and Creation*, 87. See also Briggs, *Messianic Prophecy*, 102.

Here again, as we have seen, Israel is clearly identified as a nation among nations in this fundamental reference to her future purpose. This is not to deny the spiritual dimension of Israel's relationship to God that is obviously indicated in Exodus 19:4–6. But the spiritual characteristic does not negate or preclude the national meaning.

Israel's mission of bringing God's blessing to the rest of the nations is reiterated in the later prophetic writings, especially in the so-called Servant Songs of Isaiah. The Servant's mission is to be a "light for the Gentiles" (Isa 42:6; 49:6). The identity of the Servant in these passages is not easily ascertained. Most scholars view the Servant as a fluid concept referring at times to the entire nation of Israel (e.g., Isa 42:19), at other times to the spiritual remnant of that nation (e.g., Isa 41:8–10; possibly 49:3, 5), and finally to an individual, who is best identified as the Messiah (Isa 52:13–53:12).[36]

What is important for our purposes is to see that all three uses are, in fact, related. In the first of the Servant Songs (Isa 41:1–6), Franz Delitzsch identifies the servant as the "future Christ." Nevertheless, he rightly states that "there must be a connection between the national sense, in which the expression 'servant of Jehovah' was used in ch. xli. 8, and the personal sense in which it is used here." He explains the "servant of Jehovah" in terms of a pyramid: "The base was Israel as a whole; the central section was that Israel, which was not merely Israel according to the flesh, but according to the spirit also; the apex is the person of the Mediator of salvation springing out of Israel."[37]

Certain saving functions of the servant can only be properly applied to the messianic mediator of salvation. Yet the interrelationship among the uses of "servant" allows us to identify the mission of the Servant with Israel. According to John Bright, ". . . however the Servant is pictured, the Servant mission is always laid before Israel as her destiny in history (e.g., 50:10)." As for the Servant as a saving person, Bright says,

> Israel is to follow the Servant, to take up the cross of the Servant, to share in the Servant's redemptive mission. The Servant can no more be separated from Israel than Christ can from his church. . . . Israel is to be the people of the Servant. . . . It is her destiny to be the agent of establishing God's kingdom in the world.[38]

---

[36]John Bright, "Faith and Destiny," *Interpretation* 5, no. 1 (January 1951), 24. Bright lists Franz Delitzsch, R. A. Torrey, Christopher North, and H. H. Rowley as holding this view on the identity of the Servant. These differences are obvious in certain passages, but in others the distinctions become unclear as concepts frequently blend together (e.g., Isa 49:3, 5).

[37]Franz Delitzsch, *Biblical Commentary on the Prophecies of Isaiah*, vol. 2 (reprint, Grand Rapids: Eerdmans, 1960), 174.

[38]Bright, "Faith and Destiny," 24.

Some Scripture passages (Isa 42:6; 49:6) explicitly call the Servant to the task of enlightening the Gentiles. Delitzsch is probably correct in assigning an individual messianic Servant as the first reference to both passages, but he also correctly sees the nation of Israel involved.[39] Identifying the Servant in 49:3 as a single person whom he calls the "heart of Israel," Delitzsch states, ". . . it is He . . . in whom the history of Israel is coiled up as into a knot for a further and final development, in whom Israel's world-wide calling to be the Saviour of mankind, including Israel itself, is fully carried out."[40]

Thus, the personal messianic Servant is central and necessary in the fulfillment of these passages, but Israel is involved in his mission. As Claus Westermann comments on Isaiah 42:6–7, "God has designated Israel to be a light to the world and to mediate salvation to it; she is to bring enlightenment and liberation to others."[41]

The universal ministry indicated in the Servant passages is affirmed elsewhere. The prophet does not view the day when Zion would be enlightened by the glory of the Lord as the final goal, but rather, "Nations will come to your light and kings to the brightness of your dawn" (Isa 60:1–3). In the context of Israel's restoration, God declares, "Listen to me, my people; hear me, my nation: The law will go out from me; my justice will become a light to the nations. . . . My arm will bring justice to the nations" (Isa 51:4–5). The agent in this passage is the Lord himself. But the prophet's previous statement that "the law will go out from Zion" (Isa 2:2) and the close connection with the restoration of Israel in this passage show that Israel is to be involved as God's minister when he brings salvation to the nations.

Another glimpse at Israel's mission is revealed in connection with God's purpose to glorify himself. The demand to give God glory is evident throughout history. But as Gerhard von Rad notes, "to an extraordinary degree . . . [it] is also a theme of religious hope and an established part of eschatological expectation." Although one can say even now of God's creation and historical acts that "the whole earth is full of his glory" (Isa 6:3; cf. Nu 14:21), this concept is more often expressed as a hope. With the psalmist, all God's people continue to pray, ". . . may the whole earth be filled with his glory" (Pss 72:19; cf. 57:5, 11). This eschatological display of

[39]Indications of the close relationship between the ministry of the individual Servant and the nation of Israel may be in the parallel thoughts expressed in relation to both. In Isaiah 42, for example, the verbs "call" and "take by the hand" are used in reference to God's action in relation to the Servant and also toward Israel (cf. 41:9). The ministry of the Servant to "bring justice to the nations" (42:1) is also performed through Israel (cf. Isa 2:3–4).

[40]Delitzsch, *Biblical Commentary on the Prophecies of Isaiah*, 2:258.

[41]Claus Westermann, *Isaiah 40–66* (Philadelphia: Westminster, 1969), 100–101. Although Westermann identifies the Servant in Isaiah 42 as Israel, his statement is still valid in light of the connection between the individual Servant and the nation of Israel. (fn. 39 above).

God's glory is concerned not so much with revealing the intrinsic nature of God as with revealing "the final actualisation of His claim to rule the world,"[42] the establishment of his kingdom.

According to Scripture, the means to achieve this eschatological glorification of God entails a central role for Israel. God calls the nations to restore his sons and daughters from afar and states, "I created [them] for my glory" (Isa 43:2). Christopher R. North translates the phrase "for my glory" as *that my majesty might be clearly seen*"; he explains that "Israel, ransomed and restored, is the final evidence of the majesty which all mankind is to see (cf. xl. 5) and acclaim."[43]

Along with this teaching of Israel's mission to display God's glory to the world, the prophets supply the means for its attainment. God will make his glory dwell in that people in a special way. To eschatological Israel, God declares, "I will be its glory within" (Zec 2:5; cf. Eze 43:1–5, where the glory of the Lord fills the eschatological temple). In dwelling with Israel, God will be glorified to the nations, above all in salvation, and many will be joined to him and become his people (Zec 2:11). Isaiah sees a time when God's glory will "appear over" Zion so that the nations will come to her light (60:1–3). For von Rad, Israel is inherently related to the goal of divine glorification: ". . . it makes little difference whether it is said that Yahweh will become כָּבוֹד [glory] for Israel or that Israel is created for Yahweh's כָּבוֹד [glory]."[44]

Other evidence of Israel's eschatological mission may be adduced,[45] but what we have examined is sufficient to establish Israel's having been created and chosen by God for his service to the rest of the world. Israel had at times lost sight of its mission, yet that mission was kept alive not only through prophetic rebuke, but most of all through a divinely revealed hope of an eschatological restoration and transformation through which this purpose would be realized to the glory of God and the blessing of all peoples.

Most scholars generally recognize these matters as the teaching of the prophets. The question that divides interpreters is whether these prophecies are still valid according to their original meaning. Dispensa-

---

[42]Gerhard von Rad, "δοκέω, δόξα κτλ," in *Theological Dictionary of the New Testament*, vol. 2 (Grand Rapids: Eerdmans, 1964), 241–42.

[43]Christopher R. North, *The Second Isaiah* (Oxford: Clarendon Press, 1964), 121. See also Delitzsch, *Biblical Commentary on the Prophecies of Isaiah*, 2:192.

[44]von Rad, "δοκέω, δόξα κτλ," 2:242.

[45]Walther Eichrodt, for example, sees Israel's mission in the grand honorifics that give cosmic significance to Israel's kings. "Such language was made possible only by the belief in election, which awoke the sense of the nation's special mission in the service of the unique God of Israel; the right to universal dominion could therefore be ascribed to the Israelite king as the 'son' of the covenant God without risk or megalomania" (*Theology of the Old Testament*, vol. 1 [Philadelphia: Westminster, 1961], 478).

tionalists affirm their validity on the basis of the New Testament, which on the one hand gives no evidence that Israel's mission to the world has been canceled and on the other hand positively affirms Israel's future.

B. The Future Fulfillment of Israel's Mission

If Israel does, in fact, have a future mission in God's plan of salvation for the world, how is that mission to be understood? This question is especially pertinent in light of the present universal mission of the church. We suggest (1) that the present offer of salvation does not completely fulfill the scope of the messianic salvation promised by the prophets, and (2) that the completion of that salvation is best explained as accomplished through the mediation of the nation of Israel in accord with the prophets. Israel's future service is focused on two roles that are obviously closely related, but may be distinquished for clarity: (1) the channel of revelation, and (2) the mediation or ministry of salvation to the world.

1. Israel's Role as a Channel of Revelation. Both Scripture and history disclose Israel's role as a channel of divine revelation to the nations. The psalmist praised God for declaring "his word to Jacob, his laws and decrees to Israel." And "He has done this for no other nation; they do not know his laws" (Ps 147:19–20). The apostle Paul wrote that the Jews "have been entrusted with the very words of God" (Ro 3:2).

But this privilege of revelation, as the word "entrusted" suggests, was not intended for Israel alone. The revelation had the purpose of making that nation a lighthouse of divine revelation to the nations. This was implied in the instruction Moses gave to the people prior to their entering the Promised Land: "See, I have taught you decrees and laws as the LORD my God commanded me, so that you may follow them in the land you are entering. . . . Observe them carefully, for this will show your wisdom and understanding to the nations, who will hear about all these decrees and say, 'Surely this great nation is a wise and understanding people'" (Dt 4:5–6). In these words Jan Ridderbos sees that "Israel's missionary task vis-a-vis the pagan world is indicated in a veiled manner: This respect for Israel implies respect for Him from whom Israel received these laws."[46]

Israel's mission as a channel of revelation to the nations is fully developed by the prophets, who portray that people as God's "witness" (Isa 43:10, 12; 44:8) and "a light for the Gentiles" (Isa 42:6; 49:6; cf. 51:4–5; 60:1–3). According to the prophets, this revelation will occur primarily through God's future dealings with his people. This theme is particularly

---

[46]J. Ridderbos, *Deuteronomy*, The Bible Students Commentary, trans. Ed. M. van der Maas (Grand Rapids: Zondervan, 1984), 83.

prominent in Ezekiel, whose prophetic word, according to Walther Zimmerli, "announces that what happens to Israel historically is in fact Yahweh's own dealing with both His people and the nations."[47]

Donald E. Gowan notes that Ezekiel portrays the nations as "spectators who will learn something about the true God from his works in history ('then they will know that I am Yahweh')."[48] In this theme Ezekiel and the other prophets are simply picturing the fulfillment of God's original intent to reveal himself to the world through this nation. According to T. C. Vriezen, God's deed in Christ, although having universal significance, was first his deed *par excellence* in Israel. "This is so because cosmic significance must be ascribed to revelation in Israel from the very beginning."[49] Arend Th. van Leeuwen concurs. In a fascinating discussion of God's pattern of "gathering and scattering and gathering again," which he traces throughout God's historical dealing with all mankind, van Leewen says,

> Israel . . . represents all mankind, in unity and scattering, in pride and sin and fall. God's judgment on his people is his judgment upon all the earth; and when the Lord has mercy on his people and gathers them again, the action adumbrates his blessing which he has promised to bestow on each and every nation. Israel then is the vanguard of the nations; her history is the centre and epitome of all history and the revelation of God's purposes for all mankind.[50]

a. Revelation through God's acts of judgment. In the prophetic picture, God's self-revelation will be manifest through his people in both judgment and restoration. Of judgment, Zimmerli says that

> the recurring direct association of this judgment of Israel with the strict statement of recognition virtually identifies it as the locus at which Yahweh reveals Himself in His most personal essence.

---

[47] Walther Zimmerli, *I Am Yahweh* (Atlanta: John Knox, 1982), 88.

[48] Donald E. Gowan, *Eschatology in the Old Testament* (Philadelphia: Fortress, 1986), 49.

[49] Th. C. Vriezen, "Theocracy and Soteriology," in *Essays on Old Testament Hermeneutics*, ed. Claus Westermann (Richmond: John Knox, 1963), 218.

[50] Arend Th. van Leeuwen, *Christianity in World History* (New York: Scribner's, 1964), 101. In a similar vein U. Cassuto notes the relation of Israel to the other nations in the "evidence of close ties" between Genesis and Deuteronomy: ". . . the fact is stressed that the number of nations corresponds to the number of the children of Israel. . . . The general harmony in the history of the world is paralleled by the particular harmony prevailing in Israel's history. Seventy peoples on the one side, seventy sons and seventy families on the other. The people of Israel occupies in the plans of the Divine Providence a place resembling, on a small scale, that of all mankind; it is a small-scale world, a microcosm similar in form to the macrocosm" (*A Commentary on the Book of Genesis, Part Two: From Noah to Abraham* [Jerusalem: Magnes, 1964], 180).

Yahweh's revelatory self-introduction is to be recognized in His judgment over Israel.[51]

Through Ezekiel God declares his purpose in bringing desolation to his people through Babylon: "Then all people will know that I the LORD have drawn my sword from its scabbard" (Eze 21:5). This passage together with numerous other references state clearly that God intended to make himself known to both Israel and the nations through his judgment on Israel (cf. 5:13; 6:14; 7:9; 12:15ff.; 15:7; 39:21–24). Most of these statements refer in the first place to the Babylonian exile from which Israel had returned, but they are not exhausted by that event. These statements of judgment are balanced and inherently related to statements of divine revelation as coming through Israel's restoration. Because this restoration has not yet been fulfilled in the prophetic picture, the divine self-revelation to the nations through judgment on Israel must continue until her final restoration.

That continuation is expressed in the use of identical language, as in Ezekiel's description of a patently eschatological action by God in behalf of his people, namely, the destruction of Gog and his invading hordes (Eze 38–39). Not only will God receive glory from the nations as they recognize his hand in their destruction, but they will also "know that the people of Israel went into exile for their sin, because they were unfaithful to me" (39:21, 23). God's purpose to reveal himself to the nations through his judgmental dealing with his people Israel thus remains valid for the eschatological era.

b. Revelation through God's act of restoration. The same self-revelatory purpose of God is associated with Israel's future restoration. In fact, the awareness of God that comes through judgment is heightened by his gracious acts of restoration. As we have noted in regard to Gog, it is when God intervenes in behalf of his people that the nations recognize that Israel suffered because of their sin. We cannot say that history thus far reveals *the nations* as truly recognizing God's hand in the suffering of Israel. That awakening is still in the future.

God's revelation to the nations (as well as to Israel herself) in the restoration of Israel is a prevalent theme in biblical prophecy.[52] This revelation is double-edged, effected in both the destruction of Israel's enemies and in Israel's exaltation. Isaiah declares that God will make the "oppressors" of Israel "eat their own flesh [and] . . . be drunk on their own blood," with the result that "all mankind will know that I, the LORD, am your Saviour, your Redeemer, the Mighty One of Jacob" (49:26).

Usually the emphasis is on the display of God's glory through the

[51]Zimmerli, *I Am Yahweh*, 93.

[52]In addition to the verses discussed, see Ps 59:13; Isa 41:17–20; 43:8–13; 44:23; Eze 36:22–36.

grace and power exerted in behalf of Israel. The transformation of Israel from a sinful, scattered, downtrodden people to an exalted nation following God's righteous ways and consequently blessed with spiritual and physical prosperity is frequently seen as the means by which God is going to reveal himself to the nations and to Israel herself.

Isaiah comforts the dispirited people of Israel by declaring that eventually judgment by the Lord's hand will be completed and God will visit his people with salvation. In the familiar image of raising the valleys and making the rough ground level for the arrival of the Lord, Isaiah declares, "And the glory of the LORD will be revealed, and all mankind together will see it" (40:1–5). Again, describing God's comforting his people through redemption, Isaiah wrote, "The LORD will lay bare his holy arm in the sight of all the nations, and all the ends of the earth will see the salvation of our God" (52:9–10).

Ezekiel predicted the same revelatory effect of the restoration of Israel: "When I have brought them back from the nations and have gathered them from the countries of their enemies, I will show myself holy through them in the sight of many nations" (Eze 39:27; cf. v. 7). Similarly, the psalmist anticipated the day when God will "have compassion on Zion" and "show favor to her." Consequently "the nations will fear the name of the LORD, and all the kings of the earth will revere your glory. For the LORD will rebuild Zion and appear in his glory" (Ps 102:13–16; cf. 87:1ff.).

The task of the Servant to bring light to the Gentiles, a topic discussed earlier, is also intrinsically connected to the restoration of Israel (cf. esp. Isa 49:6–7). Noting a similar theme in Ezekiel, Robert Martin-Achard concludes that the Servant passages of Isaiah give form to an idea that had already been expressed: "Yahweh's judgment—i.e., the salvation of His People—is, in the last resort, something that affects the whole world." Martin-Achard explains how this happens:

> Mankind, learning of the transformation that has taken place in Israel's fortunes, will discover the greatness of Israel's God; confronted by the work of Yahweh, the heathen, now subdued, will give Him the glory that is due to His name. The final result of the restoration of Israel is the encounter between Yahweh and the nations.[53]

In the same vein, H. J. Kraus declares, *"God reveals his sovereignty, which brings salvation, through the act of bringing Israel back from its captivity and gathering his people together. In this final act of*

---

[53]Martin-Achard, *A Light to the Nations,* 30–31; cf. also Norman K. Gottwald, *All the Kingdoms of the Earth* (New York: Harper & Row, 1964), 344–45.

liberation the saving might of God is manifest to all the world."[54] Norman K. Gottwald also notes this connection between Israel's mission and restoration as a nation, especially in Isaiah's prophecy, but observes that many scholars neglect this truth: "It is ironic that generations of Christian interpreters have lauded Deutero-Isaiah's sacrificial, missionary spirit without conceding that it is indestructibly rooted in the restored Jewish community."[55]

It is not that God *simply chooses* to reveal to all people his grace and power in the reestablishment and blessing of his people. The previous history of Israel *makes it mandatory;* God's reputation is at stake. Not to restore Israel would result in unfavorable revelation. God's holiness necessitated his judgment of rebellious Israel, yet this action rebounded against his holy name. Instead of producing fear in those who saw it, according to Ezekiel, wherever Israel went among the nations, "they profaned my [i.e., God's] holy name, for it was said of them, 'These are the LORD's people, and yet they had to leave his land' " (Eze 36:18–21). Thus God declared that he would regather his people out of the nations and bring them back to their own land, not for their own sake, "but for the sake of my holy name, which you have profaned among the nations where you have gone. . . . Then the nations will know that I am the LORD, . . . when I show myself holy through you before their eyes" (36:22ff.).

These passages in Ezekiel, with others (cf. Dt 32:27; Isa 48:9ff.), reveal that the restoration of Israel is not only a display of God's love and power in behalf of his people, but also *"an event necessary to the preservation of the honor of the true God."*[56]

c. The revelation of God through Israel's life. The eschatological purpose of God, as expressed in prophecy, to reveal himself through actions with Israel does not end with her restoration. God's purpose is reflected also in the revived life and holy character of Israel's presence before the nations of the world. "Listen to me, my people; hear me, my nation: The law will go out from me; my justice will become a light to the nations" (Isa 51:4). Compare this with the prophet's earlier teaching that

---

[54]H. J. Kraus, *The People of God in the Old Testament* (New York: Association Press, 1958), 77. Although he unduly limits it to the return from Babylon, Ronald E. Clements likewise notes the centrality of revelatory purpose of God's restoration of Israel in the prophecy of Isaiah: "The eschatological content [of 'the oracles of Deutero-Isaiah'], pointing to a new and glorious manifestation of divine power in the rebirth of Israel, stands at the centre of the prophet's thought. This new election and new wilderness journey were expected to be crowned by a triumphant homecoming of the exiles to Jerusalem, which all the nations would witness, and acknowledge as the work of Yahweh" (*Prophecy and Covenant*, Studies in Biblical Theology, no. 43 [Naperville, Ill.: Alec R. Allenson, 1965], 117).

[55]Gottwald, *All the Kingdoms of the Earth*, 346.

[56]Gustave F. Oehler, *Theology of the Old Testament* (Grand Rapids: Zondervan, n.d.), 505.

the "law will go out from Zion, the word of the LORD from Jerusalem" and that the nations will come to the mountain of the LORD, to the house of the God of Jacob to learn his ways (2:2–3; cf. Mic 4:1–2). On those grounds we conclude that somehow restored Israel is involved in the revelation of God's justice to the nations. Isaiah is only affirming the continuation of what we have already seen as the original purpose of Israel's call.[57]

According to Lothar Coenen, God purposed in Israel to create "among the nations a new, quite different type of community. . . . to show in Israel in the midst of world history God's sovereign acts, his grace, and the seriousness of his demands."[58]

Serving God's revelatory purpose by simply living as the people of God, Martin-Achard writes, sums up the mission of Israel as the Servant of the Lord in the prophecies of Isaiah: "The Chosen People's business is to exist: its presence in the world furnishes proof of Yahweh's divinity; its life declares what He means for Israel itself and for the universe." Israel is the light of the nations "because, first, and in an exceptional fashion, it has been enlightened by the glory of God."[59]

That light shines first of all in the form of a new community in which God's justice and righteousness are expressed in the totality of life and societal structure, something the world has not yet seen. Kraus finds this purpose expressed in the prophet Amos' exhortation to "let justice roll on like a river, righteousness like a never-failing stream" (Am 5:24).

> Justice and righteousness . . . are the foundations, the basic
> ordinances for the life of Israel. . . . Israel has been chosen to live
> according to the law of God, that is to say, to live under the
> sovereignty of God, as sovereignty that is *intended to cover every
> aspect of the whole of life.* Righteousness means, further, that
> behavior in accordance with the covenant relationship to God,
> through which the people bring to visible expression the fact that it
> is the chosen people of the Lord (emphasis added).[60]

Although Rowley believes (wrongly, in our opinion) that Israel forfeited her prophetic calling through unbelief, he correctly assesses the Old Testament prophets as teaching that

---

[57] See pp. 306–11.

[58] Lothar Coenen, "Elect," in *New International Dictionary of New Testament Theology,* vol. 1, ed. Colin Brown (Grand Rapids: Zondervan, 1975), 538.

[59] Martin–Achard, *A Light to the Nations,* 31.

[60] Kraus, *The People of God in the Old Testament,* 50. Israel's function as a model nation for the other nations has been well stated by the Jewish philosopher Martin Buber: "The prophets call upon a people which represents the *first real attempt at 'community'* to enter world history as a prototype of that attempt. Israel's further function is to encourage the nations to change their inner structure and their relations to one another" (*Israel and the World* [New York: Schocken Books, 1948], 170).

the life of Israel would be incomparably glorious and happy; the hand of God would protect her from all her foes and peace and prosperity would be her portion; and other nations be so moved by the sight of her happiness that they would come to her to learn its secret and would find it in her religion.[61]

d. God's revelation in Christ and the revelation through Israel. The idea of a revelatory role for Israel before the world raises the question of the how that relates to God's self-revelation in Christ. It is universally recognized that up to the coming of Christ, the people of Israel were uniquely the channel of divine canonical revelation to mankind. Both the verbal Word of God and the living Word came through the Jews. But the New Testament teaching that Christ is the complete and final revelation of God (cf. Heb 1:3) raises questions about any further revelatory function for the nation of Israel.

Does acknowledging the finality of revelation in Christ—i.e., no further revelation can be expected apart from him—mean that the Christological revelation has been totally disclosed? Should we agree with Loraine Boettner? He wrote,

> now that the Messiah has come and God's revelation to mankind has been completed, written in a book and made available to the people of all nations with nothing more to be added, there is no further need for a separate people or nation to serve that purpose.[62]

In response, we note that nowhere in Scripture do we find the idea that the close of the New Testament canon precludes further revelatory activity. Prophetic activity is clearly anticipated in the end times, for example, in the prophetic ministry of the two eschatological witnesses (Rev 11:3ff.).[63] What is precluded is any future revelation that is unrelated to Christ and his saving activity. But the suggestion that revelation of God's activity in Christ is finished is unwarranted by the biblical evidence.

---

[61]Rowley, *The Missionary Message of the Old Testament*, 29.

[62]Loraine Boettner, "A Postmillennial Response," in Crouse, ed., *The Meaning of the Millennium: Four Views*, 52–53. A somewhat similar limitation of God's prophecied revelation to the canonical Scripture is suggested by Derek Kidner in his comment on Psalm 67:1–2. There the psalmist speaks of God's blessing on Israel "that your ways may be known on earth, your salvation among all nations." Kidner finds this "hope wonderfully fulfilled in the writing of the Scriptures" (*Psalms 1–72* [London: InterVarsity Press, 1973], 237). There seems to be no valid reason, however, why this verse should not be interpreted more in conformity with its straightforward meaning, which is in harmony with prophecies such as Isaiah 2:2–3.

[63]A good case could also be made for seeing a further intensified fulfillment beyond Pentecost of Joel's prophecy of the outpouring of the Spirit, resulting in prophetic activity in the future in connection with Israel's restoration (cf. Joel 2:28–32).

Beyond the fact of future revelation, the nature of God's revelatory activity also bears on the question of Israel's role. Scripture affirms that God reveals himself not just in verbal messages but also in historical activity. Unlike the gods of the philosophers, who become known only through abstract thought, the God of the Bible shows himself by direct intervention in history. Both his actions with Israel and his message through the prophets were revelatory. Jacob Jocz says,

> Jewish history is the visible, empirical act of revelation. It demonstrates to all who want to see that the God of Israel is not a philosophical concept, but the living God. He cannot be imprisoned in a book, no matter how sacred, and relegated to the past. He is still the enactor of history; he is still a Presence in human affairs and still acts against and on behalf of his people.[64]

If this is true, there is no reason why Israel as a historical nation cannot play a role in the divine activity in line with the prophetic picture. But it is not simply that the biblical understanding of revelation including its finality in Christ *allows* for Israel's future service in divine revelation. We would argue that the prophecies involved *are best understood* as applying to the future nation of Israel.

While is may be argued that some of the passages related to Israel's function in the revelation of God may be interpreted as applying to the church, there are some which defy such an application. For example, Isaiah's picture of the nations streaming to Zion to learn the ways of God, and God judging between the nations and settling their disputes with the result of the absence of war, seems impossible to apply to the church during this age. It is very difficult to see the nations in any "national" sense as coming to the church to learn the ways of God and practice them on the "national" level. Nor is there any divinely mandated peace among nations in this age. Jesus himself predicted international turmoil, with war among the "birth pangs" that would eventually bring forth the Messiah (Mt 24:6–14). Therefore, there is no place for such peace before Christ's return.

Moreover, if the "ways" of God that result from his "law" and "word" proceeding from Zion and Jerusalem include righteousness and justice in all societal structures, we are looking at nothing less than a theocractic society. In such a society the so-called realm of the state, or "Caesar's realm," is merged with the "realm of God." But Scripture gives no indication that Christ is to assume the realm of Caesar until he returns to destroy the human government of the antichrist (cf. Mt 22:21).

If this passage is difficult to apply to the present day and impossible

---

[64]Jacob Jocz, *A Theology of Election* (New York: Macmillan, 1958), 3; cf. also Journet, "The Mysterious Destinies of Israel," 39, 42.

for the perfected state of the new earth, it is easily interpreted in accordance with a future restoration of Israel and a central role of that nation in the revelation of his ways to the nations. If such be the case with this passage, there is no reason not to take the other prophecies that depict God's self-revelation to the nations and to Israel herself as related to his activity with that people.

2. *Israel's Mission in the Completion of Salvation.* The prophetic picture of the nations coming to live by the ways of God is closely related to another aspect of Israel's future function. According to the prophets, the Messiah was to effect not only personal spiritual salvation, but the salvation of society. The very social and government structures of the nations would be transformed so as to reflect the righteousness of God. Internationally there would be peace among the nations. Since, according to the Scriptures, Israel as God's servant and priestly nation was to serve in bringing God's salvation to the world, we suggest that that nation still has a role to play in the final drama of the completion of this messianic salvation for the nations.

Some interpreters try to show that some prophecies dealing with socio-political salvation have at least begun to be fulfilled in the present age of the church as the "new Israel" (e.g., Isa 2:1–4). But it must be readily admitted that these prophecies are far from fulfillment in any straightforward understanding of the text. History thus far reveals an absence of divine salvation in the socio-political structures of earthly life. Moreover, experience offers little hope that we are in the process of a gradual fulfillment of this societal salvation during this age. This condition fits with Christ's teaching that there will be dismay among the nations until the end of the age (cf. Mt 24:6–7; Lk 21:25–28).

The issue of unfulfilled promises is a perennial point of contention with Jewish scholars, who resist the claims of Christians that prophetic fulfillment will come through the church, especially in a spiritualized form. Gershom Sholem declares:

> In all its forms and manifestation, Judaism has always held firmly to a concept of redemption which understood it as a process which takes place under the public gaze, on the stage of history and in the medium of society, that is, which definitely takes place in the visible world. . . . The reintepretation of the prophetic promises of the Bible [by Christianity] to apply to the realm of the inner life . . . has always seemed to the religious thinkers of Judaism an illegitimate anticipation of what could be manifested at best as the inward aspect of a process which essentially takes place in the external world—and which could not be manifested without this process.[65]

---

[65]Gershom Sholem, "Zum Verständnis der messianischen Idee im Judentum," *Judaica* 1 (1963): 7f.

Shalom Ben-Chorin goes so far as to say that the nature of the messianic redemption of the world is "the basic reason for Israel's rejection of Jesus" rather than "a purely external or national conception of messianism."[66]

Jewish thinkers point to the lack of fulfillment in terms of the restoration of their own nation, but also of the nations of the world. Eugene B. Borowitz expresses this sentiment: "Theologically, this is the situation: all men stand in covenant with God but though some individuals fulfill that dignifying relationship, the nations and the peoples do not."[67]

As Christians we must reject the idea that these prophecies have not been fulfilled to any degree. The Messiah has come, and the gospel message of salvation proclaimed today is the fulfillment of Old Testament promises, according to the teaching of the apostles. But in proclaiming this initial, partial fulfillment of the messianic prophecies, we as Christians should also acknowledge that the kingdom prophecies of a socio-political sort have not been fulfilled and not try to reinterpret them as somehow being fulfilled through the church during this age.

The idea that socio-political prophecies will be fulfilled in literal earthly terms has been rejected by prominent amillennialists in the church since the time of Tyconius and Augustine.[68] But the concept has been affirmed by proponents of "salvation-historical" theology from Coccejus and the heyday of Reformed federal theology through Pietism and the Lutheran Erlangen school down to the present.[69] This view is prominent among dispensationalists today, but they are not its only proponents. William La Sor writes,

---

[66]Shalom Ben-Chorin, *Die Antwort des Jona*, (Hamburg-Volksdorf: Herbert Reich, 1956), 99. Cited by Jürgen Moltmann, *The Crucified God* (New York: Harper & Row, 1974), 100.

[67]Eugene B. Borowitz, "The Dialectic of Jewish Particularity," *Journal of Ecumenical Studies* 8 (Summer 1977): 567. Martin Buber graphically makes the same point using the example of his own people: "Standing bound and shacked in the pillory of mankind, we demonstrate with the bloody body of our people the unredeemedness of the world" (*Ereignisse und Begegnungen* [Leipzig: InselVerlag, 1920], 20; cited by A. Roy Eckardt, *Elder and Younger Brothers* [New York: Scribner's, 1967], 106).

[68]According to Jürgen Moltmann, the tendency to reinterpret prophecy in terms of an individual internal salvation in preparation for heaven instead of salvation in terms of real earthly affairs came to the fore with the loss of a futuristic eschatology. He writes, "But in what historical era do we find this concept, which internalized redemption into the redemption of the saved soul? There is no doubt at all that we find it in the historical Christendom which abandoned the real futurist eschatology of the New Testament and internalized human salvation, at the same time banishing the future of God to a world beyond this one, so that redemption is no longer seen in the kingdom of God, the 'new heaven and the new earth,' but now only in the saving of the individual soul for the heaven of the blessed" (*The Way of Jesus Christ* [San Francisco: Harper, 1990], 31).

[69]Moltmann, *The Church in the Power of the Spirit*, 138–39. Moltmann summarizes this theology this way: "Israel will only be converted to the Lord through the direct and special intervention of Christ before the end. . . . Israel's conversion in the last days will be the external sign of the transition from messianic world mission to the messianic kingdom."

There are countless prophecies in the Old Testament concerning Israel and the land of promise which have not been fulfilled in the Christian church, and, in my opinion, can never be fulfilled in the church. They can be fulfilled only in Israel.[70]

Similarly, Arnold A. van Ruler, taking note of the Jewish objection, asserts,

In my view Martin Buber is completely correct to level against the Christian church throughout the centuries the accusation that it has never really been faithful to this Old Testament belief, this grand vision of the God of Israel, this visionary faith in the possibility of the sanctification of the earth.[71]

Pointing specifically to the Old Testament concept that salvation includes even the political structures of nations, James Parkes notes that every time the church makes a distinction between "secular" and "religious," she repudiates her intention of fulfilling the Old Testament.[72]

The attempt by some[73] to solve the problem by ascribing fulfillment to the new earth seems inadequate for at least two reasons. First, it does not make room for the Old Testament prophecies that speak of a particular people (whether Israel or the church) as being God's agents to bring this societal salvation to the other peoples. Surely, in the eternal state of the new earth there will be no mediation of salvation from some people to others. The provision of the new covenant salvation that "no longer will a man teach his neighbor . . . because they will all know me" will be fully realized. Under the new-earth view, any *mediatorial* ministry of the messianic salvation must only pertain to the personal spiritual salvation of this age. But the Old Testament picture, as we have seen, includes the socio-political salvation as part of the messianic salvation to be mediated through Israel. It would seem that one is left with either requiring the present fulfillment of these prophecies through the church or acknowledging a still future fulfillment before the time of the new earth.

Second, and perhaps more important, the societal salvation in the new earth would no longer be part of the Messiah's peculiar work of mediating the salvation of God's kingdom on the earth. As we have discussed,[74] the handing over of the kingdom by Christ to the Father signifies the conclusion of his work as the Messiah in mediating salvation

---

[70]William S. La Sor, *Israel: A Biblical View* (Grand Rapids: Eerdmans, 1976), 81–82.
[71]Arnold A. van Ruler, *The Christian Church and the Old Testament* (Grand Rapids: Eerdmans, 1977), 91.
[72]James Parkes, *The Foundations of Judaism and Christianity* (London: Vallentine, Mitchell, 1960), 325–26.
[73]For example, Hoekema, *The Bible and the Future*, 205–6, 275–76; Vern Poythress, *Understanding Dispensationalists* (Grand Rapids: Zondervan, 1987), 47–48.
[74]See pp. 281–82 and 290–92.

(1Co 15:24–28). If this occurs at the transition from the old to the new earth, then the fulfillment of these societal promises is placed beyond the time and, consequently, the scope of the messianic salvation. The saving work of Christ as Mediator would therefore be limited in society to what transpires during this age and to the final destruction of the false world system at his parousia. It would not include a positive restoration of society's structures.

But the prophecies clearly include the positive elements of socio-economic righteousness and international peace. Messianic salvation entails redemption from all effects of sin. For mankind this means the restoration and transformation into a full and true human nature that is not only individual, but also corporate. Salvation in the present age promises individual salvation with a regenerate heart. While the life and power of the regenerate heart works itself out in social actions, it must be acknowledged that the real salvation of the socio-political sphere—the realm of Caesar—is not promised for this age.

Thus "the problem of his [man's] collectivities," as Borowitz puts it, remains.[75] The saving work of the Messiah is yet to be brought to the problems of communal life among the peoples of the world. Pointing to a surplus of promises not presently fulfilled in the church, van Ruler identifes them with this dimension of salvation. They are "to be found in the social ideal of the Old Testament, a just society, the brotherhood of all men, the king or authority who is the true shepherd—not God on earth but the servant of God."[76]

We suggest that it is precisely here, in this socio-political salvation, that Israel still has a role to play. We have seen that from the beginning this people was formed as a nation designed to exemplify the righteousness of God in the very structures of her community existence. Borowitz expresses this idea well: "Israel is brought into history to show that the might of man unified can be subjected to and perfected through the divine sovereignty." He explains the practical effect of such a ministry for society:

> Judaism called men to subject their particularities to the covenanting King so as to make their group the sort through which universalism can become real in history. Nationhood subordinated to messianism, collectivities faithful to God, real lambs lying down with real lions. That remains the continuing vision of Jewish particularity.[77]

---

[75]Borowitz, "The Dialectic of Jewish Particularity," 568.

[76]van Ruler, *The Christian Church and the Old Testament*, 90; cf. also Journet, "The Mysterious Destinies of Israel," 42.

[77]Borowitz, "The Dialectic of Jewish Particularity," 568, 574.

That God's salvation for mankind includes the picture of a world-wide society in which justice and righteousness prevail and the nations walk peacefully in the ways of God is clear in the prophetic Scriptures. That Israel was called into the service of this salvation for the nations is also expressed in those Scriptures. Whether this "Israel" refers to the restored nation or to the church remains the primary point of dispute between dispensationalists and non-dispensationalists.

Given the nature of this salvation—i.e., socio-political—we affirm that the mediatorial ministry of witness and proclamation is best fulfilled through a real nation, the restored nation of Israel. In the words of Buber,

> ... only an entire nation, which comprehends peoples of all kinds, can demonstrate a life of unity and peace, of righteousness and justice to the human race, as a sort of example in beginning. A true humanity, that is, a nation composed of many nations, can only commence with a certain definite and true nation. Only the fulfillment of this truth in the relations between the various sections of this people, between its sects and classes, is capable of serving as a commencement of an international fulfillment of the truth and of the development of a true fellowship of nations, a nation consisting of nations. Only nations each of which is a true nation living in the light of righteousness and justice are capable of entering into upright relations with one another. The people of Israel were charged to lead the way toward this realization.[78]

3. Conclusion. God's election of Israel reveals a commission to the task of service in the divine blessing for all peoples. This is reiterated in the prophecies of the eschatological messianic salvation. While few details are given as to the exact nature of the fulfillment of this task, in some way it involves bringing the fullness of God's salvation to the world. Interpreters of Scripture have increasingly affirmed that God has been providentially involved in the historically unique preservation of the people of Israel to our point in time. That he has done so because Israel yet has a role to play in his plan for the world seems most reasonable in light of the prophetic Scriptures.

---

[78]Buber, *Israel and the World*, 186–87.

Subject Index

Abraham
  father of believing Gentiles, 50
  paradigm of genuine faith, 42
  spiritual significance of, 204
Abrahamic covenant
  foundational for N.T. history, 49
  paradigm of divine/human relationships, 40–41
  role of land promise in, 45–46
  significance of term "seed" in, 43–44
  underlying Israelite history, 46–48
  use of term "nation" in, 43–45
Ascension, relationship to Israel of, 270–71
"All Israel," interpretation of, 254–56
Augustine, millennial view of, 274, 320

Baptism, of John and Christ compared, 176
Baptism of the Holy Spirit, 143
  announced in O.T., 176–77
  defined, 180, 182
  extended to Gentiles, 182–83
  grammatical construction for, 181
  heralding the messianic age, 178
  inaugurating the church age, 174–75
  in relation to body of Christ, 181–82
  not occurring in O.T., 175
"Body" metaphor, 185–86

Christianity
  final rift with Judaism, 214
  illegal status in Rome, 214
  relationship to Jewish War, 213–14
Church
  and Israel's spiritual prerogatives, 212–13
  defined, 208
  mediating position with O.T. prophecies, 163–65
  not existing as a nation, 210
  spiritual nature of, 208
  term only for present age, 209–10
"Church age"
  defined, 26
  relationship to O.T. prophecies, 39–40
Circumcision, 202–5

Davidic covenant, 221
  compared with Abrahamic covenant, 63
  Gentile conversion in, 76–80
  in relation to human king, 60–61
  in relation to Israel, 62–63
  in relation to land promise, 61–62, 64
  summary of, 60

unconditional nature of, 65–66
universal blessings of, 64–65
Dispensationalism
  central issue with non-dispensationalism, 187–88
  defined, 13
Early church
  acceptance of O.T. scriptures by, 250
  comprised primarily of Jews, 246, 250
  millennial views of, 273–74
Election, and eschatological hope, 249
Eschatology, place of in O.T., 221–22, 236

"Fullness" and Israel's restoration, 251

Galatians, purpose of book, 199–200
Gentiles
  as a "new Israel," 111, 127
  as co-equals with Israel, 157–58
  dependence on promises to Israel, 247
  O.T. predictions of salvation, 163
  reconciled with believing Jews, 157
  salvation of in O.T., 123–24
  sharing in God's blessings, 155–57
  spiritual standing with Israel, 159–62
Glory of God, historical purpose of, 20
Grammatico-historical hermeneutic, 19–20, 29–30

History, end of defined, 290
Holocaust
  influence on eschatology, 299
  infuence on non-dispensationalism, 23
Holy Spirit in relation to baptism, 176, 181

Israel
  and God's restoring work, 313–15
  and national integrity in N.T., 195–202
  and socio-political relationships, 319–23
  as distinct from the church, 26
  as God's servant, 301–2
  as mediator of revelation, 311–19
  as mediator of salvation, 319–23
  as revealing God's judgment, 312–13
  as type of the church, 31–32
  as unique entity, 192
  definition as a nation, 193–94
  eschatological role, 305–6
  identification with Messiah, 191
  ignored by church history, 298–99
  importance of obedience to God, 303–5
  meaning of election by God, 302–3
  mediatorial role of, 307, 309, 310

significance of time of, 8–9
Restoration of Israel
and physical creation, 236–37
and relationship to sin, 234, 238, 240
and repossession of the land, 229–30
as goal of God's discipline, 222
facilitated by Gentiles, 227–28
human redemption as focus of, 241–42
in rival millennial views, 238–39
in tension with eternal state, 237–39
purpose and effects of, 234
teaching in Acts about, 268–72
teaching in Gospels about, 264–68
timing of a mystery, 270
Resurrection
physicality defended, 275
usage of term in N.T., 275
Resurrections, number of, 260, 285–87

Roman Catholic Church, view of Israel in, 23
Salvation in reconciling peoples, 165–66
Satan
future binding of, 276–77
status during church age, 277
"Seed," doctrinal use of, 44
Sermon on the Mount, views of, 17–18
"Servant Songs" and Israel, 308–9, 316
"Spiritual circumcision," 203–5
Spiritual redemption, concept of, 21–22
State of Israel (modern), influence of, 299

Types
as foreshadowings, 31–32
historical and theological relation, 32

Universal blessings,
dual N.T. fulfillment of, 57
N.T. nature of, 57

Scripture Index

62:7 232
62:12 231
63:18 266
65–66 230
65:3–7 125
65:5ff. 304
65:17 ....30, 55, 237
65:20–23 55
65:20 240
65:25 237
66:12 232
66:19–20 227
66:20 248
66:22 ....30, 55, 237

JEREMIAH

2:2 184
3:11–20 48
3:17 ....70, 116, 123, 124,
231, 236
3:18 229
3:19 229
3:20 184
4:4 198
4:14 116
6:10 203
7:24 116
9:25–26 202–4
11:8 116
12:14–17 48
14:9 78
14:21 133
15:16 78
16:10–18 48
16:14–20 123
16:14–15 224
16:15 271
17:9 116
18:12 116
22:17 116
23:1–8 48
23:3–8 224
23:5–8 228
23:5–6 229
23:5 62
23:6 64
24:4–7 226
24:6 271
24:7 ....116, 117
25:9 300
25:30 296
27:22 229
28:1–4 48
29:1–14 48
29:10–14 226
29:10 229
30:1–11 121

30:1–3 48
30:3 ....48, 225, 229
30:7–8 113
30:9 62
30:10–11 ....48, 225
30:18 118
30:20 118
31 ....111, 112, 126
31:1–26 47
31:2–14 48
31:4 118
31:5 118
31:7–14 114
31:7 ....118, 232
31:8–11 118
31:8 225
31:12–14 118
31:13 118
31:17 118
31:23–25 118
31:27–28 ....118, 235
31:31–34 ....47, 120
31:31–33 235
31:31–32 40
31:31 ....111, 112, 113,
128, 226
31:32 119
31:33–34 17
31:33 ....113, 116, 117,
127, 171, 300
31:34 ....114, 117, 262
31:35–38 114
31:38–40 118
32:1–44 48
32:15 118
32:36–44 235
32:37 118
32:37–38 114
32:38 117
32:39–40 116
32:40 112
32:41 118
32:42–44 118
33:6 118
33:8 114
33:9 232
33:11 118
33:12–13 118
33:14–17 228
33:14–15 28
33:15 62
33:16 64
33:17–22 66
33:26 121
42:1–22 48
42:6 123
50:4–5 113
50:5 112

50:17–20 48
50:19 271
50:20 ....114 X:30

EZEKIEL

5:13 313
6:14 313
7:9 313
11:16–19 118
11:17–21 225
11:19–20 235
11:19 127
11:20 117
12:15ff. 313
15:7 313
16:8 184
16:60–62 112
20:5 300
20:33–44 225
20:39–44 48
20:39–42 229
20:41 235
20:42 229
21:5 313
23:4 184
28:25 235
32:26 127
33:7–20 88
34–37 223
34:1–16 48
34:7–24 61
34:11–16 225
34:22–24 121
34:23 62
34:25 ....112, 237
34:26–27 236
34:29 236
35:1–36:15 48
36 119
36:8–15 226
36:8–12 ....118, 230
36:8–11 236
36:10–11 227
36:16–36 48
36:18–21 315
36:22 226
36:22ff. 315
36:22–38 122
36:22–36 313
36:22–23 235
36:23 123
36:24–38 118
36:25–29 235
36:25–27 115
36:26–28 47
36:26 116